The Dawn That Never Comes

STUDIES OF THE WEATHERHEAD EAST ASIAN INSTITUTE

Studies of the Weatherhead East Asian Institute
Columbia University

The Weatherhead East Asian Institute is Columbia University's center for research, publication, and teaching on modern and contemporary Asia Pacific regions.

The Studies of the Weatherhead East Asian Institute were inaugurated in 1962 to bring to a wider public the results of significant new research on modern and contemporary East Asia.

The Dawn That Never Comes

SHIMAZAKI TŌSON AND JAPANESE NATIONALISM

Michael K. Bourdaghs

COLUMBIA UNIVERSITY PRESS   NEW YORK

Columbia University Press
Publishers Since 1893
New York   Chichester, West Sussex

© 2003 Columbia University Press
All rights reserved

Library of Congress Cataloging-in-Publication Data
Bourdaghs, Michael, 1961–
The Dawn that never comes : Shimazaki Tōson and
Japanese nationalism / Michael K. Bourdaghs.
p. cm. — (Studies of the East Asian Institute)
Includes bibliographical references and index.
ISBN 0–231–12980–7 (cloth : alk. paper)
1. Shimazaki, Tōson, 1872–1943—Criticism and interpretation.
2. Nationalism in literature.
I. Title. II. Series.

PL 816.H55Z543   2003
895.6'34—dc21

2003046105

Printed in the United States of America
Designed by Audrey Smith

c 10 9 8 7 6 5 4 3 2 1

For Satoko, Sonia, and Walter

CONTENTS

Acknowledgments   ix

Introduction
I

CHAPTER ONE
Tōson, Literary History, and National Imagination
19

CHAPTER TWO
The Disease of Nationalism, the Empire of Hygiene:
The Broken Commandment as Hygiene Manual
47

CHAPTER THREE
Triangulating the Nation:
Representing and Publishing *The Family*
77

CHAPTER FOUR
Suicide and Childbirth in the I-Novel:
"Women's Literature" in *Spring* and *New Life*
114

CHAPTER FIVE
The Times and Spaces of Nations:
The Multiple Chronotopes of *Before the Dawn*
154

EPILOGUE
The Most Japanese of Things
191

Notes   199
Works Cited   247
Index   265

ACKNOWLEDGMENTS

With a project that has gone on as long as this one, a comprehensive list of acknowledgments would have to continue for many pages. With hesitation, though, I would like to acknowledge my debt to at least some of the people who have helped me along the way. This project began, almost by accident, in a paper I wrote for Brett de Bary on Tōson's *The Family* during my first semester as a graduate student at Cornell University; over the years since, she has been a remarkable mentor and model of integrity to me. I thank my other teachers at Cornell as well, especially the other members of my dissertation committee—Joel Porte and Naoki Sakai—and Karen Brazell, J. Victor Koschmann, and Kyoko Selden. My fellow students in the graduate program at Cornell also contributed (and continue to contribute) greatly to my intellectual growth—especially Mark Anderson, Richard Calichman, Tomer Inbar, Ayako Kano, Beng Choo Lim, Joseph Murphy, Antonia Saxon, Robert Steen, and Joshua Young.

Much of the research included here was conducted while I was in residence at Tōhoku University in Japan, and I thank Nihei Michiaki, Satō Nobuhiro, and Takahashi Akinori, as well as the students in the Japanese Literature program there, for their kind hospitality and guidance. I am also grateful for the support my research received at various stages, including a Fulbright-Hays Doctoral Dissertation Research Grant from the U.S. Department of Education, a dissertation-writing fellowship from the Mellon Fellowships in the Humanities, and faculty research grants from the UCLA Academic Senate and Center for Japanese Studies.

My colleagues and students at UCLA have provided a wonderful environment in which to pursue my research, and I feel blessed to have worked alongside them. In particular, I would like to thank those who have provided suggestions and other help with this project: John Duncan, Ted Huters, Seiji Lippit, Michael Marra, Fred Notehelfer, Herman Ooms, Herbert Plutschow, David Schaberg, Shu-mei Shih, Miriam Silverberg, and Mariko Tamanoi.

Over the years, I have had many invaluable opportunities to discuss my work on Tōson and nationalism with, and learn from, a large number of scholars. This list could go on for many pages, but I am especially grateful to Henry Em, Judith Farquhar, Jerry Fisher, Carol Gluck, Marta Hanson, Harry Harootunian, Hinata Yasushi, Kamei Hideo, Karatani Kōjin, Thomas Lamarre, Murai Osamu, Nagahara Yutaka, Narita Ryūichi, Richi Sakakibara, Suga Hidemi, Stefan Tanaka, and Atsuko Ueda.

Jennifer Crewe at Columbia University Press is now my ideal model for what an editor should be. I am also grateful to the two anonymous reviewers for the press for their many intelligent suggestions.

Early versions of chapter two previously appeared in *positions* and in *New Directions in the Study of Meiji Japan*, edited by Helen Hardacre and Adam L. Kern (Leiden: Brill, 1997). In Japanese, too, I have previously discussed some of the material here in articles published in *Gendai shisō* and in the following volumes: *Kindai no yume to chisei: Bungaku shisō no Shōwa 10-nen zengo (1925–1945)*, edited by Bungaku Shisō Konwa Kai (Tokyo: Kanrin Shobō, 2000); and *Sekai ga yomu Nihon kindai bungaku III*, edited by Fukuoka UNESCO Kai (Tokyo: Maruzen Books, 1999).

Finally, I would like to thank my parents, the Ogura family, and my sister for their support, both tangible and intangible, over the years. And most of all, I would like to thank Walter, Sonia, and Satoko, who have all put up with a great deal of nonsense as I tried to finish this book.

⊞

Japanese personal names appear in their original order (family name first, given name second), except in citations of translated works in which the order has been reversed. I have also followed standard scholarly practice in Japan by referring to canonical authors by their given names (e.g., "Tōson" instead of "Shimazaki"). All translations from Japanese sources are mine, except where noted. Finally, the following abbreviations are used in citations throughout:

STJ: Itō Kazuo, ed. *Shimazaki Tōson jiten* (Shimazaki Tōson dictionary)(Tokyo: Meiji Shoin, 1972).

TZ: *Tōson zenshū* (Complete works of Tōson), 18 Vols. (Tokyo: Chikuma Shobō, 1966–1971).

The Dawn That Never Comes

Introduction

Nationalism is an inspired vehicle of ambiguity.

Tom Nairn, *Faces of Nationalism: Janus Revisited*

1897 AND THE NATIONAL POET

In Japan, as in other modern nations, poets have delved into the rhetoric of national imagination. But of the many brilliant poets who have appeared since the Meiji Restoration of 1868, whose verses sing most truly the song of the Japanese? In 1921, Akita Ujaku (1883–1962) nominated his candidate for the position of Japan's "national poet" (*kokuminteki shijin*). In doing so, he tried to pin down the necessary qualifications that distinguish the national poet:

> Of course, the national poet must be someone who represents accurately the passions, the thought, the traditional taste or the particular humor of the nation [*kokumin*]. But most importantly, he must be the first to detect that which the nation wants—yet is unable—to express, and he must give voice to this on behalf of the nation. When this happens, it is always the youth of the age who first hear the voice of this representative and rise up in chorus with him. . . . Many different authors sing out on behalf of the nation in its various ages. And yet there is no one who has sung on behalf of the Japanese people in as powerful and lofty a tone as did Shimazaki in his *Rakubaishū* [Fallen plum blossoms], *Wakanashū* [A collection of seedlings], and *Hitohabune* [A leaflike boat].[1]

The praise must have been gratifying to Shimazaki Tōson (1872–1943), who by 1921 was better known as a rather scandalous novelist than as a youthful romantic poet: nearly two decades had passed since the publication of his most recent poetry collection.

What, however, does it mean to call someone the "national poet"? Is there only one kind of national poet? If not, what varieties exist, and why? Poets deal in rhetoric and imagination, the very stuff of national identity. But nations require more than one kind of rhetoric, more than one form of imagination. And if rhetoric is concerned with the effective use of genres, what are the genres specific to national imagination? Benedict Anderson has famously pointed to the modern novel as the source of the specific temporality required by modern nations—and, in fact, the following chapters in this book will mainly explore novels.[2] But the critic Suga Hidemi argues that national imagination also needs poetry.[3] The modern novel may be crucial to establishing the linear time of national narratives, but in order to rescue a sense of meaningfulness from the randomness of death, prosaic national imagination must be supplemented with poésie, a poetic strain that provides an aesthetic guarantee of the nation's eternal existence at a transcendental level. According to Suga, Anderson's failure to consider how poésie supplements the prose of nationalism prevents him from seeing the inherent connections between nationalism and fascism, between "good" and "bad" nationalisms.

Suga implies that the rhetoric of national imagination consists not of a closed system centered around a single genre, but of a field of multiple, often contradictory and shifting genres. For national imagination to function effectively, it must mobilize a whole range of genres—not just literary ones—that supplement, reinforce, and sometimes contradict one another. F. Scott Fitzgerald once wrote that the mark of a great thinker is "the ability to hold two opposed ideas in the mind at the same time, and still retain the ability to function."[4] The same could be said of national imagination.

Akita Ujaku identified Shimazaki Tōson as modern Japan's national poet, and yet others attacked Tōson precisely for failing to live up to that role. What do these contradictory assertions tell us about the field of national imagination? As a means to set the stage for the chapters that follow, let us begin by looking at how this field was aligned at the moment Tōson's first poetry collection appeared in 1897. What made some people discover in him Japan's "national poet"? What made others reject him, and what alternatives did they propose? And, most importantly, how was the field of national imagination shaped through this process?

☒

By 1897, the flames of revolutionary nationalism that had launched Japan into the Meiji era were burning out. Young Japan was becoming Middle-Aged Japan. The idealistic youths of strong will who had seized control of the state in the 1860s were now difficult old men determined to retain power, snuffing out or co-opting their opposition and busily constructing the narratives and rituals that they hoped would solidify their preferred version of national history. The main task of the state had long since shifted from a radical overturning of the Tokugawa feudal order to the mundane task of codifying the new status quo: the primary domestic political issue of the day was the writing of the massive Meiji Civil Code, to be promulgated the following year. Likewise, in foreign relations the burning desire to avoid colonization had waned; Japan was now laying the groundwork for its own empire as it took possession of its first overseas colony, Taiwan, part of the booty it received from its victory in the 1894–1895 Sino-Japanese War. If the Tripartite Intervention of 1895 enraged the nation by forcing Japan to cede back other parts of its war booty, the revision of the Unequal Treaties in 1899 would signify Japan's entrance onto the world stage as one of the great powers.

In short, at the level of the state, revolutionary nationalism was giving way to a more conservative and quotidian nationalism of common sense. And yet despite this (or perhaps because of it, perhaps even as its necessary counterpart), elsewhere the fires of popular nationalism still burned brightly—most notably in the cultural realm. In the newly expanded university system (an expansion underwritten by war reparations from China), new disciplines appropriate to cultural nationalism were emerging. Ueda Kazutoshi (1867–1937), the founder of *kokugogaku*, or "national language" studies, vowed that the Japanese language was the lifeblood of the nation. Haga Yaichi (1867–1927), the founder of *kokubungaku*, or "national literature" studies, likewise undertook the project of defining the classical canon and transforming it into the basis of contemporary national education. Japan's premodern past was being translated into a living national tradition.

Beyond the university system (which was, after all, still a part of the bureaucratic state apparatus), there appeared a new generation of young men—and some women too—who embraced cultural nationalism as a form of oppositional politics. As "outsiders" to officialdom, they decried the spineless bureaucraticism of the government and the selfish desire for personal success that seemed to dominate in civil society.[5] They hailed Japan's own cultural traditions as the source of national regeneration, self-consciously rejecting the Westernization that their seniors had advocated in earlier decades. The *genbun itchi* movement, which sought to create a vernacular literary style adequate to the Western ideal of a modern, realistic, and psychological novel—and the hot topic in literary circles in the late 1880s—even temporarily ceded centerstage to a revival of interest in the works of Saikaku in the 1890s. Young writers like Ozaki Kōyō (1867–1903) and Kōda Rohan (1867–1947) now looked to Japan's past for literary models. In sum, the meaning and shape of tradition was changing. More precisely, a new and highly selective set of traditions was being invented, traditions ironically appropriate to, and derived from, modernity, even as they harkened back to the premodern past. As Oguma Eiji has noted, Japanese nationalism in the Meiji era was created through something like a "marriage between the ancient Imperial Court and modern Western technology."[6] The Saikaku revival, after all, could not have occurred in the absence of the modern publishing industry, which made the great seventeenth-century writer's works available for the first time to a wide audience. And even in their rejection of the West, the new generation found themselves citing modern Western thought, albeit now with the stress on currents of antimodernism: Nietzsche, the German and English Romantics, Ruskin.

By 1897 the multiple forms of national imagination that would dominate early-twentieth-century Japan had begun to take palpable shape. And it was in this moment of transition that the first poetry collection by a rising young writer, Shimazaki Tōson, appeared and created a stir in literary circles: a new poetic voice was born, one that seemed adequate to the vibrant, modern yet traditional nation that cultural nationalists sought. As the poet himself would write seven years later in a preface to another anthology (a manifesto often compared to Wordsworth's 1802 "Preface" to his *Lyrical Ballads*),[7]

> At last, the time for a new poetry has come!
>
> It is like a beautiful dawn. Some cry out like the prophets of old, some exclaim like the poets of the West, and all seem intoxicated with a clear light and a new voice and the fancy of a daydream.
>
> Youthful imagination has awoken from its long slumber and adorns itself with the words of the common folk! Legends have come back to life! Nature is adorned afresh with new colors! . . .
>
> Who can rest easy in their old lives? For each to strive to open the new: that is the proper task of the young!
>
> Life is force [*chikara*]. Force is voice. Voice is words. New words can be nothing but new life.

I too seek to enter into the new, I too have passed many lonely and
dark days!   (*TZ* 1:526)

That first anthology, *Wakanashū* (A collection of seedlings), contained some
fifty-one poems, works of "new-style poetry" (*shintaishi*) that introduced
novel themes, vocabulary, and forms into Japanese poetry while retaining the
traditional 7–5 syllabic meter. It caused such a sensation that "Tōson may fairly
be called the creator of modern Japanese poetry."[8]
What sort of poetry did this new "national poet" write? Near the beginning of the collection appears the following poem:

OKINU

The fierce eagle soaring through the air
Has descended into a maiden's body
As if it sought to dwell within a flower blossom form
Thirsting for the pounding storms, hungering for the clouds,
But forbidden even to desire
The means to soar to heaven
My body with its long black hair
Sightless since birth.

If my previous self was a cotton rose
Then my tears are autumn flower's dew;
If my previous self was an *ogoto* lyre
Then my grief is a note sounded on its slender strings;
But now my previous life is as an eagle's body,
The wings that exceed a human maiden's grasp.

Aah, some times my heart
Abandons all that is,
Sees the world as dull and tasteless,
A dwelling overrun with weeds;
My body lacks all means, a cricket
Creeping through the grass of nighttime fields
Crying out to no avail,
Singing out a poem, perhaps.

When the color of passion enters my body
My maiden's heart becomes a bird;
When love enters its heart,
The bird takes a maiden's form;
A maiden, yes, but also a bird in the sky,
A fierce eagle, yes, but also a human body,
Lost between heaven and earth,
The sad fate of my body.

(*TZ* 1:6–7)

Like nearly all of Tōson's poems, "Okinu" in the original Japanese presents a strongly rhythmic pattern, achieved through consistent use of 7–5 meter and repetition of various phrases. Likewise, the poem's romantic and melancholic tone, its youthful yet autumnal quality, echoes throughout the collection. And like so many of Tōson's poems, this one employs dramatic monologue, here adopting the passionate voice of Okinu, a blind maiden.[9]

Tōson's later novels and stories (with the exception of his explicitly historical fiction) have rarely been discussed in connection with their role in the political project of nation building. In fact, a small army of critics has devoted itself to the unlikely project of demonstrating the apolitical nature of Tōson's first novel, *The Broken Commandment* (*Hakai*, 1906). But Tōson's highly personal and emotional poetry has, from early on, been linked with the politics of Meiji nationalism. By 1936, for example, Itō Shinkichi (1906–2002) declared that Tōson's poetry was inextricably bound up with the swelling sense of national identity that marked 1890s Japan:

The Meiji Restoration, accomplished by overthrowing the domination of Tokugawa feudalism, above all hastened the unification and systematization of national sentiment [*kokuminteki kanjō*], a sentiment that was subsequently fully unleashed by a spectacular burst of capitalist development. To reflect this process was the creative task of literature in that age, and it was out of this swelling of national sentiment that Romantic literature raised its head and laid the foundation for modern Japanese literature. Accordingly, *Wakanashū* [A collection of seedlings] too sings the sentiment of its age, and in so far as it boomed with this new sentiment, it had fulfilled its historical task.[10]

Taking up the poem "Eagle's Song" (Washi no uta) from Tōson's second poetry collection, Itō compares it to Walt Whitman's *Leaves of Grass* for its portrayal of the burgeoning sense of national spirit at a moment of rising capitalism.[11]

One reason that the political significance of Tōson's early poetry has been so frequently noted is the explicitly nationalistic bent that marked poetic reform movements in the 1890s. The notion of literature as a realm of autonomous aesthetic value, cut off from the politics of social reality, had not yet taken hold, and the new generation of cultural nationalists demanded a national literature, and in particular a national poetry, that would serve as a means to achieving a variety of political ends. As Suga notes, nationalist critics in the 1890s explicitly called for a new national poetry to become the voice of the national people. The early translators of Western poetry, who created the *shintaishi* genre in anthologies such as *Shintaishi shō* (Selection of poetry in the new style, 1882), worked out of an overtly political desire to produce a modern, colloquial Japanese poetry that was beholden neither to the supposedly "dead language" of archaic Japanese nor to "foreign" Chinese vocabulary. The new poetry was to sing the living daily experience of the nation, in the living tongue of the national people, and it often included explicitly political and patriotic subject matters.[12]

Reformers active in traditional verse forms such as tanka and haiku were, if anything, even more explicitly nationalistic. They inherited the ideological linkage between classical poetry and national essence that had been established by the protonationalist Nativist (*kokugaku*) schools of late Edo. Masaoka Shiki (1867–1902) and Yosano Tekkan (1873–1935), among others, launched vigorous campaigns to reform the traditional genres, which they believed had grown feminine, weak, and frivolous. Rising to a fever pitch around the time of the Sino-Japanese War (both Shiki and Tekkan traveled to the Asian continent in 1895), the reform movement championed haiku and tanka that were vigorous, masculine, patriotic—and at times bluntly militaristic. This often involved radical and deliberately provocative reevaluations of the traditional canon—as when Shiki notoriously toppled Bashō from the pinnacle of the haiku canon, replacing him with the more "manly" Buson.[13]

Given this background, it is not surprising that from early on readers interpreted Tōson's poetry within the explicitly political framework of a modern national culture. Nor is it surprising that Tōson's poems were already, by late Meiji, included in textbooks designed to introduce students in middle and higher schools to their national literature, textbooks edited by such figures as

Haga and Ueda. But not everyone saw in Tōson the ideal "national poet." In a series of essays, Takayama Chogyū (1871–1902), one of the most prominent of the new generation of nationalist ideologues, attacked Tōson's poetry for its excessively "vague" (*mōrō*) nature: it was too conservative, passive, rhetorically dense, and ambiguous. He complained that the lack of clarity in Tōson's poetic language threatened to cloud the harmonious and rational communication between poet and reader that Chogyū saw as essential to a national literature. In Tōson's place, Chogyū proposed Doi Bansui (also known as Tsuchii Bansui, 1871–1952) as Japan's national poet.[14]

But Chogyū's critique does not mean that Tōson's poetry is somehow not "national." Rather, we are dealing here with two different (yet mutually supplementary) versions of the imagined national community. As Nakayama Hiroaki points out, Chogyū's critique overlooked the way that the amorphous emotionality of Tōson's poetic language could summon up and shape individual affect in its readers, thereby intensifying their sense of belonging to a national community based on sentiment. Nakayama traces how this abstract language of affect subsequently became a kind of code that was reproduced in the poetry of a whole generation.[15]

Part of what is at issue here is the fluid gendering of national imagination. In synch with what Harry Harootunian has called the "aggressive, indeed Darwinian egoism"[16] that characterized his version of the nation, Chogyū implies that Tōson's poetry is not sufficiently masculine. But this does not necessarily mean that a "national poet" could never speak in a feminine voice. After all, women too had to be mobilized into the national community, if not in the same way as men. As Takashi Fujitani has demonstrated, for example, the public image of the Meiji Emperor was doubled and included both a masculine, modern image associated with the new capital city Tokyo, and a feminine, "traditional" image associated with the ancient court in Kyoto.[17]

The rhetoric of national imagination, then, had to include both masculine and feminine voices. Writing in a woman's voice did not prevent Higuchi Ichiyō (1872–1896) from entering the canon of national literature, and it must also be noted that the inclusion of feminine voices did not necessarily constitute a challenge to patriarchy. When Ichiyō brought her early drafts to the male novelist Nakarai Tōsui (1860–1926) for advice, he told her that the woman's voice in her prose was too coarse and that she could not simply transcribe women's actual language if she wanted to appear feminine in print.[18] The very definition of femininity in national imagination was mediated through a male gaze. The "national poet" could speak either in a masculine or feminine voice—after all, women had authored many of the premodern texts then being transformed into Japan's national literary tradition. But only certain tones of feminine voice were acceptable.

Accordingly, the field of national imagination included both the sort of "masculine" poetry advocated by Chogyū, Tekkan, and Shiki and "feminine" poetry, such as Tōson's "Okinu," quoted above. In fact, many of the poems in *Wakanashū* (A collection of seedlings) foreshadow, both in content and tone, the strong feminine voice that would appear four years later in the tanka of Yosano Akiko (1878–1942) in her *Midaregami* (Tangled hair, 1901).[19] Tōson's *Wakanashū* opens with a series of six poems that take as their subject matter the strong passions of six young maidens (*otome*), whose given names—including Okinu—provide the titles for the individual poems. Various other poems also take the form of monologues or dialogues, more often than not spoken by female characters. In contrast to the calls for an explicitly masculine national poetry in Shiki and Tekkan, Tōson focuses on the feminine as the proper object of literature (an *object* even when she is the speaking *subject* of the poem). As Kōno Kensuke notes, the use of female narrators allowed Tōson to bring into his poetry an intense focus on the realms of emotion and sensibility, realms coded as feminine under modern patriarchies, thereby using his "drag" performance to reinforce, rather than subvert, gender norms.[20] What emerged was a complex gendering of literature itself, as competing masculine and feminine forms of writing vied for the privilege of representing the nation, of assuming the mantle of national literature.

This gendered divide helped produce a fluid imagination that could figure the national community as simultaneously embodied and disembodied, spiritual and material. In this field, masculine and feminine voices were assigned a multiplicity of positions: subject, object, and abject. Tōson's poems, for example, provide a vision of feminine passion that situates it between the fleshly body and the disembodied spirit. Frequently, the female is made to represent the (otherwise disembodied) passion of the male poet, so that her body becomes the physical matter of his spiritual confession, as in the black hair and white hands of the young girl depicted in what is perhaps Tōson's most famous poem, "Hatsu koi" (First love). There, reminiscing on a youthful love, the male narrator recalls his own "innocent sighs" as "brushing against [your] locks of hair" (*TZ* 1:54). Or again, in "Sōnen no uta" (Song of a man in his prime), the male poetic voice declares:

> Even as her hair envelops me
> Even as her blood dyes me
> Even as flowers adorn my lips
> Sorrowful thoughts torment my breast
>
> (*TZ* 1:247)[21]

These sorts of multiple and often contradictory images of fleshly bodies were crucial to Japanese national imagination, helping to produce the desires it needed for both internal purity and risky contacts with alterity. Moreover, these images intersected with modern discourses of health, race, and diet to produce an array of links between individual human bodies and the "body" of the national community itself.

In its spiritual and disembodied aspect, on the other hand, this passion echoes the romantic concept of platonic love (*ren'ai*), associated most closely with Kitamura Tōkoku (1868–1894), the leading figure in the Romantic School of the 1890s, with which Tōson's poetry is conventionally associated. The notion of a nonsexual, spiritual love between the sexes, associated first with Christianity in Meiji Japan but then later a staple of a wide variety of discourses, was an ideological linchpin in contemporary movements to reform the Japanese family. These reform movements played an indispensable role in the modern project of nation building. The fierce romantic love that Okinu and her sister-maidens express invokes one of the key tropes of modern nationalism: as Ueno Chizuko argues, the "internalization of the notion of 'romantic love' by women was an indispensable condition for the establishment of the modern patriarchal system," a system that formed a primary component of national imagination in Japan.[22] But "national poets" depicted other sorts of families as well. The field of national imagination was necessarily fragmented to include multiple conflicting versions of the proper national family: extended and nuclear, traditional and modern, moralistic and romantic. To be functional, in a sense, the national family had to be dysfunctional.

Finally, the "national poet" helped provide the national community with its sense of time—its images of past, present, and future, as well as a sense of the linkages and breaks that lie between them. Here too, we find not a single coherent system, but a field that combines many contradictory versions of national time. Tōson's poems present the odd temporality of national imagination, with its characteristic blurring together of nostalgic longing for lost pasts, ceaseless striving toward future triumphs, and demands that the national people fulfill their duties in and for the present moment. Like the heroic protagonist of national histories, characters in Tōson's poems simultaneously look backward, stride forward, and stand lock-still in reflective contemplation.

The melancholic, nostalgic tone of Tōson's poetry seems odd in a volume that from its very title celebrates youth and springtime. But as Yasuda Yojūrō (1910–1981), the leader of the nationalistic Japan Romantic School (which in its valorization of classical poetry epitomized the poésie of national imagination), wrote in 1935,

> Tōkoku and Tōson were poets of autumn. Poets who sing in praise of spring must begin from desolation and ruins. *Sturm und Drang* are the dreams of a day that contrasts modernity with antiquity and that compels a certain attitude toward the ancient classics, and so they also compel a journey that begins from the graveyard of desolation and walks toward a sparkling dawn.[23]

Many of Tōson's poems place the young poetic speaker at a site of ruins, contemplating in melancholic fashion a vanished past—notably, the famous "Komoro naru kojō no hotori" (By the old castle of Komoro).[24] Other poems evoke autumn and death, mournful elegies of loss, yet almost as many poems invoke moments of awakening, of dawn and spring, moments that resonate with the image of a butterfly that graced the cover of the first edition of *Wakanashū* (A collection of seedlings). The nostalgia for a lost past links up with an expansionary, future-oriented project. Or, as one critic wrote in 1925, Tōson's poetry invokes "the youthful desire for an unconstrained outward expansion [*nobiyaka na soto e hirogatte iku kibō*]."[25] Like the wanderer depicted standing at the nation's edge, gazing wistfully at an exotic coconut that has washed ashore in "Yashi no mi" (Coconut),[26] national imagination included from its start the idea of a desirable exterior, a yearning after what lay beyond the nation's boundaries—the dream of empire.

We are clearly in the realm here of what Suga calls the "poésie" of national imagination. Sasabuchi Tomoichi analyses the following poem from *Wakanashū*, translated below in its entirety:

THE SOUND OF THE TIDES
(Chōon)[27]

Gushing up and flowing away
The countless ocean tides
Hesitating in the depths

> The *koto* of the sea
> Its music deep
> From a hundred rivers
> Their myriad waves
> Summoned to gather
> When the time is full [*toki michikureba*]
> Glorious
> Audible from afar
> The sound of springtime tide will come
>
>   (*TZ* 1:20)

Sasabuchi argues that the poem demonstrates a "messianic" form of time, a sense of anticipation for a coming revelatory moment when time will be "full."[28] Yet that final triumphant awakening remains perpetually deferred, just as the national community itself remains unsutured, unable ever to realize homogeneous self-identity.[29] Tōson himself seemed to consider this deferment the essence not only of his poetry, but of Romanticism in general. As he told Kamei Katsuichirō (1907–1966), another member of the Japan Romantic School, during a 1941 visit,

> But in the end, Romanticism seems unable to reach fruition. Whatever country you look at, that's the case—Romanticism moves from one reform to another, smashing one thing only to move on and smash another, ceaselessly surging forward, so that it always ends up something unfinished. We might call it the eternal unfinished quality of Romanticism, and that inability to come to final fruition is what's good about it, right? Isn't its failure to bear fruit the best part of Romanticism?[30]

The "national poet" sings into being a never-ending project, a passionate striving to break through the shackles of convention and to reach a future moment of triumph, a triumph that paradoxically is often figured as a return to tradition and origins. He or she sings the desire for national identity—even before, as Akita Ujaku suggests, the national people themselves have consciously felt it. The speakers in the poetry of Tōson figure the subject of national imagination as a being driven ceaselessly forward, spurred by the desire for a promised moment of awakening, a springtime of rejuvenation and rebirth—a dawn that by its very nature must never arrive.

MODERN JAPAN AND THE COMPLEXITIES
OF NATIONAL IMAGINATION

The present study of Shimazaki Tōson and his role in Japanese nationalism proceeds from my conviction that the cultural history of Japan in the early twentieth century is of crucial importance for anyone hoping to understand the
complexity and durability of national imagination. By the end of the 1930s, the
field of national ideology in Japan had managed to appropriate to itself the
energy of virtually every potential source of opposition: liberal humanism, scientific rationalism, feminism, anticolonialism, socialism, and anarchism. While
this pattern is not unique, and similar instances can be found elsewhere,
nonetheless, early-twentieth-century Japan does present, in an unusually stark
form, the patterns of densely mingled exclusion and assimilation that characterize modern nationalisms. It provides a remarkable example of the supple fluidity and intricacy that any useful understanding of nationalism must account
for.

How did national imagination acquire this flexibility, and what role did
modern literature play in this? The present study will try to provide answers
to those questions by delving into fiction produced in this period, using it to
map out the contending and often contradictory forces that came together to
produce (and sometimes trouble) an effective national imagination. I will
touch on a wide variety of writers, but mainly, I will focus on the works of
Tōson, one of modern Japan's most respected novelists and poets.[31] The
choice is deliberate, not only because Tōson during the period in question was
perhaps the central figure in the modern Japanese canon, but also because he
is not considered a particularly nationalistic writer. He is remembered, for
example, for having resisted the waves of xenophobia that arose during the last
decade of his lifetime. If we can consider him a nationalist at all, it is mainly
in terms of the "good" variety, the popular nationalism that often opposes
official state nationalism.

In *The Broken Commandment* (*Hakai*, 1906; trans. 1974), Tōson's first novel,
for example, the hero is a member of a minority group that suffers virulent
discrimination, but the villains in the novel are not the ordinary townspeople
(who in fact are largely sympathetic to the hero), but rather the representatives
of the nation-state, bureaucrats and politicians. And in *Before the Dawn* (*Yoake
mae*, 1929–35; trans. 1987), Tōson challenged the orthodox historiography that
had portrayed the Meiji Restoration as a heroic top-down revolution carried
out by the small clique that seized power in 1868. In place of that official nar-

rative, Tōson envisioned a bottom-up grassroots struggle, a popular revolution that was in the end tragically betrayed by the new ruling junta.

Such works made Tōson a hero of sorts to the youthful antistate activists who rediscovered his works in the 1960s—and who were unconsciously repeating the rediscovery made by another generation of youths in the 1930s. And it is precisely the conscientiousness of Tōson's liberal, antielitist, and cosmopolitan nationalism that makes him a suitable test case for exploring the broad questions that underlie this project. A study of ultranationalist writers (Iwano Hōmei, for example, or Hayashi Fusao) would likely reveal much less about the diverse field of national imagination.[32] My purpose here is to examine how the national community became part of the common sense of twentieth-century Japan, an unspoken assumption embedded within the rhetoric of even those who, like Tōson, were not particularly nationalistic. Moreover, I will investigate the ways that "bad" nationalism haunts even the best of "good" nationalisms. Again, this is not a problem unique to Japan. We have no right, as Etienne Balibar argues,

> to equate the nationalism of the dominant with that of the dominated, the nationalism of liberation with the nationalism of conquest. Yet this does not mean we can simply ignore the fact that there is a common element—if only the logic of a situation, the structural inscription in the political forms of the modern world

As Balibar notes, all too often nationalisms of liberation transform into modes of domination. The burden of this history requires us "to inquire into the oppressive potentialities contained within every nationalism."[33]

Following Benedict Anderson, among many others, I consider the nation to be a form of social organization that serves to differentiate the era of modern global capitalism from earlier ages. Since this form of community is new (even as it often claims to be ancient), a sense of belonging to it must be constructed, and since the typical national community is so vast as to exceed the ability of its members to perceive it directly, this sense of belonging must be produced in part through acts of imagination—hence the need for a dense rhetoric of national imagination. Images of health and illness, practices of sexuality and gender, the patterns of family life, calendars and maps: as we will see in subsequent chapters, all of these devices help produce images of the abstract national community and interweave it into the concrete practices of everyday life. Imagination here does not imply mere fantasy—the imagined national community has tremendous power to affect historical and social actualities, including the economic. In this case, at least, imagination is real.

It is also important to note that there is not one stable form of nationalism. Nationalism is not a single ideology; rather it is a bundle of ideologies, so that it has more in common with concepts such as "kinship" or "religion" than with more specifically defined ideological systems such as "liberalism" and "fascism."[34] As Eve Sedgwick notes, nationalism can be thought of "as the name of an entire underlying dimension of modern social functioning that could then be organized in a near-infinite number of different and even contradictory ways."[35] A commonplace that will appear throughout this study is that nations attempt to achieve unity by distinguishing themselves from their various others, but

> it may be that there exists for nations, as for genders, simply no normal way to partake of the categorical definitiveness of the national, no single kind of "other" of what a nation is to which all can by the same structuration be definitionally opposed.[36]

As we will see in the chapters that follow, often a single text will propose images of the nation that relate not to a single other, but to many different others, defined by varying degrees of otherness and differentiation from the national community. In studying national imagination, my goal is not to produce a single modular structure, but wherever possible to complicate matters, to map out the unstable flows and shifting boundary regions that characterize modern nations. It is precisely this fluidity and multiplicity that enables nationalism to achieve social reproduction, both at the level of individual nations and of the modern world system.

Given this multiplicity, no single epistemological or symbolic "modular" could account for the fluidity that has made national imagination such a potent ideological force. Moreover, as Partha Chatterjee has argued, the use of a modular theory like Anderson's "imagined community" threatens to reduce non-Western nationalisms to the position of passive consumers who merely import a structure originally produced elsewhere. Such a theory can blind us to the creative agency, the productive translations, the shifting differences generated in the cultural praxis of non-Western societies, with the result that even the imaginations of the non-West end up colonized.[37]

Chatterjee, in turn, argues that anticolonial nationalisms resist the Western nation-state model by producing sovereignty in the inner spiritual domain, outside the realm of the state. But the experience of modern Japan troubles this theorization as well. It shows us that the imagination of a spiritual community, even an imagination that was specifically antistate and antimodern in nature, can be complicit with modern state nationalism. In 1930s Japan, what Marilyn Ivy has aptly named the "discourses of the vanishing" became a tremendous source of energy for the expanding nation-state.[38] It may be an exaggeration to write, as Harootunian does, that "contemporary postcolonial discourse is simply a repetition of the [1930s] Japanese experience in a different historical register."[39] There is, after all, no historical law necessitating that contemporary forms of postcolonialism result in something like the fascist nationalism of 1930s Japan—but neither is there any guarantee that they will not. This danger underscores the need for us to reach a practical and sufficiently complex understanding of national imagination.

Accordingly, in the following chapters I will argue that heterogeneity and lack of identity have always been the reality of nations and nation-states. To borrow Nira Yuval-Davis's words, nations are not the stable, homogeneous entities that they sometimes present themselves as because "even the most hegemonic naturalized grand narratives in historical societies have never had homogeneous unified control over the differentially positioned members of those societies."[40] There is not one national body, national family, or national space, but several—and they overlap, fall apart, and cohere, all at once. Moreover, this multiplicity and fluidity are central to national imagination: to cover all the contradictions and antagonisms that tear apart national society and to keep the nation moving forward, it is necessary that a diversity of national canons functions together—and apart. I will also argue that the discovery of heterogeneity in nations is not by any means a new phenomenon: nations are constantly rediscovering their own hybridity. Only by forgetting empire, colonialism, and migration, ignoring the problems of uneven development, gender, class, and racialization that have been central components of national imagination, could one be led to conclude that somehow the boundaries of nations were once fixed and stable. As Tessa Morris-Suzuki notes, early-twentieth-century Japanese national imagination was marked by "an essential ambivalence" that stressed both Japan's "*uniqueness*" and "the international *commonalities* which justified Japan's claim to impose its regimes on others and to create an empire in Asia" (emphasis in original).[41]

Any social machine that could produce these results must be of enormous complexity, one that is constantly falling apart as part of its own renewal, and one that is capable of continuously neutralizing its own limits so that it can safely transgress them. To borrow the language of Deleuze and Guattari, the field of national imagination is a hybrid mixture of rhizome and tree, or, again, something like the fluid, smooth space of the game of Go articulated with the highly coded and bounded space of chess. And, "it is *in order to function* that a social machine must *not function well*" because "social machines make a habit of feeding on the contradictions they give rise to, on the crises they provoke, on the anxieties they *engender*" (emphasis in original).[42] The present study attempts to map out the diverse subject, object, and abject positions produced within the desiring machines of national imagination and to trace the ways in which those positions complement and reinforce one another. It will also examine crucial moments in Tōson's works that tend to undermine the dominant assumptions that govern national imagination.

Some may question the relevance of a study of national imagination at this point in time. A number of recent theorists have, after all, proclaimed the imminent end of the nation-state form in the wake of transnational global captialism.[43] This study, however, proceeds from a different asumption, that, in so far as capitalism is haunted by contradictions and contractions, it will need a form of subjectivity like the nation to guarantee its own reproduction. In Immanual Wallerstein's words, "Ethnicization, or peoplehood, resolves one of the basic contradictions of historical capitalism—its simultaneous thrust for theoretical equality and practical inequality."[44] The repercussions of early-twentieth-century Japanese nationalism still echo today, for both nationalists and antinationalists, in East Asia and elsewhere. We will be living with national imagination, both "good" and "bad," for the foreseeable future. Its immensity and complexity remain central problems, perhaps the central problem, to our understanding of modernity, our historical moment.

※

The chapters that follow each take up aspects of Tōson's works and their reception in Japan in terms of distinct strands from the complex field of national imagination. Chapter one focuses on the manner of Tōson's canonization, showing how the history of Tōson studies in Japan demonstrates not merely continuity between the wartime and postwar eras, but also how national imagination in Japan has been supple enough to absorb even explicitly anti-nationalist forms of thought. Chapter two then takes up Tōson's first novel, *The Broken Commandment*, and explores how the often contradictory images of the human body produced through the modern discourse of hygiene functioned as a sort of machine for simultaneously achieving the exclusion from, and assimilation into, the national community of various "others." Chapter three shows how multiple images of the family intersected in national imagination by unpacking the complex architecture of domestic space that structures *The Family* (*Ie*, 1910–11; trans. 1976), one of Tōson's best-known works. It also argues that the reception of Tōson's work has tended to efface aspects of the novel that trouble commonsense notions regarding the Japanese family and its place in national culture. Chapter four takes up the issues of gender and national literature and argues that Tōson's novels *Haru* (Spring; 1908) and *Shinsei* (New life; 1918–9) were active participants in the production of a version of "women's literature" that was not merely compatible with, but in fact necessary to, a masculinist version of the national canon of modern literature. The final chapter explores the multiplicity of chronotopes that have surrounded Tōson's great historical novel, *Before the Dawn*. It argues that the various forms of spatiality and temporality that structure national imagination help account for the process of *tenkō*, or political apostasy, whereby Japanese national imagination has been able to co-opt various antagonistic others and transform them into symbiotic variations of itself. It also locates traces within the novel of a chronotope that deconstructs many of the assumptions that inhere within national imagination.

The chapters are arranged so that the vision of national imagination they present proceeds roughly in an order of increasing complexity: from a stress on identity between two periods in the first chapter, a description of dual images of the national body in chapter two, a reading by triplication in discussing the national family, and, finally, in the concluding chapters, a depiction of the fields of national gender and temporality, which each include multiple competing images. Of course, the reality of national imagination is even more complex than such a schematic approach can account for: its field weaves together wildly divergent threads into a coherent, if continually collapsing, machine. I cannot claim to provide a systematic theorization of the problem here; instead, I will attempt to map out its complexity, as I unpack the remarkable intricacy of modern Japanese national imagination, as well as that of the works of one of its most important writers and intellectuals.

CHAPTER ONE

Tōson, Literary History, and
National Imagination

The canon serves as a utopian site of continuous textuality in which a
nation, a class, or an individual may find an undifferentiated identity. Central to its operation is the notion of founding geniuses (i.e., Homer, Shake-
speare, Dante, and Goethe) who seem to produce and validate it with their
language and authority. These founders express the spirit of the entire
nation and, in so doing, paradoxically transcend their national borders to
become universal figures. Their double role as local and global authors,
however, does not undermine the canon's national status but actually gives
it international prestige.

Gregory Jusdanis, *Belated Modernity and Aesthetic Culture: Inventing National Literature*

A convenient place to begin my exploration of the works of Shimazaki Tōson
and their relation to national imagination is the position the author has occupied in a variety of canons of Japanese literature. There is, after all, "no single
national canon, but several, each representing different communities, all striving to be officially crowned."[1] As Haruo Shirane has shown, the modern
canon of classical Japanese literature has had to stitch together texts from
widely variant domains, placing aristocratic, folkloric, and commercial texts
alongside one another in order to meet the conflicting demands of national
imagination.[2]

Just as there may be multiple versions of the national canon in the interior,
there can also be disjunctions between domestic and foreign versions of a
given nation's canon. "Japanese literature" functions not only for Japanese
readers seeking a sense of identity through encounters with the self-same, but
also for non-Japanese readers who seek various forms of identity mediated

through a foreign other. National imagination requires the representation of difference from foreign others, and canons of foreign literature are one site where such representations are produced.

In this chapter, I will examine the ways Tōson has been constructed as a canonical author and as a figure of literary history. In exploring the ways his works have been studied in the West, in prewar Japan, and in postwar Japan, I will pay particular attention to instances where studies of Tōson have provided a site for producing the rhetoric of national imagination, especially how the canonization of his works in the prewar period was implicated in processes whereby national imagination in Japan was able to co-opt and assimilate its own putative others. I also explore how that prewar history would continue to shape national imagination in Japan even after 1945.

⌗

With some exceptions, the canon of modern Japanese literature as defined by Western (primarily American) scholars has acknowledged Tōson's existence but rarely situated him as a central figure.[3] The history of his translation into European languages provides ample evidence of this tendency. In 1954, Joseph Roggendorf was assigned to write on the topic of the reception of Tōson's works in the West. He acknowledged frankly that there was none: "In fact, the sad truth is that Tōson is almost entirely unknown abroad. With the exception of the Chinese translation of *New Life*, the Russian translation of *The Broken Commandment*, and the German translation of two or three episodes from *Before the Dawn*, none of Tōson's works are available in a form that non-Japanese can read."[4]

This situation would remain unchanged for two more decades. Whereas writers such as Mishima Yukio, Tanizaki Junichirō, and Kawabata Yasunari had multiple novels appear in English translation during the 1950s and 1960s, the first English translations of Tōson's novels did not appear until the 1970s. A glance at Donald Keene's influential history of modern Japanese literature, *Dawn to the West* (1984), shows that more than half of its chapters devoted to fiction bear the names of individual writers, but Tōson does not rank a chapter of his own. He is instead one of several writers discussed in the chapter on "Naturalism," and although Keene praises a number of Tōson's works, the praise is often tempered with criticisms, usually made from the perspective of the values that predominated in New Criticism: Keene criticizes the failure of Tōson's works to function as organic, unified wholes. The characters in *The Broken Commandment*, for example, are not "successfully drawn, the female characters being particularly weak," while *Before the Dawn* is "excessively detailed" and "insufficiently absorb-ing" for readers not already fascinated with early Meiji.[5]

It is easy to suggest possible causes for the less-than-overwhelming pres-ence of Tōson in Western versions of modern Japanese literature. For exam-ple, Tōson's failure to provide the sort of benign-but-exotic images of Japan that were popular in the Cold War version of Orientalism that held sway in the 1950s and 1960s seems relevant. Again, the contrast with the works of Mishima, Kawabata, and Tanizaki, full of exotic (albeit frequently ironic) images of geisha, samurai, and cherry blossoms, is telling. As if to fill in this perceived lack of exoticism, the relatively few Western scholars who saw Tōson as central to the canon tended to stress how indelibly Japanese he was.[6] Moreover, the focus within Japanese scholarship on Tōson's "naturalism" and on the relationship between his works and his real life likely discouraged West-ern scholars working within the framework of New Criticism, which insisted on the autonomy of the literary text from both authorial biography and his-torical context, from seriously considering his works.

It has become something of a commonplace to argue that New Criticism, with its insistence on the autonomy of the literary work, functioned as an ide-ological technology during the Cold War. It reified the literary text into a har-monious and conflict-free organism that, in Terry Eagleton's words, "proved deeply attractive to sceptical liberal intellectuals disoriented by the clashing dogmas of the Cold War," providing them with a soothing "recipe for politi-cal inertia, and thus for submission to the political status quo."[7] While such cri-tiques tend to underplay the complexity of New Criticism (its stress, for example, on paradox and ambiguity) and the negative reaction it initially pro-voked among Cold War liberals,[8] nonetheless they do highlight the tendency of New Criticism to naturalize certain versions of society that were complicit with the deterritorialization and reterritorialization of society under global capitalism. Moreover, in the field of Japanese literary studies, New Criticism intersected with another pillar of Cold War ideology: the modernization-the-ory paradigm that predominated in area-studies scholarship in the United States during the 1950s and 1960s. Under modernization theory, Japan was held up as a model alternative to Marxist theories of development in the non-West. Its national culture was constructed in the West (and by advocates of modernization theory in Japan itself) as a rebuff to socialist internationalism and specifically to the Asian versions of Marxism found in Vietnam, China, North Korea, and elsewhere.

Paradoxically, the modernization-theory paradigm condemned writers like

Tōson to the relatively minor role of imitator of Western literature, especially of the "romanticism" and "naturalism" with which conventional literary history associated him. As Takashi Fujitani notes, modernization theory produced a supplemental twist on conventional Orientalism, which had previously stressed the exotic difference of the oriental other. In modernization theory, the Japanese other's similarity to the American self was now stressed, so that "the bottom line in the Cold-War revision of orientalism that became modernization discourse was that Japan could only be represented as an active, coherent, and rational subject insofar as it sought to become like the liberal, capitalist West."[9] Under this paradigm, Tōson was transformed into a rather uninteresting duplication of his Western betters. Again, those Western scholars who argued for Tōson's importance had to rebut this widespread assumption. They stressed the difference between Japanese naturalism and romanticism and their putative Western counterparts.[10]

⧉

In contrast to this Western scholarship, Japanese literary scholars typically place Tōson much closer to the center of the canon, especially in criticism produced through the 1970s. If Tōson is not the main protagonist of the narrative of modern Japanese literary history, he is at least one of the three or four figures who occupy center stage. This narrative was largely created in the 1920s and 1930s, often with the active participation of writers associated with the naturalist school, including Tōson himself. And from the 1930s through the 1960s, it seems, the best way for an ambitious young Japanese critic to make a name for himself (the field was dominated by men) was to launch his career with a book about Tōson. The list of scholars and critics who first attracted notice with book-length studies of Tōson reads like a "Who's Who" list of modern Japanese literary studies from midcentury: Kamei Katsuichirō, Hirano Ken, Yoshida Seiichi, and Miyoshi Yukio. Tōson's position in Japan has slipped some since the 1970s, displaced by, among other things, booms in scholarship on Natsume Sōseki (1867–1916) and Izumi Kyōka (1873–1939) and by the rediscovery of women writers. Nonetheless, he remains a prominent fixture in the landscape.

Contemporary Japanese readers familiar with conventional histories of modern Japanese literature might, however, be surprised by the early reviews of Tōson's *The Family* (*Ie*, 1910–1911; trans. 1976). Whereas the novel today is generally regarded as one of the masterpieces of Japanese naturalism and realism, early critics harbored reservations.[11] They found "unsatisfactory points"[12] and "cases where the author forgets his sharpness, his incisiveness, his flexibil-ity."[13] There are numerous possible explanations for the lukewarm reception the novel received in late Meiji—for example, the waning popularity of the naturalist school after 1910. And, as Jay Rubin has shown, around this time the Japanese state became increasingly concerned with policing an official canon of modern national literature, a canon that would exclude naturalist works like *The Family* because they failed to "express the glory of the Meiji era and the welling vitality of the Japanese people."[14]

But my interest here lies with another question: when, and why, was *The Family* reborn as a masterpiece and a cornerstone of the canon of Japanese national literature? This version of *The Family* was born in the 1930s. By 1938, in contrast to the criticism from the 1910s quoted above, we find an article that pronounces *The Family* one of the three masterpieces of Japanese realism—alongside Arishima Takeo's *Aru onna* (A certain woman, 1919) and Nagatsuka Takashi's *Tsuchi* (The soil, 1910).[15]

The historical timing of this reevaluation is of some significance. The 1930s, for starters, saw the publication of *Before the Dawn*, Tōson's last great work, an epic historical novel that portrayed the turbulent events of Japanese national history from the 1850s, 1860s, and 1870s. The 1930s were also the age of *tenkō*, or "political apostasy": the widespread conversion under state pres-sure of Japanese intellectuals away from Marxism and, in many cases, toward national socialist positions. (I will discuss this issue again in chapter five). *Before the Dawn* was serialized from 1929–1935, a time span that begins in a moment of radical political activism and that ends with the rise of fascism and the sup-pression of leftist thought. *Before the Dawn* not only shared a moment with *tenkō*, it sometimes shared the pages of the journal *Chūō kōron* with works that would come to be known as "*tenkō* literature," fictionalized autobiographical accounts of the experience of *tenkō* written by formerly Marxist writers who had recanted their positions. The January 1935 issue of *Chūō kōron* includes not only the serialized version of book 2, chapter 11, of *Before the Dawn*, it also contains "*Daiisshō*" (First chapter), the first of several important works of *tenkō* literature by Nakano Shigeharu (1902–1979). The canonization of Tōson in this period is, as we will see, fundamentally implicated with the problem of *tenkō*, even though Tōson himself is not typically identified as having com-mitted *tenkō*. That is to say, as in the Japan studies of postwar America, the canon of Japanese modern literature produced in 1930s Japan was implicated in the rejection of Marxist internationalism and in the celebration of a sup-posedly harmonious Japanese national culture.

In the 1930s, numerous Japanese writers and critics who committed *tenkō* found themselves, in the wake of that experience, rediscovering the works of Shimazaki Tōson, in particular his latest novel, *Before the Dawn*. In their celebration of that work, we can see them attempting to locate through it the meaning of their own apostasy, as well as to relocate their position in history following that often devastating experience. If *tenkō* is a process by which peripheral and resisting subjects are absorbed back into the national community—a process whereby national imagination demonstrates an ability to co-opt even explicitly antinational forms of thoughts—the canonization of Tōson in the 1930s helps explicate the role that national literature played in this reabsorption.[16]

⊠

As a result of the acclaim that greeted *Before the Dawn*, critics in the 1930s reevaluated Tōson's entire output. In a sense, this was planned: the first installment of that novel, in the July 1929 issue of *Chūō kōron*, was preceded by an article that celebrated Tōson as the central figure of the modern canon.[17] Earlier works such as *The Family*, which initially had met with a lukewarm assessment, were now re-read through the lens of *Before the Dawn* and pronounced modern classics.[18] It is in this same period, as already noted, that the narrative of modern Japanese literary history, a narrative that centers on the rise of "realism" and the "modern self," took the form that it would maintain well into the postwar period. Simultaneously, the various methodologies that would sustain modern literary studies in postwar Japan—*sakkaron* (author studies), *sakuhinron* (studies of a single work), literary history, comparative literature, etc.—also began to take recognizable shape. In each case, it is fair to say that Tōson's works provided the materials against which these methodologies were polished.

In that sense, although I will limit my focus here to the reception of Tōson's works, this chapter suggests a continuity between prewar and postwar studies of modern Japanese literature—and between prewar and postwar forms of national imagination. Although it was not until the postwar period that modern Japanese literature became a regular part of the university curriculum and universities began to hire specialists in modern Japanese literature,[19] I think it is valid to see this postwar development as a continuation of trends that began in the 1930s—a stance that places me in disagreement with, among others, Suzuki Sadami.[20] Suzuki argues that the standard narrative of modern Japanese literary history, centered on the heroic narrative of the rise of "modern realism," is a postwar construct, one that has been retroactively projected onto prewar history. But the example of Tōson criticism shows otherwise. To borrow Peter Hohendahl's language, although the "organization" of modern Japanese literary studies as an academic discipline may not have existed in the prewar period, the "institution" certainly did—including its characteristic narrative of literary history.[21]

For example, while academic specialists on Japanese literature in the 1930s focused mainly on classical literature, they could and did publish research on modern writers like Tōson. Okazaki Yoshie (1892–1982), one of the most influential university-based literary scholars, would write in 1936 that Tōson's style

> is an extremely Japanese style. Everywhere in it, we see the movement of things belonging to the spiritual realm marked by such words as *aware*, *yūshin*, *wabi*, and *shiori*. In such literary giants as Ōgai, Rohan, and Sōseki, too, we can spot these sorts of Japanese characteristics, yet strictly speaking, they seem more possessed of something oriental, so that if we speak of them in terms of the realm of Japanese thought, they seem in many ways medieval or samurai-like. In comparison, Tōson carries on the ancient spirit of the poets at the Nara court and of the writers of tales, diaries, and essays at the Heian court; he also bears a connection to Bashō and others who gave poetic voice to the hearts of rural peasants in the early modern period. In this sense, he seems the closest to the pure Japanese character.[22]

Likewise, in the field of literary journalism, periodicals such as *Bungaku* (published by Iwanami Shoten beginning in 1933) and *Kokubungaku kaishaku to kanshō* (published by Shibundō beginning in 1936) from the start carried articles on modern writers alongside articles on the premodern canon, articles that helped establish the standard narrative of literary history. Moreover, by the 1930s modern literature and literary history certainly existed as genres for the publishing industry. Practices such as publishing collected works of individual authors and broader series claiming to provide access to the whole canon of modern Japanese literature were already standard.

In sum, by the 1930s the project of constructing a national canon and literary history for Japan's modern literature was well under way. As I have already suggested, the rediscovery of Tōson was a central component of this process. But why in particular was the figure of Tōson so attractive to *tenkōsha*—former Marxists who had committed *tenkō*? As figures such as Kamei Katsuichirō negotiated their way from an avowedly internationalist (and therefore antinationalist) stance to a stridently nationalist one, why did they turn to Tōson?

Why did *tenkōsha* such as Itō Shinkichi make proclamations like:"The path followed by Shimazaki's literature represents the history of modern Japanese literature," and why did such proclamations become a matter of common sense?[23]
And what role did this legacy from the 1930s play in shaping postwar studies of
Tōson in Japan? By disclosing a structure of historical repetition between prewar and postwar, I hope to suggest ways in which the problem of national
imagination remains of crucial importance today.

⊠

The 1930s, then, were a crucial period in the history of the reception of Tōson's
works. Triggered by the reception of *Before the Dawn*, a buzz of activity surrounded the author throughout the decade. In 1935, the journal *Hyōron* published a special issue devoted to Tōson; the journal *Bungaku* did the same the
following year. The first of many university graduation theses devoted to Tōson
was submitted in 1932.[24] Public monuments began to be erected in places
where he had lived and worked, such as the one dedicated in Sendai in June
1937, with Tōson himself in attendance. A new edition of Tōson's collected
works issued by the Shinchōsha house during this period, the *Teihonban Tōson
bunkō* (Standard edition of Tōson's works), is emblematic of the way that *Before
the Dawn* provided a window through which his earlier works would be reevaluated: the first two volumes in the series, issued in 1935, consisted of books 1
and 2 of *Before the Dawn*, Tōson's most recent work. The final volume, volume
ten, issued in 1939, contained Tōson's oldest novel, *The Broken Commandment*.

By the middle of the 1930s, Tōson's position as one of the giants of modern Japanese literature was secure. In 1936, he was awarded the prestigious
Asahi Cultural Prize. When the Japanese chapter of the PEN Club, the international writers' society, was founded in 1935, Tōson was selected as its first
chairman. In this capacity, he later traveled to South America to attend an
international PEN conference in Buenos Aires, where he represented Japan's
modern national literature at the conference and in lectures delivered to a
variety of audiences.

Another clear sign of Tōson's canonization is the appearance during this
period of a number of book-length studies of his works. Itō Shinkichi's *Shimazaki Tōson no bungaku* (The literature of Shimazaki Tōson, 1936), while not
the first volume of criticism devoted to Tōson, has been called "the first book
of Tōson scholarship," one that is still "highly praised as one of the crucial
foundation stones in the history of Tōson scholarship."[25] Itō's study had great
influence when it first appeared, and he continued to publish important stud-

ies on Tōson in the postwar period as well, cementing his position as one of the leading interpreters of Tōson's works, especially the poetry. In terms of the problem I am addressing here, Itō quite literally embodies the continuity between prewar and postwar Tōson studies.

Before writing his study of Tōson, Itō was best known as a member of the circle of young poets associated with Murō Saisei (1889–1962). Like other young writers in Saisei's circle—Nakano Shigeharu, Sata Ineko (1904–1998), and others—Itō was active in the proletarian literature movement. But by the time he began his research on Tōson, Itō had already committed *tenkō* and left the movement. In 1932 he was arrested and then released on the condition that he renounce Marxism. Subsequently, he returned to his hometown in Gunma Prefecture and worked as a journalist.[26] It was at this time that Itō discovered Tōson. As Itō would later recall, "I had fallen away from the proletarian literature movement and was whiling away the days in my hometown with a feeling of failure. Those were days spent in a kind of drifting, lacking any spiritual vigor. Then, as my sense of spiritual starvation was growing more and more intense, by sheer chance I came across *The Broken Commandment*." Why did *The Broken Commandment* have such an impact on this *tenkōsha*? Because in it, "I saw the sturdy character of a social literature that was not proletarian literature."[27]

In sum, what Itō found in Tōson was a "sociality" (*shakaisei*) that did not rely on Marxism, a sociality that relied on "humanism" (*jindōshugi*) in place of Marxism, that spoke of "the people" (*jinmin*) in place of the proletariat. As Itō notes, when he wrote the book he had little experience as a literary scholar or critic, and hence "the book lacks a consistent critical or scholarly methodology."[28] When we read the book today, in fact, we do not find a consistent methodology. If certain sections seem to pursue what would later be called the *sakuhinron* methodology (studies that focus on a single work), other sections seem to use a *sakkaron* methodology (author studies), while yet other sections engage in comparative literature and literary history. Yet this methodological hybridity is not, I believe, a weakness; rather, it is one of the more attractive elements of Itō's work. And for my purposes here, what is of particular interest is that no matter which methodology Itō employs, his study of Tōson clearly outlines a theory of *tenkō* and attempts to resituate the *tenkōsha* within the national community.

When, for example, we look at Itō's interpretations of individual works, we find, not surprisingly, a stress on their "sociality." This is not limited to works such as *The Broken Commandment* or *Before the Dawn*, which directly thematize social problems; Itō locates sociality even in works that at first glance seem quite apolitical.[29] In *Wakanashū* (A collection of seedlings), Tōson's first poetry anthology, Itō Shinkichi finds the embodiment of "the tremendous rise in nationalist sentiment" that was unleashed by the "unceasing development of Japanese capitalism" that characterized the 1890s.[30] And while many of Tōson's works had been identified as I-novels,[31] Itō maintains that this does not render them apolitical: "They partake of I-novel characteristics. Yet when we consider the social character or the sociality of the themes that provide the contents for these I-novels, their character changes" (Itō, *Tōson*, 83).

What kind of "sociality" does Itō find in Tōson's works?

> Whenever we find his literature distinguished by its sociality, that social-
> ity is not a matter of political philosophy; we can say that it is more like
> the raw materials for a political philosophy. But it contains a rich sociality
> that arises from the way it parallels the actual level of social development,
> a stance that is achieved by the way it—grounded in the sturdiness of his
> human faith—probes the truth of human life and closes in on all facets of
> lived social reality. When we look at his concrete works and the relation
> in them between sociality and political philosophy, we see that sociality is
> always the dominant element. . . . In this, the lack of political philosophy
> avoids becoming a fatal failing, and the realistic critique of the sociality of
> desire becomes a methodology that elevates the quality of his works.
>
> (Itō, *Tōson*, 359–60).

In sum, according to Itō, Tōson's works are born out of a "skepticism or questioning of political philosophies or social movements that suddenly rise and then just as suddenly fall" (Itō, *Tōson*, 382).

In sum, in Itō's *sakuhinron*, there is an insistence on locating a sociality that does not arise from an abstract political philosophy, but rather from a firm grip on social reality itself. We begin to see, that is, the outlines of one *tenkōsha's* critique of 1930s Japanese Marxism—and his defense of his "return" to the embrace of the national community, identified as the site of social reality and authentic experience. While Itō never advocated the sort of fascist nationalism centered on emperor worship that would characterize other *tenkōsha* such as Hayashi Fusao, his version of national imagination clearly shares ground with Hayashi's ultranationalist essay, "Tenkō ni tsuite" (On *tenkō*, 1941).[32]

The nature of Itō's critique comes into clearer focus when he reads Tōson through the methodology of author studies, which seeks the unifying principle behind an author's entire oeuvre. Here, we see the emergence of a kind of allegorical figure for *tenkō*: Tōson the writer who dramatically changed course any number of times. Hence, Itō is particularly concerned with the various transitions he uncovers in the narrative of Tōson's life: his youthful conversions to and then from Christianity, from romanticism to naturalism, from poet to novelist, from I-novelist to historical novelist, and so on. In discussing the significance of *Haru* (Spring, 1908) in terms of author studies, for example, Itō declares that it represents "a changeover [*tenka*] to an affirmation of life" (Itō, *Tōson*, 123). We find a similar reading of the meaning of *Shinsei* (New life, 1918–1919) in terms of the author's lifework:

> If we ask what it was that, after forty years of human experience, suddenly plunged him into this crisis, we must say that it was his "human convictions" themselves. There is nothing paradoxical about this; we could also call it the revenge of "human convictions" on "human convictions." Something causes those convictions to reverse themselves; it comes not from outside, but from within the convictions themselves, inexorably causing them to reverse themselves: this is the tragedy that all who would live with convictions must experience at least once, a tragedy that is inescapable for anyone with convictions. When such persons stand on their convictions alone, that ground crumbles beneath them: this is the revenge of the convictions themselves. This is the chaos, the tragedy of *Shinsei* [New life]. Moreover, Mr. Shimazaki has the character of one who, no matter how painfully he will be stung, cannot forget or sidestep this. It is not merely a matter of transformation: he is a person who finds no comfort without achieving a renewal of his convictions
>
> (Itō, *Tōson*, 138)

The image of Tōson that Itō produces is one of a man who undergoes any number of disheartening reversals yet remains always able to pull out from them a new life, a new work.

Moreover, Itō suggests that Tōson is able to undergo these *tenkō*-like changes in direction without ever losing the thread of continuity that makes his life a single coherent whole. The Tōson that Itō portrays makes radical changes in direction without ever betraying his fundamental ideals. "The path Tōson has followed as a writer flows on continuously like a river," Itō writes, and "what carries on unbroken through the whole of that riverbed is his unflappable vital resolve" (Itō, *Tōson*, 109). On the surface, Tōson may commit sudden reversals, yet in his interior he never abandons his essential integrity as he steadfastly pursues the truth of human existence and sociality. It is easy to imagine how this image of an artist who maintains internal consistency even as he abruptly changes direction would have been attractive to *tenkōsha* like Itō.

An additional allegory for *tenkō* occurs at one other level in Itō's study: when he takes up Tōson's significance in literary history, particularly in terms of the position Itō assigns to naturalism. In considering this, it may be useful to examine another version of literary history produced in the 1930s by Kobayashi Hideo. In his 1935 essay, "Watakushi shōsetsu ron" (On the I-novel), Kobayashi praised the author of *Before the Dawn* for "breaking through the crisis" of the I-novel "by throwing his soul into matters of history."[33] In this and other essays, Kobayashi points out what he considers a continuity in the modern literary history of Japan. To wit, he sees a link between the naturalism school of the early 1900s and the proletarian literature movement of the 1920s. Both represent forms of thought that had a foreign origin, and both were distorted when they were imported into Japan, meaning that neither was able to form an organic connection with Japanese reality. In the case of naturalism, "this foreign school of thought was taken up by various writers solely as a matter of technique, and so it could only achieve life here as a matter of technique" (Kobayashi, 124). Because Japanese naturalist authors lacked the political philosophy that grounded the movement in the West, they could not produce masterpieces centered on the "socialized 'I' " such as were produced in Western naturalism. They could produce only "deformed" works. In the case of proletarian literature, it was the political philosophy that was imported—an achievement whose significance Kobayashi is quick to acknowledge—but since technique was lacking, the result was the same. "It produced not a single masterpiece that will last" (Kobayaashi, 132).[34]

When Itō discusses Tōson's position within Japan's modern literary history, he also points out the shortcomings of naturalism and the similarities between it and the later proletarian literature movement. But unlike Kobayashi, Itō himself had been, until quite recently, a member of the latter movement. Accordingly, there is a subtle difference between his and Kobayashi's interpretations of naturalism. To Itō, naturalism represents a necessary stage in the development of national literary history—just as the overcoming of that stage is also an unavoidable process.

The dark character of naturalist literature was probably unavoidable, whether we view it in terms of the order of historical development or of the circumstances of literary history. To pass from romanticism to realism, to reach the appearance of a humanistic literature that arose again in reaction to reality—of a newly fermented romantic spirit that is grounded in a newly discovered humanity—required the dark period during which naturalism held sway.   (Itō, 163–64)

After passing through naturalism, one moves into proletarian literature—which is, by implication, yet another necessary stage, one that in turn must be passed through. It seems that Itō is constructing here not solely an apologetic for *tenkō*, but an argument for its historical necessity, in terms of both his own life and literary history. And of course, it is after passing through the stage of *tenkō* that Itō reaches the next stage: the rediscovery of Shimazaki Tōson.

These various tendencies in Itō's interpretation of Tōson all come together in his reading of *Before the Dawn*. He reacts strongly against those who would read *Before the Dawn* as an apolitical I-novel, insisting on the "the rich historicity and sociality contained in this work" (Itō, *Tōson*, 533). He stresses the work's humanistic spirit and argues that its understanding of history arises not from some imported political philosophy, but rather from a firm grasp on historical reality itself. "Mr. Shimazaki makes the movement of history itself the central pillar of the work's structure," Itō declares, so that "the truth of the work lies not in useless interpretations of history, but in its faithful adherence to history itself" (Itō, *Tōson*, 490–91). And this firm grasp on history arises out of the long, continuous "pathway as an author" that Tōson has followed throughout his life (Itō, *Tōson*, 474–75).

In Itō's description of the novel's protagonist, Aoyama Hanzō, the idealistic follower of Hirata School nativism (*kokugaku*), we find yet again the image of a *tenkōsha*.

Hanzō is an intellectual, a man of ideals. He resisted feudal domination with the idealism of Hirata School philosophy. And yet he was unable to transform this idealism into praxis; already in his interior, this painful split between ideals and practice existed. There is no tragedy so painful as that of a person who cherishes a certain ideal and yet is not permitted to turn it into a form of praxis.   (Itō, *Tōson*, 539)

Here, perhaps, is the key for understanding why Tōson and his *Before the Dawn* became such important touchstones for *tenkōsha* in the 1930s. Attracted to the ideals of Marxism, yet forbidden from carrying them out in practice: through

Before the Dawn they could understand themselves as tragic heroes. Moreover, in portraying the act of *tenkō* as a movement away from foreign and abstract theory and toward social reality (which became a kind of leitmotif in writings about *tenkō*), the *tenkōsha*—who a few short years earlier had been advocating an explicitly antinationalist form of thought—could narrate a position for themselves within the Japanese national community. This tendency would reach something of a logical conclusion in 1941 when the *tenkōsha* Hayashi Fusao would argue that *tenkōsha*—in their ceaseless striving to achieve union with the emperor, in their understanding of the failings of Western liberalism, in their selfless devotion to society—were the most Japanese of all Japanese: "Even those *tenkōsha* who were unable to sacrifice their lives for the sake of Marxism are now—because they are Japanese—capable of gladly sacrificing themselves for the sake of a great ideal [Japan]."[35]

☷

In their 1930s rediscovery, Tōson's works were resituated in national literary history to render them suitable to the demands of wartime nationalism. Itō Shinkichi's 1936 book on Tōson was part of a general rediscovery of the writer, which in turn was part of a broader process of defining a national canon and a history of modern literature. Tōson himself took an active role in this rewriting of his career. The drastically shortened version of *Shinsei* [New life] that he published in 1938 and the revised version of *The Broken Commandment* he published in 1939 reshaped those novels in response to the needs of the new national canon that was taking shape under the crisis of Total War. Traces of colonial domination, socialist activism, and racial prejudice were erased from the works, rendering them fit to participate in the project of generating unprecedented levels of devotion and sacrifice to the nation. This process of canon formation occurred in tandem with the phenomenon of *tenkō* and the absorption of antinational thought into the field of national imagination, whereby state nationalism effectively translated antielite and anti-imperialist popular movements into its own language.

But what happened to these versions of the canon and literary history after 1945, when the authoritarian nationalism of the wartime period was discarded and a new, more democratic national imagination had to be constructed? The fate of another milestone book is instructive: Kamei Katsuichirō's *Shimazaki Tōson: ippyōhakusha no shōzō* (Shimazaki Tōson: Portrait of a wanderer, 1939).[36] In the first edition of this work, Kamei celebrated the national "blood" he discovered in *Before the Dawn* and linked it to the blood then being shed by

Japanese troops in Asia: war would renew the national community. Kamei was less impressed, however, with the recent revisions Tōson had carried out on his earlier works. "To leave behind a particular work at a given moment is a matter of fate," Kamei writes. "To append after the fact any number of corrections or explanations—isn't that really pointless? Works live on, independent of their authors. *Shinsei* [New life] too lives on today in this way, truly a great classic. Tōson's current state of mind is quite irrelevant to it." Hence, according to Kamei, the revisions and new prefaces that Tōson produced for the latest edition of his collected works were "sometimes useful, but more frequently they get in the way."[37]

Ironically, when Kamei's 1939 study was reissued after the war in 1947, it too became a revised edition. The first edition's celebration of national blood and the role of war in purifying it are edited out, replaced with the assertion that "the war has ended in defeat. But the struggle for a revolution in the minds of the Japanese people has just begun."[38] The passages where Kamei complains about Tōson's revisions of his earlier works, however, remain unaltered in the 1947 revised edition of Kamei's book. And like Itō Shinkichi, Kamei would remain an active figure in postwar Tōson scholarship.

The postwar rewriting of problematic passages in Kamei's 1939 book is symbolic of the way that Tōson figured in national canons after 1945. The basic tropes and frameworks developed in the 1930s were retained, but their connection to wartime fascism, imperialism, and state nationalism were downplayed or forgotten. The canonization of Tōson became a part of the process by which, as Yoshikuni Igarashi argues, "Japanese society rendered its traumatic experiences of the war comprehensible through narrative devices that downplayed their disruptive effects on Japan's history."[39] The postwar fate of the problematic 1939 revised edition of *The Broken Commandment* (discussed at more length in the next chapter) provides another concrete example of this process of selective forgetting. In the early postwar years, publishers continued to use the 1939 version of the text. But then, starting with a 1953 edition published by Chikuma Shobō, publishers began returning to the original 1906 text, sometimes with little explanation of the history of textual variation. By 1971, when the Shinchō Bunko edition of the novel reverted to the 1906 version, the process was complete. Since then, the 1939 revised text has been unavailable in any edition. Through a gesture that claimed to recover a lost past, a problematic segment of national history was erased: 1906 was restored to memory, but 1939 vanished. Its disappearance facilitated the drawing of a sharp distinction between "bad" exclusionary nationalism and "good" assimilationist nationalism, a distinction that was—as I will discuss below—crucial to postwar intellectuals.

❈

The postwar version of Tōson was shaped by, and in turn helped shape, a widespread resurgence in popular and cultural antistate nationalism in Japan. For members of this generation of "ambivalent moderns," national imagination has been a central problem.[40] Their critique of contemporary Japanese society relied on discovering traces of a folk or popular national culture that were being suppressed by the state, especially in its blind pursuit of economic development and in its complicity with American Cold War policies.

As a result, the 1950s and 1960s saw a revival of interest in many of the writers and thinkers who participated in the 1930s' antimodern rhetoric of national imagination. Leaders of student protests or of citizens' movements were as likely to quote folklorist Yanagita Kunio (1875–1962) as they were Marx. As Leslie Pincus notes, Kuki Shūzō (1888–1941) and his 'Iki' no kōzō (The Structure of 'Iki,' 1930) gained a "second life" in the 1960s, finding "a new place among a multitude of books offering disaffected readers shelter within the embrace of an imaginary community—comfortingly homogeneous and triumphantly exceptional, fundamentally unchanging and yet supremely adaptable to the harsh demands of modernity."[41] Likewise, Watsuji Tetsurō's 1930s works on climate and national culture were rediscovered and became an important touchstone for a whole new wave of theories of "Japanese civilization" (Nihonjinron) in the 1960s and 1970s.[42]

For the most part, the postwar generation of intellectuals and activists found Tōson an attractive figure. They read his novels with enthusiasm and also attended to new adaptations of those works appearing on stage, television, and film, including Yoshimura Kimisaburō's 1955 film version of Before the Dawn and Ichikawa Kon's 1962 film version of The Broken Commandment. In the hands of antidiscrimination activists, The Broken Commandment, with its searing accounts of the injustices of prejudice suffered by an outcast burakumin became an important document for use in liberal dōwa (assimilationist) education.[43]

Likewise, scholars of the new antielitist minshūshi (people's history) that emerged in the 1960s found much to admire in Tōson's fiction and poetry. When Irokawa Daikichi, in his pathbreaking book, The Culture of the Meiji Period, recovered the forgotten and often radically democratic constitutional drafts written by activists in the 1870s and 1880s, he was very much working within the lineage established by Before the Dawn and its vision of the Meiji

Restoration as the betrayal of a popular revolution. Likewise, Irokawa's celebration of Kitamura Tōkoku as the emblematic tragic hero of Meiji intellectual life mobilized the image of Tōkoku that Tōson had first constructed in
Haru (Spring).[44] Takashi Fujitani argues persuasively that *minshūshi* emerged as
part of a counterorientalist move to rethink Japan's history during the struggle against U.S. imperialism in East Asia during the 1960s and 1970s.[45] But in
seeking alternatives to Marxism and modernization theory, the *minshūshi* historians frequently turned to such models as Yanagita Kunio and his version of
the Japanese folk. This move was problematic partly because, as Carol Gluck
notes, Yanagita's methodology "was designed for the purposes of doing
ethnography, not history, which means that it seeks the 'fixed stream' of tradition before the many moving ones of historical change."[46] Moreover, the
return to Yanagita suggests that this postwar form of anti-imperialism might
inadvertently complement and supplement the state's own neocolonialism, as
was the case with Yanagita in the prewar period, according to Murai Osamu.[47]

During this turbulent period, right-wing nationalists (including Hayashi
Fusao, who remained quite active in the postwar period) and the state actively
promulgated their own version of a national imagination. The Japanese state,
ruled by the conservative Liberal Democratic Party, sought to naturalize the
image of a harmonious society rooted in a timeless essence—what Oguma
Eiji has called the "myth of the homogeneous nation."[48] This version tended
to delegitimize domestic dissent as being inherently un-Japanese in nature; it
also contributed to the Cold War use of Japan as a model for nonrevolution-
ary modernization in Asia.

The New Left intellectuals who rose up in protest against this state, especially in the 1960 struggle against the renewal of AMPO, the U.S.–Japan Security Pact, identified this version of nationalism with the 1930s. They "sought
to distinguish clearly between nationalism and ultranationalism," J. Victor
Koschmann writes, evoking a "popular nationalism" that was nonelite and
"rooted in the cognitive patterns of daily life" in contrast to an "ultranationalism" that they thought had been produced mainly by elite intellectuals and
foisted on the unsuspecting masses in the 1930s.[49] Recent historians have
pointed out, though, that their thought often repeated currents from the
1930s. Their "resuscitated ideal of community" undoubtedly "opened the way
for a renewed emphasis on particularism and cultural exceptionalism. The discourse on cultural exceptionalism was transformed into a social science or
'sociology' focused on explaining Japan's uniqueness."[50] While many New Left
intellectuals remained unyielding in their criticism of the state and conserva-

tive nationalism, by the time of the boom in *Nihonjinron* theories of Japan-eseness in the 1970s, it was clear that national imagination had once again managed to appropriate resisting energies into its own field.

In other words, the division between "good" nationalism (which could mean, variously, popular, antistate, antielitist, and anti-imperialist) and "bad" nationalism (statist, authoritarian, fascist, imperialist), so crucial to New Left intellectuals, could not finally be sustained. Those who in the 1960s sought to produce antiestablishment versions of Japanese culture often looked for uniqueness within the structures of the Japanese family. They focussed on aspects that were supposedly unique to Japanese domestic life in the *furusato* (native place or hometown), including its supposed division between "*uchi*" (inside) and "*soto*" (outside), and the "familialism" that was supposed to distin-guish Japanese institutions (even giant corporations) from their counterparts in other societies.[51] In the family and *furusato* these intellectuals sought reas-surance of a continuous Japanese identity lying beneath the surface of what otherwise appeared to be radical historical change, a continuity that was to provide a foundation for resistance to "bad" state nationalism. But as Jennifer Robinson notes, "the patriarchal ideology of the family-system state (*kazoku kokka*) elaborated during the wartime period persists in the [postwar] *furusato* paradigm of nation-making"; the distinction between "good" and 'bad' nationalism in the end remains suspect.[52]

❦

In tandem with this revitalized cultural nationalism, the 1950s and 1960s saw a boom in Tōson studies, both inside and outside the academy. A new gener-ation of scholars, including Yoshida Seiichi, Senuma Shigeki, and Miyoshi Yukio, published milestone works, solidifying the position of Tōson at the center of the modern canon of national literature. Often, critics from this new generation wrote quite explicitly about the role of their scholarship in sus-taining national imagination. In a 1971 article on *The Broken Commandment*, for example, Ōkubo Tsuneo revisits the history of criticism of the novel, a his-tory split between factions that interpreted it as a confessional I-novel and those that saw it as a political critique of Meiji society. Such critics, he argues, are not carrying out their proper duty. He proposes returning to the text, just as it was written. Rather than projecting external notions onto novels,

> contemporary literary historians should consider literary works as con-stituting autonomous linguistic spaces. They should unlock their inter-

nal structures and ascertain the workings of imaginative powers in them. Only through the accumulation of this sort of effort will they be able to carry out their most important task: to identify the unchanging essence [*fuhen na mono*] that persists throughout the history of Japanese literature.[53]

Katō Shūichi (b. 1919), one of the most insightful critics of the postwar period, would likewise identify in Tōson's works (and those of other I-novelists) a worldview that focused on "the countless minutiae of personal, mundane space lacking central concepts and guiding principles," a view whose origins "can be traced back through Saikaku, the *Kyōgen*, the *Konjaku monogatari* to the very beginnings of Japanese literature."[54]

When we examine the new Tōson criticism written under the sway of postwar cultural nationalism, we find the tropes and frameworks developed under the state nationalism of the 1930s reappearing, often with remarkably little alteration. But their connections to fascism, imperialist expansion, and suppression of radical thought are repressed from memory. Instead, they are invoked in the service of what is thought to be a resisting form of national imagination. Tōson emerges once again as the chronicler of the daily life of common people, the voice of the non-Marxist "sociality" that Itō Shinkichi had described in 1936. As Suga Hidemi notes, although other late-Meiji writers—including Natsume Sōseki—have been revisited in recent years as part of critiques of the rise of the concept of national literature and empire, Tōson's works have seen little of that sort of revisionism.[55]

The "blood" imagery first used in prewar Tōson criticism by such figures as Kamei Katsuichirō, for example, reappears frequently in postwar criticism.[56] In a 1972 article linking Tōson to the folk culture and "climate" (*fūdo*) of the Shinshū region, Senuma Shigeki invokes the trope of "blood," using it simultaneously to link family lineage, the *furusato* village community of Magome, and (implicitly) the nation of Japan.

> In the case of old extended families like the Shimazakis, we are reminded—along with the climate conditions of a forest region—of the internal and external causes of the melancholia, of the degenerate blood that was the great burden of Tōson's life. Tōson's fastidiousness and his melancholia marked the agony of old blood, a blood linked closely to the local climate.[57]

And, as I discuss in chapter four, Miyoshi Yukio, perhaps the most influential literary scholar in Japan in the 1960s and 1970s, would argue that foreigners are often disgusted by Tōson's novels because "reactions of both sympathy and repulsion are, in the end, problems of Japanese blood."[58]

The image of the family, or *ie*, as a trope for the Japanese national community, which I discuss in chapter three, was also carried over into postwar Tōson studies. As Morris-Suzuki argues, popular and scholarly works on the Japanese family demonstrated "the ways in which the postwar rhetoric of democratization, modernization, and scientific progress could readily be integrated with reworked prewar ideas about the centrality of the *ie* in the national order."[59] Watanabe Hiroshi, for example, in an often brilliant rereading of Tōson's *The Family* (*Ie*), locates in its portrayal of the family elements that distinguish Japan from the West. Whereas Western novels that depict father-son relations usually revolve around patricidal desires, *The Family* does not. This reveals, according to Watanabe, the difference between the family in the West and in Japan. This cultural difference is especially pronounced at the level of language. Watanabe insists that we probe "the Japanese-specific lived [*Nihonjinteki/seikatsuteki*] reality that permeates the *parole* of conversations exchanged between the characters." National difference is especially pronounced in the writing system: the use of nonphonocentric Chinese characters reveals "the fundamental difference between Japanese and European writing."[60] Likewise, Yamashita Etsuko cites *The Family* in her critique of contemporary feminism in Japan; feminist criticism of patriarchy in Japan is misplaced, Yamashita argues, because unlike the Western family, the Japanese family has been marked by an absence of patriarchy.[61] In both instances, we find tropes first developed in prewar studies, tropes that translated Tōson's works into catalysts of national imagination, recycled in the postwar era—except that they are presented in the latter version as if they were radically new and subversive recoveries of suppressed popular nationalism.

Postwar criticism also frequently replicates the allegorical use of Tōson's life as a figure for the continuity of national identity. When postwar critics locate moments of incoherence in Tōson's texts, they are frequently stitched over through appeals to the author's life. Numerous critics in the 1960s and 1970s continued the project begun in the 1930s: locating the continuity that lay behind the apparent breaks in Tōson's life. Studies were published showing, for example, how the early poetry prefigured the later novels, or how *The Broken Commandment* was, in essence, a confessional novel and therefore continuous with the later I-novels. Given the central position Tōson occupied in the national canon, this biographical continuity easily transformed into a trope for the continuity that was supposed to underlay the Japanese nation despite the radical changes it had undergone since 1868.

If there is a difference between the prewar and postwar versions of Tōson, it is that in the more recent criticism, he is identified not simply with Japaneseness, but more precisely with a Japaneseness that postwar Japan supposedly lacks. In this more melancholic mode, the image of Tōson becomes a topos for soliciting nostalgia for a Japaneseness that is apparently wanting in the postwar readers. In 1951, for example, Watsuji Tetsurō would write that "the Japanese of olden days liked to wear kimonos that were plain and simple on the outer surface that others could see, but luxurious on the inner surface that was invisible to others." This is quite different from Westerners, who "have no qualms about openly displaying extravagance." Watsuji concludes that this style "may already be old-fashioned even in Japan, but it was powerfully at work in Tōson."[62] Likewise, in 1954 the novelist Enchi Fumiko (1905–1986) wrote "among the authors of his generation, [Tōson] is the most Japanese—yet at the same time, he possesses that which Japan lacks. If Japan were grounded in a way of life as tenacious as Tōson's, it would never have fallen into its present state."[63] As linchpin in the postwar canon, Tōson became part of what Marilyn Ivy calls the "discourses of the vanishing." He became a "movement of something passing away, gone but not quite, suspended between presence and absence, located at a point that both is and is not here," one that functions to sustain the desire for desire that is crucial to national imagination.[64] Tōson himself had become the dawn (or springtime or new life) that never comes.

❈

The postwar rediscovery of Tōson occurred in tandem with a revived interest in *tenkō*. Just as *tenkō* in the 1930s operated as a device for appropriating even antinationalist thought into the project of national imagination, so too the postwar discourse on *tenkō* became a topos whereby even intellectuals who resisted the state could be co-opted into forms of cultural nationalism that ultimately were complementary to state ideology. Even in its postwar version, that is, *tenkō* and the discourse surrounding it became an important topos for the reproduction of national imagination.

In the immediate postwar era, when legal repression of Marxists was (at least temporarily) halted, Japanese intellectuals revisited the problem of *tenkō* as something shameful. The *tenkōsha* frequently found themselves reviled, especially when they were contrasted with the heroic examples of dissidents like the newly liberated Miyamoto Kenji (b. 1908) and other Marxists who had spent the duration of the war in prison rather than recant their political beliefs.[65] *Tenkō* literature produced in this era tends to be guilt-ridden. The story "Fuchisō" (The weathervane plant, 1946) by Miyamoto's wife, Miyamoto Yuriko (1899–1951), for example, describes an activist woman who had collaborated with the wartime state and the shame she feels when reunited with her husband, who had refused to commit *tenkō* and spent the entire war imprisoned.

By the middle of the 1950s, however, a different discourse on *tenkō* began to take shape. A new generation of intellectuals took up the problem, often transforming the definition of the term into a much broader concept as they sought to critique the position of Japan in the new Cold War world. Yoshimoto Takaaki (b. 1924), for example, in his 1958 essay on *tenkō* would stand the topic on its head. *Tenkō* now became an opportunity to attack Japanese Marxism in general for its elitism and lack of connection with the "people" and "tradition."

> From the perspective of my interests, it is clear what *tenkō* signifies. It refers to an intellectual transformation arising among the intelligentsia as a result of their failure to grasp the structure of Japan's modern society through a totalizing vision. Accordingly, in addition to being an intellectual compromise, submission, or corruption in the face of the terrible conditions of Japanese society, the problem of *tenkō* has another important kernel: intellectual disinterest or submission with regard to the totalizing dominant gene that is tradition.[66]

In Yoshimoto's version, *tenkō* signifies the intellectual elite's estrangement from the masses, so that the most egregious *tenkōsha* were those who had refused to renounce their beliefs and spent the war in prison. "In my view, even 'non-*tenkō*' forms of *tenkō* can be considered forms of *tenkō* in terms of this 'disinterest'" (Yoshimoto, 10). "This is because their non-*tenkō* was unconnected to actual tendencies and to the tendencies of the masses, and it amounted to nothing more than spinning ideology around in logical circles" (Yoshimoto, 26). This estrangment from the masses prevented 1930s leftists from acquiring a clear understanding of nationalism and its relation to class struggle—it prevented them, that is, from being able to distinguish "good" nationalism from "bad" ultranationalism.

In the 1958 essay, Yoshimoto was developing many of the ideas he would subsequently explore at greater length, ideas that would make him something of a cult figure among 1960s student radicals—and among critics and scholars who studied Tōson.[67] Yoshimoto sought a version of the national community grounded in the "people," one that avoided the elitism that he thought equally characterized Japanese Marxism, prewar ultranationalism, and postwar modernization theory. He advocated a form of "mass nationalism" and argued that this was precisely what present-day Japan lacked: "Mass nationalism since Meiji has lost any concept of itself; the nation in actuality no longer exists."[68]

Despite his pains to distinguish his position from ultranationalism, though, Yoshimoto's stress on the affective bonds linking the national community, his stress on the naturalness of that bond, and his identification of it with a timeless essence that had persisted throughout Japanese history, made that distinction hazy. And while Yoshimoto remained critical of the state, in the 1970s and 1980s many of his disciples translated this version of "mass nationalism" into the theories of *Nihonjinron* supported by the state itself.

In fact, we can locate moments of complicity between the authoritarian state and "mass nationalism" even in Yoshimoto's early essay on *tenkō*. In arguing that state pressure was a secondary factor in causing *tenkō* during the 1930s, Yoshimoto implicitly takes up the position advocated by the state itself: he echoes the state's assertions that its opponents were out of touch with Japan's national reality. Yoshimoto's resisting masses—for example, the father of the protagonist *tenkōsha* in Nakano Shigeharu's "Mura no ie" (House in the village, 1935)—find themselves inadvertently in league with the state, and the Marxists are condemned, finally, for being un-Japanese. Yoshimoto was unsparing in his criticism of the postwar Japanese state and of modernization theory, the ideological centerpiece of American Cold War policies. But in the end, Yoshimoto's reliance on "mass nationalism" paradoxically led him to a position that was disturbingly complicit with the state's rhetoric of Cold War anticommunism.

☒

Perhaps the most influential postwar work on *tenkō* was the three-volume series *Kyōdō kenkyū: tenkō* (Cooperative research: *Tenkō*, 1959–1962) organized by Tsurumi Shunsuke (b. 1922) under the auspices of his Shisō no Kagaku (Science of thought) group. Throughout the postwar period, Tsurumi has earned a reputation as an activist-thinker, one who asserted the importance of the philosophy of everyday life and who sought an antielitist version of a Japanese identity, one that rejected ultranationalism, communism, and Americanism.

Noting the difference between his own definition of *tenkō* and that of Yoshimoto, Tsurumi writes:

My own definition of *tenkō* is as follows: a change in the way of thinking of individuals or groups which is brought about by state compulsion. This definition allows the inclusion of various instances occurring
in various circumstances. In analyzing a particular example, we can
examine the character of state power, the means of compulsion used,
and the changes in the way of thinking of the individual in response to
compulsion. The definition does not imply any judgement as to
whether *tenkō* is intrinsically good or bad.[69]

Lawrence Olson notes that this attempt to achieve a value-free stance was
maintained only inconsistently, so that the studies published tended in general
to be unsympathetic to *tenkōsha*. Nonetheless, Tsurumi and his colleagues
were, more than most critics, "sensitive to the complexities of the whole subject, and wished to avoid self-righteous moral judgements."[70]

Tsurumi also explored the connections between Japanese *tenkō* and renun-
ciations of Marxism that had taken place elsewhere, calling for a kind of
transnational and comparative "*tenkō*-ology." But from around 1960, as he
grew increasingly critical of U.S. neoimperialism, Tsurumi's stance on *tenkō*
shifted subtly. The role of state coercion lessened, and in its wake, *tenkō*
emerged more and more as a mark of Japaneseness. He would write that

> even without the clear violence of state power, progressive ideas that
> disregard native tradition are over time changed by the force of customs.
> ...When one's native soil comes up from the bottom of one's memory,
> progressive ideas can seem unbearable and be easily abandoned.[71]

Tsurumi began to see *tenkō* as marking a kind of Japanese particularity that
persisted through history. This stress on particularity never transformed into
xenophobia; Tsurumi insisted that any return to native traditions must be
accompanied by greater international connections. Nonetheless, Tsurumi
began to find in *tenkō* the traces of an inescapable, transhistorical national culture against which all resistance was futile.

In sum, whereas Yoshimoto implicitly condemned the Marxist *tenkōsha* for
being un-Japanese, Tsurumi adopted a more sympathetic stance toward them
precisely because their experience seemed quintessentially Japanese. And
whereas Yoshimoto would argue that even Marxists who had not committed
tenkō were in a sense *tenkōsha*, Tsurumi would argue that even some admitted
tenkōsha never underwent true *tenkō*. As Brett de Bary notes, Tsurumi's version
of *tenkō* relied on "the paradoxical concept of *conversion as consistency*" (empha-

sis in original). But this required problematic assumptions about "representation": Tsurumi could find, for example, "a thematics of radical skepticism" in a work of *tenkō* literature like Haniya Yutaka's *Fugōri yue ni ware shinzu* (Credo quia absurdum, 1939–1941), but in doing so Tsurumi "fails to acknowledge the degree to which the text problematizes itself as representation."[72]

Tsurumi's problematic assumptions about representation are related to the position of national culture in his work. In using *tenkō* as part of his project to define a counterhegemonic "good" nationalism, Tsurumi had to position himself as one who could represent the unrepresented, as one who could become the voice of the voiceless. Harry Harootunian notes that Tsurumi's work evidences

> an enduring concern for the common folk and everyday life, and for the role of *tenkō* as competing codes capable of explaining Japan's modern history. The intellectual history of Japan from 1931 to 1945 reveals the operation of *tenkō* in its multiple manifestations at the same time that it discloses how ordinary people had successfully resisted assimilation into modern Western ideologies.

This stance arose as part of Tsurumi's attempt to ground a resisting popular politics in the wake of the AMPO struggle, an attempt to locate in the common people "a resistance whose absence from the hegemonic narrative is the sign of genuine political difference, suppressed alterities, new and dangerous possibilities for the ruling class to consider." Harootunian distinguishes Tsurumi's work from that of the national narrative produced by conservative historians, a narrative that stresses consensus and political quietude. Tsurumi avoids advocating Japanese exceptionalism because he refuses to define the contents of Japan's national culture beyond a declaration of its "tolerance of difference."

> But this tolerance for difference is accomplished only at the price of eliminating differences *within* the folk. Tsurumi must present this indigenous culture in the image of a unity and coherence from which the hegemonic culture has derived its own claim to authority.[73]

Tsurumi's antielite cultural nationalism, that is, complements the very state nationalism it intends to criticize. Its labors to (re)produce the imagined community of the folk that inadvertently legitimates the existence of the latter, enabling the state to claim validity as "representative" of the people. In this model of representation, small differences internal to the national community are displaced, so that difference exists only between, not within, national communities.

☒

This rather lengthy excursus on postwar debates over *tenkō* has helped, I hope, sketch in the historical framework through which postwar scholarship on Tōson recycled tropes originally developed in the 1930s. At times, the connection was quite explicit: Isoda Kōichi, for example, has argued that Hirano Ken's influential 1945 essay on *Shinsei* (New life) in fact represents Hirano's attempt to work through the problematic nature of *tenkō* and its relationship to a new postwar democratic left.[74] Moreover, the history of *tenkō* is of particular importance to the project of this book, both for the example it gives of the fluidity and complexity of national imagination and for the cautionary tale it provides for any study that would claim to stand entirely outside the object it hopes to critique.

To explore this more fully, I would like to turn now to examine one final postwar theorization of *tenkō*. In an essay on Nakano Shigeharu and *tenkō*, Karatani Kōjin (b. 1941) performs a close reading of Nakano's *tenkō* literature in order to reveal problematic assumptions underlying discourses on *tenkō* from both the 1930s and the postwar years, a reading that harbors important suggestions for any attempt to reach a critical understanding of national imagination.[75]

According to Karatani, for Nakano the central problem of both politics and literature was the way in which large, sweeping distinctions erase small differences. The key to ethical praxis, then, was to insist on the small differences that exist within both poles of a binary opposition. Moreover, Karatani argues, Nakano saw that the very structure of binary opposition was grounded in a reversible logic of identity. In it, the two poles necessarily resemble and are mutually implicated in one another. Both are locked in an attempt to achieve homogeneity through the exclusion of the other, and hence each depends on the other for its identity. It is precisely this structure that allows sudden reversals to take place between them: in a sense, there is no difference between the poles in a binary opposition. A failure to attend to the small differences that trouble each pole, in other words, allows one to switch suddenly from a socialist position to a fascist one, and vice versa.

This logic of identity conceals the ways in which each subject position is in fact created by a dense web of interlocking social relationships in which small differences exist and changes are continually occurring, making a final closure of identity impossible. The individual subject comes to conscious existence as an individual only through the friction and pressures caused by contraditions in this historical network. This understanding of subjectivity was, according to Karatani, the central tenet of Nakano's political praxis.

Other Marxist writers from the period (for example, Kamei Katsuichirō) saw Marxism as a kind of religious belief, as an ultimate guarantor of identity. Operating through the logic of identity, they had committed *tenkō* when they converted to Marxism, just as they would do again when they converted away from it. Nakano, in contrast, consistently attended to the small differences inherent in each subject position, differences that undermined any attempt to draw closure around either meaning or identity. Rather than explore the binary distinction between *tenkō*/non-*tenkō*, his *tenkō* literature explores the small differences that existed within each category, preventing either from reaching a state of self-identity.

According to Karatani, Nakano understood the abandonment of small differences as being a rejection of the central principles of Marxism—*tenkō* in the worst possible sense. Moreover, Nakano understood that one could never pin down the meaning of the small differences that were so important to him: such an act of definition would require one to resort to a binary logic, whereby the differences themselves would be erased. Nakano labored, through his fiction, to signal the existence of such small differences through the presence of incoherent feelings, through inexplicable gaps and excesses in his language. The whole point was to face up to "feelings of incompatibility" without translating them into something else, without claiming to be able to *represent* them adequately in language.

Karatani's theorization of *tenkō* is a tremendous aid to a critical rethinking of Tōson and Japanese nationalism. The phenomenon of *tenkō* demonstrates the ability of national imagination to absorb into itself even antinational forms of thought. Karatani's work suggests that any critique of Japanese nationalism that sets itself up in binary opposition to its object (either Japan or nationalism in general) risks meeting this same fate. It was such a stance that underwrote 1950s and 1960s Western scholarship on Japan, the orientalist scholarship that tended to dismiss Tōson as it rushed to introduce more properly "Japanese" writers to English-speaking audiences. A useful critique of national imagination must begin from a realization that it shares ground with its object; it cannot situate itself as the pure opposite of its object.

Moreover, such a critique must attend to the small differences, to the contradictions and fluidities that mark both national and antinational imagination—the sorts of differences that Tōson studies in Japan, both before and after 1945, have largely been unable to countenance. Such a blindness not only leads one to underestimate the complexity of Tōson's works, it also tends to mask the substantial complicity that exists between "good" and "bad" forms of nationalism. In the subsequent chapters of this book, as I turn to explore individual novels, I will labor wherever possible to bring out the complexity and lack of identity that I think is, paradoxically, crucial to the production and reproduction of modern national identities in Japan and elsewhere. A critique of national imagination can be effective only if it attends to the small differences that are lost when nationalism is posited as a form of identity and closure.

Judith Butler cites the following words from an interview by Gayatri Chakravorty Spivak:

> If I understand deconstruction, deconstruction is not an exposure of error, certainly not other people's error. The critique in deconstruction, the most serious critique in deconstruction, is the critique of something that is extremely useful, something without which we cannot do anything.[76]

The form of critical practice I will engage in here is meant as a kind of deconstruction. If this deconstruction is useful, it is so only to the extent that it meets Spivak's conditions. National imagination is the source of many of our most necessary ideals: equality, liberty, community. Moreover, the producers of national imagination I have discussed here—Tōson, his readers, and, more recently, Irokawa, Tsurumi, and Yoshimoto, among others—were selected because they are among the most useful thinkers modern Japan has produced. Their versions of national imagination have often highlighted blind spots in American national (and global) imagination. They have mobilized Japanese national imagination in effective ways to counter the impact of American hegemony in the non-Western world. Such thinkers have much to teach us, especially those of us in the United States who take Japan as our object of study. They help us to see, for example, the gap between America's Tōson and Japan's Tōson in ways that should lead to critical self-reflection. They demand that we attend to the small differences that characterize the national imagination of both self and other.

National imagination, in Japan, the United States, and other modern societies is one of those things without which we cannot do anything. As such, its critique is urgent and necessary. This critique must not begin from the exterior of its object, just as it must not end up outside of itself. Only to the degree that we acknowledge our own implication in the object can we begin to move forward into something else.

The Disease of Nationalism, the Empire of Hygiene: The Broken Commandment *as Hygiene Manual*

It [anti-*burakumin* prejudice] is truly a severe, living problem. It is a social failing born into existence over many long years, exactly like an affliction in our individual bodies, an ache that cannot be forgotten. How can we treat this ailment and restore good health? It is not a simple problem.

Shimazaki Tōson (1928)

In 1907, one year after the appearance of his first full-length novel, *The Broken Commandment* (*Hakai*), Shimazaki Tōson published an account of the experiences that lay behind the writing of the work.[1] In the passage, Tōson describes how he began work on *The Broken Commandment* when he was a schoolteacher in the rural village of Komoro, just as the Russo-Japanese War broke out. He recounts numerous visits to the Komoro depot to send off pupils and fellow teachers who were bound for the battlefield. Moreover,

In my far-off mountain home, I heard about plans of my friends in the city to observe the war, and I too decided to pick up my pen and follow along with the troops—although in the end that wish went unfulfilled. It was then that I began work on the *Broken Commandment* manuscript. Life is a battleground, and an author is nothing but its war correspondent: thinking this way, I comforted myself with the thought that I, writing my novel, and my friends, on the far-off plains of Manchuria, were engaged in the same effort. (*TZ* 2:303–5)

Tōson's account of the novel's creation has since been joined by a number of other narratives that likewise attempt to explain the appearance of *The*

Broken Commandment in 1906. In terms of Tōson's biography, the novel represents the completion of his turn toward fiction and away from the romantic
poetry that had first established his reputation in the late 1890s. In narratives of
the rise of modern Japanese literature, *The Broken Commandment* has been celebrated alternately as Japan's first truly modern novel; as the first masterpiece
of Japanese naturalism; and as the last glimmering hope for a modern Japanese
novel that would include a consideration of public concerns, a hope soon
extinguished by the rise of the I-novel with its obsessive fixation on private life.

What I find particularly intriguing about Tōson's own explanation of the
novel's appearance is the way in which he figures his writing as participating
in the national project of empire. He renarrates the literary triumph he had
achieved with *The Broken Commandment* into one incident from the greater
tale of national triumph achieved by the Japanese military on the Asian continent. This history of imperial expansion and the shifting conceptions of
national identity that accompanied it form the background of my own reading of the novel. Irokawa Daikichi has argued that the Russo-Japanese War
completed the process of bonding the national people to the state in modern
Japan.[2] Accordingly, like Tōson himself, I begin my exploration of *The Broken
Commandment* with the national triumph achieved in the war.

But of what, precisely, did that triumph consist? Dr. Louis L. Seaman, a former U.S. military surgeon who, unlike Tōson, was able to travel with the
Japanese army during the war, had no doubts. In his book, *The Real Triumph
of Japan* (which appeared in the same month as *The Broken Commandment*),
Seaman argues that while Japan had of course defeated the Russian army,
more important was the victory it had achieved against the insidious "silent
foe" of all militaries, disease.[3] The traditional ratio of battlefield deaths resulting from disease to those resulting from combat was four to one, and recent
colonial warfare had produced even worse ratios. In a stunning contrast, for
Japan in its war with Russia, the ratio was one to four, an unprecedented
achievement. This accomplishment allowed Japan to mobilize its military
resources with the highest degree of efficiency. According to Seaman, the
Japanese soldier is drilled in the techniques of modern hygiene; he

> is imbued with the idea that it is just as necessary to maintain his body
> in the best physical condition as to keep his rifle in a state of efficiency;
> that to permit either to become impaired through his own carelessness
> or misconduct is to injure the organization of which he is a part, and
> constitutes an act of disloyalty to his Emperor.[4]

Modern warfare, Seaman argues, demands modern medicine, and in this field, Japan led the way. Japan's national victory was a triumph for the universal empire of hygiene.

As Seaman notes, the success of Japanese military medicine was the result of a long, deliberate promotion of hygienic thought and practices within Japan. My purpose here is to examine *The Broken Commandment* as a participant in this process, a process that is inextricably bound up with questions of nation and empire. I will argue that the novel reproduces the symptoms of Japan's triumph, the textual *markings* of the diseases of nationalism and imperialism. By diagnosing Tōson's (probably unconscious) reinflection of the idioms of hygiene, I hope to trace out some of the contradictory ways in which those idioms function to nationalize and colonize human bodies. In particular, I will examine the ways in which Tōson depicts tuberculosis, a disease so ubiquitous in late-Meiji Japan that it was widely known as a *kokuminbyō* (national disease). Tuberculosis admittedly plays a marginal role in the novel; the disease is attached to one character from a marginalized social group. And yet I argue that this marginal disease should be understood as central to the work's depiction of human bodies—just as the marginalized social group, the *hisabetsu burakumin* (hereafter abbreviated *burakumin*),[5] became central to the ideologies through which Japanese imagined their corporate national body, on the pages of *The Broken Commandment* and elsewhere. In turn, by focusing my reading on these particular details, I hope to open up connections between Tōson's novel and much broader historical questions. The empire of hygiene, after all, spread far beyond Japan and its colonies.

The Broken Commandment is one of a number of late Meiji fictional works that describe *burakumin* characters. The setting is Iiyama, a rustic mountain village. The protagonist, Ushimatsu, is a well-educated *burakumin* who has moved to Iiyama and become a schoolteacher, all the while hiding his origins at his father's command in order to avoid discrimination. Gradually, however, Ushimatsu's secret leaks out, aided by a rumormongering campaign conducted by the novel's villains, including a corrupt politician and the principal of the school where Ushimatsu works. While rumors fly, Ushimatsu himself is haunted by a powerful desire to openly acknowledge his status. This desire arises out of Ushimatsu's interaction with his hero, Rentaro, a famous writer and political activist who publicly avows his status as a *burakumin*. Ushimatsu's struggles with his dilemma are heightened when he finds himself falling in love with O-Shio, the non-*burakumin* daughter of one of his teaching colleagues. The death of Ushimatsu's father (he is gored by a bull from the herd he tends) provides the first major crisis in the novel. As Ushimatsu stands next to Rentaro, watching the bull being slaughtered, he resolves that he cannot disobey his late father's commandment and must keep his secret, even from Rentaro. But the pressure on Ushimatsu to confess continues to mount, and as he reaches the brink of suicide, a second major crisis arises: cronies of the crooked politician murder Rentaro. Facing this corpse, Ushimatsu experiences a kind of rebirth and resolves that he must carry on his mentor's legacy. Shortly thereafter, Ushimatsu confesses to the students in his class that he is a *burakumin*. To his surprise, his students and friends rally to his support. O-Shio even declares her willingness to marry him. But rather than remain in Iiyama, Ushimatsu chooses to emigrate to Texas. The novel closes with Ushimatsu being cheered by his students as he leaves Iiyama in the company of O-Shio and Rentaro's widow.

In *The Broken Commandment*, as Ushimatsu's secret gradually leaks out and he comes to see only suspicion in the eyes that gaze at him, the narrator describes his mental condition: "At times, Ushimatsu came to feel estranged even from his own body as he forgot everything else and single-mindedly recalled his father's commandment" (*TZ* 2:246). Obviously, it is beyond my power to restore to Ushimatsu sole ownership over his fleshly body. But my readings here will try to render visible some of the ways in which national imagination transformed the human body into a possession of the national community. My goal is not to produce a systematic theory of the nationalized body, but rather to present a case study of differences produced through the often-conflicting fields of hygiene, nationalism, and imperialism. While no one has access to the "real" body prior to ideological distortion, we should begin the process of sorting through the various ideologies that attempt to construct the body in specific modes. Because, while all discussions of the body (including my own) are inevitably ideological, not all ideologies function to the same effect.

HYGIENE AND THE MODERN NATION

My diagnosis of *The Broken Commandment* must be set against a broader understanding of a shift that occurred during the period roughly coeval with Tōson's life, that is, from the 1870s to the 1940s, in which human bodies in Japan (and elsewhere) underwent a remarkable transformation. The rise of new industrial, military, educational, and medical regimens required the literal incorporation into human bodies of previously nonexistent physical lifestyles. As Narita Ryūichi argues,

In general, it was through the military, hospitals, and prisons that the training of the body into the ways of modernity was conducted. In addition, factories were sites where the division of time and the rhythm of labor were taught, and train stations where strict punctuality and the etiquette of sharing space with others were taught. . . . In particular the role played by schools was large, as they instructed in physical and spiritual standards. Along with standards of physical movement, such as how to march, how to sit in a chair, the way to achieve correct posture, they also affirmed the ambitions of individuals, bringing to fruition the notion of "success" [*risshin shusse*].[6]

Simultaneously, a broad range of often conflicting ideologies came into play, each with its own particular set of images that attempted to fix particular meanings onto bodies. Issues that became focal points of debate include the proper presentation of the body, including attitudes toward clothing and nudity; new definitions of health and illness, including considerations of diet, cleanliness, and exercise; questions of gender and sexuality that arose out of new views of sexuality and the structure of the family; and new discourses of heredity, racial identity, and racial hierarchy. Within all of these debates and regimens, the status of individual human bodies was repeatedly linked to the well-being of the nation as a whole.

The increasing medicalization of the body in post-1868 Japan accelerated this process of reconstruction. Medical science served as a primary pivot point linking the health of individual bodies to that of the nation as a whole. In particular, the new disciplines of hygiene and physical education constructed the national population into an object of medical treatment and developed norms for every aspect of daily life. These norms led to the incorporation of national policy directly into individual human bodies. Furthermore, as hygiene shifted the focus of medicine from *curing* disease in *individual* patients to *preventing* disease in *society* as a whole, it expanded the role of medicine beyond the treatment of disease to include the monitoring and regulation of healthy persons as well.[7]

The rise of hygiene as a medical discipline was accompanied by the rise of germ theory. The discoveries and techniques attributed to a Robert Koch or a Louis Pasteur provided a powerful new language through which hygienists could write socially essential roles for themselves, thereby achieving dominance over competing schools. Bacteriology and hygiene were so closely interrelated that in 1906, when *The Broken Commandment* first appeared, they were still considered a single discipline. Japan played a special role in the worldwide dissemination of the new medicine: the presence of such figures as Kitasato Shibasaburō (1852–1931) and Mori Ōgai helped germ theory achieve a hegemonic position within Japanese medical practice in a relatively short time, though even in Japan germ theory was not without its opponents.[8]

Germ theory constructed an ideological view of the human body that rigidly distinguished between "health" and "illness." A number of idioms were invented or translated from other domains, all for use in describing the diseased body as one that had been invaded by foreign elements, germs, which were defined as the causes of illness. Karatani Kōjin is a recent critic of germ theory, calling its view of illness a "theology" aimed at exorcising "evil."[9] But, as Karatani argues, this chain of binary oppositions—health/unhealth, purity/impurity, presence/absence (of microbes)—won wide acceptance and became a fundamental precept in the thought of those who concerned themselves with the health of society as a whole.[10] Human bodies and the national community were now placed in a new relationship, wherein the purity/health of each was dependent upon that of the other.

It is important to stress, as Latour does, that there was nothing inevitable or natural about the rise of germ theory. When Koch isolated the tubercle bacillus in 1882, he did not in the process locate the real cause of a disease that had previously eluded scientists; rather, he invented a new disease.[11] Where previously there had existed a variety of symptoms and conditions linked to numerous causal factors (heredity, miasma, urban environment, personal morality, and so on), now there existed tuberculosis, a unified effect produced by a single cause. After 1882—at least in the minds of germ-theory advocates—tuberculosis was defined tautologically as the disease caused by the tubercle bacillus.[12]

Moreover, the rapid diffusion of germ theory was not due to an inherent explanatory superiority. Germ theory attracted supporters only to the degree that they were able to translate its doctrines to serve their own interests. Germ theory empowered certain branches of medicine at the expense of others. Except for the worldwide flurry of activity that followed Koch's 1890 announcement (soon repudiated) that tuberculin could cure tuberculosis, clinical doctors, whose practice was built on curing patients, saw little relevance in the discovery of the tubercle bacillus. It is hardly surprising that clinical physicians were less eager to subscribe to germ theory than military doctors and hygienists, who were immediately able to write new and powerful positions for themselves through it.[13]

Another factor in the rise of germ theory was its tendency to turn the focus of public health activities away from the social causes of illness (poverty, urban overcrowding, industrial pollution, and so on) and toward purely biological agents. Accordingly, hygiene was widely promoted as an alternative to socialism: it aimed to cure both disease and social unrest. This tendency was not limited to Japan. One of the clearest statements of hygiene as an alternative to socialism comes in an American magazine article from this period, where Dr. Cyrus Edson discusses what he calls the "germ idea of Socialism": "that all members of the body politic are theoretically and should be practically joint partners in one great co-operative state. . . ." Yet socialism itself remains an unproved theory, whereas hygiene is now "a recognized science." And it is hygiene that will ultimately achieve the goals of socialism:

> The Socialistic side of the microbe is to be found, then, in the fact that we may only fight diseases in a community by meeting it everywhere. We cannot separate the tenement-house district from the portion of the city where the residences of the wealthy stand, and treat this as being a separate locality. The disease we find in the tenement-house threatens all alike, for a hundred avenues afford a way by which the contagion may be carried from the tenement to the palace. We must, if we would guard the health of the people, look on them as being one whole, not as being several communities, each complete in itself. . . . This is the Socialism of the microbe, this is the chain of disease, which binds all the people of a community together.[14]

Socialists and syndicalists, in turn, ridiculed hygiene. This was particularly true in the case of tuberculosis, a disease whose appearance was just as much a symptom of capitalism as was the rise of the proletariat. As Karatani notes, the sudden epidemic of tuberculosis that struck Meiji Japan cannot be attributed to the tubercle bacillus, which had been present in Japan since the dawn of history. Rather, in Japan and elsewhere, the disease became widespread only after the change in living patterns that accompanied the rise of industrial capitalism. This fact was well-known to socialists of the day: in 1904, the Christian Socialist activist Kinoshita Naoe attacked hygiene's politics of tuberculosis:

> "The spread of the disease germ of tuberculosis occurs mainly through the sputum of those who have the disease": this is what it says at the beginning of an official notice recently issued by the Superintendent-

General of the Metropolitan Police. But in terms of solving the problem of a social disease like tuberculosis, this approach can hardly have
any effect. . . . When we inquire into where consumption is produced,
isn't it the factories of large companies, the dormitories of male and
female workers, the back-alley tenements?[15]

Kinoshita argues that tuberculosis was merely a secondary symptom of the
diseases of poverty and industrial capitalism and that any effort to improve
public health must attack the root diseases. Hygienists, on the other hand, saw
socialism itself as a potentially devastating social disease, one that could only
be prevented through gradualist improvements in living standards and public
health. As I will discuss below, this conflict between hygiene and socialism is
played out on the pages of *The Broken Commandment*.

Germ theory bore especially important implications for national imagination. Hygiene advocates insisted that society had to be mobilized into a coherent whole in order to wage total war against its newly identified enemy, the
germ. In theory, the social totality imagined by hygienists did not have to take
national form. In practice, however, it generally did. Japanese hygienists in the
early 1900s bemoaned the lack of governmental measures to prevent tuberculosis, noting that the worsening of tuberculosis among the lower classes
revealed an alarming lack of national cohesiveness. William Johnston quotes
from the 1913 charter of the Japan Anti-Tuberculosis League:

A society for preventing tuberculosis should have been established in
our country long ago, and instead the tubercle bacillus has been negli-
gently allowed to spread. However in today's circumstances, for the
growth of industry and commerce and the development of the Japanese race, we do not have a moment to spare. Thus we hereby establish
the Japan Anti-Tuberculosis League, and with the cooperation of all the
people of Japan we devote ourselves to the prevention of our national
disease [*kokumin byō*].

These tendencies reached a sort of logical conclusion in a 1935 article in a
Japanese public health magazine that argued that only Fascism, with its ultimate unification of the people, could implement hygiene effectively.[16]

The nationalistic implications of this hygienist rhetoric is evident from the
way that national pride was staked on hygiene. Pasteur and Kitasato were glo-
rified not merely as great scientists, but also as representative national heroes:

the humiliations of the Franco-Prussian War or of the Unequal Treaties could be partly repaired by the great advances achieved by French and Japanese science. This nationalistic conception of hygiene was also reinforced by hygiene's development, especially in Japan, primarily as a form of military medicine designed to increase battle-readiness in the nation-state's wars of imperialist expansion. For example, Mori Ōgai's studies of proposals for reforming the army's diet, based on his laboratory work in Germany, were part of the highly successful effort to combat diseases that had hampered Japanese military movements in Asia.[17] The links between Japanese hygiene and imperialism are further condensed by the career of Gotō Shimpei (1857–1929). Gotō earned his Ph.D. in hygiene in the early 1890s, studying under Max von Pettenkofer. In 1898, after a spectacular career in public health in Japan, Gotō was appointed civilian governor of colonial Taiwan, where he introduced numerous hygienic reforms. In 1906, he became President of the South Manchurian Railway Company, the primary institutional apparatus of Japanese colonial administration on the continent.[18] Gotō's career linked the experimental procedures of the bacteriology laboratory to the governing practices of colonial administration. His work in hygiene served to effect both a disciplining of bodies internal to the national community and an expansion of the national body.

As I explore the human bodies constructed in *The Broken Commandment*, I will focus primarily on two distinct narrative types, both proper components of any good hygiene manual. The two are figures borrowed from somewhat contradictory hygienic techniques: quarantine, which labors to construct an impermeable boundary separating the healthy and the diseased; and vaccination, which attempts to neutralize the effects of pathological agents on the body so as to render their intermingling harmless. Since ideological struggles to define the body are always related, directly or indirectly, to struggles over the definition of the nature of the community,[19] we would expect these two versions of the body to correspond to two distinct images of the national community: translated into the idioms of national political strategy, we might call the two hygienic techniques protectionism and expansionism, respectively.

MARKINGS OF OTHERNESS

The intense concern for public health in Meiji Japan helps form the landscape of *The Broken Commandment*.[20] The school where Ushimatsu works, for example, introduces hygienic methods to control an outbreak of trachoma, and it is equipped with such prerequisites of physical education as tennis courts, a gymnasium, and gymnastics equipment. When the school celebrates the Emperor's birthday, the ceremonies also honor visiting representatives of the Red Cross, one of the primary institutional agents of hygiene in Japan.

When we examine the human bodies described on its pages, another hygienic fact leaps out at us: illness is everywhere. Questions are continually raised about the health of Ushimatsu. Other major characters, such as Rentaro (the *burakumin* activist who becomes Ushimatsu's mentor) and Keinoshin (O-Shio's father), suffer from various diseases. The head priest at Rengeji temple, where Ushimatsu lives, commits repeated sexual indiscretions, a pattern which his wife identifies as his "illness." The principal at the school where Ushimatsu works describes certain forms of thought, along with the publications that transmit them, in terms of disease.

Perhaps the most noteworthy feature of this textual epidemic is that, throughout the novel, disease is concentrated in the bodies of *burakumin* characters. This association is introduced in the opening pages. Ohinata, the wealthy *burakumin* whose expulsion from his lodgings launches the plot into motion, has traveled to Iiyama to receive treatment at a hospital there. Rentaro suffers from tuberculosis. And Ushimatsu, though apparently not physically ill, is constantly discussed in terms of illness—his friends are forever recommending that he visit a doctor because he looks sick.

This attribution of illness to *burakumin* characters formed an important component of the "*écriture* of discrimination." Watanabe Naomi, in surveying a large number of texts that discussed *burakumin*, describes a tendency they shared to construct *burakumin* bodies through a set of tell-tale, visible "markings" (*shirushi*).[21] Watanabe compares this *écriture* to Western Orientalism: its reduction of the viewed object (in this case *burakumin* bodies) to a fixed set of interchangeable markings creates a relationship of absolute, incommensurable difference between the seen object and the seeing subject. This implies that, like the Orient produced through Orientalism, the object itself does not actually exist: it is a fantasy projection of the gazing subject.[22] Producing the object via this attribution of markings also serves to construct the viewer as an unmarked, self-identical subject. Accordingly, Watanabe ties this *écriture* to the construction of a homogeneous Japanese national identity.

The texts that reproduced this *écriture* helped disseminate the dominant ideologies of heredity, which assigned inferior bloodlines to *burakumin* as a means of naturalizing their social status. In this way, meanings inscribed onto *burakumin* bodies intersected with the broader ideologies of blood lineage that underlay the Meiji *ie* (family) system and the emperor system, as well as Western attitudes toward Japan and Japanese attitudes toward other Asians.

But with regard to *burakumin* this ideology had a tremendous weak point: the distinctions that blood lineage was supposed to produce were invisible. This lack of corporeal markings became all the more troubling as other markers of *burakumin* status (dress, residence, occupation) disappeared when legal restrictions were eased following the 1871 Liberation Ordinance. Moreover, the doctrine of success (*risshin shusse*) so widely preached in this era—and *The Broken Commandment* is, among other things, a novel about *risshin shusse*—fanned fears of staus-group permeability with its promise that *anyone* could achieve success with effort. The result was an inability to visually distinguish *burakumin* from "normal" Japanese. This apparent blurring of boundaries, a deterritorialization of the feudal social order, produced an anxiety that the *écriture* of discrimination labored to overcome with its visible markings. This constructed visibility, a power/knowledge disciplinary complex, functioned to co-opt *burakumin* characters into the politics of specularity, thereby containing the social difference they seemed to threaten.Disease constituted one of the most important visual markings. Burakumin-related stories were frequently set in hospitals and clinics—for example, Tokuda Shūsei's (1871–1943) "Yabukōji" (Spear flower, 1896). More blatantly, these fictional works, and journalism from the period, tended to portray *burakumin* as diseased, an inversion typical of this *écriture* in that it shifted the cause of prejudice away from social structure and onto the bodies of those who suffered from prejudice.[23]

In discussing what sets *The Broken Commandment* apart from earlier works, Watanabe notes that Ushimatsu himself is largely free of the corporeal markings that this *écriture* assigned to *burakumin* characters. This does not mean, however, that the novel is altogether free of these markings: the features that marked earlier burakumin-related works are reproduced in *The Broken Commandment*, but here they tend to be projected onto Ushimatsu's surroundings rather than onto the protagonist himself. Ushimatsu's interiority is then constructed in reaction to this marked exterior.

In this sense, the presence of disease in other *burakumin* characters such as Ohinata and Rentaro locates *The Broken Commandment* within the *écriture* of discrimination. There is one subtle but significant difference, however: whereas the diseases most commonly attached to *burakumin* bodies were hereditary ones, those in *The Broken Commandment* (despite the obsessive concern over hereditary disease that Tōson would display in later works) tend to be contagious.[24] They are diseases whose origins are attributed to agents invisible to the naked eye and only recently rendered visible to the medical gaze via the microscopes, cultures, and dyes of Pasteur, Koch, and Kitasato.

In a sense, as Watanabe argues, this difference in type of disease is irrelevant. The *écriture* of discrimination functions regardless of the particular marking employed. The potential markers are all exchangeable, so long as the fundamental gap between the gazing subject and its object is maintained. Laclau and Mouffe maintain that a similar process is at work in colonial relations: the colonizer distinguishes him/herself from the colonized through a whole series of markings, which are arranged in a relation of equivalence. The differences between the various markings cancel each other out "insofar as they are used to express something identical underlying them all." In such a structure, the identity of the dominant colonizer "has come to be purely negative. It is because a negative identity cannot be represented in a direct manner—i.e., positively—that it can only be represented indirectly, through an equivalence between its differential moments."[25] It is precisely this imaginary equivalence that becomes the grounding of identity of the supposedly "normal" Japanese.

But a critical rethinking of national imagination should, among other things, trouble the principles of exchange that naturalize social hierarchies. While the *écriture* of discrimination may posit an equivalence between hereditary and contagious diseases, a reader is not obliged to accept the validity of that transaction. A reader can seize upon one of its terms and insist on its irreducibility to the other term. In particular, when we reread the text critically and begin to locate the small differences at work within it, we begin to distinguish between certain subgenres or narrative types that commingle on its pages. That is, we discover a heterogeneity that troubles the simple health/disease binary. This fluidity in turn helps us understand more clearly the complexity of the "national body" produced through this form of imagination.

Accordingly, it makes a difference that Rentaro is marked with tuberculosis. This particular marking brings into play yet another ideology of disease current in the period. Karatani notes that a metaphoric use of tuberculosis was established with the Romantic movement in Europe, whereby the disease "became an index of gentility, delicacy, and sensitivity among snobs and social climbers."[26] Karatani traces the spread of this vision of tuberculosis in Meiji literature, citing as a prominent example Nami-ko, the heroine in the wildly popular late-Meiji novel *Nami-ko* (also known as *Hototogisu* [The cuckoo], 1898–1900) by Tokutomi Roka (1868–1927). Clearly, something similar happens in *The Broken Commandment* with the character of Rentaro.

The question arises again and again in *The Broken Commandment*: how could an intellectual like Rentaro have risen from the ranks of the most despised social class? Each time the answer is the same: Rentaro's success is due, either directly or indirectly, to his tuberculosis. For characters who sympathize with Rentaro—for example, the newspaper journalist (himself a consumptive) who mistakenly exaggerates the gravity of Rentaro's condition—the disease and the suffering it causes are the source of a particular quality that distinguishes Rentaro's writings (*TZ* 2:63–64). The narrator echoes this sort of language (*TZ* 2:87), as does Ushimatsu in his own thoughts (*TZ* 2:118). Even Rentaro himself credits the disease for his rise as a writer (*TZ* 2:115). In these cases, we find Romantic tuberculosis: Rentaro's consumption becomes a sign of his individual genius.

Less sympathetic characters also associate Rentaro's status with his disease, but, in this context, the attribution takes on a sinister twist: the disease becomes a means for denying Rentaro himself any credit for his accomplishments. Rentaro's agency is shifted onto the tubercle bacilli that he harbors in his body; his writings become nothing more than a pathological symptom. Bumpei and Ginnosuke, two of Ushimatsu's teaching colleagues, speculate on how the *eta* could have produced a figure like Rentaro and conclude that it is not so much Rentaro as the disease that has authored his many books:"When you look at it that way, it's not that an *eta* wrote those sort of things, but rather that the illness made him write them—that's how it is, right?" (*TZ* 2:40–41). Furthermore, Rentaro's thought is itself treated as though it were infectious, an example of the metaphorical "social fevers" that Carol Gluck has shown were a prominent part of late Meiji nationalist ideology.[27] Ginnosuke and others discuss the effect of Rentaro's writings and speeches on Ushimatsu in terms of contagion:

I don't know whether, as a rule, consumptives are like that. They say that when you listen to that teacher's [Rentaro] speeches, they really strike home. . . . Well, people like Segawa [Ushimatsu] here ought best not to listen—if you listen, it's a sure thing you'll get sick again.   (*TZ* 2:163)

For these characters, bent on deriding Rentaro, his tuberculosis explains how a *burakumin* could rise in the world. In this light, Ushimatsu's ability to overcome his initial horror at Rentaro's infectious disease to the point that he willingly shares a bath with his friend assumes a new importance (although in another sense, Ushimatsu already has the "disease": his *burakumin* origins). The erotic charge of this scene, as the reserve between the two men breaks down to the point where they scrub each other's backs, is at least partially due to the risk Ushimatsu takes in exposing his own body to disease.[28]

We can take this probing a step further. Tuberculosis, prior to and even after Koch's isolation of the tubercle bacillus, was widely believed to be hereditary. Well into the twentieth century, many people (including doctors) continued to argue for heredity as its primary cause, either in the form of direct transmission of the disease or of a hereditary disposition toward it. Others tried to synthesize the two explanations, arguing that tuberculosis was in some cases hereditary and in others infectious. Johnston notes that the continued insistence on heredity hindered the efforts of Japanese germ-theory advocates to mobilize public health campaigns to halt the spread of the disease. The novel that Karatani cites as the premiere example of Romantic tuberculosis, Tokutomi Roka's *Nami-ko*, demonstrates the simultaneous presence of multiple explanations for the disease. When Nami-ko, the heroine, falls ill with consumption, her mother-in-law begins plotting a divorce. A consumptive daughter-in-law is unthinkable to her, because of the possibility of infecting her son and because of heredity—Nami might pass on her disease to future generations of the family. The novel repeatedly jumps back and forth between explanations for the disease—Nami has either been infected by or inherited the disease from her mother (who died of it), or she caught it because of unusually cold weather. When the mother-in-law confronts her son Take to demand that he divorce his beloved wife, the following exchange occurs:

> "Nevertheless, I doubt very much her speedy recovery, Take. I heard from the doctor that her mother also died of consumption."
> "Yes, she told me that, too, but—"
> "Consumption is hereditary, isn't it?"
> "They say so, but Nami got it from a bad cold. Everything depends upon one's caution, you know. People talk about infection or heredity, but, in the point of fact, there are other causes."[29]

This multiplicity of causal explanations still held sway six years later when *The Broken Commandment* first appeared.

There are important parallels between this dual accounting for tuberculosis and the status of *burakumin* in Meiji Japan (as well as, for example, that of Jews in late-nineteenth-century Europe).[30] While the official abolition of hereditary *eta* and *hinin* status classifications in 1871 did not erase the ideologies of heredity that assigned inferior bloodlines to *burakumin*, it did create an opening for new, more liberal explanations for the existence of the *burakumin*. That is to say, in addition to the ideology of heredity, a new explanation of *burakumin* status in terms of social transmission became possible.[31] In Kurokawa Midori's words, *burakumin* were now the objects of both dissimilation (*ika*) and assimilation (*dōka*).[32]

In *The Broken Commandment*, Tōson proposes a solution to this problem of the doubled *burakumin*. There are, he argues, two kinds of *burakumin*. This becomes quite explicit in "Yamakuni no shinheimin" (New commoners in the mountain districts, 1906), a newspaper article Tōson wrote to defend *The Broken Commandment* from charges that it exaggerated the extent of anti-*buraku* prejudice (charges made by, among others, Yanagita Kunio). After describing the care he had taken in studying *buraku* life and declaring that prejudice was in fact severe, Tōson concludes by saying that there seem to be two kinds of New Commoner: "high class" and "low class" (he uses the English). The former group are in "all things—facial appearance, habits, speech, and the like—hardly different from us." But the latter group show their uncivilized status "the way that lower classes of savages show wildness in their faces," the bone structure of their faces is different, and particularly "remarkable is the difference in skin color. Because they don't marry with other groups and sometimes marry even very close relatives, there seems to be a kind of skin disease rampant among them" (*TZ* 6:77–84).

These two groups are reproduced in *The Broken Commandment*, where they are distinguished as the subjects and objects of the narrative gaze, respectively. The New Commoners at whom Ushimatsu stares in the slaughterhouse scene are stamped ("branded") at birth with a hereditary marking: the "distinct color of their skin" (*TZ* 2:126). These unfortunates are doomed by blood to remain objects of the narrative (and national) gaze. But other New Commoners, such as Ushimatsu and Rentaro (those who in "all things" are "hardly different from us"), attain the status of gazing subjects—just like unmarked commoners. What distinguished *The Broken Commandment* from earlier works of Japanese fiction, according to both readers in 1906 and later critics, was the remarkable intensity with which it narrated Ushimatsu's inner life: the reader is powerfully solicited to identify with Ushimatsu and to see the world through his eyes. In Ushimatsu, Tōson constructs a *burakumin* as an interiorized subject, one who is capable of returning the national gaze, of fulfilling the desire of the national gaze for intersubjective recognition.

In other words, Ushimatsu cannot simply be dismissed as a non-Japanese, an alien, despite the school principal's repeated attempts to identify him as a "foreign element" (*ibunshi*) who must be "expelled" (*hōchiku* or *haiseki*) in order to bring unity (*tōitsu*) to the school. That is to say, whatever there is that is "foreign" about Ushimatsu cannot be attributed to his bloodlines. Ushimatsu's father, in delivering his commandment, specifically tells Ushimatsu that their family derives from samurai bloodlines, so that they are not aliens (*ihōjin*), unlike other *eta* whose ancestors, he says, came from Russia, China, Korea, and other foreign places.[33] Some other cause besides heredity must be located to explain the difference that the "high class" New Commoner is thought to introduce into the social body. It is in this context that the tubercle bacillus takes on new importance.[34]

As I have already suggested, the slaughterhouse scene presents a topos saturated with imagery that posits an equivalence between disease and *burakumin*. The scene contains brutally prejudiced language, in particular manifesting a tendency that scholars have identified in numerous *burakumin*-related literary works: such works ascribe a bestial nature to *burakumin* characters, especially in the form of an untamed, animal-like sexuality—for example, in Masaoka Shiki's (1867–1902) "Manjushage" (*Higan* lilies, ca. 1897). A metonymic connection between certain *burakumin* and animals through traditional occupations spilled over into a metaphor for the group as a whole; *burakumin* were seen as harboring an animal-like nature in their own bodies.[35]

In a brilliant analysis, Kamei Hideo discusses the slaughterhouse scene in terms of the half-animal, half-human positions it opens up, a characteristic that Kamei argues arises from the coexistence of two kinds of subject–object relationships in the work: one in which the viewing subject labors to share the "landscape" it sees with some other subject, and one in which the viewing subject tries to close itself off from all others, to achieve a position of seeing without being seen. This latter way of seeing fears the external "landscape," which it sees as filled with ill omens, and tries to dominate it. The "landscape" of the slaughterhouse situates it in this latter, more ominous mode: Ushimatsu fears that nature is looking back at him. His anxiety produces the half-animal, half-human position into which both the bull and its *burakumin* slaughterers fit.[36]

When we employ the idioms of hygiene to read the slaughterhouse scene, we produce a clearer image of the ideologies that intersect here. The bull that is slaughtered is, of course, being brought to justice for having gored Ushimatsu's father to death. As Kamei points out, the bull is a figure for Ushimatsu's father: in witnessing the death of the bull, Ushimatsu is watching a displaced reenactment of his father's death. The bull stands in for Ushimatsu, too: its killing of the father enacts the patricidal aspects of Ushimatsu's own desire to break his father's commandment. It is significant that each of the human characters projected onto the animal's body is a *burakumin*. But the interpenetration of *burakumin* and animal bodies is not limited to this sort of figural projection. Ushimatsu's father dies when the boundary of his human, *burakumin* flesh is violated by an animal—that is, a penetration of the body by a foreign agent. The guilty animal is then brought to justice under quasi-human standards, and its punishment reverses the crime: its flesh is violated by human, *burakumin* hands. The slaughterers bash in the bull's head and then cut through its flesh, hacking the corpse into four large hunks of meat that hang down from the ceiling, dripping blood across the floor. The witness to all of this is, of course, Ushimatsu, whose very name indicates the depth of the problem here: as James Fujii notes, the first character in his given name carries the meaning "cow."[37]

But there is another displaced *burakumin* character figured through the bull: the bull's carcass, as it lies bleeding in front of Ushimatsu, prefigures the appearance of Rentaro's corpse, lying in its own blood and inspected by a policeman, in chapter 20. Like Rentaro's corpse, the bull's carcass is viewed by a policeman. But prior to the slaughtering, the bull is also inspected by a veterinarian. "The veterinarian, walking this way and that, circled the cow—he pinched its hide, pressed against its neck, tapped at its horns; finally he lifted up its tail, and with that the examination was over" (*TZ* 2:128). Readers in Japan in 1906 would have understood the significance of this passage: *the veterinarian is inspecting the bull for signs of bovine tuberculosis.* The opening years of the twentieth century saw the rise of an intense, worldwide concern over the possibility that meat and milk from cattle infected with bovine tuberculosis might be an important cause of human tuberculosis. In Japan, the 1901 Domestic Cattle Tuberculosis Prevention Law implemented the first mandatory inspections of cattle, beginning with imported animals in 1901 and extending to domestic animals in 1903. It provoked a social controversy, as farmers protested the loss of income it entailed.[38]

The bull in the slaughterhouse scene, then, not only reproduces the figure of Rentaro's corpse through its violent death: it is also monitored for markings of the same disease that has invaded the *burakumin* activist's body. The ideologies that intersect on the slaughterhouse floor constitute a scandalous violation of animal/human distinctions. Bestial *burakumin* slaughterers penetrate the flesh of an oddly human cow, which in turn had penetrated (that is, fatally infected) the flesh of Ushimatsu's father. This cow is suspected of harboring within it the same germs that infect Rentaro, a *burakumin* present at the slaughtering. If tuberculosis is capable of being transmitted from cows to people, it only makes sense that the germs should be concentrated in *burakumin*, who are ideologically located somewhere between the categories of animal and human. This is consistent with modern hygiene's reorganization of Japanese society, under which *burakumin* were frequently situated as the carriers of disease. Moreover, two sorts of burakumin are present in the scene, those in whom the pathogenic status is apparently hereditary (the slaughterers) and those in who the status must be explained in terms of social transmission (Ushimatsu and Rentaro). It is the mobilization of tuberculosis as the specific marker of *burakumin* status here that renders possible this whole network of ideological distinctions and blurrings.

QUARANTINE AND NATIONAL IMAGINATION

The redefinition (at least in some cases) of tuberculosis into a contagious disease justifies the exclusion of even those *burakumin* who are "purely" Japanese from the social body. Quarantine as a hygienic technique requires just such a separation of the morbid from the healthy: infected bodies had to be isolated away from healthy ones. The social space of Meiji Japan underwent a massive reorganization as part of an effort to separate out elements that were posited as introducing difference into the national population—people with diseases, criminal offenders, poor people. A controversial network of prisons, isolation hospitals, and poorhouse labor camps was set up throughout the land to effect a separation of the morbid from the healthy, to construct a homogeneous national community, and to maintain a constant surveillance on elements that threatened to introduce heterogeneity. Germ theory, which demanded the unification of national society into a single unit dedicated to total war on the microbe, provided a major ideological rationale for this social reorganization: in Latour's words, "*Disease was no longer a private misfortune but an offense to public order.*"[39]

The conclusion of *The Broken Commandment*, in which Ushimatsu decides to emigrate to Texas after confessing his *buraku* origins, has been an object of derision since 1906, even among critics who praise the novel.[40] As many critics have noted, the ignoble body language of the confession scene and Ushimatsu's subsequent decision to emigrate undermine whatever value readers may have attributed to his and Rentaro's earlier struggles; moreover, the decision to emigrate comes so suddenly as to seem like a case of deus ex machina. The conclusion had become such an embarrassment that in 1962, when

Ichikawa Kon directed a film version, he simply rewrote it.[41] Yet when the novel is read as a hygiene manual, its conclusion does reveal a certain logic (albeit a double logic, as I will explore below): it can be read as reproducing the ideologies of quarantine in the broader spatial register discussed earlier. Just as disease is seen as the penetration of foreign elements into the body, so the carriers of those foreign elements—the novel's *burakumin* characters—are finally portrayed as the agents who introduce an unhealthy difference into the community. The diseased must be isolated, quarantined, even when they boast hereditary pedigrees "hardly different from us."[42]

Perhaps Ushimatsu did catch something from Rentaro in that bathtub after all. The promiscuous, irresponsible (that is to say, socialist) Rentaro actively tries to infect those around him with his unhealthy thought/disease, and therefore must ultimately be repressed—or, in the language of the Cold War, "contained." The rhetoric of hygiene made possible numerous equivalences between *buraku* status, socialism, and disease:

> Internationally, [Bolshevik] Russia is the special *buraku* of thought. They are carriers of a hazardous germ that takes as its ideal the smashing from the foundation up of social organizations, the instigation of revolution in all the nations of the world, and the conquering of the world with the communism in which they believe.[43]

Ushimatsu, on the other hand, exercises a sense of social responsibility and implements the self-segregation so essential to hygienic strategies for containing social diseases like tuberculosis.[44] Once again, we are presented with the conflict between hygiene and socialism. Rather than agitate for social change, Ushimatsu emigrates. In this sense, the climax of *The Broken Commandment* reproduces the ideological fantasy (as Slavoj Žižek uses the term) of hygiene: a healthy, homogeneous community in which heterogeneous agents voluntarily quarantine themselves.[45]

Accordingly, Ushimatsu is not simply a foreigner, either to Japan or to the village of Iiyama. Rather, he is a faithful subject who carries out the hegemonic duties of hygiene. The novel's conclusion can be read, paradoxically, as the successful consummation of Ushimatsu's bid for membership in the local Iiyama community. This is one of the revolutionary features of *The Broken Commandment*: whereas earlier works describing *burakumin* characters had tended to ally those characters with sympathetic members of society's elite— the aristocracy, the wealthy, and so on—against the irrational prejudice of the uneducated common folk, in *The Broken Commandment*, Ushimatsu clearly allies with the local folk against the ruling elements of society.[46]

In *The Broken Commandment*, this local Iiyama community and its nature are described in great detail. As Fujii notes, the community's identity is largely constructed via a center-periphery conflict that pits rural Iiyama and its traditions against the incursions of the centralized state and its bureaucrats.[47] The community is constructed in the face of this other, the exterior that looms just beyond its boundaries, but in order to establish those boundaries—in order to simultaneously produce and reproduce the community as a self-identical entity—the community needs a *pharmakos* figure.[48] Like the *pharmakos*, the ritual scapegoat of ancient Greek societies, Ushimatsu occupies a position simultaneously inside and outside the Iiyama community; he is the foreign element who nonetheless originates from within and whose expulsion to the exterior allows the social community to produce/reproduce its internal identity—its health. As Tessa Morris-Suzuki argues, modern national communities "encompass small groups that fail the tests of belonging because it is only through the visible failure of defined 'minorities' that the state can repeatedly reassure itself of the invisible homogeneity and loyalty of the 'majority.' "[49] In *The Broken Commandment*, hygienic discourse has so naturalized this exclusion of difference that violent rituals of expulsion are no longer needed: here, the *pharmakos* excludes himself. This is because Ushimatsu knows his place in the community. Like the school principal, Ushimatsu comes to Iiyama from outside. But unlike the principal, who represents the interests of the centralized state, Ushimatsu becomes one of the townspeople following his confession. His acceptance is signaled by the reaction to his confession shown by his students and his housemates at Rengeji. A more important sign is O-Shio's willingness to marry him in spite of his being *burakumin*. Yet this acceptance is paradoxical: under the ideologies of quarantine, the condition of Ushimatsu's becoming a member of the Iiyama community is that he leave Iiyama.

Ushimatsu's confession signals his acceptance and internalization of the *pharmakos* role. In revealing his secret to his students, Ushimatsu reminds them of two things: his difference from them (as he recounts the traditional social stratification and the rituals used to separate *eta* from the community) and his similarity to them (as he recounts the activities they have participated in together). He tells them that he is both one of them and not one of them. Ushimatsu, having accepted this position via his confession, is then accepted by the community.

Only Ushimatsu's subsequent departure from the community can fulfill the hygienic logic of his position. The language used to describe Ushimatsu's mental state as he departs from Iiyama suggests the contradictory nature of his situation:

> How Ushimatsu must have breathed in the December morning's cold air and come back to the feeling of being revived after having finally set down a heavy load. *It was like, for example, the nostalgic feeling of a sailor who kisses the soil upon returning to land following a long sea journey.* That was exactly how Ushimatsu felt. No, in fact, he felt even happier. Even sadder. Walking on snow that crunched with each step, he came to feel as if, without a doubt, this world was his own.
>
> (*TZ* 2:293; italics added)

Only when he leaves Iiyama can Ushimatsu feel that he has at last come home: his departure is figured as a homecoming. The specific use of contagious disease, as opposed to hereditary disease, as the marking of *burakumin* status both enables and necessitates this contradictory resolution.

Hence, in its conclusion *The Broken Commandment* reproduces at the level of the Iiyama community the idioms of quarantine, just as it also portrays a victory of Ushimatsu's hygiene over Rentaro's socialism. Furthermore, while the Iiyama community certainly resists the centralized state, the novel's conclusion hints at the absorption of this peripheral difference into a self-identical national community. After all, Ushimatsu does not simply leave Iiyama, he emigrates from Japan to join Ohinata's proposed ranching venture in Texas. The assumption behind Ohinata's project (and behind all the other *burakumin*-related works that proposed emigration as a solution) was that abroad, Ushimatsu would be free from the anti-*burakumin* prejudice that set him apart from other Japanese. His *burakumin* status will disappear in Texas, where in the face of Yellow Peril racism (mentioned, we are told, in Rentaro's work *Confessions*), he will likely be scorned simply as a Japanese. The logic here echoes that from an 1890 editorial aimed at New Commoners:

> Those of you with capital should go to foreign countries and engage in business. Those without capital should go to foreign countries to work and earn your keep. In foreign countries, there is no distinction between commoners and New Commoners. Foreigners will treat you in an equal manner as they do us, as subjects of Imperial Japan.[50]

The same paradox that saw Ushimatsu becoming a member of the Iiyama community when he agreed to leave Iiyama is reproduced at the level of the national community: Ushimatsu finally becomes Japanese at the moment he leaves Japan.[51]

VACCINATION AND NATIONAL EXPANSION

As I have argued, the fascination with tuberculosis found in literary works such as *The Broken Commandment* arose at least partially from its ambiguity as a disease suspended between conflicting hereditary and contagious explanations. This ambiguity situates it as a particularly potent marking for *burakumin* status.

A similar ambiguity marks many hygienic texts. Mori Ōgai's hygienic diet reforms, for example, argue that traditional Japanese foods provide the best possible diet for the Japanese Army, since they are ideally suited to the Japanese physique. In one of his first published papers, Ōgai addressed proposed reforms to the army diet. Outbreaks of beriberi had severely hampered Japanese military activities in Asia, and prevention of the disease became one of the primary tasks of military doctors. While the cause of the disease was still unclear, the navy had succeeded in drastically reducing its incidence by introducing a diet that included meat and bread. Ōgai (who believed that beriberi was a contagious disease unrelated to nutrition) argued against a similar reform to the army diet. He analyzed rice, miso, tofu, and other domestic staples and demonstrated that the desirable protein-to-carbohydrate ratios as defined by European hygiene could be obtained with them. In other words, Japanese people should eat Japanese food with no fear of decline, and without becoming dependent on imports of Western foodstuffs. Ōgai would also argue throughout his career that Japan's dietary standards should be derived using Japanese, not European, bodies as models. In the 1886 essay, for example, Ōgai cites a study that shows the intestines of "Japanese" (not "Orientals" or "Asians") to be longer than those of "Westerners": already, national identity is being mapped onto physiology.[52]

In these instances, there is an ambiguity that links the Japanese state and the bodies of individual Japanese in mutual dependence. State policies are to be grounded in the natural physique of the Japanese people. Nonetheless, that body is also simultaneously constructed as a project requiring state intervention: hygienic diet reforms are designed to mold the Japanese physique into a more efficient military tool to carry out state policy within Japan and without. That is to say, the Japanese body must become all the more Japanese.

Hygienic nationalism, then, celebrates the national body as it is handed down through heredity, and yet at the same time it calls for a transformation of that body into something else. As Mark Seltzer writes in discussing a similar complexity in bodies depicted in American Naturalist writing, what "looks like, from one point of view, a return to nature looks, from another, something like the opposite, a turn against nature," one that reveals "the unnaturalness of nature itself."[53] Rather than choose between these sets of idioms, it seems more productive to consider the nationalized body as being riddled with small differences—or, to borrow the language of Homi K. Bhabha, as being suspended in a disjunctive, liminal space between contradictory constructions, "pedagogical" and "performative" modes of narrating the body that are mutually supplementary and do not "add up."[54] The closure that would assure national, corporeal, and textual self-identity remains inevitably deferred.

A similar ambiguity marks *The Broken Commandment*. The hygienic narratives described above, which I have grouped together under the name quarantine and which effect a separation of the healthy from the morbid, are supplemented by another range of narratives. These latter can be figured through the medical practice of vaccination (or, following Bhabha, vacciNation), which I use here as a metonym for a range of techniques that increasingly sought to reconstruct the body as something fundamentally open to the exterior and hence as capable of enhancement and even expansion. In one sense, these two sets of narratives exist in a relationship of temporal succession: in 1906, the focus of hygiene was shifting from quarantine to vaccination, from curing disease to promoting health, from acute infectious diseases like cholera to chronic diseases like tuberculosis. And yet, as we see in *The Broken Commandment*, the earlier idiom retained currency even as the new idiom was introduced. As Oguma Eiji has argued, by the late 1890s, Japanese national imagination was marked by the copresence of two self-images, one that stressed internal homogeneity and purity of bloodlines, the other that stressed hybridity and the ability to assimilate putative foreigners into itself. "To close the door firmly in order to defend oneself from the outside becomes an obstacle," Oguma notes, "when one decides to go outside oneself."[55] The nationalized body, then, lay suspended between the two contradictory poles of protectionism and expansionism, each with its own form of colonialism: the leper or penal colony, on the one hand, and the paternalistically administered protectorate or colonial territory, on the other.[56]

In the narrative of vaccination, one locates or manufactures a weakened strain of some agent of disease and then introduces it into the human body so as to steel that body, to strengthen it so that it will be able to dominate the more virulent microbes it encounters in the future. As a technique, vaccination played a fundamental role in facilitating colonial expansion: to borrow William McNeill's language, immunizing Western bodies against the microparasites of tropical disease was a necessary step in the transformation of those bodies into macroparasites on non-Western regions.[57] When a body was constructed through the figure of vaccination, concern shifted away from fortifying the boundaries of the body and maintaining internal purity. The germ was no longer to be avoided or dissimilated becasue, as hygienic texts repeatedly stressed, contact was inevitable. Attention was turned, rather, toward effecting proper hierarchies between body and germ. What was essential was to discipline both the germ and the body, reconstructing them so as to enable the body to assimilate the alien germ on the most profitable terms possible.

This is true at the level of the individual human body as well as at the level of the social body: when smallpox vaccinations were introduced into colonial Bombay in 1802, the first phase focused on vaccinating European settlers and their Indian servants.[58] This was accompanied by an effort to restrict contact between these (imperfectly) protected populations and the mass of unvaccinated colonial subjects, thereby effecting a kind of quarantine. Soon, however, and with mixed results, the colonial government launched campaigns to vaccinate the entire Indian population. That is to say, instead of separating the healthy European from the diseased Asian, the new medicine was now implemented as a means of neutralizing the dangers of colonial space so as to allow further penetration by the colonizers. Accordingly, this vaccination campaign met with strong resistance from colonial subjects—just as vaccination as a form of discipline met with opposition in Britain, Japan, America, and elsewhere. Many of those who were subjected to this colonizing of the body resisted absorption into the neutralized, harmless position that vaccination attempted to assign them. Indian subjects resisted smallpox vaccination because, as a colonial official reported in 1872, they read it as a "mark of subjection to the British Government."[59]

The conclusion of The Broken Commandment, then, with Ushimatsu's decision to emigrate, can be read not only through the narrative of quarantine, but also through the narrative of vaccination and the image of the human body that it entailed. It is important to note that the novel was first published at a time when state policies toward domestic minority groups and toward colonial empire were undergoing important changes. With regard to domestic others, the late-Meiji period saw a shift in governmental policy away from isolating those groups toward a policy of actively integrating them into the national community—the beginning of official *yūwa* (integrationist) policies toward *burakumin* in the late-Meiji years is emblematic.[60] Simultaneously, Japan's colonial policy shifted from one that defined its colonies as external properties, chips it could manipulate in the game of international power politics, and toward one that stressed the integration of the colonies into Japan itself—a new policy heralded by the 1910 annexation of Korea. While these new policies were never stable and the coming decades saw much back-and-forth movement between the two strategies, nonetheless, by the time *The Broken Commandment* appeared, the narratives of vaccination were available for reinflection alongside those of quarantine. And, as Kō Yoran has shown, the discourse of colonial expansion frequently overlapped with the discourse of *yūwa*, as in, for example, the thought of Kita Sadakichi (1871–1939), a prominent exponent of both Korean annexation and *yūwa* policies.[61]

Accordingly, in *The Broken Commandment* and other works describing *burakumin* as a form of social "affliction" or "ailment" (to borrow Tōson's own words from the epilogue to this chapter), there is not simply a stress on isolating the "foreign" (quarantine), but also on disciplining and then absorbing the "foreign" to strengthen the national body (vaccination). Certain *burakumin* figures—"high class" ones who carry neither inferior bloodlines nor pathological socialist thought—are constructed for the purpose of assimilating them into the body of the national community.[62] They are as carefully monitored and manipulated as were the strains of pathogens worked over by Pasteur, Koch, and Kitasato in producing vaccines. In particular, two important conditions define their construction: that they do not actively agitate for change (i.e., evoke domestic difference) within Japan, and that they participate in the expansion of the nation beyond its present-day borders. In the language of Deleuze and Guattari, they must be migrants, not nomads, and they must mark the limit, rather than the threshold, of the national community.[63]

When such *burakumin* and other potential "pathogens" are assimilated into the national body, the result of this vaccination is a reenergized national community, one that is strengthened for its encounter with new others (Koreans, Taiwanese, Chinese, Russians). Accordingly, Ushimatsu and Ohinata emigrate to Texas; the heroine of Shimizu Shikin's "Immigrant School" emigrates with her husband and other *burakumin* to colonial Hokkaido; and—most symptomatically—in Ogura Chōrō's *Biwa uta* (Biwa song, 1905), the brother of the heroine is a *burakumin* soldier who serves the Emperor bravely on the battlefields of Asia, despite the discrimination the siblings face from other Japanese. In these works, readers are solicited not to reject the *burakumin* protagonists, but rather to sympathize with their heroic strivings on behalf of national expansion.[64]

Accordingly, two kinds of narratives are simultaneously invoked to define individual and social bodies in *The Broken Commandment* and its kindred texts. The publishing history of Tōson's novel in the 1920s and 1930s can also be read through the contradictory figures of quarantine and vaccination. By the middle of the 1920s, with the rise of the Suiheisha liberation organization (founded in 1922) and growing public awareness, open expressions of prejudice against *burakumin* began to go out of fashion in Japanese polite society (although this in no way meant an end to discrimination). With this shift, *The Broken Commandment* became controversial. It was attacked not because it urged the inclusion of Ushimatsu into the national community, but rather because its most prejudiced language had suggested a difference that excluded other *burakumin* from that same community. In response, for a 1922 edition of his complete works, Tōson made a number of minor changes in the text, revising some of the more blatantly offensive language. A 1929 edition of the work included a few similar additional changes.[65]

Then in 1929, shortly after the publication of the second revised edition, Tōson withdrew *The Broken Commandment* from publication altogether. The text, he implicitly acknowledged, was infected with the disease of prejudice. His conscientious response to the "ailment" of prejudice was to place the novel in quarantine, lest it spread the disease to the reading public. Despite its status as a classic of modern Japanese literature, it remained out of print for a decade.

But in the late 1930s, as Japan mobilized for Total War, Tōson again changed strategies. In 1939 he reissued the novel, explaining his reasons in a new preface and afterword.[66] The new preface begins: "This is a tale of the past." Tōson goes on to explain that the society and especially the *buraku* slums that he describes in *The Broken Commandment* are those of the past, not of the present. It was precisely for this reason that he had once resolved to quarantine—in his words, to "completely bury"—the novel from public view. And yet now he has changed his mind because art is supposed to convey a truthful portrait of social life. Moreover, there is a need for Japan to be confronted with this ugly image of its past, a need that can compared to the plot of the novel itself:

> When you think of it, the past can come back to life at any time. In *Hakai*
> [The broken commandment], there are two figures. One [Ushimatsu's
> father] attempts to conceal the past out of an excessive anxiety over the

future; the other [Rentaro] believes that the only way to bury the past is to expose it. Yet other people in this world fluctuate between these two positions. At any rate, I have decided to place this tale of the *buraku* before the readers of the present day with the feeling of one who renews a grave marker for the sake of those persons who would lay to rest the olden days.

Quarantining the ugly past, hiding it from view, will not work, Tōson argues. It is only by taking the cure offered by a Rentaro, a cure that involves exposing oneself to the unhealthful and ugly aspects of the past, that one can overcome that past: Tōson offers up *The Broken Commandment* as a kind of vaccination for Japan's "ailment" of prejudice (even as he claims the disease has largely disappeared). The novel may contain pathogens of prejudice, but if administered properly, it can strengthen the national body for the current national emergency.

In the 1939 "Afterword," Tōson reiterates these themes. He notes a certain form of historical repetition, what he calls a "coincidence": that *The Broken Commandment*, which was originally written at the height of the Russo-Japanese War, is being reissued in the midst of yet another war—1939 represents the third year of war in China. He then concludes:

today, on the occasion of the republication of this text, I have attempted as much as possible to preserve it in its original state and have made no significant revisions. I have done no more than revise or cut out a phrase here and there. It is the case that a number of questions have been raised about this work, but it is my intention to offer up the work itself in place of an answer to all of those.

It is hard to know what Tōson's intention was in writing that last comment because, in fact, the 1939 edition was drastically altered. An incomplete listing in the current edition of Tōson's complete works lists more than 250 distinct changes to the 1939 text, including major revisions of a number of extended passages. Like Pasteur and Koch in producing their vaccines, Tōson has labored to produce a manageable and safe form of the pathogenic agent.

When the actual changes that Tōson made to the text are examined, two dominant patterns emerge. First, there are revisions of discriminatory phrases and concepts. Derogatory words such as "*eta*" and "New Commoner" are replaced with neutral phrases such as "*buraku no mono*" (person from a buraku). Statements made by various characters that suggest that *burakumin* are racially distinct from other Japanese are cut out. The narrator's descriptions of certain *burakumin* as being "ignoble" or "branded in the skin" are cut. In sum, the pathological markings of "low class" *burakumin* characters are erased from the text.

But there are other sorts of revisions as well, unrelated to the issue of anti-*burakumin* prejudice. A number of words are avoided, repeatedly replaced by words that did not carry the echoes of radical thought and social critique, thereby producing the image of a Japan untroubled by class conflict and other forms of social antagonism. For example, *shakai* (society) becomes *yo no naka* (the world), and *kaikyū* (class) becomes *mibun* (social status). Rentaro is no longer a *shisōka* (political ideologue or social critic), but rather he becomes a *kangaeru hito* (person who thinks). *Rōdōsha* (laborers) become *kinrōsha* (devoted workers—the word loses its socialist connotations). Other words, such as *kenri* (rights, as in political rights), disappear altogether. Another significant change occurs in the list that the novel provides of the titles of Rentaro's published books. The 1906 text lists five books. The 1939 text, however, lists only four: the work titled *Rōdō* (Labor) disappears from the list. The title of another book is altered. The book that in 1906 is called *Gendai no shichō to kasō shakai* (Current trends in thought and the lower strata of society) is shortened in 1939 to *Gendai no shichō* (Current trends in thought).

In short, the 1939 edition is heavily doctored. It erases all traces of internal difference, racial or political, and replaces them with language that depicts healthy identity. The agents of disease have been cultivated and domesticated into a beneficial form. That is to say, if the suspension of publication in 1929 was a kind of quarantine, the 1939 revision employs a more aggressive technique, vaccination. This locates the revised edition within the contemporary campaigns being conducted to ensure the total mobilization of all "Japanese," including *burakumin* and other marginalized nationals—women, Okinawans, Taiwanese, and Koreans.[67] Even the radical Suiheisha movement was co-opted into this effort. At its founding in 1922, Suiheisha had taken a strong anti-imperialist stance, allying itself with Korean and Taiwanese nationalist movements that resisted Japanese colonialism. But by 1939, Suiheisha had come to define its anti-imperialism in terms of supporting the Japanese military in its crusade to liberate Asia. Symptomatic of Suiheisha's decline as an oppositional force is the role of movement leaders in approving the 1939 edition of *The Broken Commandment* prior to its publication.[68]

In the ideological fantasy presented by the 1939 revised edition, the publication of *The Broken Commandment* in 1906 was in fact a kind of vaccination, and it has been successful. Quarantine is no longer necessary; the *burakumin* have been assimilated into the national body on favorable terms, without pathological infection. Ushimatsu's status as a beneficial microbe is now extended to all *burakumin* characters, even to the (formerly socialist) Rentaro. Moreover, the text itself has been doctored so as to eliminate its pathogenicity. As a result, in 1939, difference no longer troubles the homogeneous interior of the nation; it is now permitted to exist only in the space between nations. A complicated, contradictory set of bodily images are invoked side-by-side to define the national community: diseased difference is discovered and quarantined, but then the same potential source of infection is taken internally in a domesticated form, and the body of the national community is thereby strengthened so that it can safely encounter other forms of difference (whereupon the process can be repeated). And the narrative of quarantine (Japanese "uniqueness") that separates internal homogeneity from external difference is supplemented by the narrative of vaccination ("coprosperity"), as the nation steels itself in preparation to absorb even external others into itself.

In the late 1930s, Japanese national imagination needed to sustain conflicting and contradictory desires. Morris-Suzuki notes that at least three distinct

> justifications of colonial expansion—the ideas of racial uniqueness, ethnic commonalities [with other Asians] and [Japanese] civilizational advancement—coexisted at different layers within the intellectual world of the 1920s, 1930s, and 1940s and the use of the ambiguous imagery of "nation" and "ethnos"—*minzoku*—allowed a continuous slippage backward and forward between different levels of justification.[69]

Hence, "the more one looks at literature of the 1930s and 1940s, the harder it becomes to sustain simple equations in which belief in racial purity are equated with militarism and imperialism and belief in racial hybridity with tolerance of difference."[70] Oguma Eiji has shown how the Government-General in colonial Korea pursued the destruction of Korean national identity and the assimilation of Koreans into the Japanese nation—even as it carried out policies that would maintain discrimination against Koreans.[71] The rhetoric of national imagination required both inclusion and exclusion, both vaccination and quarantine.

❖

In 1906, the socialist magazine *Katei zasshi* published a brief unsigned review of *The Broken Commandment*:

The celebrated work of recent days. Setting as its protagonist a New Commoner primary school teacher, this novel describes the extent of the hatred and abuse that the world heaps on the class of people called New Commoners. Racial prejudice is the true enemy of human sentiment, and we must struggle against it with all our might. That Japanese are looked down upon by Westerners is also due to racial prejudice. If this angers Japanese, they must first abandon their own identical prejudice. That is, they must drop their own hateful attitudes toward Chinese and Koreans. And of course the likes of the hateful attitude shown toward New Commoners are truly the height of irrationality. Accordingly, we hope that you will read this novel *The Broken Commandment* and find in it a means of overcoming racial prejudice.[72]

Rather than end my diagnosis of *The Broken Commandment* and its case of the disease of nationalism by prescribing a cure, I would rather simply iterate two theoretical positions I have attempted to sustain in my reading here, as well as in the other chapters of this book. First, I hope to contribute to the critique of modernity in a way that avoids some of the problematic assumptions that grounded classical modernization theory. Hygiene is clearly an aspect of modernity in Meiji Japan, but I have tried to demonstrate that it was not a matter of simple belated imitation of Western models: the rise of hygiene in Japan was simultaneous with (and often prior to) its rise in the West. Japan was as involved in the production of this new form of knowledge as any nation. Moreover, a critique of hygiene in Japan can (and must) be linked to a critique of Western hygiene, nationalism, and imperialism. And, as I discuss in chapter 5, the progressive form of temporality that underlay modernization theory is itself a problematic component of national imagination.

Second, I have tried to foreground the dense complexity of the relationships between ideologies that construct individual human bodies and those of communities such as nations. There is no single national body, Japanese or otherwise, that can be easily isolated and analyzed. Contradictory images of the body can be found even within a single utterance, and these contradictions will only multiply when the sphere of analysis is expanded to include plural utterances. In order to answer the call of this 1906 review, that we use *The Broken Commandment* to find "in it a means of overcoming racial prejudice," we must remain attentive to the chronic instabilities, the small differences, that haunt both the empire of hygiene and our attempts to dismantle it.

CHAPTER THREE

Triangulating the Nation: Representing and Publishing The Family

> Civilized modern societies are defined by processes of decoding and deter-
> ritorialization. But *what they deterritorialize with one hand, they reterritorialize*
> *with the other.* These neoterritorialities are often artificial, residual, archaic;
> but they are archaisms having a perfectly current function, our modern way
> of "imbricating," of sectioning off, of reintroducing code fragments, resus-
> citating old codes, inventing pseudo codes or jargons. Neoarchaisms, as
> Edgar Morin puts it.
>
> > Deleuze and Guattari, *Anti-Oedipus: Capitalism and Schizophrenia*

During the early twentieth century, one of the words most commonly used
to designate the Japanese nation, to name the cultural and political entity that
was thought to have existed continuously from antiquity to the present, was
kokutai, usually translated as "national polity." Those who stressed the continuity of the imperial line and its centrality to Japanese identity especially
favored this word. The first character in this compound, *koku*, carries the
meaning of "nation" or "country"; the second, *tai*, is usually translated as
"body." In short, the characters literally mean "national body." In fact, today
kokutai also functions as an abbreviation for KOKUmin TAIiku taikai—the
National Athletic Meet. The very characters used in the word *kokutai* summon
up the linkage between bodies and national community that formed the subject of the previous chapter.[1]

Another word used widely to designate the nation was *kokka*, usually translated "state." The word designates in particular the role of the state as representative of the national people (the *kokumin*). The first character in *kokka* is
again *koku*, while the second character, *ka*, bears the meanings "family" or

"home." A literal translation would be "national family." That second character *ka*, in its most common Japanese reading, is pronounced *ie*, which is also
the title of Shimazaki Tōson's third novel.

Since the 1930s, *The Family* (*Ie*, 1910–1911; trans. 1976) has been praised as
one of the masterpieces of Japanese realism, almost as frequently as it has been
condemned for failing to portray the political dimensions of everyday life.
Here, though, I will experiment with a different tactic of reading. As I trace
through the rhetoric of "family" that is so central to national imagination in
modern Japan, I will try to demonstrate not only the politics of the novel, but
also and more specifically its politics of representation. Since, as we have
already seen, the rhetoric of national imagination relies on certain conventional notions of representation, this rereading will find in the novel elements
that trouble commonsense ideas of national identity. We will see how the
novel both resists and reproduces important components of national imagination—both in its representations of the family and in its representations of
representation—in ways that avoid easy characterization.

BROTHERS, FATHERS, AND GHOSTS

As Tōson's third full-length novel, *The Family* followed The *Broken Commandment* (*Hakai*, 1906; trans. 1974) and *Haru* (Spring, 1908).[2] Like *Haru*, its storyline was drawn from Tōson's own life, although critics have noted a number
of passages where Tōson substantially altered real-life events in his fictional
version. The sprawling novel traces the slow decline of the Koizumi and
Hashimoto families over a period of twelve years. Unlike *Haru*, the novel provides few temporal benchmarks such as dates to situate its events historically,
although the corresponding period in Tōson's own life stretches from 1898
(when he was twenty-seven) until 1910. Book 1 focuses primarily on the
young writer Koizumi Sankichi and his older sister Otane, who has married
into the Hashimoto family. It tells the story of Sankichi's marriage to Oyuki,
the dreadful poverty they endure as Sankichi pursues a career teaching in a
rural mountain village, and the crisis that arises when Sankichi discovers that
Oyuki is secretly exchanging letters with a man she was once engaged to wed.
Book 1 also traces the decline of the traditional Hashimoto family business
and Otane's increasingly desperate efforts to hold her family together, even
after her shiftless husband runs away with a geisha.

Book 2 retains its focus on Sankichi. He moves his family back to Tokyo
and begins to achieve some success as a novelist but meets one disaster after

another, including the deaths of three of his children (apparently due to mal-nutrition caused by their poverty), increasing demands on his resources from his extended family, and continued friction with his wife Oyuki. One of the most famous incidents occurs when Sankichi finds himself on the verge of an incestuous relationship with a niece, an event that brings Sankichi to the real-ization that he too is inescapably bound to the dissipated blood of the Koizumi and Hashimoto families. While Otane remains a powerful presence in book 2, in many ways she is supplanted in her role as Sankichi's foil by her son, Shōta, who throws himself into the stock market in a doomed attempt to revive the Hashimoto family fortunes. Shōta's business failings and his increas-ingly dissipated lifestyle, including affairs with geisha, are depicted, ending with his death from tuberculosis. The novel closes on a somber note, with an exhausted Sankichi and Oyuki apparently having reached a quiet understand-ing of one another, but as the novel's famous last line tells us, "Outside it was still dark" (*TZ* 4:411).

❏❏

In the preceding chapter, I tried to complicate the notion of an imaginary national body by insisting on the copresence of two contradictory yet mutu-ally supplementary versions of that body. But much of the given wisdom about *The Family*—and about the "Japanese family" and the "family-state" (*kazoku kokka*)—is already bound up in pairs of binary oppositions. Accord-ingly, in order to achieve a similar effect here, in order to uncover small diff-erences swept away from view by these binary oppositions, my strategy will be to complicate these existing dualities by adding a third term. My goal in doing so is not to achieve a dialectical resolution of thesis and antithesis into syn-thesis, nor to channel the unruly flows of desire into tidy Oedipal triangles. Nor do I want to locate the sort of "hybridity" that posits a Japanese cultural identity suspended between Asia and the West. Such an identity arises only from the erasure of Japan's own history of imperialism, so that Japan imagined as meeting space of West and non-West erases the history of violence between non-West and non-West.[3] Rather, I hope to use this triplication to denatural-ize the two existing poles, a first step toward rethinking them, both individu-ally and in their interrelationships. In so doing, I will examine how the novel narrates the irruption of what Deleuze and Guattari call "Oedipus" in early-twentieth-century Japan; I will also map out the way in which the novel acknowledges precisely the hybridity that modern national identity (especially in its imperialist, expansionary mode) must produce—and conceal.

In fact, the novel seems to call out for this sort of reading-by-threes. It is a work haunted by ghostly third parties. Tōson began daily serialization of the first part of *The Family* (under that title) in the *Yomiuri* newspaper in early 1910. The following year, the second part of the novel was serialized in two installments under the title *Gisei* (Sacrifices) in the monthly journal *Chūō Kōron*. Tōson revised the previously serialized sections and added a new final chapter when the novel was published in book form (in two volumes) late in 1911. As he had with his two earlier novels, Tōson self-published the book version of *The Family* (borrowing 300 yen to finance it), largely for financial reasons.[4] After having received scanty manuscript fees for his four poetry collections (and quite possibly no subsequent royalty payments when the collections were reprinted in multiple editions), Tōson chose to go into the publishing business for himself, so that he could receive not only his author's fees but also the publisher's profits.[5] In the essay, "Chosaku to shuppan" (Writing and publishing, 1925), Tōson recalls his decision to enter into publishing on his own as a deliberate attempt to improve the position of authors in relation to publishing houses. He recounts the desperate financial struggles of authors from the Edo period through the mid-Meiji, noting that it was only after the Russo-Japanese War that it became possible for writers to earn a stable income through writing alone (*TZ* 13:70–77). In fact, his decision to enter into the publishing business with his first novel provides an important thread to the autobiographical narrative of *The Family*. The surviving handwritten manuscript of that novel, *The Broken Commandment*, includes detailed instructions to the typesetters for laying out the pages: even as Tōson the author was writing the novel, Tōson the publisher was designing the book he would market.[6]

Tōson and other writers at the turn of the century found themselves dealing with an increasingly commercialized and industrialized publishing world, and as Nakayama Hiroaki has argued, their fiction and critical essays from the period show an increasingly concerted effort to produce the discourse of the starving writer-genius, whose works possessed a "value" immune to the corruption of commodity exchange value.[7] In this sense, *The Family* belongs alongside such works as Natsume Sōseki's *Nowaki* (Autumn storm, 1907) and Tayama Katai's "Futon" (The quilt, 1907), fictional works that depict the struggles of writers to survive in a market economy. In *The Family*, the fictional works the protagonist produces are depicted as both artistic and business ventures, works of art and commodities. The tense relationship between these two types of production forms an important link in my own attempt to rethink the novel.

This publishing history also provides one of the ghostly third parties that haunt the novel. In a new forward to *The Family* written in 1937, Tōson notes that he had originally planned to write the novel in three books, rather than the two books that it has today. According to Tōson, the missing third book was supposed to portray the events by which the two central characters of book 2, Sankichi and his nephew Shōta, each piece together their new families. Shortly after Tōson completed serializing book 1, however, his real-life nephew (Takase Chikao, the model for Shōta) died unexpectedly, as did Tōson's own wife, Shimazaki Fuyuko, the model for Oyuki. Real life had intervened to change the anticipated course of Tōson's novel. Accordingly, after completing book 2, Tōson decided to, in his words, "put off book 3 until another day" (*TZ* 4:622–3).[8]

The absence of this ghostly third book has troubled critics who study the novel. Should we consider *The Family* complete, or is it properly read as an unfinished work? The episodic nature of its construction, with no single plot line informing its structure and no obvious moment of climax at its end, means that both answers are plausible. Moreover, other critics have used Tōson's apparent decision to modify his original plan for the novel, that is, his decision not to write book 3, as a key for explaining the striking change in tone between the first and second books of the novel that we have now.[9] In fact, the narrative structure of the novel shifts dramatically between the two books. In book 1, the narrative perspective switches back and forth between Sankichi, his sister Otane, and other characters, so that some early readers complained that they were unsure who the protagonist of the novel was.[10] In contrast, one early critic complained that book 2 was flawed because its perspectival focus stays too rigidly with Sankichi.[11] In this latter book, Otane's son Shōta emerges as a central figure, but he is almost always perceived through Sankichi's eyes: after the opening passage of book 2, Shōta rarely becomes the perspectival center of narration. Moreover, the theme that most critics see as dominating the first half of the novel—Sankichi's desire to construct a new family—largely disappears in the second half. It portrays instead the increasing burden Sankichi feels as more and more demands, especially financial ones, are placed upon him by the members of the old Koizumi and Hashimoto families.

Accordingly, the history of the writing and publication of the novel provides an example of an apparent duality haunted by an absent third party, the missing book 3. The novel's storyline, too, repeatedly revolves around pairings that are interrupted by the unexpected presence of a third party. Virtually all of the dramatic plot movement in the novel occurs by way of love triangles:

Sankichi's discovery of his wife Oyuki's love letters to her former fiancé; San-kichi's own flirtation with the unmarried Sone in book 1 and his quasi-inces-tuous relationship with his niece Oshun in book 2; Tatsuo's abandoning his wife Otane for a geisha in book 1; his son's repetition of the same act in book 2; and so on. The families in *The Family* are continually destabilized when the duality of the married couple is troubled by the appearance of a third party.

If we examine the spatial world of the novel, we see the same pattern. In book 1, two locales dominate, the space of Sankichi's household in Komoro and the space of Otane's household in another old mountain highway post-town. In book 2, likewise, there are two dominant spatial centers: Sankichi's household (now relocated to Tokyo, first in the city's western suburbs and later in lowertown Shinkatamachi) and Shōta's. Yet in both cases, a ghostly third space haunts the work: that of the old Koizumi family estate, the birthplace of both Sankichi and Otane. Sankichi actually visits his old hometown at the end of the novel, paying his respects at the graves of his parents, gazing at the ruins of the burned-out family compound and meeting people who had known his father, who died insane when Sankichi was a child. As Sankichi tells his brother Morihiko, "It's just that, somehow, I feel as if our dead father is haunting us . . . wherever we go, whatever we do, he always seems to turn up" (*TZ* 4:355–56). As in so many works of Meiji literature, the father here is a ghostly presence, one that must be sought after by the children.[12] As Watanabe Hiroshi notes, *The Family* is structured not so much around a patricidal desire, but rather a desire to find the father.[13] In a sense, the novel is situated within what Juliet Flower MacCannell calls the "regime of the Brother."[14] This does not, however, mean that patriarchy is absent. *The Family* in many ways narrates Sankichi's discovery of the missing father within himself—but with, as we shall see, a twist, one that potentially troubles the dualistic framework of modern patriarchies.

※

There is one other third party of significance in the novel. In her reworking of modern Japanese literary history as a narrative of changing forms of fam-ily and home, Nishikawa Yūko notes that the protagonist's name, Koizumi Sankichi, indicates quite literally that he is the *third [san]* son in the Koizumi family.[15] While this may seem an irrelevant detail, it is in fact of some signifi-cance when we try to map out the relationship between Tōson's *The Family* and its historical moment.

As Nishikawa argues, the protagonists of male-authored I-novels, the genre of autobiographical fiction that rose to prominence in early-twentieth-century

Japan and in which many (though not all) critics would categorize *The Family*, are almost always second or third sons.[16] Nishikawa argues that this family status forms a sort of precondition for the I-novel itself. The prototypical male-authored I-novel traces a hero who leaves the extended family estate, the *ie*, in the countryside and struggles to establish a new household, a *katei* containing only the nuclear family, in rented lodgings in the city. This is the career path of second and third sons, of course: first sons stay at home to inherit the mantle of family head, a title passed down from generation to generation. A second or third son usually has no chance to become the *ie* patriarch and can only aim to become the head of a one-generation *katei*. Early on in *The Family*, Shōta—a first son who increasingly feels the weight of responsibility for the extended family he will someday lead—envies Sankichi (his uncle, but nearly the same age as himself) the relative freedom of his life:

> Shōta felt jealous of his uncle, able to remain a student for as long as he wanted. His uncle could come here, do what he wanted, think what he wanted, and no one objected. On the other hand, even when Shōta had made up his mind to carry out a plan of study in Tokyo, he was summoned back home midway through, before he could realize it.   (*TZ* 4:25)

The *ie* could seem an implacable burden for first sons like Shōta. On the other hand, second or third sons like Sankichi (that is, the I-novelist cohorts) drift with their *katei* through the city, from one rented house to another—as Sankichi laments, "there is nothing worse than house-hunting" (*TZ* 4:188)—and their fiction focuses on their troubled relationships with members of the *katei*, in particular their wives. Nonetheless, even for them, the old *ie* remains a looming, fixed presence in the background, so that the family system for these writers consisted of a duality, the uncomfortable copresence of two different families, the *ie* and the *katei*.[17]

Accordingly, the typical male-authored I-novel is the story of a second or third son trying to escape from the *ie* to establish a *katei*.[18] A popular prewar card game in Japan (*kazoku awase*) involved assembling "ideal" hands—the two parents and three children who were thought to constitute the "ideal family." Nishikawa describes the I-novel as depicting the struggle to assemble or hold together the winning hand of an "ideal family."[19]

> In the I-novel, if you put together the winning hand of family-game cards, the novelist loses his true theme. . . . Whereas, if one continually

fails to put together the right combination of family-game cards, or if one puts together a winning hand but then loses one of the cards, it becomes possible to keep on writing I–novels as long as one likes.[20]

In this sense, the theme of Tōson's *The Family* is how Sankichi struggles with the bad hand he is dealt in this homosocial game where the places at the table are reserved for second and third sons. It is a game that also demonstrates how intricately bound up this novel is with the forces of urbanization, industrialization, and social dislocation that so profoundly altered the landscape of Meiji Japan.

VERSIONS OF THE FAMILY OF NATIONS

What, however, is the relationship between the family and national imagination? This not a matter of one relationship, but of several: a "family" of "related" problems. I will consider primarily three interconnected issues here: the family as a metaphor through which the national community is imagined; the family as a functional institution that binds together the nation and links its individual members to the nation-state; and the family as a culturally distinct entity whose particularity is used to distinguish one nation from another.

As a metaphor for the nation, the family plays an important role in ideological production and reproduction. As Benedict Anderson notes, one of the ways in which the hierarchical power relationships that structure national communities are naturalized is through the rhetoric of the family: one is bound to one's fellow nationals through a common bond of love for the Fatherland, the Motherland, or the imagined fraternal community. This language produces the image of a community that is based on sentiment rather than coercion, one that is naturally given rather than artificially constructed, and one that is arbitrarily assigned as fate rather than something that one consciously chooses. Ueno Chizuko argues that

> people do not call relationships entered into voluntarily and by free choice—relationships whose formation and dissolution are always possible—by the word "family," and accordingly when people use the simile "family-like" to describe a freely chosen relationship, we see functioning the motive of a desire to transform the foundation of that relationship from something voluntarily chosen into something absolute and necessary. . . .[21]

The rhetorical figure of the family, and especially the family as trope for the nation, performs into existence what Judith Butler calls "an ethical community based on nonartificial, i.e., natural ties," thereby covering over the nightmarish image of an antagonistic society torn apart by ceaseless conflict between self-interests.[22] In sum, the use of the family as a metaphor for the nation allows its citizens to imagine the nation as "the domain of disinterested love and solidarity."[23] It is this disinterestedness that permits the nation to ask for sacrifice on the part of its citizens, just as the family can demand sacrifice from its members—precisely the logic of sacrifice or "infinite debt" that so bedevils Sankichi in *The Family*.[24] The family becomes, for example, the site of production for the soldiers who would sacrifice themselves for the nation in the many wars that have marked Japanese modernity, soldiers who perceived themselves to be simultaneously defending nation and home.

Meiji Japan provides many remarkable examples of this use of the family as an ideological figure for the nation-state. As Carol Gluck, Irokawa Daikichi, and others have demonstrated, the notion of Japan as a family-state (*kazoku kokka*) was central to the thought of such nationalist ideologues as the philosopher Inoue Tetsujirō (1855–1944).[25] Arguments about the ideal nature of the family were often indirect discussions of the ideal nature of the nation itself—and vice versa. In such texts as the 1890 Imperial Rescript on Education, the Confucian virtues of "filial piety" and "loyalty to one's sovereign," which had always been distinct, and between which the former had generally taken precedence, were now blurred together, with loyalty to the state taking precedence over filial piety. In this way, as Tessa Morris-Suzuki has argued, the national community, imagined as family, was imbued with both "solidarity and inequality," so that all Japanese "were part of a single community, but, also as in the family, they had different rights and duties within that community."[26] The Emperor was the "parent" of the national family, and the national people were to be his obedient "children."

Such an equation of nation and family was not, however, the sole preserve of conservative ideologues. When young reformers of Tōson's generation—MacCannell's "Brothers"—advocated a new kind of family, one based on equality and romantic love rather than on hierarchy and duty, their arguments also invoked the nation. The nation that they imagined, though, implicitly—and often explicitly—took a different form from the Japan imagined by Inoue and others. One of the most common readings of *The Family* argues that it narrates Sankichi's failed attempt to break away from the old family system of feudal Japan, a system that centered on the hierarchical relation of parent to child, and his equally failed attempt to construct a new, modern family centered on a relationship of equality and affection between husband and wife. If we accept this reading, it is easy to see the novel as an allegory for the defeat of the People's Rights Movement of the 1870s and 1880s and its populist conception of the nation. That is, its narrative of the tragic triumph of the old family system over the incipient modern nuclear family can be read as an allegory for the victory of official state nationalism over popular revolutionary nationalism in Meiji Japan—the overt theme of Tōson's last completed novel, *Before the Dawn* (*Yoake mae*, 1929–35; trans. 1987).

In addition to its role as trope for the nation, the family, as a functional institution, was also central to the production and reproduction of the national community. If the Emperor was now the "parent" of the nation, the actual parents in individual families were charged with becoming the agents of the nation-state within the space of the domicile. As a technology for the division of labor within modern nations, the family in Meiji Japan—as in other modern nations—became the primary ideological apparatus for achieving the biological, economic, and cultural production and reproduction of the nation. "The vast space of the nation-state was tidily divided up into little spaces known as 'households,' " Nishikawa writes, "thereby instituting a thoroughgoing control over it."[27]

The Meiji period saw an intense interest on the part of the state and nationalist intellectuals in reforming the legal codes that defined the family. In 1871, the modern family-registry system was established as an official state institution. In 1882, the longstanding practice of classifying concubines as legal family members was abolished, the first step in a lengthy process of redefining the proper relationship between sexuality and the family.[28] The 1898 Meiji Civil Code (whose promulgation coincides with the beginning of the period narrated in *The Family*) and a host of other legislation reconstructed the supposedly "traditional" family of Japan. They redefined the position of household head so that, except in extraordinary situations, it could only be held by men, and they codified hierarchical relations between that household head and other family members. Women were banned from most forms of property ownership and from marrying without the consent of their household head. Formal legal divorce was made more difficult, with the result that the divorce rate in Japan dropped dramatically—a change that is directly depicted in *The Family*.[29] Perhaps most importantly, the Civil Code defined the family, and not the individual, as the basic administrative unit of the Japanese nation.

New practices and ideologies accompanied these legal changes. Lifelong monogamous marriage was now celebrated as a national norm (even as a sexual double standard remained in actual practice). As Takashi Fujitani has argued, the new public ceremonies commemorating marriages and wedding anniversaries for the imperial family played a central role in propagating this new norm. Such ceremonies were part of the nation-state's family discourse, "in which the imperial household and the people were mystically bound together as a family." Despite the fact that the crown prince (the future Taishō Emperor) was the biological son not of the Meiji Empress, but of one of the Emperor's concubines, public ceremonies such as the 1894 Silver Wedding Anniversary provided the image of Emperor and Empress as a stable, monogamous married couple, a model for the nation, because "it was imperative that the family itself be a properly ordered model for the nation."[30]

Likewise, changing patterns of urbanization and industrialization and the rise of large-scale bureaucratic organizations in government and business required novel forms of the family to sustain economic production. These forces tended to contradict the version of the family that had been legally installed by the Civil Code, as market forces reterritorialized domestic space. Whereas, legally and ideologically, the patriarch of the family was its moral center, for more and more Japanese families, especially those in the emerging urban middle class in the 1910s, the sole justification for his authority as patriarch was his ability to earn income.[31] As Immanuel Wallerstein argues, the household serves as the primary unit of modern capitalist societies. With its gendered division of labor and its ideological distinction between production and reproduction, the household serves as a primary mechanism for reproducing the network of unequal exchanges that underwrite the modern world-system.[32]

In a broad range of discourses and institutions, then, the Meiji project of nation building was simultaneously a project of family and house building. The new modern educational system promoted a gendered, two-tiered track for boys and girls, thereby instituting many of the ideologies that would underpin the modern Japanese family. Moreover, older patterns for marriage among nonelite rural communities, under which young people married local partners they had often chosen for themselves, broke down. In its place, a pattern previously associated mainly with the elite ruling class—of arranged marriages based on economic considerations, often linking families from spatially distant regions—increasingly became the nationwide norm, especially for the new urban middle classes.[33] In *The Family*, the arranged marriages between Sankichi and Oyuki and between Shōta and Toyose (as well as Otane's fears, discussed below, that Shōta might marry a local girl from an inappropriate class background) exemplify this new pattern.

Likewise, the mid-Meiji period saw the family reconfigured as the primary site for implementation of many of the hygienic reforms discussed in chapter 2.[34] As Jordan Sand has shown, this also meant the introduction of new architectural forms, as the space of the home was physically reconfigured in an effort to mold the lifestyle patterns desired for the new modern family.[35] Moreover, pregnancy and birthing came under a dense set of legal regulations, as the state intervened directly in the site of biological reproduction.[36]

The state's efforts to reconstruct the family as an administrative institution were not without opposition. But even intellectuals and feminists who opposed the state's actions implicitly accepted the framework of nation building. As Ken Ito notes, "the *katei* can serve the nation just as well as the *ie*."[37] Reformers argued not that the family should be freed from its subservience to the goals of nation building, but rather that their own vision of the family and home (based on equality and romantic love and centered on the nuclear family) would be more effective in achieving those goals. An 1891 article on the family declared that

> Each man and woman is a national citizen, thus a couple is also one unit of the nation. Accordingly, discord in a marriage is a grievous matter for the country. It is a national couple's duty to become as one body and soul, cooperating for social development.[38]

From the early-Meiji period, progressive reformist intellectuals demonstrated a strong tendency to equate the affection that was supposed to be the bond of the modern family with the bond of affection linking individual to the nation.

Thus, when Tōson's *The Family* depicts strains within the family, the novel is touching on one of the central institutions of the modern nation. It is ironic that this modern construct would become a symbol for Japan's ancient "tradition," an irony that Japan shares with many other modern nations. In Japan, as elsewhere, the family has become a metonym for national culture. The *ie* system became one of the "icons of Japaneseness" thought to distinguish Japanese culture from that of other nations.[39] As Harry Harootunian has noted, in the thought of such figures as the philosopher Watsuji Tetsurō, the notion of a culturally distinct Japanese family "would constitute the guarantee of Japan's continuing identity in a world marred by sameness, while its disappearance would mark the end of what it meant to be Japanese."[40] This use of the family as an example of the particularity of national culture also appears directly in *The Family*. When Sankichi discovers that his wife is still exchanging letters with her former fiancé, he visits the elderly principal of the school where he teaches, hoping for some useful advice. The principal (educated in the United States) immediately leaps to a comparison of the American and Japanese families: "American women, when it comes to this, handle things so skillfully. Even when it is an old boyfriend, they introduce him to their husband and carry on very proper relations—'*He was my lover*,' they come right out and say it—well, it's refreshingly candid. Unfortunately, Japanese women aren't that sophisticated" (*TZ* 4:80).[41]

This sort of comparison between the "Japanese family" and the "Western family" has also dominated much of the criticism written on *The Family*, especially in recent years. Such features as the division between *uchi* (inside) and *soto* (outside) that are thought to characterize the Japanese family become in turn markers that attempt to establish a clean separation between the inside and outside of Japan itself by way of the family.[42] Such a simple binary opposition overlooks the complexity and heterogeneity of the family, the small differences that characterize domestic life in both Japan and the West—heterogeneity depending on such factors as historical period, region, class, profession, religious practice, and so on. In rereading *The Family* as part of a critique of the rhetoric of national imagination, it is important not to start from the assumption of a Japanese national family that can be neatly distinguished from its Western counterpart, a distinction that the novel would then simply represent. Instead, it is necessary to look at how the novel helps produce—and contest—this component of the rhetoric of national imagination.

COMPLICATING THE DUALITIES OF TIME AND SPACE

There are two pieces of received wisdom about *The Family*, two presumptions that anyone who reads through the criticism on the novel will encounter again and again. The first is that *The Family* lacks a sense of sociality, since its narrative focus remains entirely within the private, domestic space of the family, never moving beyond the bounds of that interior into the public space of society and politics. Tōson himself is at least partially responsible for this interpretation. In 1930, he wrote about the method he pursued in writing the work:

> When I wrote *The Family*, I attempted to produce a full-length novel as
> if I were constructing a house out of sentences. I completely omitted all

things that occurred outside the house, and limited myself entirely to the scenes occurring inside. I started writing from the kitchen, or from the entryway, or from the garden. It was only when I went to a room from which you could hear a river that I would first write about that river. It was in this manner that I built my *Family*. (*TZ* 13:121)[43]

Critics have tended to accept this statement at face value and have treated *The Family* as an asocial, apolitical I-novel. In terms of literary history, the novel then becomes emblematic of the retreat from social concerns that marked earlier works such as *The Broken Commandment* and of the rise of an obsessive fixation on private life that came to dominate Japanese fiction after the publication of Tayama Katai's "Futon" (The quilt, 1907). Critics such as Hirano Ken note that although *The Family* is set during the time of the Russo-Japanese War and the social turmoil that surrounded it, these merit hardly any mention in it. Likewise, the economic and social activities of the family members when they are away from home are barely mentioned. Hirano notes the contrast between *The Family* and *Before the Dawn* and declares that, as for the former, "there is no society here, there is no history here."[44]

The second commonplace is that the storyline of the novel is constructed around the conflict between old and new versions of the family, and that it narrates Sankichi's failed attempt to break away from the old *ie* and to establish his own new, modern family—a *katei*, although in the novel Tōson prefers the phrase "new family" (*atarashii ie*).[45] Again, the origins of this commonplace can be traced to Tōson himself, both in his commentaries on the novel and in passages taken from the work itself. In one scene, Sankichi discusses with Shōta the fact that the Koizumi family line is about to be extinguished, as Oshun, the family-head Minoru's only surviving child, is going to marry into her husband's family: "The Koizumi family line, with its long history, has for all practical purposes become extinct. . . . Shōta—you, me, Oshun, we are like new buds sprouting from the old family. We are all new buds. All we can do now is for each of us to make new families" (*TZ* 4:303). Nonetheless, as Sankichi repeatedly bemoans, he is forced to take on the burden of supporting his extended family, even as he is unable to establish and preserve his own *katei*. As noted above, this suggests an allegorical reading, one that undercuts the notion that the novel lacks a political dimension: the ability of the old feudal *ie* to forestall the rise of a new modern *katei* parallels the ability of the conservative Meiji state to wrest the mantle of nation away from the People's Rights Movement during the 1880s and 1890s.

In sum, there are two commonplaces regarding the novel that I will address here: first, that its focus on *uchi*, the private and domestic space of the family elides the presence of *soto*, the public and political space of society; and second, that it narrates the tenuous relationship between "old" and "new" models of family life, between the *ie* and the *katei*. It is not the case that these readings are utterly mistaken. But I hope to show that both are based on overly simplex binary oppositions—spatial (inside/outside) and temporal (old/new)—that efface as much as they reveal. As a first step toward grasping the complexity of the relationships between family, nation, and this novel, I will try to complicate each of these pairings by locating a third term, a hybrid that confounds the attempt to draw a clean boundary between the two opposed elements, one that signals the presence of small differences that the larger opposition tends to efface.

Let me begin with the notion that the novel lacks sociality because it focuses entirely on the interior of the family house. This is of course an exaggeration. While the novel does not provide dates or details, it does in fact mention numerous events that without question occur in the public space of politics, market economies, and society: the Russo-Japanese War and the economic fluctuation it entailed, the Forestry Incident to which Sankichi's second eldest brother devotes his life, and the rise of new forms of industry (including the factory that Sankichi's eldest brother tries to launch) and finance (Shōta throws himself into a career in the stock market) are all mentioned. The drastic changes that the late-Meiji period brought to the physical appearance of both city and country are also detailed in the novel. On the outskirts of Tokyo:

> Even in that quiet suburban vista, which called to mind the landscape of the old Musashino plain, if you looked closely you could see startling changes. The tree nurseries and vegetable fields were disappearing, one after another. The earth was being dug up. New houses were appearing everywhere. (*TZ* 4:253)

Likewise, on his return visit, at the novel's end, to Otane's home in the mountains, Sankichi discovers the arrival of electricity and the railroad in that rural town.[46]

In the wake of the feminist dictum that the private is the political, too, one must be wary of claims that we can cleanly separate the practices of domestic life from questions of politics because, as Yuval-Davis notes, "the construction

of the boundary between the public and private is a political act in itself."[47]
And as we have seen, in the Meiji era there was not yet any widespread
assumption that the interior of the family constituted a domestic refuge of
private space, cut off from the demands of the public sphere. Both conservative and progressive advocates of family reform in Meiji Japan acknowledged
explicitly that their positions regarding the proper Japanese family were primarily political positions. As Jordan Sand argues, it was not until the Taishō era
that the middle-class presumption of a distinction between private and public space achieved widespread currency, whereupon the retroactive reading of
The Family's lack of sociality became possible. To write about the family in the
Meiji period was to take up one of the most highly charged political issues of
the day.

If one rereads The Family without presuming that its focus on the domestic realm renders it apolitical, it becomes possible to see that it is, in fact, a
remarkably political novel, one that maps the effects of the rise of industrial
capitalism on the lives of ordinary citizens. Moreover, it presents a kind of
political critique grounded not in the grand narrative of modes of production, but in the lived time of everyday life and the transformation it underwent with the rise of modern capitalism.[48] The Family depicts with remarkable clarity the rise of that series of interlocking economies (psychic, capitalist, literary, national, and imperial) that Deleuze and Guattari call Oedipus.
Tōson's novel records in intricate detail the process whereby the social repres-
sions characteristic of capitalism, imperialism, and nationalism deterritorialize
and reterritorialize the space of the family, decoding and recoding the flows
of desire that traverse it.

❁

For a number of reasons, then, the notion that because its focus lies mainly
with the interior, The Family lacks a political aspect is problematic. Moreover,
the novel itself produces a third space, one that is neither quite inside nor outside the family/home, a hybrid space that is highly eroticized precisely because
of the effect it has in potentially undermining the boundary between uchi and
soto: it marks the ever-present threat of deterritorialization. I am referring to
the space of the veranda (engawa), the corridor that wraps around the rooms
of the house but which in daytime and in good weather is left directly open
to the outside.[49] A number of important scenes in the novel take place on the
verandah. The first of these, occurring very early on, is emblematic. Sankichi,
visiting his sister Otane in the country, sits on the verandah with her, her hus-

band Tatsuo, and others. They are discussing Shōta, Otane's eldest son and the heir to the Hashimoto line, and the concerns his parents have that he may be sexually involved with a local girl whose family background makes her an unsuitable candidate to be Shōta's bride.

> "If that's the case, why don't you just let him marry the girl?" Sankichi blurted out, in the manner of a student.
>
> "How could we do such a foolish thing?" Otane chided. "You say such things because you don't understand anything."
>
> "Moreover, sir," piped in Kasuke [the manager of the Hashimoto family medicine business; not a blood relative but a member of the extended *ie*], looking toward the guest with his red, bloodshot eyes, "We don't like the girl's parents. . . . This, well, this may just be my own suspicious mind, but I can't help feeling that her parents are behind it all, pulling the strings. . . ."
>
> Otane, as if she had suddenly remembered something, looked threatened, but made no attempt to give voice to her feelings.
>
> "And even if that is not the case," Kasuke continued, "there is the difference in family status. How in the world, sir, could the Hashimotos bring in a bride from a family like that?" (*TZ* 4:18)

Here the verandah provides a space in which to discuss sexuality, marriage, and a potential undermining of the class identity of the Hashimoto family. Desire is threatening to deterritorialize fundamental boundaries that define the family, and the location Tōson chooses to set the discussion of this threat is the ambiguous space of the verandah, neither quite inside nor outside the family house. In order to capture this unruly desire in print, that is to say, the novel reterritorializes domestic architecture.

This is not the only strategic use of the verandah in the novel. As Sekiya Yumiko notes, many of the major characters in the novel are assigned one area of the household architecture that is closely associated with them, so that the character serves as a metonymic figure for that place, and vice versa.[50] For example, Otane is closely associated with the cooking hearth, and Sankichi (especially in book 2) is associated with the second-floor room to which he retreats when he writes. The character most closely associated with the verandah is Oshun, the daughter of Sankichi's eldest brother Minoru (the reigning *ie* patriarch). This association arises with the first mention of Oshun in the novel: when Sankichi visits Minoru after he returns to Tokyo from his visit to

Otane, the narrator notes that, "Out on the verandah, his niece Oshun was playing" (*TZ* 4:41).

The verandah suits the role Oshun plays in the novel quite well. She is a highly eroticized character, one who finds herself uncomfortably situated both inside and outside the proper space of the family, straddling the boundary between *uchi* and *soto*. That is to say, she is the object of incestuous sexual advances from a number of male relatives, including Sankichi himself. As a blood relative, she seems to belong inside the family, but as the object of sexual desire for the family's men, she should be outside of it. As noted above, she finds a way out from this unbearable situation by marrying into her fiancé's family, thereby bringing to an end the main branch of the Koizumi family line. Without its verandah, it seems, the house collapses.

Sankichi's improper advance on Oshun revolves around the perverse space of the verandah. The event occurs when Oshun comes to live with Sankichi to help with housekeeping while his wife is away visiting her family in Hokkaido. A series of encounters are briefly recounted between Oshun and Sankichi, all set on or around the verandah. Through these encounters, Sankichi finds himself increasingly drawn to his young niece. Finally, one night, after he, she, and her cousin Onobu eat watermelon on the verandah, Onobu goes to bed, and Sankichi and Oshun take a stroll through the moonlit garden. The actual moment when a "mysterious force suddenly caused him to take his niece's hand" (*TZ* 4:237) is not directly depicted. All we are given is Sankichi's guilt-ridden mental recounting of the event the next day, as he stands looking out a window (over the verandah?) toward the street. Then, the following night:

> The night was deep and quiet. Beams of moonlight shone across Sankichi's knees as he sat on the verandah. Oshun had lay down next to her cousins, but now, saying she couldn't sleep, she again came to her uncle's side, still wearing her white nightgown.
>
> Suddenly, a pack of dogs burst through the bamboo fence and into the garden. Snapping at one another, wagging their tails, they raced around the garden trees in sport. Then, from the street there arose the howl of a comrade. Hearing this, one dog rushed out after it. The other dogs followed and all rushed out. Their barking sounded through the nighttime sky.
>
> "It's almost impossible to sleep on a night like this, isn't it?" So said the uncle, sitting next to the niece who had lapsed into silent thought. He listened to the dogs' barking. The uncle was shaking like a dog. (*TZ* 4:239)

Again, the verandah provides the setting for an outcropping of intense desire, what Deleuze and Guattari would call a "becoming-animal" that threatens to erase the boundaries—spatial, sexual, and moral—that divide inside from outside in the family.

There is another reason that the association of Oshun with the verandah seems appropriate, and this moves the discussion beyond the level of the individual family house and to the broader register of the family-state, of the *kazoku kokka*. If, as I have argued, the household and the nation become tropes for one another in national imagination, then one can think about the verandah in terms of its equivalent at the level of national space. After all, at the time *The Family* was being written, the Japanese nation-state was busily constructing its own verandah, its own buffer space that was neither quite inside nor outside of the nation. In rethinking the relationship between family and nation, it is necessary to take into account Japan's expanding colonial empire, a ghostly third that haunts any attempt to define history through a simple opposition between Japan and the West. *The Family* contains no scenes directly set in the colonies, though Edward Said points out that readers must remain attentive to "the way in which structures of location and geographical reference appear in the cultural languages of literature, history, or ethnography," structures that accustom metropolitan audiences to the idea of empire even in works "that are not otherwise connected to . . . an official ideology of 'empire.' " Such a stance allows us to see "the formation of a colonial actuality existing at the heart of metropolitan life," including its domestic spaces.[51]

I have already mentioned how the deaths of Tōson's wife and nephew in the time between the writing of books 1 and 2 had a major impact on the form of *The Family*. But one other major event occurred in that same interval. Shimazaki Fuyuko died of massive hemorrhages after childbirth on August 6, 1910; two weeks later, on August 22, Japan formally annexed Korea. While the impact of the former event is widely discussed in scholarship on the novel, the latter event is largely absent from the criticism. This silence is consistent with the presumption that the novel is apolitical, but the relevance of the annexation to this narrative of family life suddenly becomes material when the novel is read without this presumption.

After all, as Murai Osamu notes, the annexation of Korea into the Japanese nation was represented through ideologies of the family.[52] The unusual word, *heigō*, that was used by Japanese bureaucrats to name the act of annexation was chosen because it seemed to indicate not a forcible conquest, but rather a union between consenting parties: it seemed to suggest, in short, the merging of two families by way of marriage. Here, the image of "family" allowed for a new model of assimilation, one that—as Tessa Morris-Suzuki notes—did not require the exclusionary elements that were inherent in a racialized version of national identity (and yet which supplemented rather than cancelled out that racialized version).

> This approach, it should be said, created considerable scope for ambiguity in the rhetoric of nationhood. When Japanese writers spoke of the national family, and of the first emperors as the founders of this family, it was often left to the listener to determine whether they were speaking in terms of biology or culture or some combination of the two.[53]

As Oguma Eiji has demonstrated, the post-1910 marriage between the two nations of Korea and Japan was further sealed by actual political marriages arranged between members of the Korean and Japanese royal families, by policies that encouraged marriages between Korean and Japanese commoners, and, in Japanese popular culture, by works that depicted romances and marriages between Japanese men and Korean women.[54] And as the linguist Tokieda Motoki would note, writing in 1942 about the problem of educating Korean subjects in the Japanese national language, assimilation would occur via the family or not at all: only if Japanese became the mother-tongue that Korean infants learned would true assimilation of the colonies become a reality. As Tokieda notes, the relationship between national language and national identity in 1942 was considerably more complex than it was in the 1890s, when Ueda Kazutoshi blithely equated the Japanese national language with a racial bloodline: "When [Ueda's] 'National Language and the Nation-State' was written [1895], Japan did not yet possess Taiwan or Korea. It was an age, as it were, when parents and children, brothers and sisters all lived together happily in one family-house. It was an age when there were as of yet no sisters-in-law or brothers-in-law."[55]

Oshun's association in *The Family* with the verandah resonates with this context because she is also closely associated with the colonies and with colonial hybridity.[56] The colonies serve in Tōson's fiction as a sort of dumping ground for problematic family members, those who have committed some violation that makes it impossible for them to remain at home. These characters can no longer stay inside the family, yet because of the familial bond that exists with them, they cannot simply be cast outside into the exterior, cut off from all ties to the family. Sending them to the colonies is the preferred solution. In *The Family*, Oshun's father Minoru meets this fate. He is the titular head of the Koizumi family, but after he is twice jailed because of his inadvertent role in shady business deals, Minoru is toppled by his younger brothers, who insist that he move to Manchuria and start over. There, in (semi)colonial space, he will have a chance to start over and at the very least will no longer burden the other members of the family. One of the few extended scenes in book 2 where the narrative perspective leaves Sankichi occurs in the scene when Sankichi and Morihiko (Sankichi's second eldest brother) confront Minoru and demand that he emigrate; the entire scene is narrated through Oshun's perspective. (In fact, all of the major male characters except Sankichi—that is to say, all of his potential rivals for the role of patriarch—have their own colonial experiences. Minoru, Morihiko, Tatsuo, and Shōta all spend time in colonial or semicolonial Asia).

As I will discuss at more length in chapter 4, this tendency to use the colonies as a hybrid space of exile is even more pronounced in Tōson's next major novel, *Shinsei* (New life, 1918–1919). In this work, another autobiographical novel, Tōson describes the incestuous relationship that Kishimoto, the protagonist, has with Setsuko, his niece (who is in fact modeled after a different real-life niece from Oshun). Unlike in *The Family*, this affair does develop to the point of sexual relations, resulting in a pregnancy. When the protagonist Kishimoto describes Setsuko physically, one of the things that attracts him is her dark skin color.

> At times, Kishimoto would leave his desk to look at Setsuko. The damp towel on her forehead naturally wiped away the white makeup. There her inborn dusky complexion showed through. Among her four siblings, her older sister Teruko and her younger brother Ichirō had been born in their rural hometown, while Jirō had been born in this suburb of Tokyo; only she had been born during the time that [Setsuko's parents] lived in Korea. The natural color of the skin on her forehead was a duskiness she had brought from Korea. (*TZ* 7:317)[57]

At the conclusion of the work, once the scandalous affair has been revealed, due to Kishimoto's publication of a confessional novel based on it (*Shinsei* itself, we are supposed to understand), Setsuko becomes an impossible, hybrid figure, one neither inside nor outside the family.[58] She is forcibly shipped off to colonial Taiwan (where her uncle lives—a character modeled after Tōson's eldest brother, or Minoru, Oshun's father, from *The Family*) in order to begin her own "new life."

In sum, once we begin to rethink of *The Family* as a work with imperial dimensions, the novel's architecture shifts. The equivalence it seems to posit between the verandah and colonial space undermines conventional interpretations that see the novel as apolitical because its focus remains inside domestic space. The binary *uchi/soto* distinction that such readings rely on is often immediately transferred into a comparison between the "Japanese family" and the "Western family," transforming a certain model of the family into a metonym of national culture. Such an opposition erases, among other things, the history of Japan's empire in Asia and the impact it had in deterritorializing domestic spaces and in producing a proliferation of small differences that undermine the possibility of a clean distinction between *uchi* and *soto*. The verandah brings this ghostly third party back into a consideration of the relationship between family and nation. *The Family* explicitly refers elsewhere—via the pictures of the Black Ships discovered at the end of the novel (*TZ* 4:381–82)—to the ghosts of the past, the West's threat to colonize Japan at the dawn of the Meiji era. But I have tried to show here that Tōson's novel also maps Japan's own imperial expansion. The *uchi/soto* opposition, which implicitly centers national history on the heroic narrative of Japan's resistance to Western colonization, is thereby supplemented by a ghostly third party, a nonlinear citation of Japan's own empire in Asia. As an instance of the rhetoric of national imagination, *The Family* traces through the ways in which colonial desires reconfigured the architecture of domestic life—in the fluid spaces of both national territory and family home.

❁

The other commonplace reading of *The Family* is that it narrates the failure of Sankichi's desire to break with the old-fashioned *ie* and to build his own modern *katei*. My goal here again is not simply to reject this reading, but to complicate it: we need to move beyond the binary *ie/katei* opposition if we want to understand the multiple ways in which family and nation were articulated onto one another in early-twentieth-century Japan.

It is, however, easy to see why this binary model has proved so attractive to critics of this novel. In fact, *The Family* clearly does portray Sankichi's desire to escape from the prisonlike atmosphere of the old family, bound by hierarchy and centered on the parent-child relationship, and into a new family bound by affection and centered on the husband-wife relationship (even as that new family typically began in a marriage between strangers, one arranged through negotiations between their respective family heads). The contrast between the novel's opening and closing scenes highlights the conflict between the two models.

In the opening pages, we are given a detailed portrait of the old *ie*, the Hashimoto clan at lunch, with Otane presiding. The key attributes associated with the old *ie* system are present here: the hierarchical ranking that determines spatial placement and temporal order for dining; the presence at the meal of the extended household, including servants, employees, and distant relatives; the lack of separation between public work space and private living space; and the hereditary disease, aberrant sexual desire, and unhygienic conditions (countless flies buzz around the food) that modern critics thought characterized the feudal *ie*. As Jordan Sand notes, rituals of dining became a central issue in the debates over the family in the late-Meiji period, and in the opening scene of *The Family* we get the characteristic model of eating for the old *ie*: each family member eats off his or her own individual tray, arranged in hierarchical order in the space of the dining area.

By contrast, when Sankichi sets up his own *katei* after marrying, one of the first pieces of furniture described is the large table around which the members of his new family will sit as they share their meals (*TZ* 4:65). The final scene of the novel likewise contrasts sharply with the opening: there, we have only the members of the nuclear family present—Sankichi, his wife Oyuki, and their surviving children. They are in the most private of spaces, the bedroom, and husband and wife engage in an intimate conversation not meant to be shared with the sorts of outsiders who were included in the extended family meal depicted at the work's opening.

In that final scene, Sankichi and Oyuki seem to have achieved some sort of understanding, so perhaps Sankichi's desires for a new family based on conjugal affection have not entirely been in vain. But, in fact, the drama of the novel largely comes from the frustrations that seem to derail Sankichi's desire to leave behind the old *ie* and establish his own new *katei*. First, in book 1, comes the dramatic moment when he discovers the letters Oyuki is exchanging with her former fiancé, meaning that the romantic love and understanding between husband and wife that are supposed to ground the new family are missing. Sankichi is thunderstruck. He suggests divorce to Oyuki, since a loveless marriage is by definition unthinkable to him. This is averted and Sankichi and Oyuki remain married, but the trust and love that were to be the foundation for their new family are severely damaged.

On top of this, Sankichi is frustrated by his inability to cut ties with his extended birth family. Book 2 in particular portrays the increasing demands

placed on Sankichi by his extended family, demands that require him to sacrifice the well-being of his own *katei* to support his extended clan through its
various difficulties. In the end, it seems, blood is thicker than water, or at least
thicker than ties based on affection, and Sankichi finds himself unable to
escape the burden of supporting an extended network of brothers and sisters,
nieces and nephews, cousins and in-laws. With the exception of that subdued
glimmer of hope at the very end of the novel, the old family seems to have
sucked all life out of the fledgling new family that attempted to escape from
its orbit.

Hence, the notion that *The Family* narrates Sankichi's failed attempt to
break with the old *ie* and to establish his own new *katei* is not without merit.
But things become more complicated when we look closely at what Sankichi
actually does in the wake of his disillusionment with marriage. In fact, what
Sankichi achieves is a kind of revolution within the family system. He is faced
with an apparent conflict between two subject positions: his role as a sub-
servient younger brother within the extended *ie* and that of a husband, the
single-generation patriarch in a nuclear *katei*. But rather than choose between
those two options, he ends up stumbling into a third option. He becomes
patriarch of an extended family, but not the old Koizumi line. Sankichi
becomes "father" to the whole range of characters present in the novel, from
both the Koizumi and Hashimoto extended families. This requires a toppling
of the old *ie* hierarchies: as youngest sibling, Sankichi usurps the authority of
his elder brothers and assumes a position to which he has no right. He
becomes the spiritual reincarnation of his father. As we will see shortly, this is
foreshadowed in the opening pages, when Otane reminisces that their father
had declared Sankichi his "true son." This status is affirmed at the novel's conclusion when Sankichi not only erects a gravestone for his father, but also is
given his father's stone seals: as the "true son" of the patriarch, Sankichi for all
practical purposes becomes the new patriarch, albeit in a different mode of
patriarchy.[59]

In what sense does Sankichi become a patriarch? Most blatantly, he
becomes the soul source of economic support for the whole network of
dependents that populates the novel. But in other ways, too, he usurps the
authority of the family head. One way to read Sankichi's incestuous advance
on his niece Oshun is as a challenge to the authority of her father, Minoru,
then still the head of the Koizumi *ie*. Just as Sankichi had assumed financial
responsibility for Minoru's family when the latter was jailed, thereby displacing his brother in economic terms, here too he seems to assert privileges over

the bodies of that elder brother's family members (a misdeed that again situates him as the true heir of his father, the ghost whose past sexual indiscretions repeatedly provide a topic of conversation in the novel). When Oshun finally does get married, after Minoru has been shipped off to Manchuria, Sankichi (along with his second eldest brother, Morihiko) stands in for her father in the various negotiations and ceremonies.

Why does Sankichi obtain this position? On this point, the novel is quite unambiguous. Sankichi rises to the position of patriarch not because of his blood ties or birth position, which define the patriarch of the *ie*; nor because of any bond of affection, such as defines the patriarch of the *katei*—in fact, Sankichi often expresses clear loathing toward family members, even as he takes them under his wing. Rather, Sankichi becomes patriarch of this third model of the family because, among all the family members present, he alone is able to negotiate successfully the new market economy that has displaced the families' traditional sources of income—the Koizumis' now-vanished landholdings and the Hashimotos' failing medicine business. Unlike Minoru, the failed businessman, or Shōta, the failed stockbroker, or Tatsuo, the failed banking director, Sankichi achieves a measure of financial success in the new industrial economy of the late-Meiji period. And the source of his ability to negotiate the market is the commodity of literature, a commodity that takes as its raw material the events of family life.[60]

Sankichi's ability to repress his desire, the "mysterious force" that causes him to grab Oshun's hand or to read Oyuki's letters, his ability to repress that desire and to transform both it and his subsequent guilt into literary representation enable his rebirth as capitalist patriarch.

"I saw Uncle's secret! I know exactly what sort of person Uncle Sankichi is!" The bone-gouging glare of his niece's eyes that seemed to speak these words was something Sankichi could not forget. Every time he remembered it, he secretly fell into a cold sweat. He was no longer the sort of person he had been before, who could think about himself without anguish.... The unspeakably deep relations, the odd shadowy relations that bound people together in family life, those relations smothered his breast....   (*TZ* 4:253)

It seems hardly coincidental that the desires that Sankichi needs to overcome are specifically incestuous ones. We see here the rise of what Deleuze and Guattari call Oedipus, under which the family is the delegated agent of psychic repression, or rather the agent delegated to psychic repression; the incestuous drives are the disfigured image of the repressed. The Oedipus complex, the process of oedipalization, is therefore the result of this double operation. *It is in one and the same movement that the repressive social production is replaced by the repressing family, and that the latter offers a displaced image of desiring-production that represents the repressed as incestuous familial drives.*[61]

Oedipus arises in tandem with Oedipal literature, where the "whole of desiring-*production* is crushed, subjected to the requirements of *representation*, and to the dreary games of what is representative and represented in the representation."[62] What emerges will be called "realistic fiction." By the early 1920s, it will be identified in Japan even more specifically as the "I-novel," a genre that grounds itself on a claim to represent truthfully the events of real life—a theater or staging of the family romance, and "not even an avant-garde theater," but rather "the classical theater, the classical order of representation."[63] It is a realism that prides itself on both its economy of expression and its economy of existence: wastefulness is not tolerated, scarcity is its presumption.[64] And it is precisely the truthfulness of the representation, especially when what is represented is scandal, that becomes the chief selling point of the I-novel genre as commodity.[65]

Sankichi's profession as a writer marks him as the true heir to his father, whose calligraphy and writings haunt the family throughout the novel. As Nakayama Hiroaki notes, when literature is discussed within the novel, it is most often discussed in terms of the business end—it is usually referred to as Sankichi's "work" (*shigoto*, but often written with the characters for *jigyō*: "enterprise" or "business").[66] The following passage provides the first discussion in the novel of Sankichi's career as a writer.

"Dear," Otane said, turning to her husband, "Look at that. The way Sankichi's sitting there, it's so much like Father. . . . His hands too— among all the brothers, his look the most like Father's."

"Dad had ugly hands, too, huh?" Sankichi laughed as he examined his hands.

Otane laughed. "According to Father, Sankichi was the only real scholar among us—*he's the one who will carry on my work* [shigoto], *he's my only true son*—he was always saying that."

Sankichi looked at his sister's face. "If Dad in all his fury were alive today and saw what we were doing, I'd really be in for it. I'd get a real whipping."

"Yes, but the work you people do is so convenient, you can take it with you anywhere you go," Otane laughed.

Tatsuo, sitting cross-legged, shifted his knees out of habit. "You young people these days, you write all sorts of things, don't you? Literature— it's interesting, of course, but you can't make a steady living at it."

"I suppose you folks try to make a business out of your hobby [*dōraku shōbai*]," Otane chipped in.   (*TZ* 4:12–13)

Ironically, by the work's conclusion Otane and all the other family members will be almost completely dependent on the income that Sankichi's writing produces.[67]

In his rise, Sankichi has a father figure in addition to his own biological father. Oyuki's father, the Hokkaido capitalist Nakura, is a self-made man whom Sankichi cannot help admiring. Nakura

was the sort of man who in a single generation had established any number of households, who had undertaken great building projects, and the life-force that swelled within his aged body wouldn't let him rest easy. . . . Sankichi, who had lost his father when still a boy, was fascinated and delighted by the visit of this elder. A "father" was something largely unknown to him. . . . This old man left behind him something that San- kichi's siblings lacked. And he made Sankichi realize that there were families and houses built by technicians according to designs completely unlike the model that the deceased Tadahisa [Sankichi's father] had left behind.   (*TZ* 4:85–87)

As a model capitalist, Nakura gives Sankichi a great deal of sage advice, includ- ing warnings against allowing his relatives to become too dependent on him. Nakura does not have much time for books—he vows that "when you sell them, all you get is their value as scrap paper" (*TZ* 4:87). He sees in them only the raw materials of the publishing business, not the raw materials of literary representation. Nakura is not interested in Sankichi's career as a writer. On the other hand, he helps launch Sankichi's career as a publisher: Nakura provides the capital that allows Sankichi to publish his novels.

The politicality of *The Family*, then, lies in part in the way it exposes the I- novel as a commodity and the genre's implication in the rise of print capitalism and industrialization. And yet, there are limits to the novel's radicalism. In it, the feudal patriarchy of the father falls, only to be replaced by the capitalist patriarchy of the brother. The boundaries of the family (both *ie* and *katei*) are deterritorialized, only to be reterritorialized within the new economy, complete with its own form of patriarchy.

Like any commodity, literature requires both raw materials and labor. As the novelist Natsume Sōseki wrote in a letter to Masaoki Shiki in 1890,

> Because prose *is an idea which is expressed by means of words on paper,* I see *idea* as the *Essence* of prose. The way of *arranging the words* is without doubt an *element;* but it is not as important as the *idea,* which is the *essence.* In order to create what in economics is called *wealth,* you need *raw material* and *labor. Labor* does no more than *modify* the *raw material.* If there is no *raw material* to begin with, no matter how skilled the *labor,* there is no use even in beginning; in the same way, if in the first place you don't have an *idea,* the *words' arrangement* is completely useless.[68]

In a bit of narrative sleight-of-hand typical of the I-novel, Tōson allows readers of *The Family* to believe that the ultimate literary commodity that Sankichi produces, that which he labors to manufacture out of the raw materials provided by both the old *ie* system and his failed new *katei,* is this novel, *The Family,* itself.[69] Sankichi acknowledges that he has been accused by a friend of using those around him as guinea pigs in his writings: "in the laboratories at the university, the doctors inject them and use them for all kinds of experiments. He said that my friends were the guinea pigs, and I was the doctor" (*TZ* 4:262).[70] Hence, all the scandals of the family become what MacCannell calls "narrative capital" for the novels that Sankichi produces as author and then markets as publisher in order to accumulate real capital.[71] Unlike friends, family members cannot distance themselves from Sankichi: in fact, they seem to line up to sacrifice themselves to the whims of their new patriarch. Note the conversation Sankichi shares with Shōta when the latter is on his deathbed:

> "Shōta, I wonder if I should try writing about your life—I just feel somehow as if I want to write it down, do you see?"
> "Please do, Uncle, please write it—by all means, please write it—the good and the bad."   (*TZ* 4:407)

Likewise, Oshun promises Sankichi raw materials: "When I turn twenty-five, I'll tell you the things I've been through, Uncle. They write all kinds of things in novels, but when I look back on my life, those things are nothing. The things I've encountered, they go far beyond what you find in novels" (*TZ* 4:227).

As noted above, the original title of book 2 when serialized was *Gisei* (Sacrifices). The various sacrifices that mark this novel are made not only in the name of family or nation, but also in the name of literature, the commodity that finally becomes the sole source of financial support for this newly reassembled extended family that is the novel *The Family*.[72] Sankichi's toppling of the patriarch does not end patriarchy, but rather founds a new patriarchal order, one grounded—at least upon first glance—on the commodity of literature and its ability to represent scandal—hence the novel's celebration since the 1920s and 1930s as one of the landmarks of Japanese realism.

And yet there is another strain in the history of interpretations of this novel, one that calls into question the protocols of realism. This strain argues for the presence of a critical rejection of the notions of representation and realism. This alternative history also places the novel at least implicitly in a more critical relationship to hegemonic forms of Japanese national imagination.

BEYOND REPRESENTATION AND REALISM

Writers in the proletarian literature movement that held sway in Japan from the late 1920s through the early 1930s frequently criticized *The Family* for its supposed lack of politicality. By this, they generally meant that it failed to *represent* realistically the contradictions of class society. Conversely, those who praised the novel did so only to the extent that they thought it represented "historical reality." As is already clear, neither position questions the notion of representation itself. That is to say, even the radical proletarian literature produced by avowed Marxists and anarchists in the 1920s and 1930s failed to achieve a revolution in poetic language. For example, when Nakano Shigeharu, the brilliant poet and theorist of proletarian literature, addressed the troubling question of why the Japanese masses did not respond to the proletarian literature that was written on their behalf, he could only propose as a solution a literature that achieved a better representation of reality. "What the masses want," Nakano declared, is not the I-novel nor any trumped up romance or historical potboiler; "it is the figure of the masses themselves, the life that the masses themselves live."[73] The most superb art is always unadorned and economic in its expression, Nakano continues. "When the object is grasped in its objectivity, then great literature is born. Only then can the thing depicted just as it is lay claim to its own destiny" (Nakano, 154).

In pronouncing the superiority of realism over more experimental forms of writing, the advocates of proletarian literature were following the critique of high modernism that characterized Marxist literary theory during the period, in Japan and elsewhere. Such a stance was understandable for a generation of writers determined to realize radical changes in society: as Hosea Hirata notes, most literary modernism in Japan remained "strictly in the domain of aesthetics," as much as possible "divorced from political implications."[74] Critics in the Japanese proletarian literature movement argued that experimental, modernist writing represented a bourgeois retreat from social reality. Committed to a notion of realism as progressive, they could not countenance the notion that a critique of representation itself might have radical political implications.

It was only in the wake of the proletarian literature movement, with its particular definition of the political—a definition that all too often failed to include any notion of gender politics—that Tōson's The Family became apolitical. Whereas criticism written since the 1930s frequently revolves around this issue, it is entirely absent from reviews written about the novel when it first appeared. Moreover, even as the novel is in some ways complicit with common ideologies of literary representation, we also can find in it the traces of an attempt to trouble those ideologies. This suggests that The Family calls into question certain orthodoxies of capitalist modernity that even explicitly "political" proletarian literature was unable to challenge. In that sense, Tōson can be reimagined as being in tandem with his contemporary, Proust, who—as Deleuze and Guattari argue—"is not wrong in saying that, far from being the author of an 'intimate' work, he goes further than the proponents of a populist or proletarian art who are content to describe the social and the political in 'willfully' expressive works."[75] To understand this, however, we must detour through the narratives of the history of Japanese realism, a history that is bound up with the rise of modern print capitalism.

According to conventional literary histories, Futabatei Shimei's Ukigumo (Drifting clouds, 1887–89) marks the beginning of the genbun itchi movement and modern realism in Japan, a beginning that reached full flower with the naturalism of Tōson and his contemporaries. Tōson may be the "father" of modern Japanese poetry, but in prose fiction, he is conventionally seen as being one of Futabatei's "sons."

The father-son relationship between the two writers extends beyond writing style. Futabatei is also Tōson's father in the sense that, with the rise of the new discourse of literature as a fine art in the 1880s, he was the first modern writer to struggle with the conflict between literary and commercial value, between intrinsic use-value and market-driven exchange value. As Futabatei wrote in 1908, when he decided to live without parental support as a young man, he needed to find a way to get money. The need drove him to produce his first novel, *Ukigumo* (Drifting clouds).

> I had to write a novel to get money, but this went against my artistic ideals. Moreover, at first I was unable to get published under my own name, and it was only by borrowing Tsubouchi's name that I was able to convince the bookstore to publish it. Accordingly, for no other reason then my selfish profit I would be making Tsubouchi commit a dishonest act. I would be using him. Moreover, I would be deceiving my readers. Like selling dog meat under the label of mutton, it was a scheme, or more properly, a swindle.[76]

Despite his moral qualms, though, he went ahead and published the book: "From the standpoint of my ideals, I had become a wicked, unprincipled person—but in the end I took the money." This struggle led Futabatei not only to mislabel his novel with the more marketable name of Tsubouchi Shōyō, but also to rename himself in the form of a curse: "More and more, I thought of myself as a worthless, disgusting person. It was then, at the peak of my torment, that a voice flew out of me: *Kutabatte shimei*—Drop dead! (Futabatei Shimei)."[77] Here, the privilege of bestowing names has been transferred from the biological father to the market. Like Bunzō, the hapless protagonist of *Ukigumo*, Futabatei must become a self-made man, a son who has no patriarch on whom to rely. It is perhaps not surprising that Futabatei would produce out of this crisis a narrative of Bunzō's inability to sustain his romantic ideals of family and marriage against the withering reality of a new economy based on market competition.

Futabatei is also Tōson's father in the sense that he provided Tōson with his own initiation into the modern world of industrialized publishing. In 1927, Tōson would look back on this father figure, recalling that he had no plans to serialize *Haru* (Spring) when he began work on that manuscript, his second full-length novel. Midway through the writing, however, he was visited by an editor for the *Asahi* newspaper, who invited him to serialize the novel in the paper—and who revealed that it was Futabatei (then in the employ of the *Asahi*) who had first suggested this. Tōson notes, "That was how *Haru* came to be serialized in the *Asahi* newspaper. That was my first attempt at writing a newspaper novel." He concludes, "Now, when I think back on the time when I was writing *Haru*," Futabatei is "the first person who comes to mind."[78]

Tōson would not forget the debt. On his 1936–1937 journey to South America, where he would represent Japan at the meeting of the International PEN Club, he made a stopover in Singapore. There, he visited a cemetery containing a memorial to Futabatei Shimei. It was as a foreign correspondent, in the employ of the *Asahi* newspaper, that Futabatei was sent to Russia to cover the aftermath of the Russo-Japanese War. In May 1909, on his way back to Japan, Futabatei fell ill and died at sea—a few months before Tōson began work on *The Family*.[79] In *Junrei* (Pilgrimage, 1937–1940), an account of this voyage, Tōson describes his pilgrimage to the Futabatei memorial, how he and his companions placed flowers at the base of the monument before leaving the graveyard, and how he felt the gaze of this ghostly father.[80]

> The monument to Hasegawa (Futabatei) was erected in the deepest part of the cemetery. The characters carved deep into the surface of the stone were vivid [*azayaka*], fitting for the author of such works as *Ukigumo* [Drifitng clouds] and *Heibon* [Mediocrity, 1907]. They were in the hand of a Doctor So-And-So, an official of the Singapore Japanese Society. It was as if that great skeptic born out of the Meiji period were even now, from the shade of these foreign trees and grass, intently watching the new transformation of Japan.   (*TZ* 14:133)

In South America a few weeks later, Tōson carried out his duties as the official representative of Japanese national literature, delivering lectures on the essence of Japanese culture and on the development of Japanese modern literature. In one talk, he cites Futabatei (along with Yamada Bimyō [1868–1910]) as the force behind the *genbun itchi* movement that launched modern Japanese literature, and notes with pride that the movement's "literary influence now extends even to our neighboring country, China."[81] Tōson here was actively participating in the production of the version of literary history that posited Futabatei as the father of modern realism, implicitly situating himself as heir to this movement.

❁

More recent criticism, however, has called into question the interpretation of *Ukigumo* (Drifting clouds) as a "realistic" novel written in supposedly "transparent" or "representational" language. Karatani Kōjin, for example, argues that *Ukigumo*, especially in its opening chapters, "has nothing 'realistic' about it" and "cannot be considered a *genbun itchi* work."[82] If the work of Futabatei, the "father," deviates from the protocols of transparent linguistic representation, what about the work of the "son," Tōson? In rereading *The Family* today, can we find traces of a nonrepresentational or even antirepresentational literature in it?

In fact, there are two dominant narratives of the history of literary realism in early-twentieth-century Japan: one is a heroic epic, the other a tragedy.[83] In the heroic version, a narrative constructed in part by naturalist writers such as Masamune Hakuchō (1879–1962), Tayama Katai, and Tōson himself, the naturalists are celebrated as marking the successful culmination of the drive to develop a realistic modern novel in Japan, carrying to fruition the project begun by Futabatei a few decades earlier. In the tragic version, associated most closely with the critic Nakamura Mitsuo (1911–88), the realistic novel develops steadily up through Tōson's *The Broken Commandment*, whereupon forward progress suddenly halts, and the supposedly degenerate form of the I-novel takes over. In this version, it is the purported turn away from the social—in I-novels such as Tayama Katai's "Futon" (The quilt) or Tōson's *Haru* (Spring) and *The Family*—that marks the tragic failure of Japanese literature to develop a true modern realist novel.

In either version, critics assign *The Family* a central place in the history of Japanese realism, for better or worse. Yet there is another branch in the history of the work's reception that is worth exploring. As I have noted, when early reviewers discussed the novel, they did not address the issues that would become central to later criticism: the novel's supposed lack of politicality or its status as realism. Instead, they were inclined to view it as a difficult experimental work. In a 1911 essay, the critic Ikuta Chōkō (1882–1936) would contrast Tōson with Katai. Whereas Katai in his fiction is mainly interested in narrative content, especially raw emotions, Ikuta argues, Tōson was more interested in formal experimentation and technique.[84] Other early critics such as Ōnuki Shōsen (1887–1922) and Kimura Sōta (1889–1950) grappled with the odd narrative structure of the novel, with its fracturing of perspective between multiple characters, and came to the conclusion that it harbored tendencies similar to those found in modern art. The landscapes it describes, for example, "are spread out before us like a beautiful impressionist painting."[85] Like an impressionist or cubist painting, the novel seemed to disrupt the transparent subject/object relationship by including multiple perspectives within a single visual field, thereby calling attention to the mechanisms of representation itself. When we pick up this line in the history of the work's reception, then, we can read *The Family* alongside, for example, the novels of Proust. Both are characterized by an "ambiguous—or rather, complex—and deliberately nonorganized position" of narrative focalization, one that presents "the antithesis of realism" and "shakes the whole logic of narrative representation."[86]

As I have hinted throughout this chapter, *The Family* can be read as falling outside the domain of conventional realism in other ways, too. It lacks a clear linear narrative temporality, preferring instead to string together apparently unrelated events within the tedious, reiterative rhythms of everyday family life. I have also suggested that it functions in part as allegory, a reading that troubles the one-to-one relation between represented signified and representing signifier that is supposed to pertain in "realistic" fiction.[87] Moreover, if the novel succeeds in the publishing marketplace by translating the raw material of domestic scandals, via realistic representation, into sellable commodities, it also parodically represents the very process of representation within its pages. If confession sells, one of the things this novel confesses is the fact that confession sells, a kind of "baring the technique" that characterizes modernist fiction.

Tejaswini Niranjana argues that the presumption of transparent representation became one of the epistemological pillars legitimizing Orientalism in its role as the intellectual counterpart of colonial rule.[88] If *The Family* calls into question the protocols of representation even as it represents the hybrid space of the colonies (the verandah, located in neither *uchi* nor *soto*) in national imagination, it seems to reach a contradiction. The novel is complicit with those protocols, and yet it also seeks a way out from them, as it gestures toward a modernist literature capable of critiquing not only representation, but also—at least implicitly—imperialism, not to mention the commodity form that is Oedipal literature. James Fujii has argued that Tōson's *The Broken Commandment* "manages, almost in spite of itself, to bring into question" the naturalized ideologies of state nationalism and the emperor system.[89] Likewise, *The Family*—perhaps inadvertently—seems to call into question the very protocols of representation upon which imperialist Orientalism and print capitalism rely.

The Family, then, contains glimmerings of possibility for a critical modernism that could call into question capitalist deterritorialization, imperial expansion, *and* the ideologies of representation that were fundamental to national imagination. We see in it foreshadowings of a modernism in which, as Seiji Lippit notes, "The bounded private space that had become a hallmark of confessional fiction is exploded, turned inside out, and the representation of enclosed space containing an internalized modernity is fragmented."[90] The failure of the proletarian literature that appeared in the 1920s and 1930s to develop these possibilities may mark the real tragedy of Japanese realism. And even this tragedy is not final. In the late 1930s, as Brett de Bary shows, Haniya Yutaka experimented with a form of Marxist literature that deliberately troubled the notion that language could transparently represent interiority, while Miriam Silverberg has demonstrated the traces of a "modernist Marxism" in the poetry, if not the theoretical essays, of Nakano Shigeharu.[91]

In postwar Japan, too, there appeared heirs to the project Tōson took up in the 1910s. Recent cultural production includes numerous creative works that link a critique of the modern family with attempts to transgress the norms of "realistic" representation. Terayama Shūji's 1974 film, *Den'en ni shisu* (Pastoral hide and seek), for example, presents a fictionalized version of the director's life as a young boy in a rural town during the war, straining to escape the demand that he sacrifice himself for both family and nation—a depiction that repeatedly breaks through its various frames to call attention to the norms of cinematic realism.[92] Likewise, Yu Miri's story "Kazoku shinema" (Family cinema), winner of a 1996 Akutagawa Prize, presents a parodic version of contemporary family life in Japan as staged for a documentary film. Her story implies that even "realistic" documentaries of the family under late capitalism are ideological fictions.

❊

In rereading Tōson's *The Family* as a work with political and modernist dimensions, I hope to have unpacked some of the complexity of the relationship between this novel and the family-oriented rhetoric of national imagination. By supplementing the conflict between the old *ie* and the new *katei* with a third version of the family, one produced through the workings of the capitalist market economy, I have argued that when one rethinks the relations of family and nation in Japan, one cannot stop with an analysis of how the family becomes a metaphor for the national community. And by exploring the hybrid space of the verandah, I have tried to demonstrate that it is likewise not enough to rest easy with a comparison between the Japanese and the Western family, the *uchi* and *soto* that are supposed to distinguish one nation from another. It is necessary to go further and explore how the ideological field of the national family was constituted out of a number of competing visions of the family. The national family cannot be understood without reference to empire and capitalism and the new modes of production and consumption that they installed. Deleuze and Guattari define capitalism as a process of deterritorialization and reterritorialization, whereby capitalist desire erases existing social boundaries, redraws and translates others, and makes up entirely new ones from scratch. Capitalism only respects the boundaries between *uchi* and *soto*, traditional and modern, to the extent that it can translate them and reterritorialize them to its own purposes. As Balibar reminds us, the nation and its structures—including the family—emerge out of a long "pre-history," and yet this pre-history "differs in essential features from the nationalist myth of a linear destiny," and its units "do not even belong by nature to the history of the nation-state, but to other rival forms (for example, the 'imperial' form). It is not a line of necessary evolution but a series of conjunctural relations which has inscribed them after the event into the pre-history of the nation form."[93]

The theme of Tōson's lifework, the replacement of one system of patriarchies by another in modern Japan, reaches beyond the boundaries of one nation. It requires a broader examination of the rise of the modern global systems of capital and empire, connecting the modern Japanese "family state" to the global "family of nations," mapping the links between various patriarchies, capitalisms, and empires. In rereading *The Family*, I have tried here to take a step toward redrawing this map. And in locating in the novel not just the ideologies of representation, but also the beginnings of a critique of representation itself, I have tried to find possibilities for a way out of some of the blind spots that marked Japanese proletarian literature in the 1920s and 1930s, blind spots that (as I explore in chapter 5) enabled Japanese national imagination to co-opt even antinational Marxist thought.

The Family may not qualify as "minor literature" in the sense that Deleuze and Guattari propose. Yet neither does it seem adequate to classify it as "major literature." It produces in its pages both Oedipus and anti-Oedipus, it reterritorializes just as furiously as it deterritorializes. If *The Family* shares one characteristic of minor literatures, "that everything in them is political" so that "the family triangle connects to other triangles—commercial, economic, bureaucratic, juridical—that determine its values,"[94] it also shares a characteristic of major literatures by being in part a literary commodity based on representation. The binary opposition between major and minor finally seems too simple to account for its complexity. The status of *The Family* depends on the way its readers articulate themselves to it, the way they materialize it through their productive acts of reading. As a ghostly third, *The Family* sits uneasily at an unmapped location somewhere between those two poles, minor and major, awaiting the next inevitably partial reading that will try to domesticate its unruly architecture.

Suicide and Childbirth in the I-Novel: "Women's Literature" in Spring and New Life

It is not in giving life but in risking life that man is raised above the animal: that is why superiority has been accorded in humanity not to the sex that brings forth but to that which kills.

Simone de Beauvoir, *The Second Sex*

Shimazaki Tōson's autobiographical novel *The Family* (*Ie*, 1910–1911; trans. 1976) seems deliberately to avoid representing childbirth, as if that were a structural principle for its narrative. Five children are born to the protagonist's family over the course of the novel, and yet not once is the moment—or even the day—of childbirth depicted. Typically, births occur during a period of time that the narrative skips over, so that the children's appearances are described retroactively and even then only in passing. This elision is perhaps most pronounced in the novel's ending—at least for readers familiar with the author's biography. As noted in the previous chapter, Shimazaki Fuyuko died in childbirth in August of 1910, midway through her husband's writing the novel. The second half of the novel, written after her death, reproduces the events in Tōson's life (including his wife's pregnancy) up through July of that year, but the narrative halts abruptly a few weeks short of his wife's death. It is as if childbirth, and in particular death from childbirth, was not proper subject matter for literature, even for naturalist literature with its intense preoccupation with the human body.

This apparent avoidance of death in childbirth should not, however, be confused with a reluctance to depict death in general. Several deathbeds are depicted in dramatic detail in the novel, notably those of the protagonist's daughters and Shōta, the protagonist's nephew. The three young girls die of various illnesses, but the novel suggests that we understand their deaths as "sacrifices" on the altar of literature, the tragic result of their father's choice to subject his family to harsh poverty in order to launch himself as a novelist. In Shōta's death, likewise, the immediate cause of death is tuberculosis, and yet this too seems only a symptom of a deeper cause. Shōta's illness provides another example of romantic tuberculosis: the disease is the result of choices he has made, choices deriving from a certain aesthetic temperament. Shōta's illness marks him as a sort of genius out of step with the modern world of capitalism, and in throwing himself into the dissipated lifestyle of a Kabuto-chō stockbroker, Shōta commits a kind of suicide.[1]

A certain distinction, it seems, is being drawn between kinds of deaths, and genres of mortality take form. Some deaths are literary, others are not. A nonliterary death arises directly out of the body and is associated with maternal reproduction. A literary death, on the other hand, arises out of the soul and is associated with paternal forms of production. A death in childbirth invokes objective necessity, imprisonment in the body, whereas a literary death—in particular a suicide—involves spiritual anguish and subjective choice, a deliberate scorning of the physical body by the disembodied soul. In short, Tōson's fiction establishes an ideological field formed around several sets of opposing pairs: literary versus nonliterary, masculine versus feminine, suicide versus childbirth, production versus reproduction. Within this field, the failure to represent childbirth and death from childbirth becomes an important ideological silence, a constructed and constructing silence—a pregnant silence, one filled with unspeakable significance.

Moreover, in examining the opposition of childbirth and suicide, it must be noted that suicide did not function only as a marker of literary value; it also functioned as a marker of Japaneseness—suicide was supposed to be one of the hallmarks of Japan's national culture, an association that was already in place by the time *Haru* (Spring, 1908) and *Shinsei* (New life, 1918–1919) were published. For example, Iwano Hōmei, a writer associated with the naturalist school, serialized the essay "Jisatsu ron" (On suicide) in the Tokyo *Niroku* newspaper from June 1 to June 5, 1908. In it, he proclaimed "Suicide itself is unfortunate, and yet by necessity a race [*jinshu*] that produces a large number of suicides thereby shows that it is in earnest contact with reality." For Iwano, suicide was a marker of national culture: "suicide should be regarded as one of the adornments of our nation." The tendency for suicide demonstrates the "ardency" (*netsuretsusei*) of the Japanese nation. Iwano goes on to connect this

to literary naturalism: "in our nation, we have a true naturalism that even sur-
passes that of the West."[2] Nitobe Inazō's English-language paean to Japanese
culture, *Bushidō* (1900), would likewise argue that suicide formed an important component of Japanese masculinity. Suicide, then, functioned as a representative metonym for Japanese national culture—a rhetoric of which Tōson
was aware and which he helped disseminate.[3]

As Alan Wolfe has shown, this version of suicide was in many ways a modern construct.[4] Moreover, Kamei Hideo has argued that *Haru* (Spring) marks
a turning point in the representation of suicide in Japanese literature, from the
passionate double-suicides of carnal love gone wrong represented by earlier
writers—such as Higuchi Ichiyō's "Nigorie" (Troubled waters, 1894) or
Hirotsu Ryūrō's "Imado shinjū" (The love suicides at Imado, 1896)—to the
modern alienated suicides, often closely related to a sense of national identity,
that would predominate in twentieth-century literature—in, for example,
Natsume Sōseki's *Kokoro* (1914).[5]

By invoking suicide, a work lays down a powerful claim for entry into the
national canon of pure literature.[6] Moreover, by claiming to represent the act
of suicide, such works efface the traces of the incoherent material body that
haunt the literary text itself: death is transformed from a meaningless silence
into a meaningful one. This is achieved, in part, through the opposition of suicide to childbirth. Pregnancy and death from childbirth are not completely
absent from this field. In fact, to function as a constructing absence, their
absence must be made noticeable: through various strategies, the absence must
be rendered present within the work. In one such strategy, pregnancy obtains
literary representation by being severed from the female body and transformed into a form of male suffering, as for example in Mori Ōgai's "Mai-
hime" (The dancing girl, 1890). To borrow Saitō Minako's formulation, it
seems that only a man's pregnancy has literary value.[7] The following passage
from *Shinsei* (New life) is instructive. The protagonist Kishimoto (whose wife
died in childbirth several years earlier) is in self-exile in Paris, where he has
fled to avoid the scandal of having impregnated his own niece. As we will see
below, the baby is born offstage, the scene of childbirth depicted only indirectly. But oddly enough, across the street from Kishimoto's boardinghouse in
1914 Paris, there is a maternity hospital. What meaning is entrusted to this
building?

[T]he landlady stood by the window in the dining room and pointed
out for Kishimoto the building of the maternity hospital, died a crim-

son-purple color in the twilight air. The landlady's niece, a girl with short red hair who had come from Limoges in the country, also stood with them, looking at the blood-like sunset.

"War may be inevitable now."   (*TZ* 7:175)

Clearly, the crimson maternity hospital begins to summon up the image of bloody childbirth and even perhaps of death in childbirth. But as soon as that possibility is evoked, it is displaced: the blood-red color signifies not death in pregnancy, but rather battlefield death in service of the nation.

Similarly, pure literature, to distinguish itself from the nonliterary, must always raise the specter of the nonliterary—but then deny it.[8] This ideological field of literature is by its very constitution an unstable one: masculine literature, both as gender and genre, could only aim at identity by distinguishing itself from its various others, so that the ground of its own identity lay outside itself. It was doomed to discover continually the traces of its own otherness within itself—its identity consisted of the repeated act of distancing itself from this otherness.[9] Hence, the distinction between suicide and death from childbirth was by necessity continually collapsing and in need of reiterated delineation: small differences repeatedly troubled the binary oppositions that structured the field. To make matters more complicated, the attempt to link the literary with masculinity and paternity was also continually challenged by the appearance of women who insisted on writing, in addition to giving birth to children. The coherence of the field was threatened, that is to say, by the appearance of monstrous, inexplicable combinations of gender and genre, both from "within" and "without." Men with queerly feminine bodies, women who produced queerly masculine texts.

As Judith Butler stresses, "these are spectres produced *by* that symbolic as its threatening outside to safeguard its continuing hegemony."[10] The problem of ideological reproduction becomes the problem of producing and then overcoming these monstrosities— straightening them out to fit the preexisting categories or creating new categories to account for them. To borrow William Haver's language, a "logic of integration" is employed, whereby an otherwise unintelligible text is integrated into the canon, allowed "to achieve its meaning in the communion of human community"—but at a price. "And that price is always death, the death of the particular *in* its particularity. And that death is a *sacrifice*. The community of the totality is achieved in the voluntary sacrifice of individuality. This is the promise, and the price, of every patriotism."[11]

When, for example, women begin to produce texts in the supposedly masculine genre of the novel, the field must create a category to integrate these potentially subversive monstrosities into the field so as not to disrupt the hierarchies it installs. It *must* name them to demonstrate that it *can* name them. Likewise, when traces of a feminine or maternal embodiment are located within the disembodied male writer and his texts, either rituals must be effected to make them go straight or new categories must be invented to name and thereby discipline any leftover remnants. Through the reiterated performance of such acts, masculinity is produced as an identity, albeit one that remains unstable and complex.

In the field I am describing here, the genre of *joryū bungaku* (women's literature) plays an indispensable role. Male Japanese writers, in order to become male Japanese writers, required this genre. As a component of the genre of pure literature—centered, as we shall see, around the masculine I-novel—and as an enunciative position for women writers in social reality, *joryū bungaku* became a category that claimed to account for the otherwise unaccountable. It became a component in the strategy by which male writers both co-opted and distanced themselves from the feminine—and thereby became (imperfectly) male writers. Although the genre of *joryū bungaku* did not emerge as an object of literary criticism until the 1920s and 1930s, here I will be looking at the strategic deployment of something like *joryū bungaku* within several of Tōson's works, in particular *Haru* (Spring) and its sequel, *Shinsei* (New life).[12] I will also explore how, in the late 1930s, one female writer (in fact, Tōson's own niece) mobilized the norms of *joryū bungaku* to establish an enunciative position for herself within social reality—a position she used to mount a critical response to *Shinsei* and its portrayal of the woman writer.

GENDER AND NATIONAL LITERATURE

In the previous chapter, I noted that anyone who reads the classic studies of modern Japanese literary history invariably encounters two standard interpretations of *The Family*. The same is true for *Haru* (Spring), Tōson's second full-length novel: again, there are two standard readings of the work. The first such interpretation argues that *Haru* represents a turn away from socially oriented fiction, such as that of Tōson's first novel, *The Broken Commandment* (*Hakai*, 1906; trans. 1974), and toward the privately oriented, confessional fiction that would subsequently become the I-novel genre. That is, *Haru* is said to mark Tōson's jumping onto the bandwagon of the new tendency that had begun with "Futon" (The quilt), published one year earlier by Tōson's close friend, Tayama

Katai.[13] Miyoshi Yukio argues that this shift can be seen within *Haru* itself: in theme, structure of expression, and narrative perspective, Miyoshi argues, the last thirty chapters of the novel present an "abrupt refraction" away from the earlier chapters, away from Tōson's original intention to write an "objective novel" and toward his new intention to write a confessional "I-novel."[14]

In this interpretation, *Haru* (along with *The Family*) marks the rise to hegemony of the new I-novel genre that would subsequently—for better or worse—claim the position of the representative genre of Japan's modern national literature. The genre could signify the failure of Japanese literature to develop a true modern novel, as the West supposedly did, or it could signify Japanese modern literature's transcending Western realism to find a more highly evolved form. But in either case, it was interpreted as marking that which distinguished Japan's national literature from those of other countries. The I-novel, premised on the ability of the new vernacular literary language, *genbun itchi*, to represent realistically the inner life of the author, was canonized as the genre that most faithfully represented the national culture of Japan.[15] As Tomi Suzuki notes, a tendency to associate the I-novel with "traditional" Japanese literary genres, thereby constructing an image of cultural continuity for the nation, was a common feature of the critical discourse surrounding the I-novel.[16] In 1935, the novelist Kikuchi Kan (1888–1948) would call the genre "typically Japanese" and lament that "it seems almost hopeless for this type of novel to be appreciated by Western readers."[17] The claim that this literature merely represented a preexisting national reality was an ideological fiction, one that ignored the way in which the concept of a national literature in fact was one form of rhetoric that helped bring into existence the very national community it claimed to represent.[18]

The second commonplace one encounters is that *Haru* is an autobiographical work that centers on the close friendship between Shimazaki Tōson and Kitamura Tōkoku, the leader of the group that published *Bungakkai*, the literary organ of the romantic school of the 1890s. The central event in the novel, in this interpretation, is the suicide of Aoki (the character based on Tōkoku), a death that leaves the protagonist Kishimoto (based on Tōson) not only the literary executor of a pile of manuscripts, but also the heir to an almost suicidal despair that he must overcome to launch himself on his career as an author.

This reading tends to underplay the importance within the novel of a second figure who is also the object of a passionate attachment on Kishimoto's part, a character who is also a writer, and whose death likewise leaves Kishimoto with a stack of manuscripts to deal with.[19] This writer is Katsuko, the female student with whom Kishimoto falls in love before she marries another man and eventually dies of complications from her pregnancy. To read *Haru* as centered around the relationship between the two male figures, then, is to engage in a kind of displacing of the voice of a female writer, to relegate her work to the status of a marginal literature within the text. It is to create within the novel itself something like *joryū bungaku* as a peripheral genre, one of importance only to the extent that it contributes to the mainstream genre of "pure literature" and enhances the literary suicide being performed center stage.

As is well known, the journal *Bungakkai* began publication in 1893 as a literary supplement to *Jogaku zasshi*, the preeminent women's magazine of mid-Meiji Japan.[20] Here, it is Adam who borrows Eve's spare rib; the male-dominated literary magazine emerges by splitting away from the women's magazine, as if mainstream literature and women's discourse could not coexist on the same page. When we think, too, that Katai's "Futon" (The quilt), the work that is supposed to have launched the I-novel genre, also narrates the displacing of a young female writer, the snuffing out of her attempt to enter into the realm of *genbun itchi* writing and her return both to her father's house and to the *sōrōbun* letter-writing style that marks her last appearance as a writer within that story, it seems that the muting of Katsuko's voice within the novel *Haru* may not be coincidental, but rather something fundamental to the I-novel, the genre that would soon claim to represent the modern Japanese literary canon. In other words, it seems that the creation of a place for a peripheral *joryū bungaku* was a component part of what would come to be called the I-novel genre.

Hence, as I trace the tense relationships between gender and genre and between birth and death, I will also connect these relationships at least provisionally to the problem of a national literature, of a canon centered (at least until the mid-1970s) on the I-novel. And with *Haru* (Spring), we are dealing with a novel regarding which Donald Keene has declared, "*Spring* has little appeal for Western readers, but Japanese readers, even those who complain about the inadequacy of the setting for the young people in the novel, can still be stirred by the youthful hopes of the Meiji past."[21] We find a similar claim made by Miyoshi Yukio for *Shinsei* (New life):

At a roundtable discussion, I once heard a well-known foreign scholar of Japanese literature dismiss the novel *New Life* with a single word: disgusting [*iyarashii*]. I imagine that many readers have the same impression, but in fact the disgusting nature of *New Life* somehow reverberates in an acute manner with the etiquette, conventions, and physiology that Japanese people carry in their own interiors. Tōson's novels dig to the bottom of his own unique decadence, thereby excavating with precision a more universal aspect. Reactions of both sympathy and repulsion are, in the end, problems of Japanese blood. No other author has unearthed the weighty topics that lurk in the climate and consciousness of Japan to the extent that Tōson did.[22]

These novels are said to be so characteristically Japanese, so representative of modern Japanese culture in all its strengths and weaknesses, that only a Japanese reader can appreciate them.

Works classified as I-novels were almost always written by men, so that the prominence of this genre in the canon produced an inherently male-centered version of Japan's national literature. But this canon would not go uncontested: it existed side-by-side with claims for a "feminine" essence to Japan's national literature, whose great classical masterpiece, *Genji monogatari* (The tale of Genji), after all, was the work of a woman. And yet, as Mizuta Noriko has argued, this claim to an essentially feminine national literature—one that would be made in reference to both male and female writers—is equally implicated in modern patriarchies as the masculinist strand of literature I will be tracing here is.[23] The essential "femininity" (read: "Japaneseness") of writers such as Izumi Kyōka and Kawabata Yasunari is, in many ways, the flip side of the "masculinist" version of national literature, an expansion of genre and gender norms for *joryū bungaku* that were laid out within the I-novel genre itself. This doubly gendered national literature found parallels in other realms of national imagination, too—for example, the images of the Meiji emperor that split his existence between a "traditional," "feminine" image centered on Kyoto and a "modern," "masculine" image centered on Tokyo.[24] For national literature to claim to represent the nation, it had to be able to account for both genders, as well as for crossings between them and for complexity within each. Male literature, centered increasingly on the I-novel and its version of realism, had to acknowledge some form of female literature in order to be national. Yet in order to be male literature, it also had to reject femininity at another level. It required a double economy of assimilation and exclusion, one that situated women as both object and abject.

The question I will ask in rereading *Haru* and *Shinsei*, then, is both "what makes a man?" and also, "what makes a specifically Japanese man?" The answer will involve matching one anachronism (the reading of these works as I-novels, a genre that did not exist when they were first published) with another. That is to say, the answer involves a detour through the genre and gender that is *joryū bungaku*—the peripheral genre that in the 1920s (at the same time that the I-novel itself was emerging as a self-conscious genre) would become a crucial component in the project of identity formation at the privileged core, be it for the male subject, for the author of so-called "pure literature," or for the modern Japanese nation.[25] In this genre, an apparent equivalence performed through the supposedly universal category of *bungaku* (literature) masks the hierarchical relationship implied with the phrase *joryū* (women's), and as a result the category *joryū bungaku* is brought into the national canon but marginalized. It becomes a peripheral source of surplus value that is constantly transferred to the core, where it reinforces the central notion of a Japanese national literature that is implicitly masculine.[26] In short, it becomes a colony of the mainstream canon. To borrow Leigh Gilmour's language, if "women's self-representation describes territory that is largely unmapped, indeed unrecognizable, given traditional maps of genre and periodization," the genre of *joryū bungaku* marks an ideological attempt to integrate that territory into the map of national literature, to provide a "truth-scape" by which such writing can be known as narrating the truth of a patriarchal national literature.[27]

Although he is more famous as one of the founders of the I-novel genre, Tōson was also central to the historical creation of the genre *joryū bungaku* as an enunciative position for women writers. Throughout his life, he was involved in the promotion of women's literature, from his days as an aspiring young writer and translator publishing in *Jogaku zasshi* to his sponsorship of *Shojochi*, a women's magazine he bankrolled in 1922 and 1923.[28] In a 1922 interview, he described his purpose in founding that journal: "I want to open up a small path for those young women who are trying to extend themselves. In Japan today, there are any number of vehicles for men to express their thoughts, but there are none for women."[29] Tōson was also interested in feminism and modern scientific studies of gender and sexology, and he read widely in the writings of such figures as Margaret Sanger, Ellen Key, and Havelock Ellis.[30] Much of Tōson's interest in the works of Henrik Ibsen, too, revolved around the role that Ibsen, a male writer, had played in awakening a feminist consciousness among women. Clearly, Tōson hoped to play a similar role in Japan.

How, then, did Tōson see women's writing? The editor's statement to the first issue of *Shojochi* (not signed by Tōson, but at least surely edited by him) sets forth the journal's position and purpose. It begins:

As you can see, our first issue is largely given over to articles in the form of letters. The letter form is unrestricting [*jiyū*] and convenient, and so we all decided to start out with letters.

We would like to place our underlying tone in this unrestricting form. We do not, however, intend to fill every issue with letters in this way. From our second issue, we plan to run a variety of articles. But for us, grown accustomed to the silence of long centuries, how can we suddenly begin to express ourselves? The faltering in our voices comes from this. We would like to think of this *Shojochi* as a small "House of Life" and plan to bring up that which is born out of our inner selves.[31]

Note the discussion of genres here: the articles in the magazine mainly take the form of letters, a genre chosen for its lack of restrictions. The implication that develops in the second paragraph is that the female writers on the magazine's staff feel uneasy about immediately tackling genres that are more formally demanding—more literary genres. Moreover, the concluding lines establish a linkage between female writing and childbirth: members of the editorial staff vow to "bring up" whatever offspring might be "born out" of them. The connection between women's writings and maternal bodies—the site of a supposedly natural form of reproduction—is set. It is a connection that Tōson would repeatedly draw in his own writings.[32]

In considering this connection, we need to remember that the maternal position to which various ideological and institutional forms assigned women was a historically specific construct. Modern pregnancy had to be constructed before it could become the "natural" destiny for females. In the Meiji and Taishō periods, women were assigned the role of passive facilitators, the proverbial "good wife, wise mother."[33] In particular, a dense and interlocking web of regulations and ideologies transformed the meaning and practice of childbirth, as preexisting norms were replaced by those of modern medicine under the watchful eye of the state, eager to expand the national population. By the 1910s, the traditional sitting-position delivery technique had largely been replaced by the lying-position delivery favored in Western obstetrics, and the locally autonomous midwife was replaced by nurses trained at a rapidly expanding network of state-sponsored schools, nurses who usually worked under the supervision of a male doctor.[34] Previously widespread practices such as abortion came under increasingly drastic penalties: in 1868, one of the new regime's first steps in its creation of a modern nation, even before it promulgated the era-name Meiji, was to issue a prohibition on the distribution of abortifacients.[35] As in other modern cultures, this constructed maternity had a dual nature as an object of both spiritual devotion and fleshly loathing. As Nina Cornyetz argues, "in modern Japan an aspect of the maternal body is repeatedly naturalized as abject, as the other side of the reification of maternity as female vocation."[36]

In sum, the undeniable libratory aspect of Tōson's promotion of female writing was accompanied by an essentializing gesture, one that sought to link female writing to biology and specifically to the maternal body. Ayako Kano has shown how the appearance of female actors on the stage in the late-Meiji period, in such roles as Nora in Ibsen's *A Doll's House*, was justified on the grounds that only a biological woman could perform a female role because there is "some kind of essential femaleness that is naturally expressed by a woman through her body and voice."[37] If suicide was the thematic that guaranteed the literary value of the masculine I-novel, then childbirth underwrote the gendering of *joryū bungaku*. Gender as a trope became a component of genre—in both the I-novel and *joryū bungaku*. Likewise, genre became a component of gender. If, following Judith Butler, we can think of gender as a kind of genre, an assemblage of attributes that form a rhetoric of performance, then writing according to the genre norms for *joryū bungaku* becomes one attribute by which one performs the role of "woman."

Accordingly, the promotion of a literary voice for women was at the same time a disciplining of women into the norms that defined *joryū bungaku*. When female writers emerged, they had to write through and against the enunciative norms that had already been laid out for *joryū bungaku* by the I-novel genre. The soliciting of a distinctly feminine literary voice was also a silencing of more troubling enunciative positions—and the creation of a space on which to displace the incoherent noise arising from the textual bodies of male writers. Yet this disciplining could never achieve seamless perfection: the need for reiteration of norms always creates the possibility for troubling them. Genres, genders, and other forms of identity—including the nation—"are forever haunted by their various definitional others."[38]

OVERCOMING SUICIDE

Haru (Spring) was serialized in the Tokyo newspaper *Asahi* in 1908; it appeared in book form with substantial revisions later that same year.[39] It narrates in fictional form the events in Tōson's life during the 1890s, when he was involved with the group that produced the journal *Bungakkai*. The novel focuses on a half-dozen or so members of the group, detailing both their literary and romantic careers. The protagonist Kishimoto finds himself involved in two particularly intense relationships. One is with Aoki (modeled unmistakably after Kitamura Tōkoku—*Haru* quotes extensively from Tōkoku's published works), the brooding poet and essayist who dominates the group. The other is with Katsuko (modeled after Satō Sukeko, one of Tōson's former pupils), a student with whom Kishimoto has fallen in love, despite her being engaged to another man. The narrative intertwines the fates of Aoki and Katsuko, even though the direct relationship between the two is negligible. By novel's end, both are dead, leaving Kishimoto to forge a new path for himself in the world. Significantly, both leave writings behind them, so that Kishimoto becomes a sort of literary executor (literally in Aoki's case, more figuratively in Katsuko's) for both. The two bodies of writing, however, receive quite different treatments, treatments that relate directly to the gendering of their respective of authors.

The contrasting status of these two sets of writing invokes a theme that dominates much of *Haru*: the relationship between literature and romantic love.[40] The fictionalized *Bungakkai* group is an exclusively male society.[41] The members of the group are keenly interested in literature and women and spend much time discussing both, often in tandem. What emerges from these discussions is a consensus that literature is a masculine pursuit bound up with spiritual love for women, a pursuit that the fleshly presence of women can only contaminate. As Ichikawa, one of the group, declares, all women, even those from the best families, "have something of the character of a prostitute about them" (*TZ* 3:19–20). For pure literature to emerge, sexuality and love must be rigidly distinguished.

This consensus harbors a number of important implications. As a masculine province, literature promises a realm in which the men in the group can transcend their own fleshly bodies—not only in relation to women, but also to each other. In literature, women are transformed into an ideal figure, a fantasy that grounds the homosocial world of the male characters: literature serves as an incorporeal realm that erases the physicality of the passionate male-male relationships that bond the group together.[42] The masculine literary text desires to be all spirit; it claims to have no body. The presence of female bodies can only degrade the spiritual love that literature is supposed to express, just as women's writing, so closely linked to the female body, can only be permitted to exist as a degraded or peripheral form of literature: *joryū bungaku*.

Accordingly, women are best loved from a distance, as an ideal. A physical relationship can only produce the sort of disillusionment that marks Aoki's marriage to Misao, a love match instead of an arranged marriage that has iron-ically robbed him of his belief in love. In a passage quoted in the novel from Aoki/Tōkoku's essay "Ensei shika to josei" (World-weary poets and women, 1892), he bemoans the fate of both himself and his wife: "The pitiful woman who represents to the world-weary poet the graceful and lofty must also at the same time become his interpreter into the ugly and dirty world of the vulgar, so that she becomes the target of his ridicule and his cruelty" (quoted in *TZ* 3:18). Likewise, Kishimoto's yearning for Katsuko shifts to a different register after their first private meeting. Whereas he previously thought of her in a "sis-terly" way, she now looks "maidenly" to him. When their hands accidentally touch, it creates a physical sensation he can't forget.

> From that day on, the pain in his breast grew. He thought it would have been better not to meet with her. When he had left on his journey, infat-uated with her image, he was satisfied just to know that Okami's sister had carried word of his feelings to her. Yet now, having met and spoken with her, he wanted all the more to hear her voice. He could no longer be satisfied with her remembered image alone. To speak frankly, now he wanted the person Katsuko.   (*TZ* 3:41–42)

After a subsequent meeting, Kishimoto will treasure the soiled handkerchief she gives him: the traces of her body that remain in it become the object of his desire. Katsuko's body comes to haunt Kishimoto, a haunting he will have to overcome to become both a man and an author.[43]

As I have already noted, both Aoki and Katsuko entrust written manu-scripts to Kishimoto. The two also grow ill at the same time, and they die almost simultaneously. But the causes of the two deaths are quite different. After Aoki's first suicide attempt, he is hospitalized, and his wife hopes that the doctors will be able to cure him of his illness. "But according to the doc-tor in the hospital, he wasn't ill; when the wound in his throat healed, that would be the end of the treatment; after that there was nothing a doctor could do for him" (*TZ* 3:126–27). What ails Aoki is not his body but his spirit; his death after another suicide attempt brings this to bear. Aoki dies not because of any corporeal failing, but because he chooses to die. His is a romantic suicide, as described by Alan Wolfe: one that demonstrates how in the modern world "artists constitute the new aristocracy by virtue of their capacity to *feel* more intensely. And suicide becomes the litmus test of sensi-tivity." Suicide brings an aura of genius and authenticity to the writer—and to "the literary establishment as a whole," too.[44] This effect was intensified when, in the midst of the serialization of *Haru*, the well-known writer Kawakami Bizan (1869–1908) committed suicide. Contemporary media coverage speculated on the cause of Kawakami's suicide, invoking such notions as the temperamental nature of literary geniuses and the romanticized notion of the struggling artist.[45]

In I-novels, suicide as a marker of national essence was largely a masculine preserve. Women died of a different set of causes. In *Haru*, around the time of Aoki's first suicide attempt, Katsuko's father becomes alarmed at her strange behavior: "Her father suspected that it might be hysteria. He even called in a doctor to examine Katsuko. In the descriptions that the family members gave to the doctor, there were certain conditions that sounded pathological, yet the doctor concluded from his examination that Katsuko was in good health" (*TZ* 3:130). As with Aoki, physiological causes are sought in vain for Katsuko's condition. But hysteria in the late-Meiji period was frequently associated with female reproductive organs: in women, hysteria was less a mental disease than a physical one.[46] And when Katsuko dies, her death is not caused by the sort of mental anguish that leads Aoki to suicide, but rather by bodily failings that arise as complications from her pregnancy: "due to her pregnancy, with severe morning sickness and the like, her body naturally weakened, and a heart condition developed, made all the more difficult by her high-strung nerves" (*TZ* 3:194). As if to maintain a hygienic distance from this pregnancy-related death, to render it present as an absence, this depiction of Katsuko's demise is doubly distanced from the narrator's voice: it occurs in a letter written by Katsuko's sister, which is subsequently published in a school bulletin, where Kishimoto encounters it.

While Aoki's death signifies his escape from his body, Katsuko's death defines her as the captive of her female body. This difference has its counterpart in the different fates met by the two characters' writings. Aoki's essays, poems, and letters (all of which are actual published works by Tōkoku) are quoted at length in the novel: *Haru* itself functions as a sort of Tōkoku anthology. For Aoki, literature exists to express a fierce encounter with the sublime that threatens to overwhelm the self (*TZ* 3:65–67). He attacks contemporary writers involved in the Genroku Revival for their writing carnal literature that lacks a religious or spiritual element (*TZ* 3:21).[47] To Aoki, literature is a form of fierce spiritual warfare, with the author a soldier who fights with writing brush instead of sword (*TZ* 3:117–18). Aoki's literary activities are not a form of giving birth; instead they are a form of creative destruction that clears the way for the creation of something new in the "fatherland" (*sokoku*) (*TZ* 3:87). After Aoki's suicide, Kishimoto takes painstaking care to prepare his manuscripts for posthumous publication: their value as literature is simply assumed. Moreover, Kishimoto sees himself as completing Aoki's unfinished task: "In front of their eyes there lay still unopened territory—vast, vast territory; Aoki had tried to open up one part of it but died leaving his work unfinished. Heartened by this thought, Kishimoto stood where the bones of that sower lie buried and resolved to carry on his work" (*TZ* 3:208).

On the other hand, Katsuko's writings (which are rarely quoted directly but rather tend to be summarized by the narrator) are born out of her with little mental struggle:

> she spread out a sheet of paper to write on. Katsuko felt that Kishimoto still did not understand her feelings. It was not quite a diary, nor was it exactly a letter; she simply wrote things down just as they were, thinking she would give them to him if the opportunity arose. She had already accumulated seven or eight such notebooks. Some days, she had even recorded such things as having washed her hair. This night too she intended to write things down just as they occurred to her. . . .
>
> "Sister, what are you writing?" said her younger sister Toyoko as she entered the room. Toyoko looked at her sister's face as if puzzled, laughed at nothing in particular, and then abruptly left the room again.
>
> Just now Sister came in. She said, "Sister, what are you writing?" Katsuko wrote this down.   (*TZ* 3:131–32)

When Kishimoto reads this "letter in diary style" that is written "in no particular order," it makes an enormous impression on him: "Now, she was teaching him." Her "everyday womanly impressions" teach him "how to stop thinking only of himself and to start thinking about the circumstances of a woman's life" (*TZ* 3:145–46). Clearly, Katsuko is portrayed in a sympathetic light in these passages, and her written texts have a powerful impact on Kishimoto: she achieves a kind of voice here. But her writings never achieve the status of literature. They are never allowed to transcend the woman's body from out of which they flow as a kind of natural excretion.

The treatment Kishimoto gives to another of Katsuko's letter (one that thanks him, among other things, for introducing her to the world of literature) deserves close inspection. In this letter, she proposes a continued platonic relationship: "They say that a pure relationship [*kiyoi majiwari*] is difficult to maintain, but relying on your heart for my strength, I want to walk the womanly path—that is what she wrote" (*TZ* 3:64).Yet for Kishimoto, a purely spiritual relationship (what he enjoys with Aoki) with Katsuko seems impossible. While still infected with the uncontrollable physical passion she has awakened within him, Kishimoto goes out to a restaurant, orders beef and gets drunk: he is brought down to the lowest form of fleshly existence. Or, as Konaka Nobutaka argues, he is rendered into a "wordless" being, one driven on by bodily impulses to which he is unable to give voice.[48] Then,

> When he searched through his pockets, he found Katsuko's letter and photograph. For some reason, Kishimoto ripped them up and threw them away. He was exactly like a thoughtless little girl who grabs the cherished doll that she hugs as she sleeps every night and plucks out its hair, rips up its clothes, breaks off its arms and legs and finally throws it away in the mud. Why had he done such a thing? He himself did not understand it. (*TZ* 3:74)

Katsuko's writings have produced a crisis: she has seized the masculine pen, in the process reducing Kishimoto to "a thoughtless little girl." Kishimoto and the narrator here manage this crisis through a three-step process of what Kristeva calls catharsis: "a purification of body and soul by means of a heterogeneous and complex circuit."[49]

First, Katsuko's letter itself is transformed from a spiritual plea invoking the category of literature into a miniature version of the body—a doll that Kishimoto dismembers. This act, however, reveals a latent femininity in Kishimoto, which he in turn attempts to redress by the action he takes immediately after destroying the letter: Kishimoto visits a prostitute. This visit functions to (re)produce gender boundaries: females are reattached to their bodies, while Kishimoto himself reasserts his masculinity. And yet this masculinity remains attached to its own sexual body, so that the visit to the prostitute must in turn be disavowed. The next day Kishimoto shaves his hair, dons a priest's robes and then later stands at the ocean shore, contemplating suicide.[50] As Kōno Kensuke notes, the encounter with the prostitute itself is never depicted, likely for fear that the description of a sexual encounter would introduce a semiotic excess into the text, an excess beyond the ability of Kishimoto to comprehend or manage: the text would visibly come to have a body. Instead, the text labors to depict the *meaning* of the encounter, which Kishimoto constructs on the following day.[51] This brush with suicide, along with his mimicking a priest, enacts a masculine transcendence of the body, placing Kishimoto squarely in the lineage of Aoki, the disembodied, suicidal writer.

Kishimoto's second brush with suicide in the closing pages of the novel follows a similar pattern. Driven into desperate straits by the bankruptcy of his family and convalescing from an illness, he feels "exactly like a badly wounded soldier collapsed on the grass of a battlefield, and yet still determined to struggle on" (*TZ* 3:232). In desperation, he writes a letter to a woman who he knows harbors passionate feelings for him. He asks her for money, acutely aware that he is trading on his youthful body for cash:

> His hair was still black, his cheeks a healthy red—surely, he thought, that black hair and those red cheeks were worth lending ten yen on. At that moment, he thought of the many weak-willed men who bow down before women, he counted up the young men who tend to amorous old widows, the male concubines who become the playthings of wealthy women, the unchaste pretty boys who would play any form of coquetry for the sake of money, and he thought that in his shameful sentiment he was not at all different from those male prostitutes.   (*TZ* 3:228)

When he finishes writing the letter, "he again felt like a dead man" (*TZ* 3:228). He loses all interest in books and literature, and when the woman's letter refusing his request arrives, he considers suicide, gazing at a dagger. But then he reaches a new resolve in one of the most famous passages from the novel: "One's parents are of course important. And yet it is even more important to discover one's own way. People must discover their own individual ways. If you don't even know why you are alive, how can you possibly act in filial piety?" (*TZ* 3:234). With this epiphany, Kishimoto resolves to set off on another journey—any destination will do. At this juncture, a job offer suddenly arises for a teaching position in Sendai.

Although Kishimoto struggles unsuccessfully to express himself in literary texts, the reader is left to understand that at the novel's end, as he prepares to leave for Sendai, he has achieved the sort of liberation (from both body and familial attachments) necessary to write literature. Readers who connect Kishimoto's career to Tōson's know that it is in Sendai that he will produce his first poetry collection. This prophesied conclusion is in fact subtly built into the mode of narration in the work.[52] The repetition of the ritual of departure and homecoming that structures the novel suggests that this departure too will end in a homecoming, one in which Kishimoto will return home to his identity as author and as Aoki's heir. Through the brush with suicide, Kishimoto is reborn as a self-made man and as an author of pure literature.

𝄞

In *Haru* (Spring), then, it seems that suicide functions as something like a manageable external limit, the sublime rendered into a useful object, one whose representation guaranteed literary value. If in a sense all literary texts are suicidal in that they must rely on the dead letter of language, then the representation of suicide in "realistic" terms attempts to mask this status.[53] This is especially the case in the I-novel genre, where, of course, the portrayal of suicide is a logical contradiction: how could a dead man write his own life's story? And yet, as Wolfe argues, suicide has always lingered around the I-novel as one of its generic attributes: "literary suicide" becomes "the logical culmination of autobiography and autobiographical fiction, especially as developed in the Japanese prototype known as the I-novel."[54] Suicide provides the sense of closure necessary to achieve narrative coherence in confession. In *Haru* and other texts that represent suicide, the radical otherness of death is displaced, integrated into the world of representation.

In contrast, within the I-novel genre a woman's body, especially a woman's body involved in the labor of childbirth, is made to represent the absolute exterior, the abject whose repression is required for the space of literature to emerge: it is represented as the unrepresentable.[55] This is especially so when childbirth coincides with death, where the binary opposition between subject and object, self and other collapses.[56] The maternal corpse in such works is situated as the abject absence that contains any trace of incoherence that might linger in the text. A pregnant silence is built into the text, a silence onto which the deathly incoherence of the literary text itself (and of the masculine body, whose transcendence the literary text was supposed to effect) can be projected. In this way, the I-novel text attempts the ultimately impossible project of accounting for its own real limits—it claims to be able to account for the incoherence that must trouble any representation, whether of individual subjective identity or of the national community. This complex mechanism ultimately functions to mask the absence of homogeneity within the represented identity, the terrifying fact that it is incoherent, riddled with difference, and has no substance. In the I-novel, the maternal corpse is an other that must be rendered absent to cement literary representation and to fix the boundary between representing subject and represented object. Yet this abject and absent other must continually be summoned up as a shadowy presence in order to sustain the value of the represented suicide.

This fluid gender structure is typical of modern national imagination in Japan and elsewhere. Representations of the national community frequently attempt to enforce a distinction that associates masculinity with a disembodied spirituality, in contrast to the supposedly corporeal nature of femininity.[57] Love for the nation, the brotherly affection between equals that binds together the national community, must be rigorously distinguished from sexual love and the hierarchies that were thought inherent in it. Even in avowedly feminist works such as Ellen Key's *Love and Marriage* (1903–1906, translated into Japanese in 1920), where female sexuality was granted public existence, its validity depended on its being disciplined into a spiritual (and eugenic) love—an ultimately asexual love in which one sacrificed one's desires for a greater good. Sexual love had validity only as a means to a higher truth, which was most often found in the nation.[58]

This distinction between patriotism and eros created a highly ambivalent status for women, as we will see in *Shinsei* (New life). In this version of national imagination, women existed as the ideal symbol of the nation, the eternal site of national purity and passive beauty that men were to yearn for and actively defend. Yet in order to define the masculine position as disembodied, the fantasy also had to assign women to a position of physical corporeality. This simultaneous stress on the mythic purity and corporeality of woman (seen in such concepts as maternity and ideal feminine beauty) inevitably brought the female body into the field of view—and with it the undeniable *corporeality* of male heterosexual desire. Woman was simultaneously the disembodied national ideal that masculine spirit desired and the erotic *body* in which that (now undisputedly embodied) spirit became entangled. The ambiguous status of women in the national community meant in turn a problematic, contradictory status for men because, as Eve Sedgwick argues, "*any* erotic involvement with an actual woman threatens to be unmanning."[59]

Accordingly, despite intensive institutional and ideological disciplining, women continued to trouble masculinist fantasies of a fraternal national community. Not only did various women speak out against their ideologically constructed position, but the masculinist fantasies themselves continually generated fears of both the feminization of men and the usurpation of masculine privileges by women. The boundary between genders was always necessarily blurring and in need of repairs: the gender system largely consisted of this reiterated process of shoring up the ever-collapsing boundary.

As I turn now to Tōson's *Shinsei* (New life), we will see again how sexual contact between men and women infects men with (feminine) corporeality, just as it turns women into (masculine) writers. In this novel, too, the literary status assigned to masculine texts is associated with disembodied spirituality, an intellectual paternity that stands in as a figure for Japan's national rise in the modern period. Pregnancy again enters into the field of literary representation only to the degree that it becomes a problem of masculine spiritual suffering because writing here is the fundamental act of the patriarch, the spiritual bond that links together the male community. And yet this status is continuously troubled by the production of texts that are literary but also apparently feminine. Not only do women write, but—as Chida Hiroyuki has demonstrated—even writing by male figures is portrayed through the imagery of pregnancy and childbirth.[60] Once again, we see the trope of *joryū bungaku* mobilized within an I-novel to hold together the ambiguous double discourses of femininity and masculinity. Female texts are described as spontaneous eruptions flowing naturally from the female body, or they are depicted as being mere parroted imitations of male textual production. Either way, they are denied what Foucault calls the "author function."[61] The female writer is assigned to the position of mother, the reproductive body that functions as the object mediating between productive male subjects. Moreover, in *Shinsei*, this gendered hierarchy of texts internal to the nation is also mapped onto the relationship of civilized (masculine) Japan and its (feminine) Asian colonies.

FROM SEXUAL BODY TO ETHNIC BODY

Tōson initially serialized *Shinsei* (New life) in the Tokyo newspaper *Asahi* from 1918–1919 and then revised it before publishing it in book form in 1919. Its publication caused a public uproar because the work was understood to be a confession of Tōson's own sexual relationship with a niece two decades his junior, including her pregnancy, his flight to Europe to avoid scandal, and his resumption of the affair after returning to Japan. Structurally, the novel takes advantage of the presumption of confession that underlay the I-novel genre and the time-lag that newspaper serialization entailed: in *Shinsei*, the serialized publication by the protagonist of a novel detailing his affair with his niece—the reader is to understand that this depicted novel is *Shinsei* itself—forms an incident in the work's latter half. The real-life public furor that arose from the publication of *Shinsei* led Tōson's brother to send his daughter Komako to Taiwan to protect her from scandal. In turn, these real-life events, triggered by the serialization of the early chapters of *Shinsei*, provided the fictional conclusion to the novel's plot—a conclusion Tōson could not possibly have known when he first began writing the novel.[62] *Shinsei* also presents itself as a sequel to *Haru* (Spring).[63] The protagonist retains the name Kishimoto, and he frequently looks back on his involvement with Aoki and Katsuko as well as the other members of the literary circle from the earlier novel. Moreover, some of the characters whom Kishimoto encounters in *Shinsei* seem to have read the earlier novel.

The opening section of *Shinsei* raises the issues of writing, masculinity, and male fears of feminization. A letter that Kishimoto, now in his early forties, receives from an old friend frames the five-chapter preface.[64] The letter sets a tone of decay, declining vitality, and death—all suggesting the "life crisis" that Kishimoto ominously feels approaching. The novel opens:

> Dear Kishimoto: I wanted to write you a part of my recent activities and thoughts. But, to tell the truth, I have nothing to write about. I had best remain silent. The deeper the relation between you and me grows, the more appropriate silence becomes. . . . The reason is that the movement of the instinctual life force in my body has become terribly faint.
>
> (*TZ* 7:4).

Kishimoto, upon reading this, remembers the long letters he and his friends exchanged in their youth; nowadays, the letters they write are short and to the point—sometimes even postcards will do. This leads to a meditation on death: Kishimoto recalls the death of his wife Sonoko,[65] the deaths of his three daughters in the years before that, and Aoki's suicide some seventeen years previously. He remembers a funeral he attended with survivors from his youthful circle (all characters from *Haru*) and their discussion of which among them would be the next to die.

An inability to write, waning bodily vigor, and premonitions of death: these are the crises that Kishimoto faces at the opening of *Shinsei*. And already in the preface, he finds himself thinking, "if I could somehow touch the stimulus of vital, primitive nature, I might be able to save myself" (*TZ* 7:11). The dread he feels is compounded when he takes a walk along the Sumida River and is told that a corpse has just been pulled from the water. He subsequently learns that the body was that of an unmarried pregnant woman who has apparently committed suicide to avoid scandal. The corpse itself has been removed before Kishimoto arrives on the scene; he never sees it. In other words, the corpse of the pregnant woman is introduced into the text only indirectly. It is via the narration of various others (witnesses and subsequent gossip) that the absence is rendered palpable in the novel.

Shortly thereafter, Kishimoto's niece announces to him that she is pregnant. Kishimoto's affair with Setsuko, twenty years his junior, and the resulting pregnancy simultaneously relieve and aggravate his crises of masculinity. Kishimoto initially achieves a kind of rejuvenation through sexual relations with her, but his masculine vitality is restored only by his becoming dangerously dependent on her feminine corporeality—her "vital, primitive nature"—thereby exposing him to the possibility of death, especially a death associated with childbirth. After learning about her pregnancy, he recalls the corpse of the pregnant woman in the river: "He was afraid even to think about that tragedy on the riverbank in connection with Setsuko. A cold, faint shiver flowed secretly across his body" (*TZ* 7:56). The memory of the pregnant corpse will continue to haunt Kishimoto, a sign of his failure to master his body and his relations with Setsuko. He comes to fear the growing fetus inside Setsuko as an insatiable evil force, "a small thing that might even try to live on by stealing away the life of its mother" (*TZ* 7:80). The crisis also results in severe writer's block and a destabilized sense of national identity. Kishimoto considers suicide as a solution (*TZ* 7:61); he even recalls the brush with suicide at the ocean shore depicted in *Haru* (*TZ* 7:65).

But as in *Haru*, Kishimoto can only brush up against suicide here; the protagonist of an I-novel can never really die. Kishimoto finds another way to overcome his crisis: it will be by going into exile in France, presented as a kind of symbolic suicide,[66] that he will rediscover both his father and his national roots. Following this catharsis, he returns to Japan and—after some initial hesitation—overcomes his writer's block to produce a literary text, an I-novel. He is restored to his masculinity, to the fatherland, and to the disembodied status of literary author. The narrative achieves this resolution though a process of shifting the other against which the Japanese male author is defined: in the opening chapters, he is defined primarily through his relations with a woman, but by the close of the novel, his identity is achieved within the boundaries of the all-male society of the patriarchal national community. His sexual body is transformed into an ethnic and racial body. As in *Haru*, this resolution is achieved through a careful managing of the relationship between gender and written texts.

Kishimoto's acknowledged misogyny defines a relationship to women's bodies that his affair with Setsuko will initially trouble, yet ultimately restore—even as Kishimoto will claim to have transcended it. Immediately after learning of Setsuko's pregnancy, Kishimoto recalls the new understanding he had reached with his wife just before her death, following the first twelve turbulent years of their marriage. Kishimoto links this warming in their relationship to the effect her body has on his:

> From around that time, Sonoko no longer feared her husband's study. To stand familiarly in that study, arranged less like the atelier of an artist than the cold, austere laboratory of a scientist, seemed to bring her a dream-like happiness. She was paying back the same familiarity to her husband that he had begun to show to her. It was in this same room now in front of Kishimoto's eyes that she would mount her husband's body across her own back and walk totteringly around in front of the bookcase there. He, who for so long had worried himself in a single-minded attempt to act as a guide to his wife, had at last learned for the first time what pleased Sonoko's heart. He learned that his wife was one of those women who wanted not to be clumsily respected with an excess of politeness, but rather to be roughly embraced in love.
>
> From that time, Kishimoto's body was like one awakened. His hair had awakened. His ears had awakened. His skin had awakened. His eyes had awakened. All of the parts of his body had awakened. He found himself next to his own wife whom he had not known until then. The disconsolate feeling that even weeping against his wife's breast failed to heal, the many overwhelming feelings that at times resembled the passions of playboys and prostitutes: all arose from the sad loneliness he found lying next to his wife, who slept on knowing nothing of it. The venom in Kishimoto's heart in fact originated in that loneliness.
>
> (TZ 7:42)

The irony of Setsuko's pregnancy, he reflects, is that he is by nature not one who is driven by desire for women; rather, he tends to feel cold scorn for them. Hence, his refusal to remarry after Sonoko's death, despite numerous offers: it is his "revenge on the opposite sex" (TZ 7:61).

Kishimoto's affair with his niece reiterates this absence of any desire. Sexual desire arises not from his interior, but instead as an involuntary bodily reaction that a female body draws out from the otherwise disembodied male. When Kishimoto learns that Setsuko is pregnant, he reflects that he "has committed this sin without any intention of committing it" (TZ 7:40). The resumption of their affair after he returns from France originates in a similar involuntary action: "Then the indescribable appearance of his niece attracted Kishimoto with a mysterious force. Almost by impulse, he drew near to Setsuko and without saying anything gave her a little kiss" (*TZ* 7:293).[67]

Like *Haru*, *Shinsei* narrates the resolution of a crisis, a crisis that begins when the boundary between disembodied males and embodied females is destabilized. The different penances paid by Kishimoto and Setsuko for their affair help reestablish this fantasy boundary: Kishimoto undergoes the spiritual, symbolically suicidal journey to France that ends in an imaginary encounter with the disembodied figure of his father, while Setsuko endures corporeal complications—not merely pregnancy, but also surgery following childbirth to correct a swelling in her breasts, as well as a mysterious rash on her hands.[68] Book 1 closes as Kishimoto, having decided to end his exile and return to Japan, hopes for a "rebirth" (*TZ* 7:237). When he does achieve this second birth in book 2, it is through his literary work. That is to say, Kishimoto achieves this renaissance (figured as the assumption of his paternal inheritance) without any maternal body involved—he produces himself as an author.[69]

The division between spiritual masculinity and corporeal femininity comes under particular threat when Setsuko takes pen in hand. She turns out to be a prodigious writer. During Kishimoto's exile, she sends him a constant stream of letters (interrupted only by a period of self-imposed silence).[70] These letters alternately delight and terrify Kishimoto—whatever the reaction, though, they produce a corporeal response on his part: "In this letter from Setsuko were written countless small things that seemed to permeate into Kishimoto's body" (*TZ* 7:99); "Every time he read Setsuko's letters, he felt as if his wound was ripped open and blood was flowing from it" (*TZ* 7:132). During Kishimoto's stay in France, they maintain an odd correspondence. She writes private letters that Kishimoto regularly rips up and burns after reading—the same destructive fate that Katsuko's letter met in *Haru*. He, on the other hand, rarely writes her directly (although she religiously preserves whatever correspondence he does send in her private "treasure box"). Most of the information Setsuko receives about Kishimoto comes from his public newspaper dispatches.

Following Kishimoto's return to Japan at the beginning of book 2, Setsuko carries on with her writing. As Kamei Hideo notes, whereas in book 1 her writings tend to be summarized indirectly, in book 2 they tend to be quoted directly, giving her a stronger sense of presence as an author.[71] Kishimoto continues to have an ambivalent relationship to her writings, expanded now beyond letters to include notebooks, diaries, poems, and other genres. On the one hand, her writings flatter Kishimoto; he is delighted to receive the attentions of a young woman, especially as they are transformed into the language of a more spiritual love. Kishimoto even trains Setsuko in a specific form of writing: as part of his self-appointed project of restoring Setsuko to a healthy existence, he hires her to take dictation. On the other hand, when Setsuko produces texts that clearly do not originate with Kishimoto, it troubles him. This is especially the case when Setsuko declares to him, "I have become a man!" (*TZ* 7:357). That is to say, due to her father's temporary blindness, she takes over her father's pen and writes letters in his name. Even her handwriting becomes masculine (*TZ* 7:366). This is very troubling to Kishimoto. He lectures her frankly, "just as if he were speaking to a man" (*TZ* 7:358). "There isn't any need for you to say rashly that you are a man. Isn't it just as well to be a woman? Think about a heart that has achieved a great enlightenment—if it is possible to purify the soul, then isn't it also possible to purify the flesh?" (*TZ* 7:360)

Later, though, when she begins to write tanka poems, works that she displays only to Kishimoto, he approves because they demonstrate that Setsuko is returning to her proper gender role:

> Kishimoto had never even imagined that her womanly life would open out in this way. He felt wonder at how Setsuko had stirred into movement from her long, long silence—she did not put it this way, but her silence had been like one practiced as a religious vow—and had sent him tanka, which she had hardly ever composed before, in the form of a letter. He read her poems again and imagined the womanly feelings concealed in the shadows of numerous words.   (*TZ* 7:372)

The poetic form Setsuko adopts is the tanka, a classical genre often (though by no means exclusively) associated with female poets. It is distinguished here from the modern literary genres that a male author would adopt—such as the I-novel. It seems to have much the same status as the *kamigata uta* genre of folk songs described early on in *Shinsei*:

> Strangely enough, what gave Kishimoto the heart to live on was when he heard old folk music. One of the women who had come to serve saké in the second floor room, knowing that Kishimoto liked *kamigata uta*, sang in accompaniment to the hushed tone of the ancient, melancholy *samisen*. . . . The lyrics to the ancient song, composed for or by whom no one knew, flowed out past the woman's lips, dulled to the color of a ripe apricot.   (*TZ* 7:50–51)

Tanka and *kamigata uta* seem to share the status of being folk art, not the genres of an individuated, alienated modern author.[72] Kishimoto seems delighted that Setsuko is now conforming to the genre norms for *joryū bungaku*. Other, more masculine forms of writing must be denied to her. Any independent voice from Setsuko would undermine Kishimoto's belief that she has become his own piece of work. When Kishimoto's eldest brother returns from Taiwan and tries to mediate the dispute between Kishimoto and Setsuko's father (eventually, he will take Setsuko back to Taiwan with him), he tells Kishimoto "Well, you can at least restore your reputation by writing some great work." Kishimoto replies, "You speak about a great work, but to bring Setsuko along to this point was for me a considerable work in itself—after all I'm only human and there's a limit to what I can do. Anyhow, please take good care of Setsuko. By hook or by crook, I have managed to carry her along this far" (*TZ* 7:485).

The road that Kishimoto follows to restore his troubled masculinity and uncertain national identity leads, of course, to France. This exile, a symbolic form of suicide from which Kishimoto does not expect to return, begins the process of restoring the boundaries of nation, gender, and authorship that the affair with Setsuko has troubled. Kishimoto's position undergoes a number of interrelated transformations during the sojourn in France. One involves Kishimoto's admiration for the culture of his host country:

> The new language that he had begun to study in order to forget his sadness, too, now started budding. When he now took up the books that had once frustrated his diligent efforts to read them and found himself suddenly able to catch their meaning, he felt the same happiness he had felt long ago in his youth. The world of art of the Latin race [*minzoku*], which he had thought of as something closed off in a great storehouse, now suddenly opened up in front of him. In that, there is the spirit of poetry; in this, there is the spirit of history: he became able to say these things.   (*TZ* 7:204)

Paris represents the height of civilization. The journey to this topos of high culture forms a step in Kishimoto's reinvention of himself as an author of high literature—a process that will reach completion with the writing of the confessional novel described in the closing chapters.

This center of advanced civilization is also the site of a powerful wartime spirit of national unity. Besides being a scandalous confessional novel and a sequel to *Haru*, *Shinsei* is also that rarity of rarities: a Japanese World War I novel, a result of Kishimoto's arriving in France in time for the outbreak of war.[73] Kishimoto finds the subsequent outburst of patriotism so enviable that he considers volunteering for the French army (*TZ* 7:178, 235). Ultimately, though, Kishimoto's discovery of a French ethnicity/race/nationality (all implied by the Japanese term *minzoku*) leads to a discovery of his own Japaneseness. What Kishimoto realizes after three years of attempting to assimilate into French society is the futility of that project:

> A person like him who had come from the farthest corner of the Orient would remain a foreigner, no matter how he tried; in the end, he could not enter into the life of the people of this land. When he first came to France, he had felt that people like him could only rely on art, that only through it could they touch the life of the people of this land. But for a bookworm like him who never approached the women of the land, there was no way to enter into the midst of these unknown people. The most natural way is to enter by way of a woman, a traveler had once told him. But he was too self-critical for that. The wound he had received through the affair with his niece was too deep.   (*TZ* 7:251)

With Kishimoto's rediscovery of his *minzoku*, his sexual body—that unwieldy entity that supposedly irrupted into existence through his relations with Sonoko and Setsuko—is converted into an ethnic body. The awakening of this ethnic body uncannily echoes the awakening of his sexual body just prior to his wife's death, as quoted above:

> Kishimoto was now not only a wanderer [*tabibito*], but also at the same time an alien [*ijin*]. Compared with when he was back in the island nation and had walked through the town of Tokyo carefree and without any self-consciousness, like an ocean fish content simply to swim in salt water, when he had thought "here comes a foreigner!" on those rare occasions when he saw a wanderer from foreign shores with different hair color, now he found his position completely reversed. For better or worse, he could not help being conscious of the difference in his own hair color, his skin color, in the shape of his face, in the color of his eyes. Each person he met eyed him with suspicion. To always be placed in the position of the observed kept him continually on edge whenever he went out.   (*TZ* 7:118)

The racialized nature of this body allows for a crucial inversion: though Kishimoto acknowledges that his awareness of his own ethnic body arose only when he went abroad, the racial definition of the body converts this awakening into a return to origins. The constitutive importance of France in this discovery of a Japanese body is thereby denied, and France merely becomes a site for discovering Japan as it has always been. Exile leads not to a discovery of the foreign (or of a self-as-foreign), but to a positing of the self as self-identical.

Accordingly, in France Kishimoto's love of woman is transformed into love of country. The Japanese national identity he finds in France is clearly gendered; the project of restoring masculine identity shifts from a male-female axis to a male-male, homosocial axis. The "rediscovery" is carried out through the medium of an all-male community of friends, the Japanese artists and academics in residence in Paris. In this community, "the small world made up exclusively of the Japanese gathered there" (*TZ* 7:142), boundaries are clearly defined. The only women allowed to enter into the daily activities of this band of male friends are foreigners, Frenchwomen. Likewise, the only direct reference to homosexuality in the novel situates it as something that French people do (*TZ* 7:195–96).

The homosociality of this national community is further emphasized by Kishimoto's imaginary rediscovery of his own father, which dominates the closing chapters of book 1. Although Kishimoto acknowledges that he hardly knew his father in real life, suddenly, the patriarch becomes a central figure in middle-aged Kishimoto's life.

> He began to long incessantly for the father from whom he had parted in his youth. When, in this inn in a foreign land, his breast filled with worries about the future, he sometimes would throw himself on the bed in the corner of the room and bury his face in the white lace bedspread. Next to the wall on which hung that ancient picture representing the death of Socrates [another suicide, of course], he would bring himself before his father, no longer of this world; he would call out to his father, he even tried praying to his father's soul. (*TZ* 7:210)

Significantly, Kishimoto's father was an activist in the nationalistic Nativism (*kokugaku*) movement of the nineteenth century. His father was as concerned about the welfare of the nation as the patriotic Frenchmen that Kishimoto sees around him; the father's last written words depict him as one who went insane with his worries over the nation (*TZ* 7:218).

The most important discovery Kishimoto makes in this imaginary return is that he himself is his father's heir. Kishimoto's own journey to France—potentially a murder of the father and his anti-Western nationalism—becomes a continuation of his father's struggles for the nation.[74] "Mysteriously," the narrator writes,

> it was at this inn in a foreign land that Kishimoto's heart drew closer than it ever had before to his father. And it was not only that. Coming to a country that worshipped Christianity, the heretical creed his father while alive had regarded with hostility and struggled with all his might to repulse: it had in fact cultivated the eyes with which Kishimoto could now see his father. When he was in his own country, he had if anything regretted that his father and the other followers of the Hirata school [of *kokugaku*]—out of dissatisfaction with the Way followed by their forebears such as [*kokugaku* scholars] Keichū and Mabuchi had carried their investigations into the realm of Shintō. But now, he began to give considerable thought to the participation by his father's circle in the then-current patriotic movements as they placed their trust in the spirit of the ancient classics and attempted to move out of academic learning and into actual practice.   (*TZ* 7:219–20)

The journey to France, Kishimoto decides, is a continuation of his father's lifework. This realization in turn prompts Kishimoto, at the conclusion of book 1, to decide to return to Japan: the exile in France does not need to be permanent, as he had first expected. "Kishimoto came to feel that in the end, it would be difficult to carry out the resolve with which he had left his country: to be buried in [literally, "to become"] the soil of this alien land" (*TZ* 7:222). The exile has accomplished the necessary step of restoring the gender and national boundaries that define Kishimoto's position. It is as a Japanese man that he will return home.[75]

Yet when he actually returns to Japan, Kishimoto initially fails to feel at home. He remains a foreigner, unable to sit or lie down comfortably on *tatami* mats, his body now accustomed to chairs and beds (*TZ* 7:266, 282, 291–292). Moreover, as we have already seen, he still finds himself unable to transcend his body: the "mysterious force" that causes him to kiss Setsuko reveals that he is not yet master of his own conduct. And Setsuko's continued writing, her becoming a man, indicate that the crisis of gender roles is yet to be resolved.

Kishimoto once again flirts with the idea of suicide (*TZ* 7:462). One more step remains before the crisis of gender and national boundaries can be truly resolved: Kishimoto must produce himself as an author, he must convert his brushes with suicide into a literary text. It is the publication of the confessional novel that finally puts everything right again.[76] Only after he has resolved to write the confessional work does his body begin to feel at home again in Japan:

> A new ray of light that he had never known before now shone in Kishimoto's heart; not only that, his body, which since his return had been so quick to tire, now at last seemed to have begun to recover. It had taken him more than a year since returning from the distant foreign land, with its different temperatures, humidity, rainstorms, frost and snow, sunlight, to feel that he had really regained his own body.   (TZ 7:404)

It is not until the day he actually begins writing the novel that Kishimoto finally feels he has returned home (TZ 7:437).

At the conclusion of *Shinsei*, Kishimoto celebrates Setsuko for having relieved him of his hatred of both women and his own flesh, and for achieving a purely spiritual love with him:

> At last, there was no longer any need to torment himself with doubts over whether it was possible to combine learning and the arts with love between man and woman. Setsuko demonstrated such familiarity with him that sometimes, while he was watching, she would pull hairpins out from her *obi*, fix the hair that hung down over her forehead and reshape her hairdo. He could now without hesitation shift his eyes from looking at that deeply lustrous hair back to his book; he was now able to devote himself to his own work with that womanly, lithesome countenance at his side.   (TZ 7:420)

Despite this claim, Kishimoto carries out a plan of actions that he knows he will result in Setsuko's exile to Taiwan; he participates in the plot to make her physically absent. This simultaneously means that she will be silenced, or at the very least, limited to the norms of "womanly" speech genres. In Taiwan, Setsuko will no longer present the possibility of competition for control over the genre of pure literature.[77]

Tellingly, after Setsuko's exile to Taiwan is decided, Kishimoto learns that his incestuous relationship with Setsuko was never, in fact, a turning away from patriarchal authority. When his eldest brother informs him that their father had also committed incest, Kishimoto understands that his own sexual indiscretions mean that he is his father's heir (*TZ* 7:481). His incest was not a form of displaced patricide, but rather a continuation of the father's life. In sleeping with Setsuko, Kishimoto was—he learns—cementing his homosocial bonds with the patriarch.

But the resolution that Kishimoto achieves by taking up the masculine authorial pen is not limited to the realm of gender. It also reestablishes national boundaries. When Kishimoto first returns from Paris, he is at times unsure whether he is in Japan or the colonies:

> he found—as does every traveler who has wandered through the wide world—that the emotions raised by his journey had not faded. When he looked over his own country, those emotions caused him to feel as if he were looking at a foreign country. At times, he felt he was still at sea. He felt as if he had come ashore in some land to sojourn for a few months. His heart went out to Cape Town in South Africa, to Durban, to the towns around Singapore where Malaysians, Indians, and Chinese lived together indiscriminately with Europeans. At times he doubted his own eyes: sometimes, he would look at a woman walking near him and begin to wonder if she was in fact not a Japanese woman, but rather a native woman from the Malay peninsula.   (*TZ* 7:302)

After producing the novel, however, Kishimoto feels securely located within the boundaries of metropolitan Japan. Conversely, Setsuko must go to colonial Taiwan.

With this resolution, everyone seems to end up where they belong. Kishimoto has become a Japanese male author, his father's son. Setsuko leaves for Taiwan. And just as Kishimoto's journey to France restores him to his original identity, so too Setsuko's journey to the colonies is portrayed as a return to origins that are written directly into the flesh of her body:

> At times, Kishimoto would leave his desk to look at Setsuko. The damp towel on her forehead naturally wiped away the white makeup from her forehead. There her inborn dusky complexion showed through. Among her four siblings, her older sister Teruko and her younger brother Ichirō had been born in their rural hometown, while Jirō had been born in this suburb of Tokyo; only she had been born during the time that [Set-

suko's parents] lived in Korea. The natural color of the skin on her fore-
head was a duskiness she had brought from Korea.   (*TZ* 7:317)

Kishimoto and Setsuko both travel to recover origins, but the hierarchical
nature of their respective destinations mirrors the asymmetries of their sexual
and literary relationship. Kishimoto, the male Japanese author, travels back and
forth through the colonies to reach two centers of civilization, France and
Japan—just as he travels through Setsuko on his way to overcoming his crisis
of declining virility. Setsuko, on the other hand, comes from the silence of the
colonies and the darkness of her body, and to them she must return.

The novel's concluding lines present a powerful image of what Kishimoto
assumes is Setsuko's only possible future role in the homosocial national community. With Setsuko en route to Taiwan, Kishimoto receives one last letter
from her, plus a package containing her "treasure box" of his letters. Walking
out into the garden of his new home, he remembers planting four begonia
roots that Setsuko gave him as a keepsake. Kishimoto worries that he may have
planted them incorrectly; the future health of the plants seems somehow intertwined with his future relations with Setsuko. And so he digs them up, "the four
sooty, unseemly begonia roots that looked as if they had sprouted hair," and
reburies them deeper into the dirt. The novel concludes: "Now Setsuko was
not only inside Kishimoto, she was also in the soil of the garden" (*TZ* 7:496).
Setsuko can live as an imaginary ideal for Kishimoto; she can permeate the
national soil (with her abject corporeality buried out of sight). She cannot,
however, remain in Japan as a physical presence, because eroticism has been
transformed into patriotism. Kishimoto must distinguish between the urge he
felt upon returning to Japan to kiss the national soil (*TZ* 7:262, 303) from the
"mysterious force" that led him to kiss Setsuko again: "He thought again of the
time when he reached his homeland after his long journey of wandering. He
remembered how he had felt then: the feeling on board the ship, wanting to
throw himself down onto the ground and kiss the beloved soil. Now such a
time had at last arrived. . . . When he looked back now, the world of love which
Kishimoto had finally reached was far away from the place where he had
begun, far from the suffering over sins committed" (*TZ* 7:437).

And yet, if *joryū bungaku* as a trope internal to the I-novel genre served to
colonize writings by women, as Naoki Sakai points out, such "imperialist
maneuvers" have "never failed to generate more than they were designed to
achieve."[78] The performance of the role of the woman writer, even in its most
limited form—taking dictation, "a form of practice in which the learner

imitates and attempts to reproduce utterances not so much in order to say what she means as to say what she is expected to say *without meaning it*"—nonetheless leads to unintended results. Dictations are "utterances that do not even qualify as speech acts" and yet they "do things: they perform and achieve certain perluctionary effects, so to speak. By saying things in these nonluctionary speech acts, the speaker does something and brings about some transformation in the world."[79] Starting from the enunciative position opened up for her within the text of a male author—having become his "work," as Kishimoto claims—a woman writer can begin the process of rereading and rewriting herself. Even within the closed-circle structure of *Shinsei*, where writing the I-novel is itself supposed to be narrated within the book's pages, a surplus of meaning will always exceed the stratagems set out to guide its interpretation. When the trope of *joryū bungaku* within an I-novel is used as the starting point of enunciation for a woman writer in social reality, the process of ideological reproduction is potentially troubled by the production of an excess. It was precisely such an excess that would return to haunt Tōson in the coming decades.

THE RETURN OF THE REPRESSED

In the 1910s and 1920s, the rise of popular women's magazines in Japan created a new space for literary publication.[80] The relatively high manuscript fees they paid made them popular with male writers like Tōson, and they also paved the way for the rise of a new generation of professional female authors. Writers such as Miyamoto Yuriko, Sata Ineko, Hayashi Fumiko, Hirabayashi Taiko, Nogami Yaeko, and Uno Chiyo now competed with their male counterparts for shares of the rapidly expanding readership that the new mass magazines (along with more literary counterparts, such as *Nyonin geijutsu*) cultivated. Even before this, the notion of *joryū bungaku* existed as a trope immanent to the genre of the I-novel, but with this new development in publishing, the formal emergence of *joryū bungaku* as an actual enunciative position for women writers became possible. In their works, these women writers frequently constructed new literary versions of pregnancy, as if in order to emerge as authors, they needed first of all to work through the form of embodiment that had been written in for them in the I-novel genre. Yosano Akiko in her essay "Ubuya monogatari" (Tale of the birthing room, 1911), for example, expressed rage at her husband for causing her the pain of childbirth.[81] Likewise, the majority of the stories contained in a 1910 special issue of *Chūō kōron* devoted to works of *joryū bungaku* depict pregnancies or child-births.[82] Perhaps the most radical rewriting of childbirth comes in Hirabayashi Taiko's "Seryōshitsu ni te" (In the charity ward, 1927). As Linda Flores has argued, the story's heroine achieves a (limited) measure of self-empowerment not through childbirth, but rather through an act of quasi-infanticide.[83]

The increased prominence of women's magazines and the possibilities they created for publication by female authors also provided the necessary precon-ditions for the eruption of what has come to be called "the second *Shinsei* [New life] incident." In March of 1937, newspapers and magazines exploded into print with shocking news: Hasegawa Komako, Shimazaki Tōson's niece and the model for Setsuko in the infamous novel *Shinsei*, was now destitute and had checked herself into a charity hospital in suburban Tokyo. Komako became a cause célèbre, widely discussed in the press as a pitiful victim of cir-cumstances. The ambivalent reputation Tōson had obtained through the pub-lication of *Shinsei* only worsened with the news of his niece's plight. Even a staid journal like *Chūō Kōron*, which only two years earlier had been the site of Tōson's triumph with the serialization of *Before the Dawn* (trans. 1987), weighed in critically on the debate over the scandal.[84]

The scandal took a new turn in May, when Komako began serializing her "Higeki no jiden" (A tragic autobiography) in the women's magazine, *Fujin Kōron*.[85] Komako's autobiography (as opposed to I-novel) was literally a piece of writing from the asylum.[86] The strategy of silencing Setsuko by shipping her off to the colonies had backfired: the publication of *Shinsei* had trans-formed Komako into a public figure, a status that she now mobilized in order to become a published author.[87]

[*Shinsei*] may be an inspired masterpiece that transforms into art the relations between my uncle and me, almost exactly as they happened. Yet for me, it meant only suffering. For my uncle, this "mistake of a life-time," the cause of the acclaim he received upon publishing one of his most respected works, turned into one of the greatest harvests in his experience of life. For my uncle as a philosopher and as an artist, an indiscretion returned to him in the form of a great harvest. But for me, an ordinary, talentless woman, dragged out in front of the public in the form of a shameful photograph, didn't it mean the end of my ability to live the life of an ordinary woman? What the novel records is almost entirely true. Yet whatever was inconvenient to my uncle was expunged. It is not truthful in the way that Rousseau's autobiography is. From my

standpoint, all I see in it is a work of self-justification as a man, as a man
who pursues philosophy.   (1:285)

Komako portrays herself as a New Woman, taking on activities that had been
barred to earlier generations of Japanese women. She discusses her careers, for
example, in the predominately masculine realms of radical politics and business. Additionally, even as she criticizes Tōson for the impact *Shinsei* had on
her life, she refuses to renounce the sexual desire she felt for him. In fact, she
decries her life after the novel's publication because it required her to repress
her sexual desires. A woman's sexuality, Komako implies, is not wholly passive.
The disembodied spiritual love that Tōson had labored to produce in his novel
is here returned to the realm of eros.

Komako's autobiography is also striking in the way it seeks empowerment
through the very ideologies that assign women to an inferior, passive social
role. Autobiography, like the I-novel, is a genre fraught with a gendered relation to truth. Leigh Gilmour has argued that when women participate in this
male-centered genre as writing subjects, they must produce themselves as
objects whose legibility depends on generic norms for what constitutes truth.

> Thus the ways in which an autobiographer variously acknowledges,
> resists, embraces, rejects objectification, the way s/he learns, that is, to
> interpret objectification as something less than simply subjectivity itself
> marks a place of agency. It is in this act of interpretation, of conscious-
> ness, that we can say a woman may exceed representation within dom-
> inant ideology. She exceeds it not because she possesses some privileged
> relation to nature or the supernatural. Rather, the discourses and prac-
> tices that construct subjectivity through hierarchy must always be
> defended, their boundaries guarded, their rights maintained. Within
> these discourses exist unruly subjects who are unevenly objectified and
> who represent identity in relation to other values and subjectivities.[88]

Komako takes up the status she has inadvertently acquired as an objectified
writing subject within the pages of *Shinsei*, and she transforms it into a means
for producing an enunciative position for herself in reality. Even as her autobiography in many ways adheres to the generic norms of *joryū bungaku*, it
avoids simply reproducing the image of herself created in her uncle's I-novel.
The work unleashes what Iwami Teruyo calls a "shriek," a noise that exceeds
genre norms.[89] Yet to produce that effect, her narrative must rely on precisely

the ideologies of self-representation that underwrote the I-novel and its marginalization of writing by women.

The autobiography opens, not surprisingly, with a scene of letter writing. Komako describes a letter she is writing to her four-year-old daughter. This invocation of motherhood and the properly feminine genre of letter-writing provides the first step in the process by which Komako turns the tables on her uncle: by invoking the "figure of mothering," she is able "to present herself as a legitimate author," a tactic frequently employed by women writers.[90] Komako relies on prevalent norms of gender to formulate a critique of men precisely for failing to live up to those norms. Her business career, for example, is described mainly as the activity of a devoted wife who selflessly supports her husband, imprisoned for his radical political activities. And even as she affirms her own sexual desire, Komako proclaims her own sexual faithfulness, first to Tōson and then to her husband, the political activist Hasegawa Hiroshi. It seems she can only legitimate her sexuality in the context of monogamous romantic love. In both cases, it is the men who fail to remain loyal, and Komako attacks them for it.

Komako avoids any claim to be writing a piece of universal pure literature. Instead, she declares, she is writing specifically for a female audience, for her "sisters" (1:286) who have shown sympathy for her plight. *Joryū* takes precedence over *bungaku* here. "In my heart, then and now, I have never believed that I should be ashamed of what I did," she writes. "I want to open my true heart to those people of my sex in this society who seek a genuine love. If that is not a woman's protest, then what is?" (1:290). Tactically bowing to the norms of *joryū bungaku* enables her to take up the position of narrating subject, whereupon she can transform Tōson into the object of her gaze. From that position, she is able to narrate how a drunken Tōson made his first sexual advances and the terror she felt at the time.

It seems that as a woman writer, Komako's enunciative position is based on her claim to represent a woman's experience, an experience that is grounded ultimately in the female body. Rather than overtly challenge the notion of self-representation in language, she insists that hers is a more truthful self-representation than that presented by her uncle. Her reproduction of conventional gender and genre norms in some ways suggests the vision of an ideal national community in which women and men coexist in harmony. We can accordingly situate Komako in relation to the widespread collapse of Japanese feminism into cooperation with state-sponsored nationalism and imperialism in the 1930s and 1940s.[91]

Yet to transcend the image of herself presented in her uncle's novel, Komako must also demonstrate—perform—her ability to become a literary narrator herself. To borrow Mary Elene Wood's words, Komako must somehow become "the author of her own actions" so that her life "will be read in a particular way by those around her."[92] The most fascinating passage in the autobiography describes in detail a scene barely sketched in *Shinsei*: Komako's giving birth to her and Tōson's son (2:203–5). As we have seen, Tōson's novels are characterized by an apparent inability to portray scenes of childbirth. But in Komako's version, we get neither an abject absence nor the "perverse maternities" that Nina Cornyetz has described so powerfully in the writings of Izumi Kyōka and others, the grotesque maternal bodies whose breasts leak not milk but blood.[93] Nor do we get the highly aestheticized version of childbirth as a kind of natural (and hence, neither cultural nor intellectual) beauty that appears in Shiga Naoya's *Wakai* (Reconciliation).[94] In Komako's writing, we get not a man's pregnancy, but a woman's.

Komako describes her experiences in painful detail. Moreover, she takes care to demonstrate that childbirth is not experienced in the same way by all women; individual circumstances shape each pregnancy differently. Pregnancy and childbirth are not natural or biological, but rather events overdetermined by their social and cultural positioning:

> It was June, 1914. At that time, my mother too was seven months pregnant with my youngest brother. My sister too was six months pregnant, as was I. These three women with swollen bellies gathered in one house. My mother gave birth on August 26, my sister on September 14, and I on September 3. But while my sister, born of the same mother as I, proudly envisioned a "delivery day filled with joy," I—as a result of my eugenic concerns for the forthcoming child and of my life of an inhuman lust denied by the oppressive atmosphere around me—was dominated by different emotions, even as I faced the same pregnancy and delivery as my mother and sister. How jealous I was of the young married couple who awaited their happy, beloved child, a crystallization of their love.   (2:203–4)

Writing about pregnancy formed one of the norms of *joryū bungaku*. Yet the attention Komako pays to the difference between pregnancies has the effect of individualizing that form of production, of troubling the distinction between mother and author, between maternal reproduction and literary production. The physical pain of pregnancy and childbirth was trying, Komako declares, but her spiritual anguish was the worst part of the ordeal. And the very writing of this scene challenges the boundary, characteristic of the genre norms for pure literature, between masculine literary production and feminine maternity: here, childbirth itself is explicitly narrated into a literary text. Moreover, her adoption of the genre "autobiography" and its truth claims allows her to publicly challenge the preexisting master narrative that had attempted to objectify her within an "I-novel."

In many ways, Komako's "tragedy" has a happy ending. Her son with Tōson ends up belying her "eugenic" fears: he is a healthy boy who is adopted by prosperous, loving parents. Moreover Komako herself believes that at the moment of her writing, she has turned the corner in her life and that her future is bright.[95] And yet another tragedy seems concealed here. "Part 2" of Komako's text ends quite abruptly. Surely I am not the only reader who turned the page, expecting more, upon reaching its conclusion. But a search through the remaining pages of that issue of *Fujin kōron*, as well as of subsequent issues of the journal, reveal that, for whatever reason, the autobiography was suspended at that point. This is particularly distressing because in the closing pages of part 2, Komako is trying to incite the reader's interest in a new narrative, one that will apparently revolve around her betrayal at the hands of her husband and a young female comrade in the proletarian movement. It seems that Komako here is trying to demonstrate that her life exceeds that of Setsuko from *Shinsei*; she is trying to establish herself as a narrator of events that have no direct connection to the earlier novel. But the editors of the journal apparently disagreed, for the serialization is not continued (nor is any definite statement of its conclusion appended). Perhaps herein lies the true tragedy of Komako: her inability to narrate beyond the confines of her inadvertent representation as Setsuko. To borrow Mizuta Noriko's language, when Komako was confronted with Tōson's "twice-told tale," she could produce only a "thrice-told tale."[96]

There is clearer evidence of the impact that Komako's intervention had on *Shinsei* itself. When Tōson reissued *Shinsei* in 1938, one year after Komako's autobiography appeared, he deleted all of book 2 and retitled the work *Nezame* (Awakening). Though Tōson did not explicitly acknowledge Komako's work, its impact is felt throughout the new "Afterword" he wrote for the truncated edition.[97] Tōson admits that he is somewhat reluctant to republish this "text of pathos and suffering" and details what he sees as its many failings. The title change is due to Tōson's realization that a "new life" is not so easily won, as the novel in its original form seemed to suggest: "A new life is a new life only when it has yet to be attained. Something that can be easily attained is not a new life" (*TZ* 7:500).

Among other things, the deletion of book 2 meant that the text no longer contained the story of Setsuko's exile to Taiwan. This of course alters the image of national community that the work provides. But as if some circuit of Asian travel were necessary to the work, Tōson spends a part of the 1938 "Afterword" discussing the 1927 publication of *Shinsei* in a Chinese translation. Now it is not Setsuko but the novel's text itself that journeys to the Asian mainland. If the publication of *Shinsei* in 1919 and its invocation of *joryū bungaku* had helped reproduce the imaginary framework for Japanese colonialism, by 1927 the novel itself had expanded onto the continent as a representative work of Japan's national literature.

❁

What, finally, did Komako achieve with her autobiography? A measure of self-representation and agency, to be sure, and probably also a degree of financial independence. Her work, like that of many other modern female writers in Japan, as Sharalyn Orbaugh has argued, "makes visible the ways in which the body has been used in the production and maintenance of economies of power, even while its role in such production has been simultaneously denied or erased."[98] Komako's self-representation, however, was grounded in the very ideologies of representation that underwrote the master narrative from which she sought to escape. In a sense, her fate resembles that of another women writer from the period, Miyamoto Yuriko, whose massive autobiographical novel *Nobuko* (1924–1926) ultimately failed to connect its challenge to gender norms with historical reality because, according to Mizuta, it remained entirely within the ideology of self-representation. Unable (as later women writers would be) to summon up nonrealistic genres that made no claim to represent reality (such as the premodern *monogatari*), it could not relativize the truth claims of the I-novel; it could only reproduce them.[99]

And yet, while Komako could not immediately bring into view the limits of representation, her intervention did expose some of the contradictions and incoherencies that riddled the gendered field of national literature, a field that by the late 1930s was increasingly centered on the I-novel genre, including works such as *Haru* (Spring) and *Shinsei* (New life). Those canonical works, through an unstable economy that opposed suicide to childbirth, paternal production to maternal reproduction, and pure literature to women's literature, sought to realize the always receding fantasy of a Japanese male author. In contrast, Komako, by producing alternative versions of herself as narrated object and narrating subject through the genre of autobiography, forced the field of literature to make room for her alongside the image of Setsuko. In this dense network of intertexts played out on a field of overlapping national, gender, and literary identities, I think that finally Komako's text should be considered not only a form of writing from the asylum, but also a form of colonial mimicry, both an acceptance and a parodic subversion of the literary and gender norms that constitute the genre of *joryū bungaku*. In shifting the genre from the divine comedy of Tōson's *Shinsei* to her own "Higeki no jiden" (Tragic autobiography), in shifting the object of literary representation from the achievement of rebirth through a brush with suicide to the achievement of rebirth through the experience of motherhood, Komako skillfully invokes the instabilities that haunt the endless, and perhaps suicidal, project of becoming a Japanese man.

CHAPTER FIVE

The Times and Spaces of Nations: The Multiple Chronotopes of Before the Dawn

"Time doesn't pass on, we pass on," are the words of a Russian writer. One time, I asked my family who was the oldest member of our household. When the maid said it was me, I pointed to the old clock hanging on the wall and said, that clock is the eldest—in human years it is already sixty or seventy. Look at the wrinkles on its face, I laughed. The old clock brings to mind the words of that Russian writer. After all, it isn't clocks that move; we are the ones who move.

Shimazaki Tōson ("Toki" [Time], 1913)

The January 1930 issue of the journal *Chūō kōron* featured two articles that are of interest to us here. The first was the fourth installment of Tōson's new novel, *Before the Dawn* (*Yoake mae*; trans. 1987).[1] Tōson had begun serialization the previous year and would continue to produce chapters at the rate of one every three months until the final installment appeared in 1935. *Before the Dawn* provided a sweeping portrait of Japan during the middle of the 1800s, portraying the events of the Meiji Restoration from the perspective of the rural village Magome. As we saw in chapter 1, the epic was immediately proclaimed a modern masterpiece, and the bottom-up version of history it proposed continues to have a palpable impact on Japanese national imagination to the present day.

The second article of interest was by Hayashi Fumio, "Koyomi no bunka shikan" (A cultural history of the calendar).[2] Hayashi traces the development of calendars in Europe from antiquity through the Enlightenment, as lunar-based calendars gave way to increasingly reliable solar calendars. He also discusses variant calendars produced by revolutionaries in France and Russia. Finally, Hayashi discusses the history of calendars in China and Japan, concluding his article with a discussion of the controversies surrounding the 1872 promulgation of the Gregorian calendar as Japan's standard by the new Meiji government—an event that would figure prominently in a later chapter of *Before the Dawn.*

While Hayashi's article is premised on the existence of a variety of calendars in different times and places, it is hardly written from a position of cultural relativism. He acknowledges the existence of only one form of time (that marked by the movement of certain astronomical bodies) as being valid in all places at all times. Moreover, his history traces a linear development of increasingly accurate scientific methods for measuring that time, as well as the progressive spread of those methods across the face of the earth. That is to say, Hayashi maps the discovery of the cycles of solar time onto the linear temporality of a world-historical narrative of enlightenment. For Hayashi, the invention of the calendar is the "first step from natural man toward cultural man."[3] He quotes approvingly from Fukuzawa Yukichi's 1872 essay "Kaireki ben" (On calendar reform) to the effect that only backward, ignorant people would resist the Meiji calendar reform: it is a "test for distinguishing between the learned men and the fools in Japan."[4]

Nationwide coordination of time for railroad and telegraph services was effected in 1888 in Japan, continuing the process of temporal "Civilization and Enlightenment" that had begun with the calendar reform. Yet despite Fukuzawa's claims, this period also saw many learned people in Japan and elsewhere who were critical of the notion of a universally valid "clock time." Even before Einstein's theory of relativity, European intellectuals such as Henri Bergson had begun to question the homogeneous, atomistic, and mechanistic notions of time that underlay much positivist and empiricist thought.[5] As Stephen Kern notes, the increasing standardization of public time, a result partly of the increased prevalence of clocks and watches as well as other forms of technology (railroads, telephones, cinema) and social organization (factory labor, standardized public education, the military) that required widespread synchronization, produced a reaction in the form of "an affirmation of a plurality of times" and "an affirmation of the reality of private time."[6]

Some challenges to the notion of a universally valid form of temporality focused not so much on time as on space. Many non-Western intellectuals came to reject the strategies of Enlightenment proposed by the likes of Fukuzawa, realizing that Western narratives of universal progress concealed an unbridgeable spatial gap, what Partha Chatterjee calls the "colonial difference," that guaranteed eternal Western superiority over the non-West.[7] The

West, as figured by these narratives, was progressive, historical, modern. The
East was stagnant, "natural" and without history; it might advance some by
imitating the West but could never quite catch up. As Stefan Tanaka argues,
when modern Japanese intellectuals confronted this version of history, they
were forced into "an awareness that such territorial categories, especially those
defined by Europe, are not neutral or objective," a realization that prompted
them to create their own versions of the time and space of world history.[8]
These intellectuals insisted on the spatial specificity of various forms of temporality, thereby challenging the validity of Western temporal concepts for
measuring time and narrating history in non-Western spaces.

Okakura Tenshin (1862–1913), for example, argued that Japan's unique and
unbroken imperial line guaranteed its national and racial continuity into the
present. This not only made it the sole legitimate heir to Asian civilization, it
also permitted Japan to absorb Western technologies without losing its self-
identity—without being absorbed into the time and space of Western historical narratives.[9] Likewise, the aesthetic theoretician Kuki Shūzō in "Tōyōteki
jikan" (Oriental time, 1936) argued that the Orient was marked by a cyclical
temporality distinct from the linear time of the West—and within which
Japan represented the "active" principle in contrast to the "passive" principle
found on the Asian mainland.[10] Perhaps the most influential such attempt was
found in the work of Watsuji Tetsurō, especially his *Climate and Culture* (*Fūdo*,
1935), to which I will return below.[11]

Novelists in early-twentieth-century Japan, like their counterparts around
the world, liked to bend time, sometimes even to fracture it. James Fujii has
shown how Natsume Sōseki, in *Wagahai wa neko de aru* (I am a cat, 1905–1906),
constructed a unique "chronotope" that "expunges time as an active force,"
cutting all links with the past in order to create a narrative determined mainly
by space, especially the "ahistorical and anonymous 'space'" of modern urban
life.[12] One of Sōseki's disciples, Akutagawa Ryūnosuke (1892–1927) carried
out similar experiments in a brilliant series of short stories set in Japan's past,
stories that questioned the nature of the relationship between past and present, most famously in "Yabu no naka" (In a grove, 1922). As Seiji Lippit has
argued, Akutagawa's writings fractured the narrative and historical structures
that legitimated hegemonic notions of modernity.[13] Literary works that
explored the ramifications of Einstein's theory of relativity in time and space
began to appear during the 1920s, including Yokomitsu Riichi's *Shanhai*
(Shanghai, 1928–1931) and "Jikan" (Time, 1931), and Miyazawa Kenji's "Ginga
tetsudō no yoru (Night of the Milky Way railroad, 1927?).[14]

Like so many of his contemporaries, Tōson was keenly aware of the problems of time and returned to them in his writings again and again.[15] By the time he set to work on *Before the Dawn*, he had spent decades thinking and writing about the problems of plural temporalities and the impacts of the past and future on the present moment. Tōson's prior novels all dealt with questions of temporality. *The Broken Commandment* in particular is structured around a perceived conflict between the encroachment of a standardizing nationwide clock time and the faltering resistance offered by local, traditional cyclical time.[16] In his essays and children's stories, too, Tōson frequently explored questions of temporality.[17] And the acclaimed short story "Arashi" (The storm, 1926) is an extended meditation on the relationship between clocks, biological time, and family history, all set against the backdrop of an attempt by the narrator to reestablish ties to a lost past.[18]

In this chapter, I explore *Before the Dawn* in relation to these controversies over the nature of time, particularly as they intersect with the problem of national imagination. I will discuss a variety of what Bakhtin calls chronotopes that are employed in it in order to construct (or trouble) images of the national community.[19] Each chronotope posits a different sort of subject position, for both the nation and individual members of the national community. This epic work narrates a decisive period of national history as experienced across vast segments of national space, spaces that are moreover portrayed as undergoing a radical transformation with the rise of new transportation and communication technologies. The novel explores the possibility of transcending modernity through the restoration of antimodern, specifically national forms of time and space. In doing so, it intersects with the discourse on *tenkō*, or "political conversion," in which, as I discussed in chapter 1, leftists and liberals in 1930s' Japan, often under intense state pressure, publicly renounced their political beliefs. I examine why *tenkōsha* (people who had committed *tenkō*) found the novel so attractive, particularly as they sought to integrate themselves into the national community. I will also examine alternative readings of the novel, readings that enable a more critical stance toward the chronotopes of national imagination.

THE TIMES AND SPACES OF NATIONS

The debates over the nature of time discussed above—the relationships of "clock time" to other forms of time; the spatial plurality of times; the nature of the link between past, present, and future—were intimately connected with national imagination. Time presents a fundamental problem for any notion of a stable subject, individual or communal. Time is both the grounding and the disruption of any subject's existence, since it is the medium that both links the distinct moments of subjective experience into unity and holds those moments apart. How can any subject be certain that its present existence is identical to its past or future existences?

Accordingly, any attempt to imagine the nation as a coherent subject of history must somehow neutralize the corrosive effects of time. A number of strategies can be employed. One can construct an ahistorical subject, one that coexists with nature and is conceived of in spatial rather than temporal terms. One can construct narratives that map discontinuous points of time onto linear continuity, thereby forming a single national history. One can invent rituals and traditions (or reconceptualize the habitual practices of everyday life into an unchanging ritual) so as to posit the nation as existing in a temporality of cyclical repetition, where nothing ever really changes. One can conceive of the nation as a living spirit, a desire that ceaselessly moves toward the future, capable of absorbing any novelty into itself without losing its own self-generated identity.

Each of these versions of time configures the image of the national community differently. That is to say, a temporal framework does not function as a neutral medium for the nation as a unified subject, but rather is productive of it. Here we can see one reason why nation-states attempting to generate nationalist energies (such as Meiji Japan) frequently install a new calendar. This gesture should not be understood so much as an attempt to harness a preexisting national subject but as a technology for hailing, for calling into being, a certain type of national subject.

Benedict Anderson argues that the rise of modern nationalism was accompanied by the emergence of a new concept of time. According to Anderson, the temporality of prenational existence was a heterogeneous, "filled" time. Premodern, prenational temporality "had no conception of history as an endless chain of cause and effect or of radical separations between past and present."[20] Relying on Walter Benjamin's "Theses on the Philosophy of History," Anderson describes this time as "a simultaneity of past and future in an instantaneous present" (B. Anderson, 30).

This temporality is heterogeneous in at least two senses. First, it is not standardized across space. Different regions, towns, even families exist within different times. Secondly, it is heterogeneous because not all units of time are seen as being of similar quality or importance. Some moments are seen, for example, as particularly lucky or unlucky. Furthermore, this prenational time is "filled" because it makes no rigid distinction between the past, present, and future. Omens of the past and future are seen as "filling in" the present moment. Simultaneity in this temporal framework occurs on the temporal axis: the past, present, and future are all seen as existing simultaneously within a single moment of time.

According to Anderson, with the emergence of the modern nation, this premodern time gives way to a new temporality,

> an idea of 'homogeneous, empty time,' in which simultaneity is, as it were, transverse, cross-time, marked not by prefiguring and fulfilment, but by temporal coincidence, and measured by clock and calendar. . . .
> The idea of a sociological organism moving calendrically through homogeneous, empty time is a precise analogue of the idea of the nation, which also is conceived as a solid community moving steadily down (or up) history. (B. Anderson, 30–31)

Again, homogeneity here exists in at least two senses. First, the new time is spatially homogeneous; simultaneity now occurs along the spatial axis, and every inch of the national soil shares a single calendar and clock. Secondly, this new national time is homogeneous because its units are seen as being utterly similar. It is "empty": each temporal moment is seen as an empty container or slot. This new time also has a linear structure, one that serves as the infrastructure for narratives of progress. Past, present, and future are distinguished from one another, yet linked in an unbroken chain.

Anderson's work provides us with powerful analytical tools, especially his critique of the ways in which the linear time of historical narratives serves to legitimate existing social hierarchies. Yet his argument is also problematic: Anderson posits a coherent temporal structure to nationalism that seems at odds with the confusion and variety that exist in nationalist utterances, where appeals to hoary tradition and youthful vitality can exist side-by-side. The words that Sasaki Masanobu uses to describe the image of "spring" as a trope for youth in Tōson's *Haru* (Spring, 1908) can be borrowed to describe the complexity of national time:

> This thing 'spring' ceaselessly exists in [the characters from the novel] and at the same time it is ceaselessly absent from them, they already have it and yet they do not have it—therefore it is the eternally pursued, and

in that sense it is something that belongs to the far side of infinity. Moreover, if this is so, perhaps this thing 'spring,' which like a mirage of water
in the road continually slips away ever farther into the distance, can only
truly be grasped on the absolute far side, that is, in death.[21]

These words capture the ambivalent time structure of the nation—and the subjective desires that this temporality elicits. Nationalism cannot be reduced to a
single temporality, linear or cyclical; its utterances frequently present an ambiguous field on which multiple temporalities coexist and, at times, collide. As
Prasenjit Duara reminds us, "The nation as the subject of History is never able
to completely bridge the aporia between the past and the present. At one level,
the ideology of the nation-state even finds it politically serviceable."[22] That is
one reason that narratives of restoration are such powerful tools for nationalism:
they promise both to break with the existing present and to reunite with some
lost past, thereby delivering both continuity and discontinuity.

In the introduction to this volume, I described Suga Hidemi's critique of
Anderson's theory of national time. Here, I would like to take up another
intriguing revision of the theory of nationalist temporality: Homi K. Bhabha's
essay, "DissemiNation: Time, Narrative, and the Margins of the Modern
Nation."[23] Strategically shifting the terms of discussion, Bhabha posits the
modern nation as "split between the continuist, accumulative temporality of
the pedagogical, and the repetitious, recursive strategy of the performative"
(Bhabha, 297). It is precisely the need to represent itself, to narrate itself that
brings the nation to a split. Language is both internal and external to a speaking subject; therefore, any attempt to represent in narration the (national) subject's own authority must immediately become ambiguous, because that
authority lies in part outside the subject.

According to Bhabha, the pedagogical aspect of a national narrative is
grounded "in a tradition of the people," a form of "becoming designated by
itself, encapsulated in a succession of historical moments that represents an
eternity produced by self-generation." But the performative disrupts things: it
"intervenes in the sovereignty of the nation's *self-generation* by casting a
shadow between the people as 'image' and its signification as a differentiating
sign of Self, distinct from the Other" (Bhabha, 299). As a result,

In place of the polarity of a prefigurative self-generating nation itself
and extrinsic Other nations, the performative introduces a temporality
of the 'in-between' through the 'gap' or 'emptiness' of the signifier that

punctuates linguistic difference. The boundary that marks the nation's selfhood interrupts the self-generating time of national production with a space of representation that threatens binary division with its difference. The barred Nation *It/Self*, alienated from its eternal self-generation, becomes a liminal form of social representation, a space that is *internally* marked by cultural difference and the heterogeneous histories of contending peoples. . . .   (Bhabha, 299; italics in original)

The act of national narration opens up a gap between the (pedagogical) narrated content and the (performative) act of narrating, a gap that Bhabha identifies as the liminal, heterogeneous *space* of the nation. This nation-space is a site of heterogeneity, of small differences that disrupt the homogeneity that the pedagogical assumes. The act of representing the nation forces the self-generating nation to open itself to those others from which it distinguishes itself, resituating them into the nation's interior and inadvertently opening up marginal spaces from which performative practices are mobilized as a means of "supplementing" (in a Derridean sense) the pedagogical temporality of the nation, thereby displacing its self-presence to itself.

In sum, Anderson's description of nationalism as a shift away from "filled time" toward "empty, homogeneous time" requires revision. The yearning for the past hinted at in Anderson's comparison of "filled" and "empty" times echoes the nostalgia for a vanishing tradition characteristic of much modern nationalism—a criticism raised by Suga Hidemi. That is to say, Anderson does not so much narrate the rise of nationalism and its temporalities as he seems to narrate from *within* the fractured temporal field of nationalism, a field that is simultaneously modern and antimodern.[24] One way to conceive of the temporality of national imagination is that it consists precisely of this "discovery" that a modern linear time is in the process of burying a traditional cyclical time—a discovery that immediately implies a project of restoration.

Moreover, time and space fluidly interpenetrate one another in any national imagination. The linear versions of time, which are so fundamental to national narratives, amount to a spatialization of temporality, as Bergson argued. Yet, as Tessa Morris-Suzuki notes, the creation of the clear geographical boundaries of the Japanese nation in the Meiji period also required the temporalization of space. Peripheral regions such as Okinawa and Hokkaidō, whose cultural differences had previously been thought to mark spatial exteriority, were now integrated into the space of the nation by means of time.

Their cultural particularity was renarrated, so that it now signified not spatial exteriority, but rather earlier stages of development in the linear time of a single national history. Similar attempts were made in the twentieth century to narrate the relation between Japan and its new overseas colonies.[25]

In attempting to stabilize the fluctuating image of the nation, national imagination frequently mobilizes a chronotope that presents the space of the nation as existing at a transhistorical level. As such, this space is capable of containing within itself multiple temporalities (linear, cyclical, vitalistic, continuous, discontinuous, public, private, domestic, foreign) without ever losing its self-identity. But this attempt to achieve stability by mobilizing space is itself troubled by the need to produce alternative versions of national space to address different concerns. That is to say, just as nationalism requires several temporalities, it also requires plural spatialities.[26] While national space is frequently defined in terms of geographical territory, a monolithic definition of national space would produce a lifeless imagined community: rigor mortis. In the language of Deleuze and Guattari, striated space must be supplemented with smooth space; national space undergoes continual deterritorialization and reterritorialization.[27] Accordingly, in national imagination the space of the nation is conflated with other forms of identity that function as supplemental forms of national space: a racial bloodline, a national language, or a unique form of subject/object relationship—that is, with a metaphysical form of desire that is continually capable of transforming other into self. The overlapping of geographical national space with a transhistorical Hegelian desire in particular allows the narration of national space as an inherently expansionary entity, a space that retains its identity even as it absorbs territory that was previously external to it.[28]

In sum, national imagination requires not one chronotope, but several. The multiple versions of time and space supplement, reinforce, and sometimes contradict one another. To attempt to map out this complexity more concretely, I will turn now to Tōson's *Before the Dawn*. In the versions of national history produced in the novel and by its readers in the 1930s, various chronotopes exist side-by-side. As we examine the early critical reception of the novel, we will also see how these various forms of time and space implicate the novel in the 1930s discourse on *tenkō*. We will see how chronotopes became one of the means that enabled Japanese national imagination to absorb into itself even antinational thought and desires, as well as one of the weapons used by those who would trouble hegemonic forms of national imagination.

CHRONOTOPES FOR IMAGINING EDO AND MEIJI JAPAN

Japan in the 1920s and 1930s saw a boom in what Carol Gluck calls "Edofying," the reimagining of the Edo period (1600–1867), as well as the transitional period of the early Meiji.[29] Edo Japan and the Meiji Restoration functioned as storehouses of tropes capable of supporting multiple forms of national imagination. For those critical of modernity from the right, these periods signified what had been lost; for those on the left, they signified the source of the feudal remnants that still underlay social domination in Japan.

Edo became a dominant presence in both mass and high culture of the early twentieth century—in, for example, the new popular medium of cinema.[30] Popular fiction in this period, too, saw a return to Edo and early Meiji in such enormously successful works as Nakazato Kaizan's *Daibosatsu tōge* (Daibosatsu pass, 1913–1935) and Yoshikawa Eiji's *Miyamoto Musashi* (1935–1939).[31] In high culture as well, Edo proved a source of fascination, often in the mode of what Marilyn Ivy calls the "discourses of the vanishing." Nagai Kafū (1879–1959) frequently returned to the imaginary landscape of Edo (or to its vanishing traces within modern Tokyo). In the critical essays he published as *Edo geijutsu ron* (A theory of Edo arts, 1920), Kafū sought a coherent national aesthetic in the visual, literary, and performing arts of the Edo period. According to Kafū, who openly acknowledged he was piecing these ideas together in part from Western sources, this aesthetic drew its strength from the spirit of resistance of Edo craftsmen toward feudal oppression, a spirit that was waning under modern consumer culture. Kuki Shūzō likewise creatively translated the phenomenological training he received in Europe to construct a Japanese national aesthetic out of materials inherited from Edo culture. In *"Iki" no kōzō* (The structure of 'Iki,' 1930) and "Fūryū ni kansuru ichi kōsatsu" (A consideration of *fūryū*, 1937), he sought in the Edo period a national aesthetic sensibility that was equivalent to, yet distinct from, that of Western cultures, one that resolved in advance the contradictions that would bedevil Western modernity—and one that was in immediate danger of vanishing.[32]

In various ways, these cultural products responded to the sense of crisis that marked the period: fears of rampant mass culture, rising feminism, economic dislocation, anticolonial movements in Japan's empire, socialist and anarchist activism at home. These "Edofying" works both solicited and responded to an increasing tendency to conceive of modernity as a kind of loss. And of all the cultural products that reimagined Edo, probably none had as deep an impact as Tōson's *Before the Dawn.* With its bottom–up version of the Meiji Restoration, the work jolted commonsense notions about Japan's modern history.[33]

The work provided a new way to imagine the Meiji Restoration, and therefore the time and space of the modern Japanese nation. It solicited (and continues to solicit) a range of conflicting desires among readers and critics. It does so, in part, by offering up more than one chronotope for imagining the nation. As Bakhtin argues, "Within the limits of a single work and within the total literary output of a single author we may notice a number of different chronotopes and complex interactions among them," so that chronotopes "are mutually inclusive, they co–exist, they may be interwoven with, replace or oppose one another, contradict one another or find themselves in ever more complex interrelationships."[34] To understand the role this work had in producing and troubling national imagination, then, is largely a matter of unpacking the overlapping forms of space and time that appear on its pages and in the readings provided by critics when it first appeared.

The most obvious chronotope in the novel is one shared by the work's characters and narrator, although they adopt a variety of stances toward it. Framed within this chronotope, the narrative of the Meiji Restoration presented in *Before the Dawn* resembles the model for nationalist temporality proposed by Anderson: it describes the replacement of a temporality of repetition by one of linearity.[35] But because the nation is conceived primarily in terms of an ahistorical space, one that can contain multiple forms of time, one dominant form of temporality can replace another without substantially altering national identity. Within this overarching framework, the story of Aoyama Hanzō, the protagonist, becomes not simply the tragedy of a man who loses his social positions as family patriarch, village headman, and station-post official. It also becomes the tragedy of a man who is unable to make the transition to the new form of temporality required by the modern nation-state. Hanzō's doomed attempt to interpret emerging linear history through a cyclical temporality of restoration prevents him from reaching a viable understanding of his (and the nation's) present in relation to past and future, and it is this failing that leads to the tragedies of his involuntary confinement and death.

From this perspective, book 1 of *Before the Dawn* describes in detail the collapse of both the spatial and temporal orders that had sustained the Tokugawa period. The dominant time of the earlier period is delineated in the work's opening pages. They construct the image of a world underwritten by an understanding of the present as a repetition of the past. It is within this tem-

poral framework that characters such as Kichizaemon (Hanzō's father) and
Kinbē (Kichizaemon's friend) are represented as finding meaning in their own
lives. A primary marker of this temporal regime is the annual pilgrimage from
the imperial court in Kyoto to Nikko to pay homage to the spirit of Ieyasu,
the founder of the Tokugawa shogunate. Throughout book 1, it is the greatest desire of the *bakufu* (the central feudal government in the Edo period) and
of the generation of Kichizaemon and Kinbē that this temporal order continue looping through its cycles of repetition indefinitely.

But the opening pages of the work also provide numerous signs that the
existing spatial and temporal order was breaking down, most notably the first
appearance of the Black Ships in 1853. The Kiso Road, too, on which Kichizaemon (and later Hanzō) serves as station head, is confronted with unprecedented occurrences, especially new kinds of movement—the Princess
Kazunomiya's journey to Edo, for example, or the Shogun's journey to Kyoto.
"This was no longer the Kiso road of the Kaiei or Tempō eras" (*TZ* 11:191).
The phrase that Kinbē repeatedly trots out to describe the state of the world
summarizes this succinctly: "unheard of in days of old" (*zendai mimon*). For the
novel's characters, these events defy explanation under a temporality of repetition. The dominant temporality has lost its ability to connect events seam-
lessly.

Perhaps the most emblematic example of this broken temporality occurs
in chapter 2. Against a backdrop of harried movement along the Kiso Road
provoked by the second Black Ship crisis in 1854, a series of unexpected dis-
asters strike, betraying the nostalgic desires of village elders for a "continuation of the present state of affairs" (*TZ* 11:66). In an attempt to restore order,
the townspeople throw themselves wholeheartedly into their annual autumn
kyōgen performances, a tradition with a "long history" (67). But soon after,
even before talk of the festival has died down, a terrible earthquake of a mag-
nitude "unheard of in days of old" strikes (70). In this "time of emergency"
(74) even the coming of a new year fails to break the string of bad luck: news
of epidemics, famine, and terrible storms buffet the town. In March, the
townspeople try to restore temporal order by holding a second New Year's festival: "If we re-start the year, we can escape from these calamities" (75). But
this "untimely New Year" only raises further temporal complications, such as
the farmer who asks Kichizaemon, "if we celebrate New Year twice, does that
mean we get older by two years?" (75).

The breakdown of the existing concept of time is also represented in the
desperate attempts the *bakufu* makes to retain its grip on power. Its forced cel-

ebration of the 250th anniversary of the death of Ieyasu clearly attempts to revitalize the steady cycle of annual imperial pilgrimages to Nikko. In particular, the *bakufu*'s disastrous attempt to repeat Ieyasu's victory at Sekigahara in the Shogun's punitive mission against the Chōshu domain is portrayed as ending in farce.

As a disciple of Hirata School Nativism, Hanzō welcomes this breakdown of the *bakufu* order.[36] He believes that the present-day disorder cannot be understood through a temporality of repetition. Instead, he organizes the significance of these unprecedented occurrences via a temporality of restoration, a narrative of decline that is to end heroically, in a moment of final redemption at the end of history. For Hanzō, the "middle ages" represent warrior usurpation of authority from the imperial court, and hence they must be rejected. What is required is a "restoration" of "antiquity." The false consciousness of repetition that sustains *bakufu* rule must be replaced by a restoration of what Hanzō sees as "naturalness itself" (*onozukara*), the static identity that marked Japan in antiquity, when there was no gap between high and low, between subject and object. The restoration of antiquity in turn will mark the onset of the modern age (*chikatsuyo*): "This can only be reached by returning to high antiquity, when there was only the ruler and the people in this world, and starting over again from that point of origin. . . . We must abandon the middle ages. We must greet the modern age" (*TZ* 11:436–37). At the conclusion of book 1, with the news of the restoration of imperial rule, Hanzō believes that the new temporal order he has longed for is finally in place.[37]

Book 2, of course, narrates the collapse of Hanzō's historical understanding. Hanzō's absence from the first two chapters of book 2 (which focus on Western machinations in Japan) already suggests that forces beyond Hanzō's grasp have taken control of the novel's temporality. By the novel's conclusion, a dejected Hanzō is forced to acknowledge that the temporality of restoration he dreamed of is nowhere to be found, despite the overthrow of the *bakufu*. "What was unfolding in front of his eyes was not a return to antiquity, but rather a truly unexpected modernity" (*TZ* 12:345).

If Hanzō's temporality of restoration fails to appear, then what temporality dominates the novel's latter half instead? It is hinted at early on in book 2: one of the "gifts that were quite curious in Japan at that time" that Commodore Perry presents to the *bakufu* is a "wall clock" (*TZ* 12:16). Chapter 7 in particular narrates the dissemination of a new form of time that is to legitimate the new nation-state: "In the spirit of this 'international law,' the new government greeted the new age by discarding the old calendar used up until then and introducing the solar calendar then in common use throughout the world" (*TZ* 12:237).

The narrative locates the seeds of Hanzō's tragic ending in the emergence of this new temporality. It is the introduction of the new calendar and Hanzō's reaction to it (he petitions the new government) that directly set off his decline into madness:

> Hanzō had put a great deal of thought into his proposal for calendar reform. When the new government adopted the solar calendar, it did not seem necessary that something as deeply rooted in the lives of the nation [*kokumin*] as the calendar be switched to the Western style. Out of the belief that it was a good thing for this country to have a calendar suited to its own climate [*fūdo*], he submitted a proposal for use by the authorities. It was a calendar constructed with the first day of spring as its New Year's Day. He had provisionally named it the "Imperial National Calendar." Unfortunately, because the proposal seemed ill matched to the desire for a reformed calendar that would have international currency, the authorities paid it no heed. . . . At any rate, Hanzō's proposal became a topic of conversation among the villagers. In this narrow mountain country, it was not so much the content of his opinions as the making of a proposal itself that led to talk, and there was all sorts of gossip about how that was not normal behavior. Some even suggested that his excessive disappointment had caused a mental disturbance. (*TZ* 12:251–52)

This is the first clear mention in the work of Hanzō having a "mental disturbance" (*seishin no ijō*), so that the theme that will dominate the closing chapters—Hanzo's mental illness—arise directly out of the calendar reform incident.[38]

At the work's conclusion, Hanzō's insanity is described as leaving him "cut off from the outside world." (*TZ* 12:510). He is represented as lacking any temporal framework that might render meaningful the otherwise chaotic events of his life (precisely the role that Benedict Anderson assigns to national temporality). In the final pages of the work, Hanzō's disciple Katsushige stands over his master's grave and muses over the meaning of this tragic life, cast adrift in the "dark," "transitional period" of early Meiji (note the hint of yet another narrative contained in this word, "transitional"). Katsushige clearly understands the temporal framework that now rules: "plans for private railroads were springing up in every region, as the reforms in transportation and communications that would shrink time and distance permeated into each and every life, like the flood of the new century that was pressing toward them" (*TZ* 12:535).[39] Hanzō, of course, is cut off from this new temporality. Having gambled his life on another form of time, he is left with nothing when it fails to appear. The tragedy of Hanzō is that of a man who cannot answer the simplest yet most fundamental of questions: "What time is it?"

THE CHRONOTOPES OF *TENKŌ* AND NATIONAL IMAGINATION

As in Anderson's argument on the rise of nationalism, one finds at the level of characters and narrator in *Before the Dawn* a narrative in which a temporality of repetition is violently elbowed out of the way by a new temporality of "homogeneous, empty time." But obviously, this means that national imagination is riddled with discontinuity, and there is a split between premodern and modern temporalities. In the chronotope shared by these characters, this split is stitched over by situating it on an ahistorical space of the nation, one that guarantees continuity.

In a number of essays and interviews, Shimazaki Tōson stressed his intention to write a novel that described the continuity of Japan's nineteenth century. For example, as early as 1915 he wrote:

> I would really enjoy reading it if somebody would write on what we could call research into our nation's nineteenth century. The Meiji period is usually divided off from the Tokugawa era, but if we think of the past century as a whole, a new and different aspect emerges. I would like to read a study of the period that begins around the time of Motoori Norinaga's death. Studies of the *Manyōshū*, the revival of the spirit of songs and poems from antiquity, the ideal of affection and respect for our national language. . . . I would like to read how these things formed the basis for an awakened national consciousness in those days.[40]

In centering his narrative on the forgotten grassroots activism that helped lead to the Meiji Restoration, Tōson was attempting to place the Restoration on a continuum of Japanese popular history. Moreover, while Tōson avoided the xenophobia that characterized many of his contemporaries, still the notion of national history as something self-generated (*naihatsuteki*), and therefore inherently continuous, was crucial to him, both at the level of the individual and the nation.[41]

Most critics who wrote on the novel in the 1930s also celebrated its portrayal of the unbroken continuity of Japanese history and of the self-generated identity of the Japanese people. One reason for this reception was the prevalence in the early 1930s of similar reinterpretations of the Restoration, especially in the famous debates between Marxist historians of the Kōza and Rōnō factions.[42] As Takahashi Akinori has argued, the debate had a demonstrable influence on Tōson's understanding of history, which underwent significant changes over the course of the turbulent six years during which the novel was serialized. Certain passages in *Before the Dawn*, for example, are clearly adapted from the writings of the Kōza faction historian Hani Gorō.[43]

The early criticism on the novel intersects with another 1930s phenomenon in Japanese intellectual life, the question of *tenkō*, or ideological conversion. Often as a condition for release from prison, numerous activists (sometimes voluntarily, more often under coercion) publicly renounced Marxism and promised to abandon all political activism. Their number included some of the most prominent leaders in the proletarian movement, and the widescale collapse of leftist activism in the 1930s has ever since been a key problem of modern Japanese intellectual history. Why did the Japanese left cave in so quickly?

Although some students of *tenkō* (notably Tsurumi Shunsuke) have sought parallels to *tenkō* in other nations, the phenomenon is often portrayed as being characteristically "Japanese" in nature. That is to say, the discourse on *tenkō* itself has become a component part of Japanese national imagination. This was true in the 1930s, among the actual *tenkōsha* (those who underwent *tenkō*) and those who wrote about them; it was also true of the postwar discourse on *tenkō* carried out by such figures as Tsurumi and Yoshimoto Takaaki, as I discussed in chapter 1.

The 1930s phenomenon of *tenkō* was accompanied by the rise of what was called *tenkō* literature. This loosely defined genre is usually portrayed in literary history as a particularly ironic return of the repressed.[44] Writers from the proletarian literature movement who had earlier condemned the apolitical and bourgeois nature of confessional, interior-oriented I-novels (such as Tōson's *The Family* or *Shinsei* [New life]), now in the 1930s found themselves writing confessional, interior-oriented fictions that depicted the psychological processes of *tenkō* and its aftermath. *Before the Dawn*, of course, is not typically thought to belong to this genre: Tōson was never associated with socialism or anarchism, nor was he arrested in the 1930s, nor did he undergo a moment of sudden political conversion.

In a sense, though, *Before the Dawn* is the masterpiece of *tenkō* literature. Many of the critics who celebrated *Before the Dawn* in the 1930s were themselves *tenkōsha*. In fact, in a famous 1936 roundtable discussion of *Before the Dawn*, Hayashi Fusao implied that only a *tenkōsha* was truly capable of appreciating *Before the Dawn*.[45] Clearly, *Before the Dawn* provided a vision to these troubled figures for how they could integrate themselves into the national community on an ethical basis. The novel is *tenkō* literature, too, because the discourse surrounding it evidences the forms of time and space that were central to that genre. This chronotope, which we will explore below, helps explain why so many Japanese Marxists emerged from the process of *tenkō* not just as renounced socialists, but as fascists and ultranationalists—that is, as national socialists.

※

A 1932 article that appeared in the journal *Mita Bungaku* begins to suggest why this conversion was possible.[46] Its author, Hara Minoru, denies the existence of any fundamental difference between the Marxist and fascist agendas: both share the same rational goal, a desire to bring about a "realm of freedom," and both utilize irrational tools to achieve that goal. While Marxism relies on the irrational force of the proletariat as its tool for achieving solidarity across national lines, fascism uses irrational nationalism as a means to achieve solidarity within the national community. Fascism's rational, scientific desire for a "realm of freedom" qualifies it "as one kind of socialist thought" (Hara, 92). In this sense, Hara argues, *Before the Dawn* is potentially the literary masterpiece of the rising Japanese fascist movement because it stresses that the Meiji Restoration was as much a moment of national self-awakening as it was a revolution driven by class conflict.

Hara's reading of *Before the Dawn* suggests that one of the reasons Marxist intellectuals could transform themselves into nationalists was that the two poles of the political spectrum shared a similar chronotope for narrating Japanese history. In this chronotope, class and nation blurred together: the Marxist teleology of world history was retained, but the role of the proletariat, the final subject of history, was now taken by the Japanese nation, which must arise to overthrow the chains of Western imperialism in Asia:

Tōson in this work does not fail to acknowledge the reality of class struggle in the Restoration revolution. Yet in the work the author also states, borrowing the thought of the Nativists, that it was not merely a power struggle. Class struggle needed to move forward through the demand for authentic sovereign-subject relations. Moreover, it was the lower classes that most clearly grasped this authentic sovereign-subject relationship. An authentic sovereign-subject relationship: that is, to return to antiquity, to have a renewed consciousness [*saininshiki*] of the unique form of the Japanese people [*minzoku*]. (Hara, 91–92)

Or, as Hara argues elsewhere, "humankind is a class-bound existence, yet it is also—perhaps even more importantly—an ethnic existence [*minzokuteki son-zai*]." *Before the Dawn* demonstrates that the driving impulses behind the rise of the oppressed classes were the "ideals of the essence [*honzen*] of the Japanese race [*minzoku*]" (Hara, 93). Hara posits Japan as an ahistorical, transcendent identity that is simultaneously geographic space, an ethnically pure community, and a unique form of subject/object relationship. This allows him to supplement the narrative of class awakening with a history of national reawakening, one identified largely in spatial terms as a return to origins. Moreover, this transcendental space is capable of retaining identity even as it expands to absorb others:

Nonetheless, to renew the consciousness of the unique form of the race is in no way to turn one's back on other races. To fuse the Japanese tradition with the traditions of other races does not merely amount to painting over the surface of the earth with a single color, but rather means to dig down that unique tradition to the center of the earth and then to take one's departure from there. (Hara, 92)

The version of Marxism that is employed here grounds its historical narrative in a reified concept of space, the space of geography and climate, as well as of racial blood. It is not my intention to argue that Marxism necessarily rests on a reification of space—Walter Benjamin, among others, argued for a materialist theory of history that stressed the need to *create* a space in the present moment that would cut through, rather than ground, the linear temporal continuities of history.[47] Like Bhabha's search for spatial antagonisms in peripheral resistance movements, Benjamin's historical materialism utilizes a spatiality that must be produced in the present moment and that can never be justified through an appeal to past or future: either would depend on a progressive notion of linear time, which Benjamin sees as precisely the mode of oppression that must be overthrown.

But when the historicity of spatial divisions is denied, and those divisions are instead reified as the transcendent ground of history, then a framework is in place whereby a socialist history can be transformed into a fascist one. Such a framework pervaded Japanese Marxism, whether it was the "national socialism" advocated by Takabatake Motoyuki (the Japanese translator of *Das Kapital*), the Rōnō-ha with its insistence on a Japanese particularity that was intrinsically external to Leninist forms of Marxism, or the sophisticated Kōza-ha version of the Meiji Restoration produced by Yamada Moritarō.[48] All these various forms of Marxist thought shared a problematic tendency to ignore what Morris-Suzuki calls "the rather obvious observation that Japan in its present form is a modern artifact, whose frontiers were drawn in the middle of the nineteenth century."[49] They ignored that the existence of a (fluid) geographic entity known as "Japan" in the premodern era cannot be equated with the existence in that period of a Japanese national community.[50] And as Harry Harootunian notes, the result is that "Japanese Marxist explanations of Japan's modernity in the 1930s often risked resembling the interpretations of more strident ultranationalists" because rather than seeing capitalism as a global phenomenon, they saw it only within the framework of national history, thereby "implying the existence of a state prior to the introduction of capitalism" and "privileging the race nation as the principal unit of analysis." Instead of "attending to the place of production" in their analyses, they tended to resort to "the production of place" and as a result the "temporal process was incorporated into space."[51]

This is not a problem limited to Japan or the 1930s. All too often, Etienne Balibar reminds us, "the socialist ideology of class and class struggle, which did develop in constant confrontation with nationalism, has ended up copying it, by a kind of historical mimicry."[52] The reification of national space sets in place a narrative structure that permits equating the proletariat with the nation. Hara, in his reading of *Before the Dawn*, provides a prototype for the many *tenkōsha* who converted from socialism to national socialism: the Marxist narrative framework of a continuous world history was retained, but the role of the proletariat, the engine driving the final stage of history, was now taken by Japanese nation, whose unbroken cultural tradition situated it in a unique position to overthrow the chains of Western imperialism in Asia.[53]

What emerges, finally, is a second chronotope for narrating national history. Like the first chronotope discussed above, it presumes the nation's spatial existence at a transcendental, ahistorical level. But unlike that first chronotope, it presumes a single form of temporality existing on this space: that of a linear,

progressive time. Hara's insistence on the progressive, "scientific"—and therefore not "reactionary"—nature of fascism implies an evolutionary model of
history, which, as Slavoj Žižek argues, is the chronotope of Stalinism (and of
many other forms of modern thought, including neoliberal free-market doctrine and modernization theory). Stalinism justifies even the most monstrous
deeds in the present through reference to the utopian future moment that
those deeds will eventually lead to. It is a view of history that is fundamentally
progressive and linear, mechanically evolutionary: the ground of history is in
place from the beginning, rather than being produced through retroactive
construction in the present. Stalinist historiography results in the production
of a fantastic sublime body of the People, an indestructible body that "can
endure even the most terrible ordeal and survive it intact," a body that is
repeatedly identified with national space and blood.[54]

❁

Another early review of *Before the Dawn* that is symptomatic of this tendency
appeared in 1934 in *Kogito*, a journal associated with the Japan Romantic
School, whose members included a large number of *tenkōsha*.[55] In this review,
Takayama Shigeru lauds what he calls Tōson's "scientific" analysis of the Meiji
Restoration—which he in turn promises to read through a "scientific" form
of criticism. This requires that one adopt "the serious-minded weapons of science" (Takayama, 5) and closely investigate the relationship between Tōson
and the Meiji Restoration, first by reaching a scientific understanding of the
Meiji Restoration, and then by using this understanding to evaluate the literary condensation of the Restoration that appears in *Before the Dawn*.

A scientific approach to history, according to Takayama, involves taking the
whole of history as a single unbroken continuity. At present, he argues, the
pressing issue that faces Japanese historiography is the particularity of Japanese capitalism and its relation to the Meiji Restoration. The problem relates
not only to the difference between Japan and Europe, but also Japan's difference from the rest of Asia. "In other words, why is it that, while India, China,
Korea, etc., were also opened up in response to foreign demands and forced
to engage in trade, none of them saw the development of capitalism as an
independent nation, as did Japan?" (Takayama, 7). Takayama acknowledges
that he is conceiving of history in Marxist terms. Hence, in explaining why
Japan alone among the Asian nations was capable of rising as an independent
capitalist power, Takayama focuses on the distinct structures of the Japanese
economy under feudalism, which he argues provided the necessary precondi-

tion for Japan's rise as a capitalist power in the wake of Meiji. That is to say, even prior to the arrival of the Black Ships, the Japanese economy had developed on its own to a point where capitalism was the necessary next stage (although Takayama maintains that capitalism in fact came into Japan from outside). It was precisely the failure of China and India to develop out of primitive communism and into a centralized feudal economy prior to their encounter with the West that doomed them to colonial subjection. Hence, for example, the Chinese Revolution of 1911 was, in world historical terms, equivalent to the Japanese Warring States period of the sixteenth century, not to the Meiji Restoration of the nineteenth century (Takayama, 13).

On the surface, Takayama's reading of Japanese history is antinationalist. He explicitly rejects historical explanations that rely on such agents as a "Yamato soul" or a "national spirit." Takayama even goes so far as to question the relevance of discussing a unified Japanese nation as existing prior to the Ashikaga and Warring States Periods, that is, prior to Japan's emergence from primitive communism into English-style, decentralized feudalism. Moreover, Takayama argues that "any judgment on historical reality that does not express itself in relation to the task [*kadai*] that is given in the present moment is false" (Takayama, 11). He vows he will take his "point of departure from the present day [state of affairs] which no one can deny": the disorder and chaos of China, contrasted with "the autonomy of Japanese capitalism" (Takayama, 12).

But having started from antagonisms existing in the present, Takayama proceeds to dehistoricize this spatial division. As a result, he projects the space of the modern Japanese nation into the prefeudal past, what Duara calls the "already-always nation-space" that becomes the unspoken premise of any national history.[56] Japan's development out of primitive communism and into feudalism, always argued through contrast with China's supposed failure to do the same, necessarily posits a Japanese space distinct from that of China and the other nations of Asia, a spatial unit that is uniquely capable of sustaining this development.

In Takayama, then, the space of Japan retains an unbroken identity across history as the transcendental stage on which the teleology of history can unfold. Ultimately, the space of geography (which Takayama equates with the space of racial blood) determines the unfolding of history:

> The difference between China and Japan too should be clear. As with England, the Japanese people [*minzoku*], who occupied isolated islands separated from the continent, were relatively free from interference by

foreign enemies and were able to move forward smoothly, step-by-step. That the cities on the continent—both in Europe and Asia—were normally surrounded by walls is of interest, but be that as it may, in contrast to this situation of being left defenseless against the constant incursions and influx of neighboring peoples, with whom there was continual quarreling, Japan enjoyed smooth progress in its development.

(Takayama, 14)

The greatness of *Before the Dawn*, according to Takayama, lay in the way it condensed in literary form this continuous development that marked Japan's national history.

Tōson himself frequently discussed this supposed continuity of Japanese history in contrast to the discontinuity of the histories of other Asian nations. In *Tōhō no mon* (The gate to the East), the sequel to *Before the Dawn* that Tōson had begun serializing (again in *Chūō kōron*) at the time of his death in 1943, the narrator argues that among all the nations of Asia, only Japan has retained its cultural tradition intact, despite the fact that movements for a restoration of antiquity had risen across the Orient. This was because only Japan had a true "Middle Ages," allowing a smooth transition between antiquity and modernity, while China and India were forced to jump directly from antiquity to modernity, thereby losing the thread of cultural continuity.[57] Here again, it is the geographical space of Japan, figured as its national "backbone" (*koshibone*: literally, "hipbone," but with the nuance of "perseverance"), that makes this possible.[58] This version of the Meiji Restoration renarrates it into a world historical event, the potential awakening of the people of the Orient to their historical destiny.

While Tōson does not explicitly make the connection, this chronotope easily leads to an argument for the necessity of Japan, the sole modern power in Asia, to "rescue" its fellow Asians from Western imperialism.[59] In other words, it can become an apologetic for the violence of Japan's military conquest of Asia. Both Kamei Katsuichirō (another *tenkōsha*) and Kobayashi Hideo in their 1930s writings on *Before the Dawn* celebrate the Japanese "blood" that they locate flowing beneath the surface of the novel's text.[60] In Kamei's famous 1939 study of Tōson, in particular, the trope of "blood" encompasses a dense interweaving of meanings. It refers to both personal and national heredity, as well as to a form of passion. Kamei also mobilizes blood as a sign of a perceived decline or corruption of Japan in the 1930s.[61] Finally, Kamei finds in blood the solution to this crisis of Japan's modernity: specifically, he reads the

blood that Japanese troops are spilling on the battlefields of China as symbol-
izing a process of national renewal, a purifying of the contaminating elements
that have corrupted the national bloodstream.[62]

The increased prominence in the late 1930s of a reified version of space in
Tōson's understanding of national history has to be situated in the context of
a general emphasis on the spatial aspect of history in early Shōwa Japan. As we
have already seen, Japanese intellectuals since the Meiji Restoration were
increasingly forced to recognize that the supposedly universal linear temporality of Western historiography concealed an unbridgeable spatial divide, a gap
that guaranteed occidental superiority over the Orient. Figures such as
Okakura Tenshin reacted to this by creating a new spatial grounding for world
history, one that rejected the validity of Western temporalities in Eastern spaces,
and one in which the Orient now possessed superiority over the Occident.
This tendency grew more pronounced in the 1930s, and anecdotal evidence
from Tōson's own life demonstrates how closely he was involved with it.

For example, it is well known that the Japan Romantic School rediscovered
and reinterpreted Okakura's writings in the 1930s. The key role that Tōson
played in this rediscovery is less well known. Asano Akira, a member of the
School who translated Okakura's English-language works into Japanese, notes
in his autobiography that it was through the writings of Tōson that he first discovered Okakura's *Ideals of the East*.[63] Tōson published a number of works relat-
ing to Okakura in the 1930s, including the brief 1936 essay "Okakura Kakuzō"
(*TZ* 13:271) and the extended description in *Junrei* (Pilgrimage, 1937–1940) of
the journey he made to Okakura's former dwellings in Boston in 1936. Most
significantly, the notes for the unfinished *Tōhō no mon* (The gate to the East)
indicate that Okakura was to play a major role, perhaps even become the protagonist, of that world-historical sequel to *Before the Dawn*.

Another prominent example of this tendency to spatialize history can be
found in Watsuji Tetsurō's 1935 study, *Climate and Culture*. In it, Watsuji criticizes his former teacher Heidegger for lacking a spatial element in his philosophy. An exclusive emphasis on time leads one into the error of considering
only individual consciousness, in isolation from community. For Watsuji, spatiality provides the communal ground of human existence. The "inseparability of time and space," Watsuji writes, "is the basis of the inseparability of history and climate. No social formation could exist if it lacked all foundation in
the space-structure of man, nor does time become history unless it is founded
in such social being, for history is the structure of existence in society."[64]

In discussing climate, Watsuji takes pains to distinguish this spatial concept from an objective, ahistorical dimension: climate is a matter of subjective experience, not objective existence. Like time for Heidegger, it is a realm in which the human subject comes face-to-face with itself outside of itself, in a state of "ex-sistere." Moreover, climate is fundamentally a communal space: it is primarily "we," not "I" that discovers cold or rain. Its space is also the realm of human freedom, in that the "we" that Watsuji locates in climate is a "we" that freely creates joint measures to cope with climate.

Nonetheless, this communal space possesses a deterministic aspect, what Watsuji calls "the climatic limitation of human life" (Watsuji, 13). For example, each local climate leads the human beings who dwell in it to produce a distinct style of clothing. A particular local style may eventually be exported to other communities living under different climatic conditions. "But to whatever locality it may be transplanted, the fact that the style is conditioned by the climate which produced it can never be effaced. European-style clothes remain European, even after more than half a century of wear in Japan" (Watsuji, 7). This is true not just for clothes, food, and cultural entities, but even for the character of human subjective existence and self-understanding, which are also limited by climate. In *Climate and Culture*, as Naoki Sakai has demonstrated, the space of climate overlaps with the image of a homosocial and ahistorical national community based on mutual sympathy.[65]

Given the increasing prominence of spatiality in Tōson's later writings, it is hardly surprising to learn that during the writing of *Before the Dawn* he became close friends with Watsuji, or to learn that Watsuji was an admirer of *Before the Dawn*, nor that Tōson admired *Climate and Culture*.[66] In 1932, after receiving a copy of book 1 of *Before the Dawn*, Watsuji wrote an admiring letter to Tōson, expressing not only his thanks for the present of the book, but also his gratitude "as one Japanese" to Tōson for finally capturing the events of the Meiji Restoration in a literary masterpiece, an artistic feat which Watsuji says he had begun to fear would never be accomplished. Watsuji in particular praises the novel's lyrical, poetic tone.[67] Likewise, Tōson wrote admiring letters to Watsuji after reading *Climate and Culture*, including a postcard that he included when he sent the complete two-volume edition of *Before the Dawn* to Watsuji in 1936.[68]

ALTERNATIVE READINGS: THE DISRUPTIONS OF SPACE

Accordingly, the many readings of *Before the Dawn* that attempted to spatialize the history of Japan should be situated within the broader currents of intellectual life in the 1930s, including the phenomenon of *tenkō*. Moreover, the shift in historical approaches between *Before the Dawn* and *Tōhō no mon* (The gate to the East)—already indicated by the two titles, one describing a temporal moment, the other a spatial position—implicates Tōson himself as an active participant in this tendency toward the spatialization of historical time. But not all critics of *Before the Dawn* in the 1930s read it in this manner. Here, I will focus on two in particular, Aono Suekichi and Hayashi Tatsuo, and use their early writings on *Before the Dawn* to map the outlines for a third chronotope in the novel, one that troubles many of the assumptions that allowed Japanese national imagination to equate proletariat with nation.

Aono Suekichi (1890–1961) was one of the most influential critics involved in the proletarian arts movement in early Shōwa. While he was instrumental in bringing a more rigorous Marxist approach to the movement, Aono himself was repeatedly at odds with the Japan Communist Party, and as a some-time member of the Rōnō faction, he increasingly distanced himself from orthodox Marxist positions throughout the 1930s. His Marxist ties were so distanced that his arrest (and subsequent *tenkō*, although many would argue that Aono never did commit *tenkō* did not come until 1938, several years after most left-wing voices had been silenced. Harootunian, in surveying Aono's work from the early 1930s, credits him with taking "a strategy that distanced the memorative past, as such" and with insisting instead on "a vigorous engagement of a performative present."[69]

We find traces of this stress on the performative over the pedagogical in Aono's two essays on *Before the Dawn*, as well as his 1935 interview with Tōson. These works in many ways set the standard for subsequent discussions of the novel.[70] Even critics who rejected Aono's approach found themselves reading the work through the categories that Aono had established. His influence on the 1936 roundtable discussion in *Bungakkai*, for example, is palpable. Nonetheless, Aono's own reading of the novel contained elements that distinguish it from the other early criticism discussed above.

Aono praises *Before the Dawn* as a work of art, in particular as a work of bourgeois art, which he argues has its own value. Nonetheless, Tōson's class limitations lead to the work's primary weakness: its inadequate grasp of historical objectivity. Although he praises Tōson for stressing the element of change in the period surrounding the Meiji Restoration, Aono criticizes Tōson for failing to dig beneath the surface phenomena of change to locate the historical "necessity" driving events: Tōson ultimately fails to grasp the "internal social necessity within which these phenomenal forms developed"

("Daiichibu," 311).While Tōson correctly stresses the importance of examining historical movements from a "bottom-up" perspective, in *Before the Dawn* he fails to identify the true driving force behind the Restoration: the active resistance of low-level samurai and the passive resistance of the peasant and merchant classes.[71] Hirata School Nativism held a powerful attraction for young persons like Hanzō in the years leading up to Meiji, but "to see it as the 'intention' moving within the tendency toward the Restoration is by no means an objectively correct view" ("Daiichibu," 309).

Aono's insistence on studying history in terms of objective necessity employs the Stalinist mode of history, which insists on a unilinear, progressive temporality grounded in a transcendent space (though here, at least, that space is not identified immediately with the Japanese nation).While not wanting to deny this aspect of Aono's approach, I want to highlight another aspect that distinguishes Aono's reading from those of many of his contemporaries.Aono insists that *Before the Dawn* and its portrayal of Hanzō are as much a commentary on 1930s Japan as they are a portrait of Japan's nineteenth century: the two eras are "identical (at least in form)" ("Daiichibu," 306), and Tōson uses the novel to comment on the contemporary world in which he lived:

> In this vast work which takes up the period of gestation of the Meiji Restoration/Reform, it isn't hard to detect the interior expression of the elder author, who lives in the present. Far from it, depending on one's perspective, this vast work locates its stage within history, and yet the figure of the author, gazing intently at the present age, lies across it. In this sense, it is not merely a historical novel, it is also an I-novel by way of the window of history.   ("Kanketsu," 315)

In this sense, by insisting on the presence of both pedagogical and performative strands to its narrative, Aono reads *Before the Dawn* and the tragedy of Hanzō in Japan's nineteenth century as an allegory for Japan's twentieth century.[72]

This is a point of some importance. Read as allegory, *Before the Dawn* seriously undermines the nationalist readings of it discussed above: it suggests that the drive for a "Shōwa Restoration" is ultimately insane.[73] Accordingly, in the 1936 *Bungakkai* roundtable, the nationalist *tenkōsha* Hayashi Fusao must deny any allegorical intent behind the tragedy of Hanzō:

> He's simply writing things just the way that they appear there, to the utmost of his abilities. It's nothing like a metaphor for the present day.

The social consciousness that Tōson does show by borrowing the Nativists is the rejection of the middle ages. He repeatedly uses the words "reject the middle ages, return to antiquity." But in book 2 this "antiquity" is clearly defined as being a "new antiquity." While they expect the Restoration to open up a "new antiquity," in fact it doesn't. That the longing for a "new antiquity" is carried forward into the present is Tōson's beautiful, powerful Japanese-style utopianism. This longing is internal and very powerful, so it was only natural that he had to write a history of the development of Japan's early-modern period. He isn't using the past as a metaphor or parody of the present, he is writing about the past itself. When he writes about the present, he writes about it head on—that's the sort of novel it is.[74]

This insistence on the transparent literalness of *Before the Dawn*, and the denial of any allegorical aspect, empowers Hayashi to maintain that the novel projects an ahistorical, transcendent space of the Japanese nation:

He writes in there something like, things Japanese can never be understood by a foreigner–he uses words like that repeatedly.[75] What was just said about seeing Japan anew from France, or what he said to Aono Suekichi—what he said in that interview: he realized that France and Japan were always going to be different, and since this was so, he wanted to try in his own way to see Japan's own, Japan's way of moving toward "the dawn." It's different from both Marxism and Fascism. As a native Japanese, and as a person who directly participated in the growth of Japanese culture, he wanted in his own way to reexamine Japan's movement and progress.[76]

Hayashi must reject an allegorical reading of *Before the Dawn* because such a reading would suggest the futility of the desire for a return to pure origins— be they national or literary. Hanzō, after all, dies a madman—and not Deleuze and Guattari's "schizo," but rather the psychotic whose desire is no longer productive, but rather organized around a lack.[77] Moreover, to admit an allegorical aspect to *Before the Dawn* would be to undermine the possibility for a seamless synthesis of *Before the Dawn* and the national community via an aesthetics of mimesis or representation—because allegory "is material or materialistic, in Benjamin's sense, because its dependence on the letter, on the literalism of the letter, cuts it off sharply from symbolic and aesthetic syntheses."[78]

While Aono uses the concept of allegory in a sense different from Benjamin's, he nonetheless insists on locating a second, nonliteral meaning behind the text, one that is linked to present-day antagonisms. The novel's language does not simply represent the past; it produces something new: a double language of past and present. Through this reading of Hanzō's tragedy, Aono uses *Before the Dawn* to produce a commentary on Japan of the 1930s, as well as on Tōson's role as an intellectual in that world. The novel describes the spirit of resistance of the Nativist movement and its longing for a restoration of antiquity. And yet "the Nativist movement ends in failure, and Hanzō's life draws to a tragic close" ("Kanketsu," 320). Aono then considers this narrative as an allegory. Does the novel attempt to "restore" or resuscitate Hanzō within the context of early Shōwa Japan? Does *Before the Dawn* call for a restoration of antiquity in the 1930s? There are two levels to this: we find in the novel, according to Aono, both an indication of Tōson's own position as an intellectual and a "warning to the present day" ("Kanketsu," 320).

Aono argues that Tōson in the 1930s in a sense repeats Hanzō's role. Both see the urgency of the crisis in which they live, and both fall back on a romantic ideology, a desire for a "return to naturalness" (one bound up with a mystical sense of tradition) that renders them into passive spectators of history ("Daiichibu," 309–10). In short, Tōson represents one type of bourgeois intellectual, the introspective observer who struggles against all social fluctuations to preserve a single, fixed position from which to observe the world in peaceful detachment. Aono contrasts this type not only with the Marxist intellectual, who stands in the vanguard of history, but also with another more reactionary type of bourgeois intellectual. Intellectuals of this latter type, represented by Masamune Hakuchō (with whom Aono had engaged in a fierce literary debate in the late 1920s), feel continually compelled not to observe, but rather to assert: they engage in struggles even before they understand the issues at hand, a dangerous tendency that only grows more pronounced in unstable periods ("Daiichibu," 314). In an implicit refutation of Hara Minoru's thesis that *Before the Dawn* was the potential masterpiece of the rising fascist movement in Japan, Aono argues that it is intellectuals like Hakuchō who are likely to link hands with fascism, whereas those like Tōson merely retreat further inward.[79] The authorial intention that Aono locates in *Before the Dawn* manifests one form of reaction to the "storm" of 1930s Japan. Like Hanzō in the Meiji Restoration, Tōson in the 1930s does not express the driving force of history—but neither does he serve the forces of reaction.

Secondly, Aono finds in *Before the Dawn* a warning to the present day. Aono distinguishes Tōson's (and Hanzō's) position from "the bunker-mentality, exclusionary [concepts] such as Japanese spirit or national spirit that are commonly being trumpeted these days" ("Kanketsu," 320–21). While Tōson and Hanzō do not embody the objective agency of history, there is a "progressive direction" to their thought, especially in their morality, their longing for an ideal return to nature, and their avoidance of simple anti-Western solutions. To equate *Before the Dawn* with a call for a revival of nationalism in the 1930s is to miss the point twice over: not only does it misread the potentially progressive aspects of Hanzō's thought, but it also mistakes the true historical significance of Hanzō's (and Tōson's) life, that of a spectator rather than active agent in history.[80]

⧈

Another early reviewer, writing from a different perspective, picked up on the problem of Tōson's relation to history. A philosopher and social critic, Hayashi Tatsuo (1896–1984) was noted for his cosmopolitan, liberal stance. He came to prominence in early Shōwa and is especially remembered for resisting the late-1930s trends toward rejecting modernity and foreign thought. In the essay "Shisō no unmei" (The destiny of thought, 1938), for example, he used the analogy of gardening to criticize contemporary attempts to root out "foreign" thought and return to purely "native" schools of thought: he notes that transplanted plants and trees often take stronger root than "native" ones. The implication was that the "sacred soil" of the Japanese nation did not guarantee any sort of historical continuity, nor was such continuity necessarily desirable.[81]

Hayashi discussed *Before the Dawn* in two brief essays. In a 1936 article, he complained that critics focused too narrowly on the motive Tōson gave for writing the novel, ignoring the very real possibility that the finished work had deviated from the author's intention. Literary works commonly stray from their authors' intentions,

> therefore it is hardly mysterious when the phenomenon arises in Tōson's case, too, that while he may have intended to produce a work that was a kind of historical epic poem [*rekishiteki jojishiteki sakuhin*], in fact what most readers find pressing relentlessly on them is more a climate-driven lyric poem [*fūdoteki jojōshiteki na mono*].

The way that history gives way to climate (the allusion is, of course, to Watsuji's *Climate and Culture*) in the novel leads Hayashi to declare that you cannot understand the work through its *motif*, but must consider instead its *quiétif*.[82]

Hayashi expanded on these ideas in another article, "Tōson Sédentaire," tucked away at the very back of the 1936 *Bungaku* special issue devoted to Tōson.[83] There, Hayashi complains about the passivity and quietude that mark all of Tōson's works, including *Before the Dawn*. Reading Tōson's works, Hayashi writes, you always imagine a man sitting motionless at his desk, buried away from the world inside his room. Tōson's social imagination is that of a man who sits immobile, peering out at the world from his window, and it is this lack of "dynamism" in Tōson's works that Hayashi criticizes:[84]

> Let's make Tōson go for a walk. Let's make him take a trip. He is forever dragging his feet as he walks around his dimly lit room, and if you look closely, you will be surprised to see that even as he walks around the room, he is sitting—you might even say that he is walking while he is sitting. This is Tōson's own unique posture.[85]

Hayashi Tatsuo's notions of a dynamic history, one in which the observer necessarily participates and in which utterances often take on unintended meanings, are very suggestive. He anticipates Deleuze and Guattari's insistence that a "schizophrenic out for a walk is a better model than a neurotic lying on the analyst's couch."[86] The space through which Hayashi wants Tōson to walk is not that of climate or national geography, but rather a new space that is continually undergoing active reconstruction in the present. In place of the sedentary who sits still even when he walks, he wants Tōson to become a nomad, one who produces a new space through the very act of walking.[87]

⌗

In fact, when *Before the Dawn* is read with these issues in mind, it reveals traces of another more critical version of time and space built into its narrative alongside the various chronotopes discussed above. In the remaining pages of this chapter, I would like to explore this final chronotope, one that is potentially quite troubling to hegemonic versions of national imagination current in 1930s Japan—and elsewhere, too.

There is a curious moment at the conclusion of book 1. It occurs in 1867, when Hanzō receives word of what he calls the "restoration of antiquity," that is, the *bakufu*'s surrendering of its authority to "restore" direct rule by the Emperor. This seems to be the fulfillment of the desire that has guided Hanzō throughout book 1. As he celebrates the news of this "restoration" with another activist in the Nativist movement, Hanzō remarks, " 'But, Kōzō, about what you just said. About how the restoration occurred without any great bloodshed. Doesn't that bring to light our national character? I can't imagine it happening this way in foreign countries' " (*TZ* 11:537).

What is curious about this statement is that the pages of book 1 that lead up to it are saturated with bloodshed. Moreover, much of this violence is directly witnessed by Hanzō himself. Throughout book 1, Hanzō closely follows a seemingly endless string of bloody battles, purges, and assassinations. In many cases, due to his role as a station official on one of the main highways connecting the cities of Edo and Kyoto, he has met the figures involved in the disputes, so that each bloodletting has its own personal ties for Hanzō.

Hanzō's first appearance in the novel comes as witness to an act of state violence so extensive that Kichizaemon, Hanzō's father, "would never forget it as long as he lived" (*TZ* 11:9). On this day, eighteen-year-old Hanzō spies from a corner of his family's courtyard as feudal authorities interrogate and punish sixty-one impoverished villagers for cutting down restricted trees. Actually, despite the large number of people involved, the convicts get off relatively lightly: the worst penalty administered is being shackled for twenty days. The customary saying, that one head will be taken for each tree poached, suggests that earlier such incidents had resulted in bloodier resolutions.

This and other examples of local conflict take place against the backdrop of even greater discord occurring at the national level. The 1859 Ansei Purge that follows in the wake of the Treaty of Kanagawa, as the strongman Ii Naosuke stifles all opposition to his policy of opening ties with America, provides the first appearance of a rhetorical figure that will become familiar to the reader by the conclusion of book 1, a listing up of casualties:

> Beginning with the Retired Lord of Mito (Nariaki), the ringleader of the so-called Treaty Opponent faction, the *daimyō* [feudal lords] and officials who had joined in it were reprimanded and ordered to undergo house arrest, and that was not all: the ferocious repression reached down to the seed bed of the newly rising forces that had begun to swirl around Kyoto. Three noblemen from Kyoto—Takatsukasa, Konoe, and Sanjō— were forced to take the tonsure, while other court nobles who were suspected of opposing Kantō were all reprimanded. Some were conveyed to Edo as convicts, transported under the status "elderly woman." Among commoners, including samurai, *rōnin* [masterless samurai], peas-

ants, and townspeople, arrests and severe punishments came one after the other. One was ordered to commit *seppuku* [suicide], one was imprisoned, five were sentenced to death, seven were exiled, eleven were banished, nine were ordered confined, four were exiled to the countryside, three were placed in manacles, seven were pardoned, three were given a severe scolding. In addition, there were six others who died of illness in jail, including Umeda Unbin of Wakasa, widely viewed as the cutting edge of the "Revere the Emperor, Expel the Barbarians" movement. Ajima Tatehaki of Mito, Hashimoto Sanai of Echizen, Rai Abukai of Kyoto, and Yoshida Sōun of Chōshu all met their ends as they tasted the bitterness [of Ii's purge]. (*TZ* 11:134–35)

In 1860, Ii is himself assassinated in an ambush by retainers from the Mito domain—the first of countless political assassinations related in book 1.

The violence that marks all of book 1 culminates in the 1864 rebellion of the Mito Loyalists. In the course of its desperate running battle with the military forces of the *bakufu*, the Loyalist army passes through Magome and is aided by Hanzō and his Hirata School colleagues. The noble anecdotes through which the Mito Loyalists are described only serve to highlight the bloody tragedy of their demise. After surrendering their weapons to representatives of the *bakufu*, the Mito Loyalists are betrayed, and all 353 surviving members are beheaded. The tragedy is compounded when the shocking news reaches Magome that not only the warriors, but the sons of two leaders (and the wife of one) were executed. The five boys range in age from three to twelve; two are also sentenced to having their severed heads placed on public exhibition. Kichizaemon, stunned by the news of this unprecedented violence, vows that he has "lived to see the end of the world" (*TZ* 11:454).

What can it mean, then, when Hanzō speaks of a bloodless restoration? Let me stress that Hanzō is aware of the bloody history that leads up to the Restoration, but it seems here that he forgets what he has seen with his own eyes. I am suggesting that *Before the Dawn* permits a reading that exposes the necessity of historical forgetfulness for any national community that seeks to imagine itself as a coherent whole.[88] A radical heterogeneity, marked by violent social antagonisms from within and ruthless external interventions from without, is described in great detail in book 1; all of this must then be processed through a selective memory before any image of a coherent national community can rise to view.

This is as much a spatial problem as it is temporal. We find here a chronotope similar to what Karatani Kōjin calls an "inversion," whereby the rise of a new spatial configuration ("landscape") leads to a "discovery" of the subject, a discovery that is immediately forgotten as the subject comes to believe it has existed all along.[89] The anti-*bakufu* slogan is "Revere the Emperor, Expel the Barbarians," and Hanzō insists on the primacy of revering the emperor, that is, on the self-generated ("pedagogical"), internal continuity of a Japanese identity. But much to Hanzō's consternation, both before and after 1868, it is the latter demand—the violent ("performative") differentiation of the interior from the external other—that seems to guide events. To Hirata School disciples, this betrays the true moral hierarchy between the two parts. Hence, they continually dismiss the "Expel the Barbarians" movement as secondary, even as duplicitous: it is merely a pretext used to justify attacks on the *bakufu*. Hanzō's repeated insistence on the primacy of revering the Emperor requires that any troubling conflict located within the Japanese interior be narrated as an incursion of the heterogeneous foreign into the homogeneous interior, corrupting its original purity. Hence, to call for a military uprising against the Black Ships, to focus on expelling the barbarians, is to act in an un-Japanese manner. Hanzō's narrative of contamination and restoration projects this fantasy spatial division between a harmonious interior and a chaotic exterior back to the dawn of history.

Hanzō's insisting that it is essential to "Revere the Emperor" is meant to signify a return to the "national character" (*kokuminsei* or *kunigara*) that existed in antiquity, prior to the usurpation of authority by the military clans and even to the introduction of "Chinese thought." The novel's narrative, however, repeatedly provides information that troubles Hanzō's pedagogical vision of history. It repeatedly demonstrates that it is only the threat of foreign intervention that brings internal unity to Japan, so that the external intervention is a necessary precondition. As Geoffrey Bennington argues,

> in order to have a name, a boundary and a history to be told at the centre, the state must be constitutively imperfect. The closure of the state becomes the frontier of the nation, and, as we have seen, the frontier implies that there is more than one nation.

Moreover, this complexity "is not an *accident* which befalls the state in its ideal purity." It "is not an empirical but a *necessary* possibility, so national differentiation does not come along to trouble the state *after* its perfect constitution, but precedes the fiction of such a constitution as its condition of possibility." A nation is "always opened to its others: or rather, it is constituted only in that opening, which is, in principle, violent."[90]

There are direct echoes of this logic in passages from *Before the Dawn*. As the Emperor travels the Tōkaidō road on his way to Edo in 1868, he sees the ocean for the first time: "What opened before him was no longer the vast, endless seas of the period of the isolated hermit nation, but already oceans that had opposite shores to which one could cross" (*TZ* 12:178). It is precisely this transformed nature of Japan's boundary, and of its spatial articulation with the exterior, that provides the necessary precondition for an image of internal unity, for Japan's pedagogical narration of itself as a nation.

In short, *Before the Dawn* undermines Hanzō's narrative of restoration by revealing that the images of a unified national spirit and an uncontaminated national space are not self-generated, but in fact are dependent upon the present-day encounter with other nations. It is only in response to foreign demands that Japan enters into treaties and speaks with a single voice that the Emperor displaces the Shogun as the ruling figure. Accordingly, "the day that brought restoration of imperial rule was also the day on which international relations began" (*TZ* 12:71). The movement to "restore" antiquity in this light stands as a prime example of ideological inversion: the Japanese national subject that is hailed into existence by the violent intervention of the Western powers misrecognizes itself as having existed since the dawn of history.

If book 1 narrates the discord leading up to the Meiji Restoration, the violence that Hanzō subsequently forgets, book 2 of the novel demonstrates the fragility of the national narrative that Hanzō produces through his acts of forgetting and disavowal. Gaps and discontinuities, conflict and disorder continue to trouble the interior of the nation even after 1868. While Hanzō continues to believe that Japan is on the verge of a grassroots awakening that will signal a true restoration of the harmonious "naturalness" of antiquity, what actually arises is more conflict as the new ruling factions fight among themselves and with other nations in Asia. Hanzō bemoans the proposed punitive expeditions against Korea and Taiwan because they miss the point of restoration—they are examples of the militaristic, "medieval" thought that the nation must overcome. Hanzō attempts to interpret this continued internal and external conflict in terms of *karagokoro*, that is, foreign Chinese thought that has contaminated the harmonious Japanese interior. But this fiction becomes increasingly difficult to maintain.

Hanzō's final decline into madness is punctuated by a series of increasingly violent actions through which he attempts to enforce the distinction between internal homogeneity and external heterogeneity, including the calendar reform proposal and his direct appeal to the Emperor (for which he is arrested). The last straw comes when Hanzō, increasingly subject to paranoid hallucinations, attempts to burn down a Buddhist temple that was founded by his own ancestors: to him, it is a symbol of the foreignness that continues to pollute the interior of Japan, even after the Meiji Restoration. In the wake of this incident, Hanzō's family locks him away, and, at the novel's end, he dies a pathetic death after years of confinement. This conclusion suggests a troubling possibility for any nationalist ideologue: the dream for a coherent and homogenous national identity is in fact a suicidal fantasy, a form of desire that ultimately destroys the desiring subject. In retrospect, it seems now that the novel's warning had an almost eerie prescience for Japan in 1935.

꠸

The 1930s *tenkōsha* who read a vision of reified national space in Tōson's writings transformed them into a call for Japan to liberate Asia from Western domination. This meant rewriting the supposed universal of Marxism itself into something particular, something national—National Socialism. Hence, the admonition from *tenkōsha* Sano Manabu: "To Orientalize, to Japanize, Western European socialist principles is most important of all."[91] The *tenkōsha* constructed an image of Japan through what Mary Louise Pratt calls narratives of "anti-conquest,"[92] transforming imperial expansion into something else. In the 1930s, they repeatedly narrated for Japan the role of a "Creole" nation, mobilizing claims of independence from and cultural equivalence to Europe to justify the domination (or "liberation") of Asia.[93] Within a few years, this led to calls for the ultimate sacrifice, repayment for what Deluze and Guattari call the "infinite debt" that national imagination demands in its most extreme forms.

But Aono Suekichi and Hayashi Tatsuo, among others, tried to locate in the novel a different version of history, one implying a different chronotope and a different model of literary production. They acknowledge the importance of Tōson's challenge to elitist versions of the Meiji Restoration, his creation of a bottom-up vision of social transformation. The problem they faced, especially the 1930's Marxist critics, in reading Tōson's works was how to arrive at a language by which they could speak to the revolutionary energies generated by groups other than the proletariat—precisely the sort of narrative presented in *Before the Dawn*.

As Harootunian has demonstrated, this situation arises from the unevenness inherent to modern capitalism and is by no means unique to Japan (neither, for that matter, was *tenkō*).[94] Ernst Bloch, writing about Germany in the 1930s, bemoaned the inability of Marxist movements to speak to the legitimate complaints farmers and others had with contemporary capitalism.[95] Their complaints, according to Bloch, arose from their contradicting the dominant mode of production from the past instead of the future (that is, from the position of the proletariat). Their contradiction was "nonsynchronous" to the present historical moment, demonstrating the simultaneous existence of a multiplicity of times. In the absence of a political practice that could link their nonsynchronous negation to what Bloch calls "the engine" of the proletariat, their revolutionary energy would be usurped by fascism, which at least pretended to take their complaints seriously.

Likewise, in looking back at the role of the Nativists in the Meiji Restoration, Marxist critics like Aono find something attractive in *Before the Dawn*. In Miyamoto Yuriko's words, "doesn't Hanzō's disillusionment present one facet of the masses' tragedy?"[96] They saw that the novel captured a part of the violence produced by the mid-nineteenth-century rise of modern capitalism and imperialism and that it linked this to the crisis facing Japan in the 1930s—even if the novel failed (from the perspective of Marxist historiography) to identify correctly the class forces at work behind history. In their essays, these critics struggle to find a language for reading the novel, for articulating its narrative to their political practice in useful ways. What they lacked and what Bloch lacked (and what Hayashi Tatsuo at least in part possessed) was a chronotope divorced from a teleological view of world history. What was needed was not a linear railroad journey to a predestined terminus, in which all social agents are pulled along behind a single "engine," but something different: a walk through smooth space, in which the final destination is to keep walking. These critics lacked a chronotope that enabled an understanding of history that began with the production of space in the present moment, a space riddled with small differences—one that troubled the pedagogical aspects of national and international narratives, even as it could never completely escape them.

In its multiple chronotopes, *Before the Dawn* both solicits and undermines the desire for an imagined national community. It simultaneously anticipates the dawn and warns that the dawn must never arrive. In the ways the novel and its early reception intersect with issues of class-based politics and anti-imperial struggles, it serves as a potent reminder of the fluidity and complexity of the rhetoric of national imagination, in Japan and beyond. And it reminds us that when we critique national imagination, our critique must remain an immanent critique, one that shares ground with its object. To do otherwise, to underestimate the complexity of national imagination and to imagine we can easily escape its field, would put us at risk of being inadvertently absorbed back into that field. It would leave us in danger of repeating the tragedy of not only Aoyama Hanzō, but also of the *tenkōsha*.

The Most Japanese of Things

It is the dead of winter in the southern hemisphere, and Shimazaki Tōson, age sixty-five, has just come ashore for a brief stopover. One year earlier, the new Japanese branch of the International PEN Club chose Tōson—riding the wave of acclaim that greeted *Before the Dawn*—as its first chair. Hence, it is as the official representative of Japan's modern literature that he is now traveling to Buenos Aires to attend the International PEN Club meeting the following month. This is in fact Tōson's second visit to Cape Town; he stopped over on his return to Japan from France in 1916 as well.

Befitting his status as one of the grand old men of modern Japanese literature, Tōson is feted by the resident Japanese community at each port of call on this journey, often by the local consul or ambassador. In Cape Town, he is hosted by "Mrs. E," a local Japanese resident.[1] He visits a monument to Cecil Rhodes, and he notes with surprise the severity of winter here in the southern hemisphere. But what most attracts his notice is the virulent racism he encounters.

The African in the driver's seat who guided us around was of mixed blood, Portuguese and the native Bushman tribe. Supposedly, all blacks are untrustworthy and steal, and that is why whites look down on them. But this African who was employed in Mrs. E's house served as driver when they went out on excursions, and when they were at home he tended to the hearth fire. He was of a gentle nature, honest, and truly

affectionate toward the family's children. If only he could have received
an education, he might well have become a great man, but blacks are not
permitted to receive education, nor are they permitted to enroll in
schools. In their discriminatory nature, the local practices were even
more severe than I had imagined.   (*TZ* 14:157)

The blatant prejudice shocks Tōson: in children of mixed blood from the same
family, he has been told, the accident of skin color is decisive: "Suppose, for
example, among the children of an African family [of mixed blood], there
were born two daughters, one resembling the white ancestors on her father's
side, the other the black ancestors on her mother's side. The lighter-skinned
daughter would receive a normal education, whereas the darker-skinned
daughter could not" (*TZ* 14:161).

As he reflects on his South African experience, Tōson connects it to Western racism against people from Africa, India, and East Asia. All through the trip,
he will encounter troubling instances of racism: anti-Japanese sentiments in
Brazil, the snubbing of an Indian passenger on board ship by a white passenger, the ill treatment suffered by "persons of color" in Baltimore, and so on.[2]
Such incidents help strengthen Tōson's own sense of Asianness, of standing on
the side of those who are scorned because of their skin color and the West's
Eurocentrism. He expresses strong sympathy, for example, for anticolonial
resistance movements in India against British rule, a sympathy he finds natural because "we are comrades of the Orient [*onaji tōyōjin nakama*]" (*TZ*
14:144). Likewise, when he finally reaches South America, he is delighted to
find that "here, there is no particular anti-oriental dogma such as we heard in
Durban and Cape Town. In that sense, this is truly a land of freedom" (*TZ*
14:176). Brazil appeals to Tōson—at least upon first impression—because it
seems a multicultural, multiracial melting pot.

And yet in addition to Western racism, Tōson makes another discovery on
this journey, one that is considerably more gratifying. As troubling as the Western tendency to hierarchize people on the basis of race and culture may be,
everywhere he goes Tōson finds evidence (especially in contrast to his visit to
many of the same ports some twenty years earlier) that Japan is rapidly moving up in this hierarchy. When he visited Cape Town in 1916, the Japanese
community there consisted of a lone bureaucrat who had been sent on an
exploratory mission by the Foreign Ministry. In 1936, however, Tōson finds
more than two thousand Japanese living in the city, engaged in all sorts of
activities. Japanese influence is rapidly spreading southward—here too, as he

had in earlier stops at Hong Kong, Singapore, and Colombo, Tōson sees concrete evidence that the much vaunted Southern Advance, Japan's widening of its sphere of influence across the Pacific, is becoming reality.[3] At many stops along his journey, he visits Japanese schools, Japanese community associations, and even Japanese cemeteries—all signs, along with the eight hundred Japanese emigrants bound for South America who are Tōson's shipmates, that Japan's global influence is rapidly increasing.

Tōson himself enjoys the privileges of this enhanced status during his stay in Cape Town. During his visits to the various sights of the city, Tōson and his party decide to stop for refreshments at a charming teahouse.

We were about to enter the teahouse when we found ourselves standing in front of a small sign that caught my eye.

"European only"

it said. This meant that non-Europeans were not supposed to enter. But we paid this no heed and walked right in, sitting down and taking our rest just like Europeans. There are a great many things to be said about the absurd prejudice that Europeans have toward Orientals, but among all oriental peoples, only we receive the same treatment as Europeans; I was strongly struck by the fact that wherever we go, we can be proud to be Japanese [warera Nihonjin no katami hiroi]   (TZ 14:158)

A few pages later Tōson returns to this subject of "honorary white" status: "I learned that among oriental peoples only the Japanese enjoy freedom from restrictions on residence or commercial activities. This was thanks to the efforts and influence of Consul Y, who was previously dispatched here from our country" (TZ 14:161).

On the one hand, classifying people by hierarchies of race and culture represents an evil legacy of Western imperialism in Asia, Africa, and South America. As an Asian nation, Japan must protest this and ally itself with the subalterns of the world. On the other hand, within this framework, Japan is making out pretty well. What does it mean, then, to be Japanese? Tōson wrestles with this dilemma throughout his journey. Is it acceptable, for example, for Japan simply to spread out horizontally, absorbing a greater and greater part of the globe's surface into its sphere of influence, or is it more important that Japanese settlers abroad put down roots and become firmly intertwined with the local cultures of their new homes? Tōson expresses dissatisfaction with Japanese settlers in Brazil and in Japan's own colony of Korea for failing to build permanent dwellings—a sign that they consider their stay abroad as something only temporary (*TZ* 14:226–28). Yet he reacts against a proposal in Brazil to require the second- and third-generation children of Japanese immigrants to attend classes taught in Portuguese rather than in Japanese. This proposal is somewhat understandable, since Brazil (unlike, according to Tōson, colonial Taiwan and Korea) possesses its own autonomous national culture, into which immigrants are expected to assimilate. Yet even if they live abroad, the Nisei and Sansei are after all Japanese and should be allowed to maintain their cultural roots. Tōson concludes that "it is desirable that they contribute to the development of South American culture with hearts that are, to the very end, Japanese-like [*doko made mo Nihonjin-rashii kokoro*]" (*TZ* 14:229). When he meets with the Brazilian Foreign Minister, Tōson pleads that the children of Japanese immigrants be allowed to continue their education in Japanese language and Japanese history (*TZ* 14:237–38).

This ongoing meditation on what it means to be Japanese, on what it means to call something "Japanese-like," crystallizes into a lecture that Tōson delivers at the Japanese embassy in Buenos Aires: "Mottomo Nihonteki naru mono" (The most Japanese of things).[4] Tōson has brought with him reproductions of paintings by the great Zen artist Sesshu (1420–1506), which he uses in an attempt to win appreciation for the cultural traditions of Japan and Asia. "I don't know how these matters sounded to the Argentineans, but at the very least I hoped that the artifacts of my and other oriental countries would become more widely known around the world and that there would be a deepening awareness of the Orient in terms of art" (*TZ* 14:210–11).

Tōson is gratified to find a receptive audience, not just among local Japanese but among others in attendance—including (although Tōson never identifies him by name) a member of the Italian PEN Club delegation, almost certainly the fascist ideologue and Futurist poet F. T. Marinetti. "When I presently finished my talk, one of the audience members came up to greet me. It was the Italian representative I had met at the PEN Club meeting. He was a poet who also, I have heard, writes art criticism, and he told me that my talk that evening had been most interesting and shook my hand warmly" (*TZ* 14:211).

This praise will subsequently trouble Tōson. When he leaves South America for New York City, he finds himself shipmates with another PEN Club delegate, this one a Jewish writer in exile from Nazi Germany (probably H. Levick):

> the PEN Club meeting gathered delegates from more than forty nations around the world, so that if there were some like this man who brought

with him an appeal against the injustice of his having been driven into exile by the Nazis, then too there were also men like the Italian representative who trumpeted the fascist spirit, and so conflicts of opinion between the various delegates were unavoidable....At any rate those like this person [the Jewish delegate] don't have to worry about the problem of a national language, as we do, nor does he have to worry about struggles of his country. Even among Jews, not all are willing like him to sacrifice humanity for the sake of principles. In the end, his struggles are not like ours, and his lack of sympathy toward Japan after our withdrawal from the League of Nations, and his apparent misunderstanding of our position, seemed to arise largely from far distant origins.   (*TZ* 14:245–46)

Again, Tōson struggles, somewhat more uncomfortably, to find a workable and yet ethical definition of what it means to be Japanese.

As the journey continues, Tōson discovers that ambivalence of national identity is not unique to Japan. After traveling through the Eastern United States, climbing to the top of the Empire State Building, touring the Hudson car factory in Detroit (where he is struck by the efficiency and scale of the assembly line), visiting such cultural landmarks as Harvard University and the Library of Congress, and spending election night 1936 among the crowds in Times Square, Tōson looks back with mixed feelings on this nation. He recalls the warm respect that was shown when a former Japanese ambassador to the United States passed away and his body was returned to Japan on a U.S. warship with full state honors. Yet he cannot help also remembering that this is the same United States that has produced violent Yellow-Peril racism against Japanese. Just as it is also the same United States that used brute force but also showed great understanding in opening up Japan during the days of Matthew Perry and Townsend Harris: "the conduct of those two men already told of this contradiction. America is by no means always a warm country, and yet neither is it always a cold country" (*TZ* 14:277).

❀

In seeking the most Japanese of things, Tōson found himself entangled in the complexity of national imagination. The rhetoric of national imagination weaves together the most contradictory strands of thought and perception into a single, often irregular, fabric of experience. As Tōson discovered, it can be simultaneously warm and cold. It invokes implacable opposites within a single breath: anti-imperialism *and* colonial expansion, antiracism *and* racial superiority, cosmopolitanism *and* national essence. On the field of national imagination, liberalism finds itself shaking hands with fascism—and with Marxism, too. In this work, I have tried to unpack this complexity and fluidity across a variety of domains—hygiene, the family, gender, literature, the fields of time and space. We have seen how national imagination simultaneously assimilates and excludes, how it claims homogeneity yet is able to translate into its own terms even specifically antinational thoughts and acts. We have also seen how it insinuated itself across a spectrum of genres, from romantic poetry and confessional I-novels to historical fiction and literary criticism.

In recent years, in the wake of globalization and "postmodernity," critics from across the political spectrum have announced the imminent demise of the nation as a hegemonic form of identity. The left-leaning historian E. J. Hobsbawm proclaims that nationalism and the nation are "no longer a major vector of historical development,"[5] while Japanese management guru Kenichi Ohmae avers that "traditional nation states have become unnatural, even impossible, business units in a global economy."[6]

I have pursued this project, however, under the belief that we have not transcended the age of the nation and nation-state. I have approached nationalism and globalization not as opposing tendencies, but rather two aspects of a single overarching process, what Wallerstein calls the modern world-system.[7] As Frederick Buell argues, contemporary nationalism should be perceived as "a concomitant of intensified globalization," so that intensified global "integration has thus paradoxically meant, and continues to mean, proliferation of asserted [national] differences."[8] Nagahara Yutaka has usefully theorized this problematic as "the subtending tautness between, on the one hand, globalization as an innately impossible dream of capital to liberate and release itself totally from territorial closure and, on the other, the nation-state (or national economy) as the result of capital's incessant and reiterative negotiation with the actuality that capital must discover . . . or inherit from the past," a necessarily irresolvable contradiction crucial to social and economic reproduction.[9]

Unlike Hobsbawm and Ohmae, then, I interpret the enormous changes we have seen in the half-century since Tōson's death not as a paradigm shift but as the intensification of a process that has been underway since the beginning of the modern world-system in the sixteenth century. This process has been flexible enough to incorporate not only colonialism, but also anticolonial resistance and neocolonialism. In sum, it has only been in tandem with the global expansion of capitalism that the modern nation and national imagination have emerged, and what we have witnessed in recent decades is a quantitative intensification of those forces, not the introduction of a qualitatively new tendency.

In this light, Tōson's struggles to maintain his balance on the uneven and shifting field of national imagination remain quite relevant to our own efforts to maintain an ethical stance today. A productive and ethical critique needs to locate itself among the small differences that are simultaneously produced and concealed through large binary oppositions central to the functioning of modern societies—including the distinction between nationalism and antinationalism. Perhaps the most important lesson we can learn from the example of Tōson and his readers is that it is often at the moment when we think we are finally free of the rhetoric of national imagination that we are in fact most densely enmeshed in it.

NOTES

Introduction

1. This passage is quoted in Nakayama Hiroaki, "*Wakanashū* no juyōken: Tōson-chō to iu seido" (The sphere of reception of *Wakanashū* [A collection of seedlings]: The system that was the Tōson style), *Kokugo to kokubungaku* 70, no. 7 (July 1993): 26–27. It comes from Akita's article "Saisho no kokumin shijin toshite no Shimazaki Tōson-shi" (Shimazaki Tōson as the first national poet), first published in a special issue of *Ningen* (April 1921) devoted to Tōson and his works.

2. Benedict Anderson, *Imagined Communities: Reflections on the Origin and Spread of Nationalism* (London: Verso, 1983).

3. See Suga Hidemi, *Nihon kindai bungaku no "tanjō": genbun itchi to nashonarizumu* (The "birth" of Japanese modern literature: *Genbun itchi* and nationalism), (Tokyo: Ōta Shuppan, 1995), especially pp. 16–56.

4. F. Scott Fitzgerald, *The Crack Up* (New York: New Directions, 1945), 69.

5. On the "outsider"/"insider" distinction, see Andrew Barshay, *State and Intellectual in Imperial Japan: The Public Man in Crisis* (Berkeley: University of California Press, 1988). On the changing shape of nationalism in the mid-Meiji period, see Daikichi Irokawa, *The Culture of the Meiji Period*, trans. Marius B. Jansen (Princeton: Princeton University Press, 1985); Carol Gluck, *Japan's Modern Myths: Ideology in the Late Meiji Period* (Princeton: Princeton University Press, 1985); and Kenneth Pyle, *The New Generation in Meiji Japan: Problems of Cultural Identity, 1885–1895* (Stanford: Stanford University Press, 1969).

6. Eiji Oguma, *A Genealogy of "Japanese" Self-Images*, trans. David Askew (Melbourne: Trans Pacific Press, 2002), xxi.

7. Tōson would eventually publish four poetry collections (which also contain essays and brief works of fiction): *Wakanashū* (A collection of seedlings, 1897), *Hitohabune* (A leaflike boat, 1898), *Natsukusa* (Summer grass, 1898), and *Rakubaishū* (Fallen plum blossoms, 1901). The "Preface" quoted here was written for *Tōson shishū* (Tōson's collected poems, 1904), which included poems from all four previous collections.

8. Donald Keene, *Dawn to the West: Japanese Literature in the Modern Era: Poetry, Drama, Criticism* (New York: Henry Holt, 1984), 204. See also James R. Morita, "Shimazaki Tōson's Four Collections of Poems," *Monumenta Nipponica* 35, nos. 3–4 (1970): 325–69; Steve Rabson, "Shimazaki Tōson on War," *Monumenta Nipponica* 46, no. 4 (1991): 453–81; and Jutta Kuhnast, *Das Epische im Fruhwerk des Shimazaki Toson: die Gedichtsammlung* (Hamburg: Gesellschaft fur Natur- und Volkerkunde Ostasiens, 1973).

9. Critics have speculated that the predilection for dramatic monologue in Tōson's

poetry was one factor that eventually led him to abandon poetry for prose fiction, where he could more fully realize his narrative imagination. See, for example, Gotō Kōji, "*Wakanashū* no shutai hyōgen ni tsuite" (On subjective expression in *Wakanashū* [A collection of seedlings]), *Gobun ronsō* 8 (September 1980), 46–61.

10. Itō Shinkichi, *Shimazaki Tōson no bungaku* (The literature of Shimazaki Tōson) (Tokyo: Daiichi Shobō, 1936), 310. I refer to a facsimile reproduction of the first edition, reprinted as vol. 5 of *Kindai sakka kenkyū sōsho* (Tokyo: Nihon tosho sentā, 1983).

11. Itō, *Shimazaki*, 323–25. For another early reading of the poetry in terms of nationalistic spirit, see Yoshie Takamatsu, "Jōnetsu no shijin Tōson" (Tōson the poet of passion), *Bunshō ōrai* 1, no. 4 (April 1925): 16–18.

12. Keene, *Poetry*, 194–204.

13. On Meiji haiku and tanka reform movements, see Keene, *Poetry*, 7–57 and 88–118; Janine Beichman, *Masaoka Shiki* (Boston: Twayne, 1982); and Robert H. Brower, "Masaoka Shiki and Tanka Reform," in *Tradition and Modernization in Japanese Culture*, ed. Donald H. Shively (Princeton: Princeton University Press, 1971), 379–418. It should be noted that Tōson implicitly rejected Shiki's version of the classical canon; Bashō, along with the twelfth-century tanka poet Saigyō, would remain central to Tōson's own vision of traditional Japanese poetry.

14. Takayama's review-essays were originally published in the journal *Taiyō* and are reprinted in *Chogyū zenshū* (Complete works of Chogyū), (Tokyo: Hakubunkan, 1926): "Doi Bansui ni ataete tōkon no bundan wo ronzuru sho" (For Doi Bansui: On the current literary world; originally published February, 1900), 2:498–511; "Mōrō-ha no shijin ni atau" (To poets of the vague school; July, 1897), 2:545–48; "Mōrō-tai no matsuro" (The last days of the vague style; September, 1897), 2:548–52; and "Bansui no shi" (Bansui's poems; December, 1897), 2:575–80. I thank Satō Nobuhiro for his assistance in helping me understand Takayama's critique and other issues related to Tōson's poetry.

15. Nakayama, "*Wakanashū* no juyōken."

16. H. D. Harootunian, "Between Politics and Culture: Authority and Ambiguities of Intellectual Choice in Imperial Japan," in *Japan in Crisis: Essays on Taishō Democracy*, ed. Bernard S. Silberman and H. D. Harootunian (Princeton: Princeton University Press, 1974), 140.

17. T. Fujitani, *Splendid Monarchy: Power and Pageantry in Modern Japan* (Berkeley: University of California Press, 1996), especially 171–194.

18. Seki Reiko, "Tatakau 'chichi no musume': Ichiyō tekusuto no seisei" (Fighting "Daughter of the father": The formation of Ichiyō's texts), in *Onna ga yomu Nihon kindai bungaku: feminizumo hihyō no kokoromi* (Modern Japanese literature as read by women: An attempt at feminist criticism), ed. Egusa Mitsuko and Urushida Kazuo (Tokyo: Shinyōsha, 1992), 31–54. See also Rebecca Copeland, *Lost Leaves: Women Writers of Meiji Japan* (Honolulu: University of Hawaii Press, 2000), 44.

19. There are foreshadowings of Akiko's poetry in many of Tōson's poems—for example, the following stanza from "Kasa no uchi" ("Under the umbrella"): "Face and face brought together / each step summoning fond memories / her black hair with plum-blossom oil / tangled, fragrant under the umbrella" (*TZ* 1:56). This is not to say the two are completely similar: Akiko demonstrates, for example, a greater willingness to violate the rules of rhythm with irregular "lines" that explode the metric norms of the tanka genre.

By contrast, Tōson's poems, especially in the early anthologies, stick methodically to 7–5 patterns (with occasional forays into 7–7 and 8–6) and contain almost no irregular lines. One of the pleasures of Tōson's poetry is its use of refrain and regular rhythm; conversely, one of the pleasures of Akiko's is her creative destruction of conventional patterns.

20. Kōno Kensuke, "Joshi kyōiku to *Wakanashū*: ren'ai no seijigaku" (Women's Education and *Wakanashū* [A collection of seedlings]: The political science of romantic love), *Nihon no bungaku* 12 (December 1993), 27–44.

21. For a partial translation of this lengthy poem, see Morita, "Four Collections," 367–68.

22. Ueno Chizuko, *Kindai kazoku no seiritsu to shūen* (The rise and fall of the modern family) (Tokyo: Iwanami Shoten, 1994), 88. For a reading of Tōson's poetry that historicizes it against shifting practices of marriage, see Koseki Kazuhiro, " 'Ren'ai' to iu gensō: ren'ai shi no ken'iki" (The fantasy of romantic love: The sphere of love poetry), *Kokubungaku* 41, no. 13 (November 1996): 42–48.

23. Quoted in Kimata Satoshi, "Tōson no romanchishizumu" (Tōson's romanticism), in *Nihon bungaku kōza 10: shiika II (kindai hen)* (Lectures on Japanese literature 10: Poetry II [modern]), ed. Nihon Bungaku Kyōkai (Tokyo: Taishūkan Shoten, 1988), 103–19. I thank Nosaka Akio for sharing with me his insights into the thought of Yasuda Yojūrō.

24. For translations, see Morita, "Four Collections," 358–59; and Donald Keene, ed., *Modern Japanese Literature* (New York: Grove Press, 1956), 201.

25. Yoshie, "Jōnetsu no shijin Tōson," 17.

26. For translations, see Morita, "Four Collections," 359–61; and Hiroaki Sato and Burton Watson, eds., *From the Country of Eight Islands* (New York: Columbia University Press, 1986), 429.

27. The Chinese characters used in the poem's title can be read more than one way, and there is some disagreement among scholars as to which is the correct reading. Some scholars cite the poem as "Shione."

28. Sasabuchi Tomoichi, *Shōsetsuka Shimazaki Tōson* (Novelist Shimazaki Tōson) (Tokyo: Meiji Shoin, 1990), 91–96.

29. On the concept of "suturing," see Ernesto Laclau and Chantal Mouffe, *Hegemony and Socialist Strategy: Towards a Radical Democratic Politics* (London: Verso, 1985).

30. Shimazaki Tōson in 1941, as quoted in Kamei Katsuichirō, *Shimazaki Tōson ron* (On Shimazaki Tōson), (Tokyo: Shinchōsha, 1953), 312.

31. The most comprehensive English language critical biography is William E. Naff, "Shimazaki Tōson: A Critical Biography" (Ph.D. diss., University of Washington, 1965). Other good sources include Edwin McClellan, *Two Japanese Novelists: Sōseki and Tōson* (Chicago: University of Chicago Press, 1969); and Janet Walker, *The Japanese Novel of the Meiji Period and the Idea of Individualism* (Princeton: Princeton University Press, 1979). A standard biography in Japanese is Senuma Shigeki, *Shimazaki Tōson: Sono shōgai to sakuhin* (Shimazaki Tōson: His life and works), (Tokyo: Kaku Shobō, 1953).

32. Iwano Hōmei (1873–1920) was an author of Naturalist fiction and somewhat occult theoretical essays. His later writings in particular invoke a mystical and protofascist form of Japanism. Hayashi Fusao (1903–1975) was a Marxist author who in the 1930s underwent *tenkō* (ideological conversion) and became a right-wing nationalist, a position he maintained even in the postwar period. Both writers will be discussed again in later chapters.

33. Etienne Balibar and Immanuel Wallerstein, *Race, Nation, Class: Ambiguous Identities* (London: Verso, 1991), 45–46.

34. Anderson, *Imagined Communities*, 15.

35. Eve Kosofsky Sedgwick, "Nationalisms and Sexualities in the Age of Wilde," in *Nationalisms and Sexualities*, ed. Andrew Parker et al. (New York: Routledge, 1992), 238.

36. Sedgwick, "Nationalisms and Sexualities," 241.

37. Partha Chatterjee, *The Nation and Its Fragments: Colonial and Postcolonial Histories* (Princeton: Princeton University Press, 1993).

38. Marilyn Ivy, *Discourses of the Vanishing: Modernity, Phantasm, Japan* (Chicago: University of Chicago Press, 1995).

39. Harry Harootunian, *Overcome By Modernity: History, Culture, and Community in Interwar Japan* (Princeton: Princeton University Press, 2000), 422n28.

40. Nira Yuval-Davis, *Gender and Nation* (London: SAGE Publications, 1997), 4.

41. Tessa Morris-Suzuki, *Re-Inventing Japan: Time Space Nation* (Armonk, N.Y.: M.E. Sharpe, 1998), 170.

42. Gilles Deleuze and Félix Guattari, *Anti-Oedipus: Capitalism and Schizophrenia*, trans. Robert Hurley, Mark Seem, and Helen R. Lane (Minneapolis: University of Minnesota Press, 1983), 151.

43. See, for example, E. J. Hobsbawm, *Nations and Nationalism Since 1780: Programme, Myth, Reality* (Cambridge: Cambridge University Press, 1990); and Kenichi Ohmae, *The End of the Nation State: The Rise of Regional Economies* (London: Harper Collins, 1995).

44. Balibar and Wallerstein, *Race, Nation, Class*, 84. See also Frederick Buell, *National Culture and the New Global System* (Baltimore: John Hopkins University Press, 1994); and Karatani Kōjin, *NAM: Genri* (NAM: Basic principles), (Tokyo: Ōta Shuppan, 2000).

Chapter 1. Tōson, Literary History, and National Imagination

1. Gregory Jusdanis, *Belated Modernity and Aesthetic Culture: Inventing National Literature* (Minneapolis: University of Minnesota Press, 1991), 76.

2. Haruo Shirane, "Introduction: Issues in Canon Formation," in *Inventing the Classics: Modernity, National Identity, and Japanese Literature*, ed. Shirane and Tomi Suzuki (Stanford: Stanford University Press, 2000), 1–18.

3. For a more extended discussion of these issues, see my "Kokusaika no naka no Tōson: Ōbei no baai" (Tōson and internationalization: The case in the West), *Shimazaki Tōson kenkyū* 29 (2001), 51–59.

4. Joseph Roggendorf, "Yōroppajin no mita Shimazaki Tōson" (Shimazaki Tōson as seen by Europeans), *Bungei* 11, no. 12 (September 1954): 23. Roggendorf had earlier published one of the first English-language articles to discuss Tōson at length: "Shimazaki Tōson: A Maker of the Modern Japanese Novel," *Monumenta Nipponica* 7, no. 1–2 (1951): 38–66.

5. Donald Keene, *Dawn to the West: Japanese Literature in the Modern Era: Fiction* (New York: Henry Holt, 1984), 254–71.

6. For example, Edwin McClellan declares that while Natsume Sōseki is "an essentially 'Western' novelist," Tōson is more "traditional," because in writing I-novels, he "might very well have been giving expression to the traditional Japanese conviction that

poetry and the essay are the respectable literary forms, while fiction is for the vulgar." "Tōson and the Autobiographical Novel," in *Tradition and Modernization in Japanese Culture*, ed. Donald H. Shively (Princeton: Princeton University Press, 1971), 353–54.

7. Terry Eagleton, *Literary Theory: An Introduction* (Minneapolis: University of Minnesota Press, 1983), 50.

8. See Douglas Mao, "The New Critics and the Text-Object," *ELH* 63, no. 1 (1996): 227–254; and Frank A. Ninkovich, "The New Criticism and Cold War America," *The Southern Quarterly* 20, no. 1 (fall 1981): 1–24.

9. Takashi Fujitani, "*Minshūshi* As Critique of Orientalist Knowledges," *positions* 6, no. 2 (1998): 310. For other critiques of modernization theory in Japan Studies, see John Dower, "E. H. Norman, Japan, and the Uses of History," in E. H. Norman, *Origins of the Modern Japanese State: Selected Writings of E. H. Norman*, ed. Dower (New York: Pantheon, 1975), 3–101; and H. D. Harootunian, "America's Japan, Japan's Japan," in *Japan in the World*, ed. Masao Miyoshi and Harootunian (Durham, N.C.: Duke University Press, 1993), 196–221.

10. Hence, William F. Sibley would conclude his important article, "Naturalism in Japanese Literature," (*Harvard Journal of Asiatic Studies* 28 [1968]: 157–69), with the following declaration: "Neither imitations of Western literature nor throwbacks to an eclipsed Japanese tradition, these works stand on their own."

11. On the early criticism of *Ie* (The family), see Yoshida Seiichi, *Shimazaki Tōson*, vol. 6 of *Yoshida Seiichi chosakushū* (Selected works of Yoshida Seiichi) (Tokyo: Ōfūsha, 1971), 93–94; and Ōida Yoshiaki, "*Ie* no jikan: chichi to no kaikō" (Time in *Ie* [The family]: Chance encounters with the father), *Bungei to hihyō* 6, no. 3 (March 1986): 44–55.

12. Maeda Akira, "*En* to *Gisei* gōhyō: egaku saku to kataru saku" (*En* [Relation] and *Gisei* [Sacrifices]: Works that describe and works that narrate), originally published in *Waseda bungaku*, February 1911; reprinted in *TZ* 18:164–66.

13. Nakamura Seiko, "Shimazaki-shi no *Ie* to Shusei-shi no *Kabi*" (Shimazaki's *Ie* [The family] and Shusei's *Kabi* [Moss]), originally published in *Waseda bungaku*, March 1912; reprinted in *TZ* 18:203–7.

14. Jay Rubin, *Injurious to Public Morals: Writers and the Meiji State* (Seattle: University of Washington Press, 1984), 214.

15. See Itō Shirō, "Shimazaki Tōson ron" (On Shimazaki Tōson), *Yuibutsuron kenkyū* 63 (January 1938): 78–96.

16. On *tenkō*, see Shunsuke Tsurumi, *An Intellectual History of Wartime Japan, 1931–1945* (London: KPI Limited, 1986); and Patricia Steinhoff, *Tenkō: Ideology and Societal Integration in Prewar Japan* (New York: Garland, 1991).

17. Mizukami Ryūtarō, "Shimazaki Tōson sensei no ashiato (kaigara tsuihō)" (In the footprints of Shimazaki Tōson [leaving the shell behind]), *Chūō kōron* 44, no. 7 (July 1929): 289–302.

18. Kawabata Yasunari (1899–1972) had already detected this tendency in 1929, with only one installment of *Before the Dawn* in print. He complained that what was needed at the time was a serious reevaluation of Tōson's works, not the sort of hagiography that Mizukami (see previous note) writes. Kawabata Yasunari, "Bungei jihyō" (Literary arts today), originally published in *Bungei shunjū*, August 1929; reprinted in *TZ* 18:297–300.

19. On the rise of modern literary studies in the postwar Japanese university, see

Kamei Hideo, "Author's Preface to the English Translation" in Kamei, *Transformations of Sensibility: The Phenomenology of Meiji Literature*, trans. Michael Bourdaghs (Ann Arbor: University of Michigan Center for Japanese Studies Publications, 2002). On the history of academic literary scholarship in 1930s Japan and its links to nationalism, see Murai Osamu, "Kokubungaku no jūgonen sensō" (The fifteen years war in Japanese literature studies), parts 1 and 2, *Hihyō kūkan* 2d ser., no. 16 (1998): 170–87; no. 18 (1998): 170–81.

20. Suzuki Sadami, *Nihon no "bungaku" gainen* (The concept of "literature" in Japan) (Tokyo: Sakuhinsha, 1998).

21. Peter Uwe Hohendahl, *Building a National Literature: The Case of Germany, 1820–1870*, trans. Renate Baron Franciscono (Ithaca, N.Y.: Cornell University Press, 1989), 202.

22. Okazaki Yoshie, "Tōson ron joshō" (Preface to a study of Tōson), *Bungaku* 4, no. 8 (August 1936): 12. *Aware, yūshin, wabi,* and *shiori* are all terms widely used in premodern Japanese discourses on literature to describe certain aesthetic qualities. Mori Ōgai (1862–1922), Kōda Rohan, and Natsume Sōseki are all major canonical literary figures, more or less contemporary with Tōson.

23. Itō Shinkichi, *Shimazaki Tōson no bungaku* (The literature of Shimazaki Tōson) (Tokyo: Daiichi Shobō, 1936), 104. A facsimile reproduction of the first edition is reprinted as vol. 5 of *Kindai sakka kenkyū sōsho* (Tokyo: Nihon Tosho Sentā, 1983).

24. This is according to the bibliography of Tōson scholarship, Saeki Yūichirō, "Tōson kenkyū bunken," published in the special Tōson issue of *Bungaku* (4, no. 8 [August 1936]: 157–69). In fact, the issue lists four university theses that were devoted to Tōson in 1932.

25. Senuma Shigeki, as quoted in Kakita Tokiya, "Kaisetsu" (Afterword), afterword to *Shimazaki Tōson no bungaku*, by Itō Shinkichi, a new essay appended to the 1983 facsimile reprint edition.

26. For details on Itō's life in this period, see Kakita, "Kaisetsu." See also Tōkoku Atsushi, " 'Haiboku' no mukō: Itō Shinkichi to tenkō," *Shakai bungaku* 18 (2003): 26–37.

27. Itō Shinkichi, "*Shimazaki Tōson no bungaku* shuppan wo meguru kaisō" (Reminiscences about the publication of *Shimazaki Tōson no bungaku* [The literature of Shimazaki Tōson]), 13. The piece is a brief memoir appended to the 1983 reprint of the first edition.

28. Itō Shinkichi, "*Shimazaki Tōson no bungaku* shuppan wo meguru kaisō," 6.

29. Many Marxist critics were less enthusiastic about the version of "sociality" found in *Before the Dawn*. In 1938 Itō Shirō, for example, praises *Before the Dawn* for being Tōson's first novel with real "sociality," yet he argues that this arises more from the material that Tōson dealt with in the book than from his approach. While Tōson had clearly engaged in much research, he failed to organize his material according to a single, fixed standard, and as a result failed to grasp the true historical forces behind the Restoration (see Itō Shirō, "Shimazaki Tōson ron" (On Shimazaki Tōson), especially 86–87). It was precisely this sort of reading that Itō Shinkichi was attempting to counter in his book on Tōson.

30. Itō Shinkichi, *Shimazaki Tōson no bungaku*, 308–9. Further references to this work in this chapter are cited parenthetically.

31. The I-novel (*watakushi shōsetsu* or *shishōsetsu*) was a genre of autobiographical fiction that enjoyed wide popularity in Japan in the 1920s and 1930s. It will be discussed at greater length in subsequent chapters.

32. Hayashi Fusao, "Tenkō ni tsuite" (On *tenkō*), in *Shōwa hihyō taikei* (Anthology of *shōwa* criticism), ed. Muramatsu Takeshi, Saeki Shōichi, and Ōkubo Tsuneo, (Tokyo: Banchō Shobō, 1968), 2:239–61. Originally serialized in *Bungakkai* in 1941

33. Kobayasi Hideo, *Kobayashi Hideo zenshū* (Complete works of Kobayashi Hideo), (Tokyo: Shinchōsha, 1968), 3:127. Further references are to the original Japanese version of this work and are cited parenthetically. The essay is available in English translation in Kobayashi Hideo, *The Literature of the Lost Home: Literary Criticism, 1924–39*, trans. Paul Anderer (Stanford: Stanford University Press, 1995).

34. A similar link between naturalism and proletarian literature is made in another essay from the period, one that explicitly takes up the problem of *tenkō*: Nakamura Mitsuo's "Tenkō sakka ron" (On *tenkō* authors), In *Shōwa hihyō taikei*, ed. Muramatsu, Saeki, and Okubo, 2:314–29. Originally published in *Bungakkai* (Feb. 1935).

35. Hayashi Fusao, "Tenkō ni tsuite," 242. On Hayashi, see Kevin Michael Doak, *Dreams of Difference: The Japan Romantic School and the Crisis of Modernity* (Berkeley: University of California Press, 1994), 107–30.

36. Kamei Katsuichirō, *Shimazaki Tōson: ippyōhakusha no shōzō* (Shimazaki Tōson: Portrait of a wanderer) (Tokyo: Kōbundō Shobō, 1939), reprinted as *Kindai sakka kenkyū sōsho*, vol. 124 (Tokyo: Nihon Tosho Sentā, 1993). I am using this facsimile reprint of the 1939 first edition. On Kamei, see Doak, *Dreams of Difference*, 78–106; and Tomone Matsumoto, "From Marxism to Japanism: A Study of Kamei Katsuichirō (1907–1967)," (Ph.D. diss., University of Arizona, 1979).

37. Kamei Katsuichirō, *Shimazaki Tōson: ippyōhakusha no shōzō*, 134.

38. From the 1947 revised edition, reprinted in Kamei Katsuichirō, *Kamei Katsuichirō zenshū* (Complete works of Kamei Katsuichirō), (Tokyo: Kōdansha, 1972), 3:226.

39. Yoshikuni Igarashi, *Bodies of Memory: Narratives of War in Postwar Japanese Culture, 1945–1970* (Princeton: Princeton University Press, 2000), 3.

40. See Lawrence Olson, *Ambivalent Moderns: Portraits of Japanese Cultural Identity* (Savage, Md.: Rowman & Littlefield, 1992).

41. Leslie Pincus, *Authenticating Culture in Imperial Japan: Kuki Shūzō and the Rise of National Aesthetics* (Berkeley: University of California Press, 1996), 5.

42. Tessa Morris-Suzuki, *Re-Inventing Japan: Time Space Nation* (Armonk, N.Y.: M. E. Sharpe, 1998), 145. I will discuss Watsuji Tetsurō (1889–1960) at more length in chapter five.

43. There were, however, exceptions, notably Shibata Michiko, who attacked the novel for its discriminatory nature, arguing that it had no place in a humanistic curriculum. See, for example, her *Hisabetsu buraku no denshō to seikatsu: Shinshū no buraku korō kikigaki* (Folklore and lifestyles of the *hisabetu buraku*: An oral history of elders in the *Shinshū buraku*) (Tokyo: San'ichi Shobō, 1975), 84–86. For a rebuttal, see Higashi Eizō, *Hakai no hyōka to buraku mondai* (Evaluation of *Hakai* [Broken commandment] and the *buraku* question) (Tokyo: Meiji Tosho Shuppan, 1977), 34–76.

44. Daikichi Irokawa, *The Culture of the Meiji Period*, trans. Marius B. Jansen (Princeton: Princeton University Press, 1985).

45. Takashi Fujitani, "*Minshūshi* As Critique of Orientalist Knowledges."

46. Carol Gluck, "The People in History: Recent Trends in Japanese Historiography," *Journal of Asian Studies* 38, no. 1 (November 1978): 32.

47. Murai Osamu, *Nantō ideorogii no hassei* (Origins of the South Islands ideology), rev. ed. (Tokyo: Ōta Shuppan, 1995). For a more sympathetic reading of Yanagita's work, one that locates an anti-imperialist impulse in it, see Eiji Oguma, *A Genealogy of "Japanese" Self-Images*, trans. David Askew (Melbourne: Trans Pacific Press, 2002), 175–202.

48. See Oguma, *Genealogy of "Japanese" Self-Images*, especially xxviii–xxxi.

49. J. Victor Koschmann, "Intellectuals and Politics," in *Postwar Japan as History*, ed. Andrew Gordon (Berkeley: University of California Press, 1993), 411.

50. Tetsuo Najita and H. D. Harootunian, "Japan's Revolt Against the West," in *Modern Japanese Thought*, ed. Bob Tadashi Wakabayashi (Cambridge: Cambridge University Press, 1998), 271.

51. On the ideological use of the "family" in postwar Japanese cultural nationalism, see Morris-Suzuki, *Re-Inventing Japan*, 110–139; and Kosaku Yoshino, *Cultural Nationalism in Contemporary Japan* (London: Routledge, 1992), 89–94 and 219–225.

52. Jennifer Robinson, "It Takes a Village: Internationalization and Nostalgia in Postwar Japan," in *Mirror of Modernity: Invented Traditions of Modern Japan*, ed. Stephen Vlastos (Berkeley: University of California Press, 1998), 116.

53. Ōkubo Tsuneo, "*Hakai*: sono soko ni aru mono" (*Hakai* [The broken commandment]: Getting to the bottom of it), *Kokubungaku* 16, no. 5 (April, 1971), 110.

54. Shuichi Katō, *The Modern Years*, vol. 3 of *A History of Japanese Literature*, trans. Don Sanderson (Tokyo: Kodansha International, 1979), 168. See also Katō's "Tōson to iwayuru shizenshugi" (Tōson and so-called naturalism) in *Sekai ga yomu Nihon kindai bungaku* (The world reads modern Japanese literature), vol. 3, ed. Fukuoka UNESCO Kyōkai (Tokyo: Maruzen, 1999), 17–36.

55. Suga Hidemi, "Kokumin to iu sukyandaru: 'Teikoku' no bungaku 1" (The scandal that is the nation: The literature of empire 1), in *Hihyō kūkan* 2d ser., no. 13 (1997): 226–46.

56. On the "blood" trope in Tōson criticism, see Kotani Hiroyuki, *Rekishi to ningen ni tsuite: Tōson to kindai Nihon* (On history and humanity: Tōson and modern Japan) (Tokyo: Tōkyō Daigaku Shuppankai, 1991), especially 42–48.

57. Senuma Shigeki, "Chi ni tsunagaru furusato" (The *furusato* linked by blood), *Taiyō* 195 (March 1972), 48.

58. This is from the 1983 essay, "Tōson: hito to bungaku" (Tōson: The man and his literature), reprinted in Miyoshi Yukio, *Shimazaki Tōson ron* (On Shimazaki Tōson), vol. 1 of *Miyoshi Yukio chosaku shū* (Collected works of Miyoshi Yukio) (Tokyo: Chikuma Shobō, 1993), 346.

59. Morris-Suzuki, *Re-Inventing Japan*, 126.

60. Watanabe Hiroshi, *Shimazaki Tōson o yominaosu* (Rereading Shimazaki Tōson) (Tokyo: Sōjusha, 1994), 115, 123.

61. Yamashita Etsuko, *Mazakon bungakuron* (On literature of the mother complex) (Tokyo: Shinyōsha, 1991), especially 41–55.

62. Watsuji Tetsurō, "Tōson no kosei" (Tōson's individuality) reprinted in *Watsuji Tetsurō zenshū* (Complete works of Watsuji Tetsurō), vol. 3 (Tokyo: Iwanami Shoten, 1962), 441.

63. This comes from the response Enchi made to a questionnaire published in a special Tōson issue of the magazine *Bungei* 11, no. 12 (September 1954), 227–32.

64. Marilyn Ivy, *Discourses of the Vanishing: Modernity, Phantasm, Japan* (Chicago: University of Chicago Press, 1995), 20.

65. On late-1940s Marxism in Japan, see J. Victor Koschmann, *Revolution and Subjectivity in Postwar Japan* (Chicago: University of Chicago Press, 1996).

66. Yoshimoto Takaaki, "Tenkō ron" (On *tenkō*, 1958), reprinted in *Seiji shisō* (Political thought), vol. 3 of *Yoshimoto Takaaki zenshūsen* (Collected works of Yoshimoto Takaaki) (Tokyo: Yamato Shobō, 1986), 10. Further references are to the reprint edition of this essay and will be cited parenthetically.

67. See, for example, the discussion of whether Tōson's *The Family* fits the mode of "family novel" that Yoshimoto had proposed in his *Kyōdō gensō ron* (Theory of communal illusion, 1968) in a 1971 symposium on Tōson and Japanese modernity: Miyoshi Yukio et al., "Shimazaki Tōson to Nihon no kindai" (Shimazaki Tōson and Japanese modernity), *Kokubungaku* 16, no. 5 (April 1971): 8–49.

68. Yoshimoto, quoted in Olson, *Ambivalent Moderns*, 102.

69. Tsurumi, *An Intellectual History of Wartime Japan*, 120.

70. Olson, *Ambivalent Moderns*, 134.

71. Tsurumi, quoted in Olson, *Ambivalent Moderns*, 141.

72. Brett de Bary, " 'Credo Quia Absurdum': *Tenkō* and the Prisonhouse of Language," in *Culture and Identity: Japanese Intellectuals During the Interwar Years*, ed. J. Thomas Rimer (Princeton: Princeton University Press, 1990), 154–67.

73. H. D. Harootunian, review of *An Intellectual History of Wartime Japan* and *A Cultural History of Postwar Japan*, by Shunsuke Tsurumi, *Journal of Japanese Studies* 15, no. 1 (winter 1989), 248–54; emphasis. For Tsurumi's thoughtful response, see his *Gendai Nihon shisō shi* (Contemporary Japanese intellectual history), vol 5 of *Tsurumi Shunsuke shū* (Tsurumi Shunsuke Anthology) (Tokyo: Chikuma Shobō, 1991), 493–98.

74. Isoda Kōichi, *Hikaku tenkō ron josetsu* (Preface to a theory of comparative *tenkō*), 2nd rev. ed. (Tokyo: Sōkōsha, 1980), 5–6.

75. Karatani Kōjin, "Nakano Shigeharu to tenkō" (Nakano Shigeharu and *tenkō*), in *Hyūmoa toshite no yuibutsuron* (Humor as materialism) (Tokyo: Chikuma Shobō, 1993), 163–200.

76. Quoted in Judith Butler, *Bodies That Matter: On the Discursive Limits of "Sex"* (New York: Routledge, 1993), 27.

Chapter 2. The Disease of Nationalism, the Empire of Hygiene: The Broken Commandment *as* Hygiene Manual

The epigraph to this chapter is from "Yūwa mondai to bungei" (The assimilation problem and literary arts, 1928), *TZ* 9:601. An earlier version of this chapter was published in Japanese translation in August 1997. After I had completed writing that article, but before it was published, Suga Hidemi published an article that reached many similar conclusions about *The Broken Commandment*: "Kokumin to iu sukyandaru: 'Teikoku' no bungaku 1" (The scandal that is the nation: The literature of empire 1) in *Hihyō kūkan* 2d ser., no. 13 (1997): 226–46. For Suga's response to my article, see his "Bungaku wo yōgo shi, shi wo hoshu suru: posutokoroniaru hihyō/karuchuraru sutadiizu to 'bungaku' " (Defending literature, preserving poetry: Postcolonial criticism, cultural studies and "literature"), *Gendai shi techō* 40, no. 9 (September 1997), 38–46. Three other useful English-language studies of the image of *burakumin* in literature have appeared since that earlier version of this chapter was published: Edward Fowler, "The *Buraku* in Modern Japanese Literature: Texts and Contexts," *Journal of Japanese Studies* 26, no. 1 (2000), 1–39; René Andersson, *Burakumin and Shimazaki Tōson's* Hakai: *Images of Discrimination in Modern Japanese Literature* (Lund, Sweden: Department of East Asian Languages, Lund University, [2000]); and Sayuri Oyama, "Shimazaki Tōson's *Hakai:* (Re)writing and (Re)reading the Canon," *Issues of Canonicity and Canon Formation in Japanese Literary Studies: Proceedings of the Association for Japanese Literary Studies* 1 (2000), 59–75.

1. *Hakai* is reprinted in *TZ* 2. There is a translation by Kenneth Strong: *The Broken Commandment* (Tokyo: University of Tokyo Press, 1974). To avoid confusion, I have followed Strong's translations for character names (dropping macrons, "O-Shio" instead of "Oshiho," etc.).

2. Irokawa Daikichi, *The Culture of the Meiji Period*, trans. Marius B. Jansen (Princeton: Princeton University Press, 1985).

3. Louis Livingston Seaman, *The Real Triumph of Japan* (New York: D. Appleton, 1906).

4. Seaman, *Triumph*, 143.

5. That is, descendents (not solely in the biological sense) of those persons classified as *eta* and *hinin* during the Edo period. Despite the official abolition of those pariah-status groups in 1871, the derogatory terms *eta* (much filth) and *hinin* (not human) remained in wide use in 1906. *Hisabetsu burakumin* (literally, people from the discriminated-against districts [district = *buraku*]) is a polite modern term. In *The Broken Commandment*, another discriminatory name is also frequently used: *shinheimin* (new commoners). This term was introduced in early Meiji to distinguish burakumin from "ordinary" commoners (*heimin*) following the official abolition of the *eta* and *hinin* categories. Although this group faced ostracization in both the premodern and modern periods, the nature of that discrimination shifted radically with the rise of the modern nation-state and its presumption of equality between citizens. See Hirota Masaki, "Nihon kindai shakai no sabetsu kōzō" (The structure of discrimination in modern Japanese society) in *Sabetsu no shosō* (Various aspects of discrimination), ed. Hirota, in *Nihon kindai shisō taikei* (Anthology of modern Japanese thought), (Tokyo: Iwanami Shoten, 1990), 22:436–516.

6. Narita Ryūichi, "Kindai toshi to minshū" (The modern city and the masses) in *Toshi to minshū* (The city and the masses), ed. Narita (Tokyo: Yoshikawa Kirofuni-kan, 1993), 19.

7. See Bruno Latour, *The Pasteurization of France*, trans. Alan Sheridan and John Law (Cambridge: Harvard University Press, 1988), 121–122. Also see Date Kazuo, *Ishi toshite no Mori Ōgai* (Mori Ōgai as doctor) (Tokyo: Sekibundō, 1981) on the rise of hygiene as a form of military medicine in Japan.

8. On Ōgai, see Date, *Ishi toshite no Mori Ōgai*; Richard Bowring, *Mori Ōgai and the Modernization of Japanese Culture* (Cambridge: Cambridge University Press, 1979); and Thomas Lamarre, "Bacterial Cultures and Linguistic Colonies: Mori Rintarō's Experiments with History, Science, and Languages," *positions* 6, no. 3 (Winter 1998), 597–635. On Kitasato, see James R. Bartholomew, "Science, Bureaucracy, and Freedom in Meiji

and Taishō Japan," in *Conflict in Modern Japanese History: The Neglected Tradition*, ed. Tetsuo Najita and J. Victor Koschmann (Princeton: Princeton University Press, 1982), 295–341; and Andrew Cunningham, "Transforming Plague: The Laboratory and the Identity of Infectious Disease," in *The Laboratory Revolution in Medicine*, ed. Cunningham and Perry Williams (Cambridge: Cambridge University Press, 1992), 209–24.

9. Karatani Kōjin, *Origins of Modern Japanese Literature*, trans. ed. Brett de Bary (Durham: Duke University Press, 1993), 106.

10. Foucault argues similarly that the prestige of biological sciences in the nineteenth century derived mainly from their deployment of "a space whose profound structure responded to the healthy/morbid opposition." Michel Foucault, *The Birth of the Clinic: An Archaeology of Medical Perception*, trans. A. M. Sheridan Smith (New York: Vintage, 1975), 35.

11. The rise of laboratory-based medicine led to a radical reconstruction of diseases, so that, for example, plague became something entirely different once scientists isolated its causal agent: "The identities of pre-1894 plague and post-1894 plague have become incommensurable. We are simply unable to say whether they were the same, since the criteria of 'sameness' have been changed. As I have been arguing, this is not a technical medical issue, but a logical, philosophical and historiographic one." Cunningham, "Transforming Plague," 242.

12. On tuberculosis in Japan, see Fukuda Mahito, *Kekkaku no bunkashi* (A cultural history of tuberculosis) (Nagoya: Nagoya Daigaku Shuppankai, 1995); William Johnston, *The Modern Epidemic: A History of Tuberculosis in Japan* (Boston: Council on East Asian Studies, Harvard University, 1995); and J. Keith Vincent, "Masaoka Shiki to yamai no imi" (Masaoka Shiki and the meaning of disease), *Hihyō kūkan* 2d ser., no. 8 (1996), 160–87. On tuberculosis in general, see Rene Dubos and Jean Dubos, *The White Plague: Tuberculosis, Man and Society* (Boston: Little, Brown, 1952); and Susan Sontag, *Illness as Metaphor and AIDS and its Metaphors* (New York: Doubleday, 1990).

13. On political and economic factors in the debate between contagion and anticontagion theories in the decades leading up to the rise of germ theory, see Erwin H. Akerknecht, "Anticontagionism Between 1821 and 1867," *Bulletin of the History of Medicine* 22 (1948), 562–92. See also Roger Cooter, "Anticontagionism and History's Medical Record" in *The Problem of Medical Knowledge*, ed. Peter Wright and Andrew Treacher (Edinburgh: Edinburgh University Press, 1982), 87–108.

14. Dr. Cyrus Edson, "The Microbe as Social Leveller," *North American Review* 161 (1895), 421–26.

15. Quoted in Fukuda, *Kekkaku no bunkashi*, 52–53. On similar radical political critiques of the germ-theory version of tuberculosis in France, see chapter seven in David S. Barnes, *The Making of a Social Disease: Tuberculosis in Nineteenth-Century France* (Berkeley: University of California Press, 1995).

16. Johnston, *Modern Epidemic*, 272.

17. See Mori Ōgai, "Nihon heishoku ron taii" (Outline of a theory of the diet of the Japanese soldier), in *Ōgai zenshū* (Complete works of Ōgai) (1886; reprint, Tokyo: Iwanami Shoten, 1974), 18:11–18. Ōgai's dietary research is described in Date, *Ishi toshite no Mori Ōgai*, especially 101–20 and 177–202. Ōgai himself, incidentally, labored throughout his life to conceal the fact that he had tuberculosis. See Fukuda, *Kekkaku no bunkashi*, 57–97.

18. Gotō's medical career is discussed in Seaman, *Real Triumph of Japan*, 220–21 and Johnston, *The Modern Epidemic*, 180–81. His colonial career is discussed in Stefan Tanaka, *Japan's Orient: Turning Pasts into History* (Berkeley: University of California Press, 1993) and E. Patricia Tsurumi, *Japanese Colonial Education in Taiwan, 1895–1945* (Cambridge: Harvard University Press, 1977).

19. See Mary Douglas, *Purity and Danger: An Analysis of the Concepts of Pollution and Taboo* (1966; reprint, London: Ark, 1984); and Peter Stallybrass and Allon White, *The Politics and Poetics of Transgression* (Ithaca: Cornell University Press, 1986).

20. Some of the most interesting recent scholarship on Tōson has focused on images of disease in his novels. See for example, two essays included in *Shimazaki Tōson: bunmei hihyōka to shi to shōsetsu* (Shimazaki Tōson: Cultural critic, poetry, and novels), ed. Hiraoka Toshio and Kenmochi Takeo (Tokyo: Sōbunsha, 1996); Nakayama Hiroaki's "Kettō no monogatari: Ie no 'yamai' ron" (Tale of blood lineage: Theory of "disease" in *Ie* [The family]), 182–97; and Iwami Teruyo's "Setsuko no monogatari: *Shinsei* no topogurafii" (Setsuko's tale: The topography of *Shinsei* [New life]), 215–29.

21. Watanabe Naomi, *Kindai Nihon bungaku to "sabetsu"* (Modern Japanese literature and "discrimination") (Tokyo: Ōta Shuppan, 1994). See also Umezawa Toshihiko, Hirano Eikyū, and Yamagishi Takashi, *Bungaku no naka no hisabetsu buraku zō: senzen hen* (The image of *hisabetsu buraku* in literature: Prewar) (Tokyo: Akashi Shoten, 1980); and Kawabata Toshifusa, *Hakai to sono shūhen* (*Hakai* [The broken commandment] and its contexts), (Kyoto: Bunrikaku, 1984).

22. Edward Said, *Orientalism* (London: Routledge, 1978). See also Edward Said, *Culture and Imperialism* (New York: Knopf, 1993) for a rethinking of this thesis.

23. See Kurokawa Midori, *Ika to dōka no aida: hisabetsu buraku ninshiki no kiseki* (Between dissimilation and assimilation: Traces of the cognition of hisabetsu buraku) (Tokyo: Aoki Shoten, 1999), esp. 51–53. I thank Jeffrey Bayliss for introducing me to Kurokawa's work.

24. The following argument is a belated answer to a question raised by Tomoko Steen in response to an earlier version of this chapter. I thank her for her insightful comments.

25. Ernesto Laclau and Chantal Mouffe, *Hegemony and Socialist Strategy: Towards a Radical Democratic Politics* (London: Verso, 1985), 127–28.

26. Karatani, *Origins of Modern Japanese Literature*, 101.

27. Carol Gluck, *Japan's Modern Myths: Ideology in the Late Meiji Period* (Princeton: Princeton University Press, 1985), 157–78.

28. *TZ* 2:113–15. Ushimatsu's inability to reveal his origins to his mentor here also masks the presence of another secret: the scandalous contact with disease overlaps with the scandal of Ushimatsu's homosexual desire for Rentaro's body. In fact, the relationship between Ushimatsu, his father, and Rentaro, can be read as an all-male, quasi-family romance, as an Oedipal struggle set in motion by the father's command. See Chida Hiroyuki, "Fusei to dōsei kara no kaihō: *Hakai* no kōzu" (Liberation from patriarch and the same sex: The composition of *Hakai* [The broken commandment]) in *Shimazaki Tōson: bunmei hihyō to shi to shōsetsu to*, ed. Hiraoka and Kenmochi, 154–66. The text will eventually control this irruption of unspeakable desire by murdering the desired male body and displacing Ushimatsu's desire onto O-Shio, the non-*burakumin* heroine. This displacement is effected through the mediation of a textual corpus: O-Shio, upon

agreeing to marry Ushimatsu at the conclusion of *The Broken Commandment*, suddenly expresses a desire to read Rentaro's writings. See Kōno Kensuke, *Shomotsu no kindai: media no bungakushi* (The modernity of printed matter: A literary history of media) (Tokyo: Chikuma Shobō, 1992), 124; Idehara Takatoshi, "Rengeji no kane" (The bell at Rengeji Temple), *Kokugo kokubun* 56, no. 1 (January 1987), 1–23; Watanabe Hiroshi, *Shimazaki Tōson wo yominaosu* (Rereading Shimazaki Tōson) (Tokyo: Sōjusha, 1994), 17–61; and Shinoda Kōichirō, *Shōsetsu wa ika ni kakareta ka* (How were novels written?) (Tokyo: Iwanami Shoten, 1982), 20–27.

29. Kenjiro [Roka] Tokutomi, *Nami-ko: A Realistic Novel* trans. Sakae Shioya and E. F. Edgett (Boston: Herbert B. Turner, 1904), 154. The novel suggests repeatedly that the real disease infecting this family is capitalism and the deterritorialization of the samurai ethical code by money. In fact, the novel provides many examples of the rhetoric of national imagination discussed in this and other chapters: not only hygiene, but also the impact of capitalism and market values on the family and marriage; the use of the family as a metaphor for the nation and vice versa; crises of unstable gender boundaries, and so on. Moreover, these issues are all placed against the backdrop of the Sino-Japanese War, Japan's first major war of imperial expansion. In the novel, it is victory in the war that restores the proper boundaries of the nation, and Nami's corpse becomes the medium through which the homosocial patriarchal order is restored.

30. On the contradictory etiologies assigned to tuberculosis in European anti-Semitism and of "the stereotype's peculiar power to accomodate antitheses" (59), see Sander Gilman, *Franz Kafka: The Jewish Patient* (New York: Routledge, 1995).

31. Moreover, the pariah status assigned to potentially infectious tubercular patients under germ theory enhanced the functioning of tuberculosis as a marker of *buraku* status. This was not unique to Japan. Despite Karatani's attempt to link germ theory and Romantic tuberculosis, in fact germ theory brought an end to Romantic tuberculosis and instead made the disease into "a contagion, something unclean," so that "the infected individual became *almost an untouchable*, a character stimulating repulsion or fear" (Dubos and Dubos, *White Plague*, 66; italics added). We see a similar example of how the rise of a contagious understanding of disease displaces an earlier romantic view in Tōson's *Shinsei* (New life, 1918–1919). There, the protagonist's perception of his father shifts when he realizes that the father's insanity might be due not to "romantic" hereditary blood, but rather the effects of a sexually transmitted disease: "He thought about the cause of the mental illness that his father had suffered. But now he did not look for it in romantic [*romanchikku*] directions, as he had allowed himself to imagine when he was young, but rather sought it in simple hygienic carelessness. Yet even if his father's insanity came from some external pathogenic germ [*gairai no byōdoku*], it did not change the affection he felt for him." (*TZ* 7:220). This passage is discussed in Kotani Hiroyuki, *Rekishi to ningen ni tsuite: Tōson to kindai Nihon* (On history and humanity: Tōson and modern Japan) (Tokyo: Tōkyō Daigaku Shuppankai, 1991), 43–48.

32. Kurokawa, *Ika to dōka no aida*.

33. *TZ* 2:9. Foreign origins were a popular (and false) explanation for the presence of *burakumin* in Japan. See Emily Ohnuki-Tierney, *The Monkey as Mirror: Symbolic Transformations in Japanese History and Ritual* (Princeton: Princeton University Press, 1987), especially 77–78. References to foreign origins were edited out of the 1939 edition of *The Broken Commandment*.

34. The story "Imin gakuen" (Immigrant school, 1899) by Shimizu Shikin (1868–1933) is also of interest. In it, an ambitious *burakumin* father hides from the world in order to allow his daughter to succeed in society, and—as in *The Broken Commandment*—it is the father's death that causes the strategy to unravel. When the daughter learns of her father's illness, she rushes to him, thereby revealing her origins in the *buraku*. Here, too, the father's unspecified disease is almost surely contagious: the father was not born of *burakumin* parents but was adopted into the community when he fled his own non-*buraku* family in his youth. For a translation, see Rebecca Sue Jennison, *Approaching Difference: A Reading of Selected Texts by Shimizu Shikin* (Masters' thesis, Cornell University, 1990), 78–118. For a discussion of the story, see also Rebecca Copeland, *Lost Leaves: Women Writers of Meiji Japan* (Honolulu: University of Hawaii Press, 2000), 196–207. Many scholars have speculated that Tōson was influenced by the story as he constructed the plot of *The Broken Commandment*.

35. Hence, the call to arms of the Suiheisha *burakumin* liberation movement's "Sengen" (Declaration, 1922): "We were the victims of ignoble class policies, and we were the manly martyrs of industry; as recompense for having flayed the skin off beasts, we were flayed of our living human skin; as the price for having cut the hearts out of beasts, we had our own warm human hearts cut out of us. . . ." Quoted in Watanabe Naomi, *Kindai Nihon bungaku to "sabetsu,"* 77–78. There is a full English translation in Ian Neary, *Political Protest and Social Control in Pre-War Japan: The Origins of Buraku Liberation* (Atlantic Highlands, N.J.: Humanities Press International, 1989), 226. Tōson himself was sympathetic to Suiheisha. See the 1923 essay, "Mezameta mono no kanashimi" (The sorrow of those who have awakened, *TZ* 9:249–52).

36. See chapter eleven in Kamei Hideo, *Transformations of Sensibility: The Phenomenology of Meiji Literature*, trans. ed. Michael Bourdaghs (Ann Arbor: University of Michigan Center for Japanese Studies Publications, 2002).

37. Fujii, *Complicit Fictions: The Subject in the Modern Japanese Prose Narrative* (Berkeley: University of California Press, 1993), 94. See also Shinoda, *Shōsetsu wa ika ni kakareta ka,* 16–20.

38. Johnston, *The Modern Epidemic,* 216–20 and Fukuda, *Kekkaku no bunkashi,* 69–71. By about 1910, the inspection system fell into disuse, due both to farmer resistance and growing doubts among hygienists of the relevance of bovine tuberculosis to the disease in humans. The bloodlines of the bull in *The Broken Commandment* further complicate matters. Is bovine tuberculosis hereditary or contagious? The bull's owner says that although he owns many cattle, "none is of bloodlines superior to this one's. Its sire was American-born, its dame was such-and-such, and if only it hadn't any bad habits it would have been the prized bull of the Nishinoiri pastures" (*TZ* 2:127). The bull's American lineage not only foreshadows Ushimatsu's emigration, but also renders the animal more suspect. Under the Unequal Treaties, Japan was prevented from enforcing any effective quarantine, and U.S. cattle growers were known to dump infected cows onto the Japanese market.

39. Latour, *Pasteurization of France,* 123, emphasis in original. On Meiji period policies toward supposedly heterogeneous elements, see Hirota, "Nihon kindai shakai no sabetsu kōzō," and Narita, "Kindai toshi to minshū."

40. Most early critics, including those who praise the novel, see its conclusion as a literary failure. Even reviewers who evidenced little sympathy for Rentaro's politics

bemoaned—for aesthetic reasons—Ushimatsu's behavior during his confession and his decision to emigrate rather than to remain in Japan and carry on his mentor's struggle. Hasegawa Tenkei (1876–1940) in his review, "Handō no genshō" (A reactionary phenomenon, 1906), is typical: although Hasegawa believes the novel overstates the extent of anti-*burakumin* prejudice, he argues that "because the novel on the one hand provides us with the figure of Rentaro, fiercely struggling against society despite his status as an *eta*, there is a tendency for us to feel less and less sympathy for Ushimatsu's suffering" (*TZ* 18:102–5). Burakumin liberation activists have also long attacked the novel's conclusion, for more overtly political reasons. See, for example, Burakumin Kaihō Zenkoku Iinkai, "*Hakai* shohanbon fukugen ni kansuru seimei" (Statement on the reprinting of the first edition of *Hakai* [The broken commandment], 1954), reprinted in *TZ* 2:535–40.

41. Yet as Kō Yonran notes, the ending was historically realistic: emigration from Japan reached a peak in the years around the publication of *The Broken Commandment*, and in the discourse surrounding emigration, Texas in particular was represented as an ideal site for Japanese settlers. Kō Yonran, " 'Tekisasu' wo meguru gensetsu ken: Shimazaki Tōson *Hakai* to bōchō keifu" (The sphere of discourse about Texas: Its genealogy in Shimazaki Tōson's *Hakai* [The broken commandment] and beyond) in *Disukūru no teikoku: Meiji sanjū nendai no bunka kenkyū* (Empire of discourse: Studies on the culture of the Meiji thirties), ed. Kaneko Akio, Takahashi Osamu, and Yoshida Morio (Tokyo: Shinyōsha, 2000), 273–302.

42. A large number of Meiji works on the *buraku* problem suggested emigration as a solution. This proposal not only nullified the possibility of a domestic *burakumin* political movement, it also tended to mobilize *burakumin* into the government's overseas expansionary policies. See Kawabata Toshifusa, *Hakai to sono shūhen*, especially 21–22 and 58–75; Kurokawa, *Ika to dōka no aida*, 61–65; Suga, "Kokumin to iu sukyandaru: 'Teikoku' no bungaku 1"; and Kō, " 'Tekisasu' wo meguru gensetsu ken."

43. Fukui Kōji in 1925, as quoted in Kamishima Jirō, *Kindai Nihon no seishin kōzō* (The spiritual structure of modern Japan) (Tokyo: Iwanami Shoten, 1961), 57. Kamishima also quotes (131–32n132) an extended metaphor from a 1955 autobiography by the Japan Romantic School figure Asano Akira (1901–1990) comparing the ideologies of left-wing intellectuals to the tubercle bacillus. Fukui and Asano's statements are discussed in Johnston, *Modern Epidemic*, 271.

44. "So long as tubercular patients are allowed the freedom of social intercourse they must be held to the moral obligation of certain restrictions." A. L. Benedict, M.D., "Consumption Considered as a Contagious Disease," *Popular Science Monthly* 48, no. 1 (November 1895), 38.

45. "Ideology is not a dreamlike illusion that we build to escape insupportable reality; in its basic dimension it is a fantasy-construction which serves as a support for our 'reality' itself: an 'illusion' which structures our effective, real social relations and thereby masks some insupportable, real, impossible kernel (conceptualized by Ernesto Laclau and Chantal Mouffe as 'antagonism': a traumatic social division which cannot be symbolized)." Slavoj Žižek, *The Sublime Object of Ideology* (New York: Verso, 1989), 45.

46. Kawabata Toshifusa, *Hakai to sono shūhen*, 29–75.

47. Fujii, *Complicit Fictions*, 76–102. In many places, the 1939 revised edition softened or omitted the language in which this resistance to the centralized state was couched.

48. Jacques Derrida, *Disseminations*, trans. Barbara Johnson (Chicago: University of Chicago Press, 1981), 128–34.

49. Tessa Morris-Suzuki, *Re-Inventing Japan: Time Space Nation* (Armonk, N.Y.: M. E. Sharpe, 1998), 204.

50. Quoted in Kawabata Toshifusa, *Hakai to sono shūhen*, 73n12.

51. Suga (in "Kokumin to iu sukyandaru: 'Teikoku' no bungaku 1") reaches a similar conclusion. See also Katharina May, "Das Motiv des Aussenseiters in der modernen japanischen Literatur," in *Bochumer Jahrbuch zur Ostasienforschung* 4 (1981): 110–29.

52. Mori Ōgai, "Nihon heishoku ron taii," 14.

53. Mark Seltzer, *Bodies and Machines* (New York: Routledge, 1992), 154–55.

54. Homi K. Bhabha, "DissemiNation: Time, Narrative, and the Margins of the Modern Nation," in Bhabha, ed., *Nation and Narration* (London: Routledge, 1990), 291–322. For another useful study of Derrida's notion of the "supplement" as a way of understanding the fluid, split nature of national imagination, see Prasenjit Duara, *Rescuing History from the Nation* (Chicago: University of Chicago Press, 1995), esp. 60–65 and 229–33.

55. Eiji Oguma, *A Genealogy of "Japanese" Self-Images*, trans. David Askew (Melbourne: Trans Pacific Press, 2002), 41. On the widespread presumption of hybridity in Western racist and imperialist discourses, see Robert J. C. Young, *Colonial Desire: Hybridity in Theory, Culture, and Race* (London: Routledge, 1995).

56. I am indebted to Mark Anderson for pointing out these two forms of colonization. On the fluctuating discourses of assimilation and imperialization in Japan's colonies, see Leo T. S. Ching, *Becoming "Japanese": Colonial Taiwan and the Politics of Identity Formation* (Berkeley: University of California Press, 2001).

57. William H. McNeill, *Plagues and Peoples* (Garden City, N.Y.: Anchor Press, 1976).

58. David Arnold, *Colonizing the Body: State Medicine and Epidemic Disease in Nineteenth-Century India* (Berkeley: University of California Press, 1993), 116–58.

59. Quoted in Arnold, *Colonizing the Body*, 143.

60. On *yūwa* policies, see Neary, *Political Protest and Social Control in Pre-War Japan*; Watanabe Naomi, *Kindai Nihon bungaku to "sabetsu"*; and Kurokawa, *Ika to dōka no aida*. For accounts of a similar shift with regard to another domestic minority group, Okinawans, see Murai Osamu, *Nantō ideorogii no hassei* (Origins of the ideology of the South Islands), rev. ed. (Tokyo: Ōta Shuppan, 1995); and Tomiyama Ichirō, "Kokumin no tanjō to 'Nihon jinshu,' " (The birth of the nation and the "Japanese race"), *Shisō* 845 (November 1994), 37–56.

61. On Kita Sadakichi, see Kō Yonran, "*Hakai* kaitei katei to minzokuronteki gensetsu" (The process of revision of *Hakai* [The broken commandment] and the discourse on ethnicity), *Gobun* 100 (March 1998), 70–82; and Oguma, *Genealogy of "Japanese" Self-Images*, especially 95–109.

62. Kō (" 'Tekisasu' wo meguru gensetsu ken") notes, however, that even Meiji-period socialists bought into the discourse of emigration as a means of achieving national expansion. Hence, the antiwar essays of such figures as the socialist Katayama Sen (who established a "model village" for Japanese immigrants in Texas) promoted emigration as a peaceful—and more effective—alternative to war as a means for achieving national growth.

63. Gilles Deleuze and Félix Guattari, *A Thousand Plateaus: Capitalism and Schizophrenia*, trans. Brian Massumi (Minneapolis: University of Minnesota Press, 1987). "The

nomad is not at all the same as the migrant; for the migrant goes principally from one point to another, even if the second point is uncertain, unforeseen, or not well localized. But the nomad goes from point to point only as a consequence and as a factual necessity; in principle, points for him are relays along a trajectory" (380). The limit, in turn, "marks the exact point at which the assemblage must reproduce itself, begin a new operation period or a new cycle, lodge itself on another territory," whereas the threshold marks the ultimate—the "ultimate is when the assemblage must change its nature," go beyond reproduction to produce a qualitatively different and new assemblage (438).

64. For discussions of Ogura Chōrō (1879–1944) and his *Biwa uta*, see Watanabe Naomi, *Kindai Nihon bungaku to "sabetsu"*; Kurokawa, *Ika to dōka no aida*, 71–72; and Umezawa et al., *Bungaku no naka no hisabetsu buraku zō*.

65. The most detailed discussion of the publishing history of *The Broken Commandment* is contained in Kō Yonran, "*Hakai* kaitei katei to minzokuronteki gensetsu." See also Umezawa et al., *Bungaku no naka no hisabetsu buraku zō*, 1–20; Kawabata Toshifusa, *Hakai to sono shūhen*, 210–30; and Kitahara Daisaku [1954], "*Hakai* to buraku kaihō undō" (*Hakai* [The broken commandment] and *buraku* liberation movements) in *Nihon bungaku kenkyū shiryō sōsho: Shimazaki Tōson* (Collection of research materials on Japanese literature: Shimazaki Tōson), ed. Nihon Bungaku Kenkyū Shiryō Kankō Kai (Tokyo: Yūseidō, 1971), 220–24.

66. The 1939 preface and afterword are reprinted in *TZ* 2:533–35.

67. On the campaigns to assimilate *burakumin* into Japan's "Total War" in the 1930s and 1940s, see Kurokawa, *Ika to dōka no aida*, 236–80. Suga (in "Kokumin to iu sukyandaru: 'Teikoku' no bungaku 1") argues that the split status of the *burakumin* allows them to provide the ideological grounding for the theories of Japan as a multiethnic society that were used in the early twentieth century to legitimate Japan's expansion into Asia.

68. As I discussed in chapter 1, in the postwar era, as the needs of national health again shifted, the 1939 text was in turn quarantined. In the mid-1950s, Japanese publishers began returning to the 1906 text, often with little explanation of the history of textual variation. The 1939 revised text has been unavailable in any edition since 1971.

69. Morris-Suzuki, *Re-Inventing Japan*, 87.

70. Morris-Suzuki, *Re-Inventing Japan*, 94.

71. Oguma, *Genealogy of "Japanese" Self-Images*, especially 210. See also Ching, *Becoming "Japanese."*

72. "Shinkan shōkai" (Introducing new publications), *Katei zasshi* 4, no. 5 (May 1906), 51. The review is unsigned, but may well be written by the magazine's editor, the socialist activist Sakai Toshihiko (1870–1933).

Chapter 3. Triangulating the Nation: Representing and Publishing The Family

1. For a history of the usage of the term *kokutai*, see Eiji Oguma, *A Genealogy of "Japanese" Self-Images*, trans. David Askew (Melbourne: Trans Pacific Press, 2002), especially 110–24.

2. *Ie* (The family) is reprinted in *TZ* 4:5–411. It is available in English as *The Family*, trans. Cecilia Segawa Seigle (Tokyo: University of Tokyo Press, 1976).

3. Yoshikuni Igarashi, *Bodies of Memory: Narratives of War in Postwar Japanese Culture, 1945–1970* (Princeton: Princeton University Press, 2000), especially 73–103.

4. The novel, published in two volumes, was the third title in the *Ryokuin sōsho* series that Tōson had begun with *The Broken Commandment*. For each of the three volumes, Tōson had to borrow money to bankroll publication, loans he was largely unable to repay since profits from the books were soaked up by his extended family—the very incidents that provided the material for the narrative of *The Family*. In 1913, shortly before his departure for France, Tōson sold his copyrights for the series to the Shinchōsha firm for 2,000 yen (the copyrights reverted to him after he returned to Japan). It was not until around 1920 that Tōson's royalties finally brought in enough money to allow him a measure of financial security.

5. Tōson received fifteen yen in manuscript fees from the Shunyōdō publishing house for each of his first four poetry collections; contrast this with his monthly salary of thirty to forty yen as a schoolteacher during the period he began work on the *Broken Commandment* manuscript. Kōno Kesuke, *Shomotsu no kindai: media no bungakushi* (The modernity of printed matter: A literary history of media)(Tokyo: Chikuma Shobō, 1992), 101–3.

6. Kōno, *Shomotsu no kindai*, 98–99.

7. See two articles by Nakayama Hiroaki, " 'Shōsetsu' no shihonron: Kōzu Takeshi no patoronēji" (The capitalism of the "novel": The patronage of Kōzu Takeshi), *Bungei to hihyō* 7, no. 10 (October 1994): 67–80; and " 'Komoro' to iu basho: Shimazaki Tōson ni okeru kinsen to gensetsu" (The place called "Komoro": Money and discourse in Shimazaki Tōson), *Nihon bungaku* 42, no. 7 (July 1993), 54–66.

8. See Kawashima Hidekazu, *Shimazaki Tōson ronkō* (Regarding Shimazaki Tōson) (Tokyo: Ōfūsha, 1987), 110–11.

9. Kawashima, for example, notes the shift in narrative structure between books 1 and 2 but argues that the novel is a coherent whole in that it pursues from beginning to end Sankichi's rediscovery of the father (Kawashima, *Shimazaki Tōson ronkō*, 82–117). For another reading that explicitly rejects the notion of a break between the two books, one that stresses the continued importance of Otane even in book 2, see Sasaki Masanobu, "*Ie* no josetsu: kōsei wo megutte" (Introduction to *Ie* [The family]: Concerning its construction), *Kokubungaku kaishaku to kanshō* 55, no. 4 (April 1990): 82–87.

10. In a 1910 review of the serialized version of book 1, Kimura Sōta mentions this complaint, though he disagrees with it, arguing that in fact this feature represents one of the formal artistic breakthroughs that Tōson had realized in the work. Kimura Sōta, "*Ie* ni tsuite no inshō to kansō" (My impression and observations on *Ie* [The family]), reprinted in *TZ* 18:153–58. The fragmented nature of the narrative perspective in book 1 has caused some critics to compare Tōson's technique here to that of the impressionist-school painters. See, for example, Ōnuki Shōsen's 1910 review, "*Ie* o yomu" (Reading *Ie* [The family], *TZ* 18:149–53) and Hirano Ken, *Shimazaki Tōson* in *Hirano Ken zenshū* (1947; Reprint, Tokyo: Shinchōsha, 1975), 2:41. I will return to this issue below.

11. Nakamura Seiko, "Hitotsu no me to tasū no me" (1911; Reprint, *TZ* 18:166–68).

12. On the weak or missing fathers that characterize so much Meiji fiction, see Yabu Teiko, "Meiji bungaku to kazoku: oboegaki" (Meiji literature and the family: A memorandum), *Nihon kindai bungaku* 41 (October 1989): 80–93; and Suga Hidemi, *Nihon kindai*

bungaku no "tanjō": genbun itchi to nashonarizumu (The "birth" of modern Japanese literature: *Genbun itchi* and nationalism) (Tokyo: Ōta Shuppan, 1995), especially 130–68. The figure of the mother in Tōson's works has received relatively little attention, although one exception is Ōida Yoshiaki, "*Haru* ni okeru komyunikeishon no mondai" (The problem of communication in *Haru* [Spring]) *Bai* 7 (July 1991), 33–47. I will explore this problem of the absent mother at greater length in chapter 4.

13. Watanabe Hiroshi, *Shimazaki Tōson o yominaosu* (Rereading Shimazaki Tōson) (Tokyo: Sōjusha, 1994), especially 114–15. (See also Kawashima 82–117.)

14. Juliet Flower MacCannell, *The Regime of the Brother: After the Patriarchy* (London: Routledge, 1991). MacCannell argues that contemporary Western societies are post-Oedipal, governed not by the openly acknowledged hierarchies of patriarchy, but rather by the false equality of the brothers, the narcissistic fraternal order that refuses to acknowledge its own desires or even the existence of the Other, in particular the Sister. Her argument is in many ways persuasive, and yet history provides repeated examples of the collapse of patriarchy from earlier periods: patriarchy, like nationalism, is always falling apart. Hence, I will frame my argument not in terms of the loss of patriarchy, but of the rise of new forms of patriarchy, as well as of the coexistence of multiple forms of patriarchy: not "the patriarchy," but rather "patriarchies," both in premodern and modern societies. I have learned much about MacCannell's ideas from the work of Mirana May Szeto.

15. Nishikawa Yūko, *Shakuya to mochiie no bungakushi* (A literary history of rental housing and private homes) (Tokyo: Sanseidō, 1998), 28. Actually, Sankichi is a fourth son given a third-son-sounding name, but Nishikawa's point is still valid.

16. For another recent study of the difference between first, second, and third sons as distinct semiotic codes in early-twentieth-century Japanese fiction, see Ishihara Chiaki, *Sōseki no kigōgaku* (The semiotics of Sōseki) (Tokyo: Kōdansha, 1999), 45–120.

17. For another recent study of the relationship between *ie* and *katei* in Meiji fiction, see Ken Ito, "The Family and the Nation in Tokutomi Roka's *Hototogisu,*" *Harvard Journal of Asiatic Studies* 60, no. 2 (December 2000): 489–536. Yamamoto Yoshiaki also provides a useful reading of *Nami-ko* (*Hototogisu* [The cuckoo], 1900), arguing that the novel functions as an ideological apparatus for reproducing patriarchy in the late-Meiji period, soliciting desire for the father as a "solution" to the nihilism that was thought to have infected the educated male youths who made up the novel's readership. See his " 'Chichi' no shōzō: Tokutomi Roka *Hototogisu*" (Portrait of the "father": Tokutomi Roka's *Nami-ko*), *Kokubungaku* 40, no. 11 (September 1995), 42–49. Yamashita Etsuko, on the other hand, rejects readings of Tokutomi's novel that see in it ideologies of patriarchy (although her definition of "patriarchy" is suspiciously narrow), arguing that it presents instead the story of a heroine who is primarily oppressed by other women in families that are governed by mothers in the absence of a functional patriarch, a structure Yamashita argues is typical of the Japanese *ie* system. See her *Mazakon bungakuron* (Theory of mother-complex literature) (Tokyo: Shinyōsha, 1991), 28–40. I am inclined to read *Nami-ko*, however, as depicting capitalist speculation as the root source of the disease that is eating away at the fiber of the national family. In this light, the novel foreshadows Tōson's *The Family*, although it portrays a turn away from the market as its solution to the crisis in patriarchy. *The Family*, as I will argue below, offers the market itself as the source of the solu-

tion. On the economics of the family in the "domestic mode of production" that characterizes precapitalist societies, see Marshall Sahlins, *Stone Age Economics* (Chicago: Aldine Publishing, 1972).

18. Nishikawa argues that I-novels by female authors (e.g., Uno Chiyo or Sata Ineko) demonstrate a different typical pattern: in them, the female protagonist attempts to escape from the constraints of the *katei*, often by experimenting with new forms of family and household space. See Nishikawa Yūko, *Shakuya to mochiie no bungakushi*, 27–39 and 331–336.

19. For another critical account of the *kazoku awase* game, including a discussion of Tōson's *The Family* and the ideological linkages of family to nation, see Terayama Shūji, *Iede no susume* (An encouragement of running away) (Tokyo: Kadokawa, 1972), 64–78.

20. Nishikawa, *Shakuya to mochiie no bungakushi*, 26.

21. Ueno Chizuko, *Kindai kazoku no seiritsu to shūen* (The rise and decline of the modern family) (Tokyo: Iwanami Shoten, 1994), 40. Ueno is in fact discussing religious communities here, but her point remains valid for national communities as well.

22. Judith Butler, *Subjects of Desire: Hegelian Reflections in Twentieth-Century France* (New York: Columbia University Press, 1987), 242–43n18. For another useful reading of the Hegelian concept of the family in terms of national imagination, see Partha Chatterjee, *The Nation and its Fragments: Colonial and Postcolonial Histories* (Princeton: Princeton University Press, 1993), especially 230–34.

23. Benedict Anderson, *Imagined Communities: Reflections on the Origin and Spread of Nationalism* (New York: Verso, 1983), 131. See also Nira Yuval-Davis, *Gender and Nation* (London: SAGE Publications, 1997), 15–16.

24. On the concept of "infinite debt," see Deleuze and Guattari, *Anti-Oedipus: Capitalism and Schizophrenia*, trans. Robert Hurley, Mark Seem, and Helen R. Lane (Minneapolis: University of Minnesota Press, 1983), 212–17.

25. Carol Gluck, *Japan's Modern Myths: Ideology in the Late Meiji Period* (Princeton: Princeton University Press, 1985); Irokawa Daikichi, *The Culture of the Meiji Period*, trans. Marius B. Jansen (Princteon: Princeton University Press, 1985).

26. Tessa Morris-Suzuki, *Re-Inventing Japan: Time Space Nation* (Armonk, N.Y.: M. E. Sharpe, 1998), 84. For numerous examples of this family-state discourse, see also Oguma, *Genealogy of "Japanese" Self-Images.*

27. Nishikawa, *Shakuya to mochiie no bungakushi*, 44.

28. On the rise of modern discourses of sexuality in Meiji Japan, see Sabine Frühstück, *Die Politik der Sexualwissenschaft: Zur Produktion und Popularisierung sexologischen Wissens in Japan, 1908–1941* (Vienna: Instituts für Japanologie der Universität Wien, 1997); Ueno Chizuko, "Kaisetsu" (Afterword) in *Fūzoku sei* (Public morals and sexuality), vol. 23 of *Nihon kindai shisō taikei* (Anthology of modern Japanese thought), ed. Ogi Shinzō, Kumakura Isao, and Ueno Chizuko, (Tokyo: Iwanami Shoten, 1990), 23:505–50; and Oshino Takeshi, " 'Yamai': Tayama Katai 'Shōjobyō' " ("Disease": Tayama Katai's "The girl watcher"), *Kokubungaku* 40, no. 11 (September 1995): 72–76.

29. In book 1, after Sankichi discovers his wife's secret correspondence with her former fiancé and considers divorce, he immediately realizes the legal complexity that this would entail, since Oyuki's name has already been transferred into his family registry, and he considers consulting a lawyer (*TZ* 4:79).

30. Takashi Fujitani, *Splendid Monarchy: Power and Pageantry in Modern Japan* (Berkeley: University of California Press, 1996), 191–92.

31. Matsushita Hiroyuki, "1910 nendai ni okeru *Michikusa* to *Wakai*: sono 'shussan' ga imi suru mono" (*Michikusa* [Grass by the wayside] and *Wakai* [Reconciliation] in the 1910s: What birth signifies in them), *Meiji Daigaku daigakuin kiyō: bungaku hen* 30 (February 1993), 47–66.

32. See Immanuel Wallerstein, *Historical Capitalism with Capitalist Civilization* (London: Verso, 1983), especially 23–28. See also Etienne Balibar and Immanuel Wallerstein, *Race, Nation, Class: Ambiguous Identities* (London: Verso, 1991), especially 107–12.

33. On the new marriage patterns that became dominant in the 1890s, see Ueno, *Kindai kazoku no seiritsu to shūen*, 114 and Koseki Kazuhiro, "Ren'ai to iu gensō: ren'ai shi no ken'iki" (The fantasy of romantic love: The sphere of love poetry), *Kokubungaku* 41, no. 13 (November 1996): 42–48.

34. On hygiene and the family in Meiji Japan, see Narita Ryūichi, "Women and Views of Women Within the Changing Hygiene Conditions of Late-Nineteenth- and Early-Twentieth-Century Japan," *U.S.-Japan Women's Journal English Supplement* 8 (June 1995): 64–86.

35. Jordan Sand, "House and Home in Modern Japan, 1880s–1920s," (Ph.D. diss., Columbia University, 1996). See also Jordan Sand, "At Home in the Meiji Period: Inventing Japanese Domesticity" in *Mirror of Modernity: Invented Traditions of Modern Japan*, ed. Stephen Vlastos (Berkeley: University of California Press, 1998), 191–207.

36. Miyasaka Yasuko, " 'Osan' no shakai shi" (A social history of birthing) in *Bosei: Nihon no feminizumu 5*, ed. Inoue Teruko, Ueno Chizuko, and Ehara Yumiko (Tokyo: Iwanami Shoten, 1995), 89–124.

37. Ken Ito, "The Family and the Nation in Tokutomi Roka's *Hototogisu*," 506.

38. Watagaki Kenzō, as quoted in Muta Kazue, "Images of the Family in Meiji Periodicals: The Paradox Underlying the Emergence of the 'Home,' " trans. Marcella S. Gregory, *U.S.-Japan Women's Journal English Supplement* 7 (1994): 53–71.

39. Marilyn Ivy, *Discourses of the Vanishing: Modernity, Phantasm, Japan* (Chicago: University of Chicago Press, 1995), especially 10–12.

40. Harry Harootunian, *Overcome By Modernity: History, Culture, and Community in Interwar Japan* (Princeton: Princeton University Press, 2000), 282–83.

41. The words italicized here appear in English in the original, except in the present tense: "He is my lover."

42. Recent examples of criticism on the novel that rely on this perspective can be found in Watanabe Hiroshi, *Shimazaki Tōson o yominaosu*, 109–42; Yamashita Etsuko, *Mazakon bungakuron*, 41–55; and (in a more historically nuanced and intriguing version), Konaka Nobutaka, "Ie no chiyuryoku" (Healing power of the family), *Nihon kindai bungaku* 53 (1995): 96–107. Perhaps the most influential reading of *The Family* in terms of the *uchi/soto* divide is found in Togawa Shinsuke's classic study, *Shimazaki Tōson* (Tokyo: Chikuma Shobō, 1980), 119–55.

43. There is an apparent misprint in the *TZ* (13:121) version of this quotation, which I have corrected here, based on the version of this same passage that appears on *TZ* 4:622. Note also that the last sentence in the quotation is more effective in Japanese, where the title of the novel carries both the meanings of "family" and "house," so that Tōson is building both the novel (*Ie*) and his metaphorical "house" ("*ie*").

44. Hirano Ken, "*Ie*"(*Ie* [The family], 1946), in *Shimazaki Tōson: hito to bungaku* (Shimazaki Tōson: His life and literature) in *Hirano Ken zenshū* (Complete works of Hirano Ken) (Tokyo: Shinchōsha, 1975), 2:39–44. This quotation appears on 2:42.

45. "*Katei*," however, does appear several times in the novel. For example, Sankichi uses the word twice to describe his household with Oyuki in the letter he writes to her former fiancé after discovering their correspondence (*TZ* 4:83).

46. For a useful reading of the role of the expanding transportation network in *The Family*, with special attention paid to the shifting urban-rural relationships that characterize early-twentieth-century Japanese writing, see Stephen Dodd, "The Railway as Rupture: The Writings of Shimazaki Tōson," in *Disrupted Borders: An Intervention in Definitions of Boundaries*, ed. Sunil Gupta (London: Rivers Oram Press, 1993), 42–54.

47. Yuval-Davis, *Gender and Nation*, 80.

48. See Ōida Yoshiaki, "*Ie* no jikan: chichi to no kaikō" (Time in *Ie* [The family]: Chance encounters with the father), *Bungei to hihyō* 6, no. 3 (March 1986): 44–55.

49. For a discussion of the role of the verandah in another late- Meiji novel, Natsume Sōseki's *Mon* (The gate, 1910), see Ishihara, *Sōseki no kigōgaku*, 163–64.

50. Sekiya Yumiko, "Kanyu toshite no *Ie*" (*Ie* [The family] as metonym), *Kokugo to kokubungaku* 66, no. 4 (April 1989): 46–59. Sekiya's article first alerted me to the importance of the verandah in *Ie*, though my interpretation of its significance differs from hers. See also Ishihara Chiaki, " 'Ie' no bunpō" (The grammar of "the family"), *Kokubungaku kaishaku to kanshō* 55, no. 4 (April 1990), 24–31.

51. Edward Said, *Culture and Imperialism* (New York: Knopf, 1993), 52 and 9.

52. Murai Osami, *Nantō ideorogii no hassei* (Origins of the South Islands ideology), rev. ed. (Tokyo: Ōta Shuppan, 1995), 39–47. For a survey of how the annexation was reported in the Japanese media in 1910, see Oguma, *Genealogy of "Japanese" Self-Images*, 81–92.

53. Morris-Suzuki, *Re-Inventing Japan*, 92.

54. On the promotion of marriages between Japanese and Korean subjects, see Oguma, *Genealogy of "Japanese" Self-Images*, especially 203–36. As Oguma notes, the figure of adopted children was also widely used to explain the absorption of other nations into the Japanese national family. On images of such marriages in Japanese popular culture, see Ayako Kano, "Japanese Theater and Imperialism: Romance and Resistance," *U.S.-Japan Women's Journal English Supplement* 12 (1996): 17–47.

55. Tokieda Motoki, "Chōsen ni okeru kokugo seisaku oyobi kokugo kyōiku no shōrai," (National language policy and the future of national language education in Korea), *Nihongo* 2, no. 8 (July 1942): 59. The work by Ueda that Tokieda refers to here, "Kokugo to Kokka" (National language and the nation-state), is the first section of his book *Kokugo no tame* (For a national language, 1895), widely considered the beginning of modern linguistics in Japan.

56. In *Colonial Desire: Hybridity in Theory, Culture, and Race* (London: Routledge, 1995), Robert Young argues that a fascination with "hybridity" is not so much a recent theoretical construct that distinguishes the postcolonial from the colonial, but rather one of the fundaments of colonial desire. "The question is whether the old essentializing categories of cultural identity, or of race, were really so essentialized, or have been retrospectively constructed as more fixed than they were. When we look at the texts of racial theory, we find that they are in fact contradictory, disruptive, and already deconstructed.

Hybridity here is a key term in that wherever it emerges it suggests the impossibility of essentialism. If so, then in deconstructing such essentialist notions of race today we may rather be repeating the past then distancing ourselves from it or providing a critique of it" (27). For useful discussions of the hybridities produced in Japanese colonial imagination, see two articles by Thomas Lamarre, "Bacterial Cultures and Linguistic Colonies: Mori Rintarō's Experiments with History, Science, and Languages," *positions* 6, no. 3 (Fall 1998): 597–635; and "The Deformation of the Modern Spectator: Synaesthesia, Cinema, and the Spectre of Race in Tanizaki," *Japan Forum* 11, no. 1 (1999): 23–42.

57. If we use the real-life models to connect characters in *The Family* to those in *Shinsei* (New life), Setsuko's father in the latter corresponds to Morihiko in the former. Morihiko's colonial career is briefly mentioned in *The Family*: "For a long while, Morihiko was in Korea. He kept his eye on the conditions of East Asia, but the members of the family knew only the broad outlines of his activities—that he had many acquaintances in a variety of fields, and that he had tried his hand at the import/export business." (*TZ* 4:63).

58. Though as Sekiya Yumiko notes in "Shinsei no shinwa kōzō: tozasareta shosai no monogatari" (The mythic structure of *Shinsei* [New life]: Tale of the closed-off study), *Nihon kindai bungaku* 45 (October 1991): 147–61, in *Shinsei* the spatial setting of the incestuous encounter has shifted from the verandah to the second-floor study.

59. The notion that Sankichi emerges as the new patriarch has been argued by a number of scholars. See, for example, Seki Ryōichi, "*Ie*: maboroshi no sanbusaku" (*Ie* [The family]: The phantom trilogy), in *Nihon bungaku kenkyū shiryō sōsho: Shimazaki Tōson II*, ed. Nihon Bungaku Kenkyū Shiryō Kankō Kai (Tokyo: Yūseidō, 1983), 152–64; and Kotani Hiroyuki, *Rekishi to ningen ni tsuite: Tōson to kindai Nihon* (On history and humanity: Tōson and modern Japan) (Tokyo: Tokyo Daigaku Shuppankai, 1991), 14–19. See also Kōno Kensuke, "Onna no kaiwa, otoko no kaiwa: *Ie* ni okeru kaiwa no gihō" (Women's conversations, men's conversations: The technique for conversations in *Ie* [The family]), in *Shimazaki Tōson: Bunmei hihyō to shi to shōsetsu to*, ed. Hiraoka Toshio and Kenmochi Takehiko (Tokyo: Sōbunsha, 1996), 167–81. Kōno argues that in the work, a mostly silent, predicative, and standardized language of patriarchy (and of narration) that claims to ground meaning is supplemented by a matrilineal, nonpredicative stream of female conversations spoken in nonstandard dialect. This dual structure sustains the family through the repeated failures of its patriarch, whose position is reduced to that of an empty sign. Sankichi's ability to step into and claim this vacancy allows him—via the mediation of the female characters' language—to assume the role of patriarch.

60. See Konaka, "Ie no chiyuryoku," for another interpretation of how Sankichi's rise to the position of quasi-patriarch represents the incursion of market competition into the domestic space of the family. Likewise, Dodd argues we should read *The Family* in the context of "a new economic order emanating from the capital from which Tōson gained one form of power even as he was denied another," so that Tōson, as a part of the "new Tokyo-centered social and economic hierarchy," was "able to exploit a newly emerging market need for nostalgic literary evocations of rural life" (Dodd, "The Railway as Rupture," 53).

61. Deleuze and Guattari, *Anti-Oedipus*, 119. Italics in original.

62. Deleuze and Guattari, *Anti-Oedipus*, 54. Italics in original. What follows is my

attempt to answer questions Mark Anderson and Miryam Sas raised separately about the status of representation in Tōson's works. I thank them for their perceptive criticism.

63. Deleuze and Guattari, *Anti-Oedipus*, 55. In fact, many so-called "I-novels" can be read against their presumptive genre norms; see Tomi Suzuki, *Narrating the Self: Fictions of Japanese Modernity* (Stanford: Stanford University Press, 1996).

64. For an analysis of Tōson's ethic of "simplicity" (*kanso*), see Nakayama, " 'Komoro' to iu basho." Arguing that this forms one tenet of the rationalization that modern industrial societies require, Nakayama argues that "simplicity" became the central ethic of Tōson's writing style, an ethic that repressed from view its complicity with the rising market economy. Nakayama notes how a comment that schoolteacher Tōson's wrote in correcting a student's essay reveals the link between literary style and commerce: Tōson encouraged his student to use simple "vocabulary like those on a merchant's order form, which anyone can understand" (63).

65. Sankichi's rise to the position of patriarch can be read through the schema of nineteenth-century European discourses on madness that Michel Foucault describes in *Madness and Civilization*, trans. Richard Howard (New York: Vintage, 1965). In *The Family*, the father's hereditary madness is split into two, between a corporeal madness that will respond only to physical therapy (the madness that Otane inherits and whose traces mark her body) and a spiritual madness that will respond only to psychological therapy (the madness that Sankichi inherits). This latter therapy interrogates the guilt of the subject, who is now held responsible for the moral failings that spiritual insanity is thought to signify. For example, "Just as when one goes to a great historic temple and the acolyte-guide narrates the life of a great priest while leading the pilgrims past pictures hanging on the ancient walls, so too did the anguish arising from Sankichi's flesh lead his mind past a variety of memories. . . . They were not like the chronicle of the life of a great priest. They were all without exception mental pictures of women. They were all memories he wanted to hide. Sankichi felt deeply, deeply disgusted with himself" (*TZ* 4:250). As Foucault argues, in this new discourse of madness, the very "prestige of patriarchy is revived around madness in the bourgeois family" (253). Sanity becomes the ability both to accept the domination of the father and (for the male child) to assume in turn the position of patriarch; spiritual insanity is conquered by subjecting it to "an infinitely self-referring observation; it was finally chained to the humiliation of being its own object" (265). These words of Foucault's might serve as a definition for the I-novel genre.

66. Nakayama Hiroaki, "*Ie* no shikaku: 'jigyō' to 'kannen' " (Perspective of *Ie* [The family]: "Enterprise" and "concept"), *Kokubungaku kenkyū* 89 (June 1989): 57–67. Nakayama historicizes *The Family* against the shift from family-run businesses to the modern enterprises that were an object of fascination in late-Meiji literature. Nakayama argues that in this historical context, the "family," which was in fact being torn apart by the external forces of modern capital, was reconfigured as a space that would compensate for the world that was being lost, and that *The Family* portrays this historical shift even down to the level of individual consciousness.

67. For example, Sankichi's reaction to a telegram from Minoru, demanding a huge amount of money: "Even if it wasn't the whole sum, he decided to send some money. For this purpose, he decided to sell the manuscript that he had just finally completed after three months' work" (*TZ* 4:123). Or again, later, Sankichi speaking to Shōta: "[Morihiko]

ordered me to raise two hundred yen. . . . If it will really help him, I'll figure out a way to raise it. I'll write something special to get it" (*TZ* 4:359).

68. Natsume Sōseki, *Sōseki zenshū* (Complete works of Sōseki), (Tokyo: Iwanami Shoten, 1966), 14:15. The words in italics here appear in English in the original. I first encountered this passage in the discussion of it in chapter 11 of Kamei Hideo, *Transformations of Sensibility: The Phenomenology of Meiji Literature*, trans. ed. Michael Bourdaghs (Ann Arbor: University of Michigan Center for Japanese Studies Publications, 2002).

69. The novel contains one passage of direct self-reference: near the end of book 2, when Sankichi is summoned to Nagoya to visit Shōta on his deathbed, he is reluctant to leave Tokyo for long because of his reluctance to interrupt the "work" he is in the midst of producing (*TZ* 4:403). Readers familiar with the details of Tōson's life would understand that this referred to *The Family* itself.

70. In *Shinsei* (New life), after the protagonist has published a confessional novel exposing his illicit relations with his niece, her father—the protagonist's elder brother—makes a similar accusation: "To blanch pale, to blush crimson, to have to write down everything you've done in order to pay the bills—what a pitiful business!" (*TZ* 7:452–53).

71. MacCannell, *Regime of the Brother*, 57.

72. The deaths of Sankichi's three daughters, of course, represent yet another sacrifice. It is implied that their various illnesses arose due to the poverty they endured after Sankichi quit his teaching job to devote his energies to writing. The short story "Mebae" (Seedlings, 1909), a first-person narrative of the deaths of the protagonist's three daughters that contains much language that would subsequently find its way into *The Family*, makes this connection even more explicitly. As the narrator resolves to resign from his teaching post he notes, "watching my daughters, I wondered how I could complete my work, how could I support my children during that time" (*TZ* 3:401). In the heat of composition, he even blurts out that he does not care what happens to his children, so long as he can produce his novel: "At busy times, I even felt that way. No matter what I had to sacrifice, I was determined to achieve as much as I could achieve" (*TZ* 3:410).

73. Nakano Shigeharu, "Iwayuru geijutsu no taishūka ron no ayamari ni tsuite" (On the mistaken notions of the so-called massification-of-literary-arts debate), originally published in *Senki* (June 1928), reprinted in *Nakano Shigeharu zenshū* (Complete Works of Nakano Shigeharu), (Tokyo: Chikuma Shobō, 1959), 6:150; further references to this work will be cited parenthetically. It should be noted, though, that Nakano's own poems and stories often deploy dense language that calls attention to its own productivity, thereby at least implicitly contradicting the stance he took in the above-mentioned essay. On Nakano's relation to a Marxist form of modernism, see Miriam Silverberg, *Changing Song: The Marxist Manifestos of Nakano Shigeharu* (Princeton: Princeton University Press, 1990).

74. Hosea Hirata, *The Poetry and Poetics of Nishikawa Junzaburō: Modernism in Translation* (Princeton: Princeton University Press, 1993), 134. On Japanese modernism, see also Miryam Sas, *Fault Lines: Cultural Memory and Japanese Surrealism* (Stanford: Stanford University Press, 1999); and Seiji Lippit, *Topographies of Japanese Modernism* (New York: Columbia University Press, 2002).

75. Deleuze and Guattari, *Anti-Oedipus*, 98.

76. Futabatei Shimei (1864–1909), "Yo ga hansei no zange" (Confession of my life's

story), in *Futabatei Shimei/Saganoya Omuro shū* (Anthology of Futabatei Shimei/Saganoya Omuro), vol. 17 of *Meiji bungaku zenshū* (Tokyo: Chikuma Shobō, 1971), 17:112–16. Tsubouchi Shōyō (1859–1935) was Futabatei's mentor and a better-established writer, and it was under his pen name that the first book of Futabatei's *Ukigumo* (Drifting clouds) was published.

77. Futabatei, "Yo ga hansei no zange." See the discussion of this essay and of Futabatei's career, as well as of Tōson's relation to Futabatei, in Dennis Washburn, *The Dilemma of the Modern in Japanese Fiction* (New Haven: Yale University Press, 1995). See also Marleigh Grayer Ryan, *Japan's First Modern Novel:* Ukigumo *of Futabatei Shimei* (Ann Arbor: Center for Japanese Studies, University of Michigan, 1965). On Futabatei's difficult relationship with commercial publishing toward the end of his life, see Komori Yōichi, *"Yuragi" no Nihon bungaku* ("Wavering" Japanese literature) (Tokyo: NHK Books, 1998), 62–63. On *Ukigumo* as publishing commodity and as media technology, see Kōno, *Shomotsu no kindai,* 28–34.

78. *TZ* 13:116. For more information on Tōson's entry into the world of corporate publishing, see Takagi Takeo, *Shinbun shōsetsu shi: Meiji-hen* (History of the newspaper novel: Meiji period) (Tokyo: Kokusho Kankōkai, 1974), 456–62.

79. In the May 28, 1909, issue of the Tokyo *Asahi* newspaper, Tōson published a brief eulogy for Futabatei. See "Hasegawa Futabatei-shi wo itamu" (Mourning Hasegawa/Futabatei), *Asahi,* 28 May 1909, reprinted in *TZ* 6:88–90.

80. *Junrei* (Pilgrimage) is reprinted in *TZ* 14:121–331. No English translation is available.

81. "Nihon kindai bungaku no hatten ni tsuite" (On the development of modern Japanese literature), reprinted in *TZ* 13:415–18.

82. Karatani Kōjin, *Origins of Modern Japanese Literature,* trans. ed. Brett de Bary (Durham: Duke University Press, 1993), 50–51. For a survey of works of modern Japanese fiction that foreground the act of narration over the narrated content, and hence subvert the norms of realism, see Atsuko Sakaki, *Recontextualizing Texts: Narrative Performance in Modern Japanese Fiction* (Cambridge: Harvard University Asia Center, 1999).

83. For a succinct history of these literary historical positions, see Tomi Suzuki, *Narrating the Self,* 48–95.

84. Ikuta Chōkō, "Tōson-shi no shōsetsu" (Mr. Tōson's novels), originally published in *Mita bungaku,* June 1911; reprinted in *TZ* 18:175–86.

85. Ōnuki, "Ie o yomu," 150. For more recent readings of the impressionistic techniques of description in the novel, see Donald Keene, *Dawn to the West: Japanese Literature of the Modern Era: Fiction* (New York: Henry Holt, 1984), 263–64; and Takahashi Masako, "*Ie* no jojutsu" (Description in *Ie* [The family]), *Nagoya kindai bungaku kenkyū* 2 (December 1984): 22–35.

86. These comments on Proust are from Gérard Genette, *Narrative Discourse: An Essay in Method,* trans. Jane E. Lewin (Ithaca: Cornell University Press, 1980), 210–11.

87. In his 1911 review of the serialized version of book 2, Ōnuki Shōsen explicitly compares Tōson's use of figurative language to "Maupassant's allegories." See his "*Gisei* wo yomite" (Reading *Gisei* [Sacrifices]), reprinted in *TZ* 18:158–60.

88. Tejaswini Niranjana, *Siting Translation: History, Post-Structuralism, and the Colonial Context* (Berkeley: University of California Press, 1992).

89. James A. Fujii, *Complicit Fictions: The Subject in the Modern Japanese Prose Narrative* (Berkeley: University of California Press, 1993), 98.

90. Lippit, *Topographies of Japanese Modernism*, 32.

91. Brett de Bary, " 'Credo Quia Absurdum': *Tenkō* and the Prisonhouse of Language," in *Culture and Identity: Japanese Intellectuals During the Interwar Years*, ed. J. Thomas Rimer (Princeton: Princeton University Press, 1990), 154–167; Silverberg, *Changing Song*.

92. On Terayama, see Carol Jay Sorgenfrei, "Shuji Terayama: Avant Garde Dramatist of Japan" (Ph. D. diss., University of California at Santa Barbara, 1978).

93. Balibar and Wallerstein, *Race, Nation, Class*, 88.

94. Gilles Deleuze and Félix Guattari, *Kafka: Toward a Minor Literature*, trans. Dana Plan (Minneapolis: University of Minnesota Press, 1986), 17.

Chapter 4. Suicide and Childbirth in the I-Novel: *"Women's Literature"* in Spring *and* New Life

1. The significance of Shōta's tuberculosis, and of illness in general in the novel, is interpreted in its connection to masculine desire and the "virus" of money in Nakayama Hiroaki, "Kettō no monogatari—*Ie* no 'yamai' ron" (A tale of blood lineage: Disease in *Ie* [The family]) in *Shimazaki Tōson bunmei hihyō to shi to shōsetsu* (Shimazaki Tōson: Cultural critic, poetry, and novels) ed. Hiraoka Toshio and Kenmochi Takehiko (Tokyo: Sōfunsha Shuppan, 1996), 182–97.

2. Iwano Hōmei, "Jisatsu ron" (1908), in *Iwano Hōmei zenshū* (Complete works of Iwano Hōmei), (Kyoto: Rinsen Shoten, 1995), 9:242.

3. For example, in the travel narrative *Junrei* (Pilgrimage, 1937–1940), after recounting his visit to Shanghai and the haunts of the recently deceased writer Lu Xun, Tōson notes the following: "Lu Xun, the writer born out of the Republic of China, left behind him the following words, spoken on his final sickbed: In Japan, they have the thing known as love suicides [*shinjū*]. Japanese people possess a temperament that makes them take matters that seriously. That is why I am envious of the Japanese. We don't find that in Chinese people. No matter what is at issue, they are always happy to let matters slide. If we don't change that attitude, we will never be able to renew China." (*TZ* 14:327).

4. See Alan Wolfe, *Suicidal Narrative in Modern Japan: The Case of Dazai Osamu* (Princeton: Princeton University Press, 1990) for a critique of this notion and for citations of numerous examples of this discourse.

5. See chapter 7 in Kamei Hideo, *Transformations of Sensibility: The Phenomenology of Meiji Literature*, trans. Michael Bourdaghs (Ann Arbor: University of Michigan Center for Japanese Studies Publications, 2002).

6. "Pure literature" (usually *jun bungaku*) was a term coined first in the Meiji period to distinguish literature in the narrow sense (fiction, poetry, drama, and so on) from literature in the broad sense (all writing), although starting in the Taishō period its definitional other shifted: it came to signify high literature in opposition to popular or mass literature (*taishū bungaku*). One of the hallmarks of "pure literature" in this latter sense was its truthful, confessional nature: that is, the centrality of the I-novel to it. See Suzuki Sadami, *Nihon no "bungaku" gainen* (Japan's concept of "literature") (Tokyo: Sakuhinsha, 1998), especially 38–40 and 253–257.

7. Saitō Minako, *Ninshin shōsetsu* (Pregnancy novels) (Tokyo: Chikuma Bunko, 1997), esp. 28–40. I am grateful to Yamazaki Yoshimitsu for pointing out the relevance of this study to my work.

8. For a study that argues that canonical literature must always summon up its opposite, popular culture, in order to prove its distance from it, see Thomas Strychacz, *Modernism, Mass Culture, and Professionalism* (London: Cambridge University Press, 1993).

9. On the relation of gender and genre, see Leigh Gilmour, *Autobiographics: A Feminist Theory of Women's Self-Representation* (Ithaca: Cornell University Press, 1994), especially 16–64. See also Judith Butler, *Gender Trouble: Feminism and the Subversion of Identity* (London: Routledge, 1990). See Suga Hidemi, *Nihon kindai bungaku no "tanjō": genbun itchi to nashonarizumu* (The "birth" of modern Japanese literature: *Genbun itchi* and nationalism) (Tokyo: Ōta Shuppan, 1995) on this problem in Meiji literature. For Suga's own reading of *Haru* (Spring), see his " 'Onna' to iu hikokumin: 'teikoku' no bungaku 2" (The non-national called "woman": The literature of "empire" 2), *Hihyō kūkan* 2d ser., no. 14 (1997): 229–46.

10. Judith Butler, *Bodies That Matter: On the Discursive Limits of "Sex"* (New York: Routledge, 1993), 104; italics in original.

11. William Haver, *The Body of This Death: Historicity and Sociality in the Time of AIDS* (Stanford: Stanford University Press, 1996), 41–42. Italics in original.

12. For a critical history of the genre of *joryū bungaku*, see Joan E. Ericson, *Be a Woman: Hayashi Fumiko and Modern Japanese Women's Literature* (Honolulu: University of Hawaii Press, 1997), as well as her "The Origins of the Concept of 'Women's Literature' " in *The Woman's Hand: Gender and Theory in Japanese Women's Writings*, ed. Paul Gordon Schalow and Janet A. Walker (Stanford: Stanford University Press, 1996), 74–115. See also Tomi Suzuki, "Gender and Genre: Modern Literary Histories and Women's Diary Literature" in *Inventing the Classics: Modernity, National Identity, and Japanese Literature*, ed. Haruo Shirane and Suzuki (Stanford: Stanford University Press, 2000), 71–95. Other recent useful studies of modern Japanese "women's literature" include Victoria V. Vernon, *Daughters of the Moon: Wish, Will, and Social Constraint in Fiction by Modern Japanese Women* (Berkeley: Institute of East Asian Studies, University of California, 1988); Nina Cornyetz, *Dangerous Women, Deadly Words: Phallic Fantasy and Modernity in Three Japanese Writers* (Stanford: Stanford University Press, 1999); and Rebecca L. Copeland, *Lost Leaves: Women Writers of Meiji Japan* (Honolulu: University of Hawaii Press, 2000). Perhaps the most devastating attack in Japanese criticism on the very notion of *joryū bungaku* is the parodic study of "men's literature" found in Ueno Chizuko, Ogura Chikako, and Tomioka Taeko, *Danryū bungaku ron* (Theory of men's literature) (Tokyo: Chikuma Shobō, 1992).

13. For example, see Irmela Hijiya-Kirschnereit, *Rituals of Self-Revelation: Shishōsetsu as Literary Genre and Socio-Cultural Phenomenon* (Cambridge: Council on East Asian Studies, Harvard University, 1996), 67.

14. Miyoshi Yukio, *Shimazaki Tōson ron* (On Shimazaki Tōson), vol. 1 of *Miyoshi Yukio chosaku shū* (Collected works of Miyoshi Yukio) (1966; reprint, Tokyo: Chikuma Shobō, 1993), 1:145–73.

15. For a critique of the I-novel and the critical discourse that grew up around it, see Tomi Suzuki, *Narrating the Self: Fictions of Japanese Modernity* (Stanford: Stanford University Press, 1996). For a close analysis of the linguistic forms used in I-novels to produce a

sense of immediacy, see Edward Fowler, *The Rhetoric of Confession: Shishōsetsu in Early Twentieth-Century Japanese Fiction* (Berkeley: University of California Press, 1988). For critiques of the constructed nature of interiority in I-novels and other genres of modern Japanese fiction, see Karatani Kōjin, *Origins of Modern Japanese Literature*, trans. ed. Brett de Bary (Durham: Duke University Press, 1993); and James A. Fujii, *Complicit Fictions: The Subject in the Modern Japanese Prose Narrative* (Berkeley: University of California Press, 1993).

16. Tomi Suzuki, *Narrating the Self*, 3–5.

17. Kikuchi Kan, "Contemporary Japanese Literature," (published in both English and Japanese) *Bungei shunjū* 13, no. 12 (December 1935): 237–38.

18. Gregory Jusdanis, *Belated Modernity and Aesthetic Culture: Inventing National Literature* (Minneapolis: University of Minnesota Press, 1991). On the formation of national literature as a modern ideological institution in Meiji Japan, see Mark Anderson, "National Literature as Cultural Monument: Instituting the Japanese National Community," in *New Directions in the Study of Meiji Japan*, ed. Helen Hardacre and Adam L. Kern (Leiden: Brill, 1997), 45–59; and Suzuki Sadami, *Nihon no "bungaku" gainen*. Other important studies of the rise of national literature as an institution include Peter Uwe Hohendahl, *Building a National Literature: The Case of Germany, 1830–1870*, trans. Renate Baron Franciscono (Ithaca, N.Y.: Cornell University Press, 1989); and Gerald Graff, *Professing Literature: An Institutional History* (Chicago: University of Chicago Press, 1987).

19. An exception to this tendency can be found in Ōida Yoshiaki, "*Haru* ni okeru komyunikeishon no mondai" (The problem of communication in *Haru* [Spring]), *Bai* 7 (July 1991): 33–47. Ōida tends to treat Katsuko and Aoki in parallel. For a representative example in English-language scholarship of the tendency to downplay Katsuko's role, see Edwin McClellan, "Tōson and the Autobiographical Novel," in *Tradition and Modernization in Japanese Culture*, ed. Donald H. Shively (Princeton: Princeton University Press, 1971), 347–78. McClellan's sole mention of Katsuko's significance in the novel in this essay is as follows: "Kishimoto is in love with a girl whom he had come to know while teaching in a women's college. However she hardly ever appears in the book. She marries someone else, and dies soon thereafter" (369).

20. See Copeland, *Lost Leaves*, 7–51; and Michael C. Brownstein, "*Jogaku zasshi* and the Founding of *Bungakkai*," *Monumenta Nipponica* 35, no. 3 (1980): 319–36. See Kobayashi Akiko, "Shimazaki Tōson no joseikan: Iwamoto Yoshiharu no joseikan to no kakawari" (Shimazaki Tōson's view of women: Its relation to Iwamoto Yoshiharu's view of women), *Tōkyō Joshi Daigaku Nihon bungaku* 76 (September 1991): 38–49, for an exploration of the impact that Iwamoto Yoshiharu (1863–1942), the (male) Christian intellectual founder of *Jogaku zasshi*, had on Tōson's fiction.

21. Donald Keene, *Dawn to the West: Japanese Literature of the Modern Era: Fiction* (New York: Henry Holt, 1984), 260.

22. This is from the 1983 essay, "Tōson: hito to bungaku" (Tōson: His life and literature), reprinted in Miyoshi Yukio, *Shimazaki Tōson ron* (On Shimazaki Tōson), 345–63. This quotation appears on 346.

23. See Mizuta Noriko, "Josei jikogatari to monogatari" (Women's self-narration and tales), *Hihyō kūkan* 1st ser., no. 4 (1992): 64–79. Arguing that one must distinguish gender as a trope that becomes one component of genre in various premodern narrative genres

(Japanese *monogatari* tales as well as such European forms as the gothic tale) from, on the other hand, gender as a constitutive element of enunciative subjectivity in social reality, she argues that male writers were able to adopt feminine gender as a trope immanent to various genres without altering the gendering of their actual enunciative subjective positions. For a discussion of Mizuta's work and a sustained critique of the modern construction of femininity as representative of Japanese tradition, see Cornyetz, *Dangerous Women, Deadly Words*.

24. See T. Fujitani, *Splendid Monarchy: Power and Pageantry in Modern Japan* (Berkeley: University of California Press, 1996), especially 171–194.

25. A typical example of this tendency can be found in Yanagita Izumi, "Meiji jidai ni okeru josei bungaku" (Women's literature in the Meiji period), *Kokubungaku kanshō to kaishaku* 6, no. 12 (December 1941): 48–56. Yanagita argues that writing by women in the Meiji period achieved a relative autonomy from men's literature yet goes on to argue that developments in women's literature tended to be nothing more than repetitions of the developments in men's literature, except on a smaller scale and a few years delayed.

26. Or, to borrow Julia Kristeva's language, so-called "pure literature" amounts to a "secondary repression" that "attempts to transfer to its own account . . . the resources of primal repression"; that is, the resources arising from the repression of the infant's attachment to the maternal body. Julia Kristeva, *Powers of Horror: An Essay on Abjection*, trans. Leon S. Roudiez (New York: Columbia University Press, 1982), 15. Here, though, we need to keep in mind that the "primary repression" too is a socially and historically constructed component of subjectivity.

27. Gilmour, *Autobiographics*, 5–7.

28. On *Shojochi*, see Makino Noriko, "Tōson to fujin undō: *Shojochi* o chūshin toshite" (Tōson and the women's movement—With special focus on *Shojochi*), in *Tōson Kinen Kan kōen shū* (Collected lectures from the Tōson Memorial Museum), ed. Tōson Kinen Kan (Magome, Nagano Pref.: Tōson Kinen Gō, 1994), 176–184; and the entry "Shojochi" in *STJ*:214–16. The editorial stance of the magazine was in many ways a continuation of the liberal, humanistic line of middle-class feminism that had characterized *Jogaku zasshi*, a stance that was much less radical than its more famous predecessor, the feminist journal *Seitō* (published 1911–1916).

29. Quoted in Makino, "Tōson to fujin undō," 178.

30. On Meiji-period feminism, see Sharon L. Sievers, *Flowers in Salt: The Beginnings of Feminist Consciousness in Modern Japan* (Stanford: Stanford University Press, 1983). On Taishō-period feminism, see Laurel Rasplica Rodd, "Yosano Akiko and the Taishō Debate over the 'New Woman,' " in *Recreating Japanese Women, 1600–1945*, ed. Gail Lee Bernstein (Berkeley: University of California Press, 1991), 175–198.

31. "Dokusha e" (To the reader) from *Shojochi* 1 (April 1922), reprinted in *TZ* 9:539–40. "The House of Life" is a sonnet sequence by Dante Gabriel Rossetti; it is referred to in numerous works by Tōson and is quoted at length in *Shinsei* (New life; *TZ* 7:418–20).

32. One work that is important in this respect is the 1925 short story "Nobijitaku" (Preparations for growth), reprinted in *TZ* 10:53–61. It describes the tremendous change that occurs in its female protagonist with the onset of her first menstrual period—"Now

Sodeko came to see clearly the difference between men and women" (60)—as well as the sense of helplessness her widower father feels as a man, unable to aid her.

33. On the role of women in Meiji Japan, see Ueno Chizuko, "Kaisetsu" (Afterword), in *Fūzoku sei* (Public morals and sexuality), vol. 23 of *Nihon kindai shisō taikei*, ed. Ogi Shinzō, Kumakura Isao, and Ueno Chizuko (Anthology of modern Japanese thought) (Tokyo: Iwanami Shoten, 1990), 23:505–50; and Sharon Nolte and Sally Ann Hastings, "The Meiji State's Policy Toward Women, 1890–1910," in *Recreating Japanese Women, 1600–1945*, ed. Gail Lee Bernstein (Berkeley: University of California Press, 1991), 151–74.

34. See Egusa Mitsuko, "*Kusamakura* no ninshin shussan wo megutte" (Regarding pregnancy and childbirth in *Kusamakura* [Grass by the wayside]), *Sōseki kenkyū* 3 (1994): 102–17; and Miyasaka Yasuko, " 'Osan' no shakai shi" (A social history of birthing), in *Bosei: Nihon no feminizumu 5*, ed. Inoue Teruko, Ueno Chizuko, and Ehara Yumiko (Tokyo: Iwanami Shoten, 1995), 89–124. On the rise of modern sexology, including reforms in birth control law, regulation of midwifery, and population management, see Sabine Frühstück, *Die Politik der Sexualwissenschaft: Zur Produktion und Popularisierung sexologischen Wissens in Japan, 1908–1941* (Vienna: Instituts für Japanologie der Universität Wien, 1997).

35. Saitō, *Ninshin shōsetsu*, 17. See also Egusa Mitsuko, "*Shinsei* nōto: Furansu ni iku made" (Note on *Shinsei* [New life]: Up to the departure for France) in *Nihon kindai bungaku* 49 (October 1993): 61–73; and Iwami Teruyo, "Setsuko to iu tekusuto: *Shinsei* no sekushuariti" (The text called Setsuko: sexuality in *Shinsei* [New life]), *Nihon kindai bungaku* 53 (October 1995): 108–21, for readings of *Shinsei* that situate it against the historical "sexuality" specific to Meiji and Taishō Japan.

36. Cornyetz, *Dangerous Women, Deadly Words*, 7.

37. Ayako Kano, *Acting Like a Woman in Modern Japan: Theater, Gender, and Nationalism* (New York: Palgrave, 2001), 21.

38. Andrew Parker et al., "Introduction," in *Nationalisms and Sexualities*, ed. Andrew Parker et al. (New York: Routledge, 1992), 5.

39. *Haru* is reprinted in *TZ* 3:3–246. No English translation is available.

40. For a useful study of *Haru* that uses Roland Barthes's theory of semiotic coding to unpack the relationship the novel posits between eros and literary representation, see Watanabe Hiroshi, *Shimazaki Tōson wo yominaosu* (Rereading Shimazaki Tōson) (Tokyo: Sōjusha, 1994), 65–105.

41. Hence women remain in the background of the group: "She was called 'Denma-chō' and she was sympathetic to her elder brothers' work and earnestly read the group's writings. Kyōko, Minako, Katsuko, and there was also one they called 'Aomori': these young women stood like sisters behind the group, bravely trying to assist them, sometimes offering up their adoration, at other times their sympathy, and always trying to draw near to their spirit" (*TZ* 3:43). The one briefly mentioned exception is the elder Tsutsumi sister (modeled after Higuchi Ichiyō), a writer whose works were first introduced to the world through the group's magazine, and who comes from a family sustained not by men but by women (*TZ* 3:202). On Ichiyō's relation to the norms of *joryū bungaku*, including the way she molded her literary voice to fit masculine expectations, see Seki Reiko, "Tatakau 'chichi no musume': Ichiyō tekusuto no seisei," (Fighting "Daughter of the father": The formation of the Ichiyō text) in *Onna ga yomu Nihon kindai bungaku: fem-*

inizumo hihyō no kokoromi (Modern Japanese literature as read by women: An attempt at feminist criticism), ed. Egusa Mitsuko and Urushida Kazuo (Tokyo: Shinyōsha, 1992), 31–54; and Copeland, *Lost Leaves*, especially 44.

42. Chida Hiroyuki notes the homoerotic relationship between Aoki and Kishimoto. See his "Fusei to dōsei kara no kaihō: *Hakai* no kōzu" (Liberation from patriarch and the same-sex: The composition of *Hakai* [The broken commandment]) in *Shimazaki Tōson: bunmei hihyō to shi to shōsetsu to*, ed. Hiraoka and Kenmochi (Tokyo: Sōbunsha, 1996), 154–66.

43. In his reading of the networks of communication and miscommunication that structure *Haru* (Spring), Ōida ("*Haru* ni okeru komyunikeishon no mondai") pays close attention to the role that nonverbal communication, that is, body language, plays, particularly in the communication between Aoki and Kishimoto. In it, the bodies of the male characters are foregrounded—and yet only to the degree that they function as transparent signifiers, providing access to the otherwise unspoken interiority. Male bodies are depicted only insofar as they function as windows on the soul.

44. Wolfe, *Suicidal Narrative in Modern Japan*, 68 and 75; emphasis in original.

45. See Nakayama Hiroaki, " 'Shōsetsu' no shihonron: Kōzu Takeshi to patoronēji" (The capitalism of the novel: Kōzu Takeshi and patronage), *Bungei to hihyō* 7, no. 10 (October 1994): 67–80; and Igari Akira, "Kawakami Bizan no shi: Meiji bunshi no keizai seikatsu" (The death of Kawakami Bizan: The economic life of Meiji writers), *Nihon kindai bungaku* 12 (May 1970): 89–100.

46. See Kawamura Kunimitsu, "Onna no yamai, otoko no yamai" (Women's diseases, men's diseases), *Gendai shisō* 21, no. 7 (July 1993), 88–109. In nineteenth-century America, too, "women's insanity was often thought to be a danger inherent to the female body, particularly the reproductive system, while men's insanity was attributed more commonly to bad habits," so that "insanity could result from women's very constitution, their very femaleness, while for men it would most likely be caused not by who they were but by what they did." Mary Elene Wood, *The Writing on the Wall: Women's Autobiography and the Asylum* (Urbana: University of Illinois Press, 1994), 7.

47. The Genroku Revival, also known as the Saikaku Revival, dominated literary circles in Japan in the early 1890s. Grounded in a rediscovery of the works of the Edo period, especially those of Ihara Saikaku, whose collected works were published in four volumes by Hakubunkan as part of its *Teikoku bunkō* series from 1894–1895, the movement was represented by such as figures Higuchi Ichiyō and Ozaki Kōyō.

48. Konaka Nobutaka, "*Haru* ron: shinwa no shūen" (On *Haru* [Spring]: The end of myth), *Nihon kindai bungaku* 36 (October 1987): 30–43, especially 34–35.

49. Kristeva, *Powers of Horror*, 28.

50. For an interpretation of Kishimoto's decision to forego suicide that explicates how his behavior is guided by a blind vital force, one that brings him both to the brink of death and then back to the world of life, see Sasaki Masanobu, "*Haru* wo megutte: Kishimoto Sutekichi zō no ichimen" (Regarding *Haru* [Spring]: One aspect of the figure of Kishimoto Sutekichi), *Nihon kindai bungaku* 25 (October 1978): 168–79.

51. Kōno Kensuke, " 'Seishun' to iu tekusuto: Shimazaki Tōson *Haru* wo megutte" (The text that is "youth": Regarding Shimazaki Tōson's *Haru* [Spring]) in *Bungaku ni okeru nijūdai* (Twenty-somethings in literature), ed. Satō Yasumasa (Tokyo: Kasama Shoin, 1990), 123–44.

52. Ōida ("*Haru ni okeru komyunikeishon no mondai*") notes that the narrator in *Haru* (Spring) uses expressions that seem to identify him as Kishimoto writing a decade or so after the events described and notes that this structure serves to legitimate the Kishimoto depicted: the novel itself serves as proof of the eventual success of his initially failed attempts at writing.

53. On the suicidal nature of literature, see Wolfe, *Suicidal Narrative in Modern Japan*. See also Naoki Sakai, *Translation and Subjectivity: On "Japan" and Cultural Nationalism* (Minneapolis: University of Minnesota Press, 1997), 177–92.

54. Wolfe, *Suicidal Narrative in Modern Japan*, 14–15.

55. I thank Sharalyn Orbaugh for pointing out to me that several works conventionally considered I-novels, including Natsume Sōseki's *Michikusa* (Grass by the wayside, 1915) and Shiga Naoya's *Wakai* (Reconciliation, 1917), do depict pregnancies and childbirths in more detail than we find in Tōson's works. Particularly in the former, the husband's flustered inability to cope with his wife's delivery has been read as a relativizing of his authority, a deliberate deconstruction of masculinity and its claims to represent rationality. See Matsushita Hiroyuki, "1910 nendai ni okeru *Michikusa* to *Wakai*: sono 'shussan' ga imi suru mono" (*Michikusa* [Grass by the wayside] and *Wakai* [Reconciliation] in the 1910s: What "childbirth" signifies in them), *Meiji Daigaku daigakuin kiyō: bungaku hen* 30 (February 1993): 47–66. But see also Egusa, "*Kusamakura* no ninshin shussan wo megutte." Egusa argues that this can be read as simply a more nuanced strategy for privileging the masculine position and distinguishing its spirituality from the embodied suffering of the wife, a strategy complicit with modern forms of patriarchy. Following Egusa's reading, *Michikusa* and *Wakai* do not so much undermine the patriarchal I-novel strategies I am finding in *Haru* (Spring) and *Shinsei* (New life) as they represent alternative strategies for achieving similar results.

56. See Haver, *Body of This Death*, 66, on the abject nature of death in childbirth.

57. My argument here is influenced by George Mosse, *Nationalism and Sexuality* (Madison: University of Wisconsin Press, 1985) and Eve Kosofsky Sedgwick, *Between Men: English Literature and Male Homosocial Desire* (New York: Columbia University Press, 1985).

58. Takahashi Masako, "Taishō-ki no ryōsei mondai: ren'ai ron to *Shinsei*" (The problem of the two genders in the Taishō period: On theories of romantic love and *Shinsei* [New life]), *Nagoya Daigaku kindai bungaku kenkyū* 3 (November 1985): 10–23.

59. Sedgwick, *Between Men*, 36; emphasis in original.

60. Chida Hiroyuki, "Sei/'kaku' koto no seijigaku: *Shinsei* ni okeru masukyuriniti no senryaku" (The political science of sex/"writing": Strategies of masculinity in *Shinsei* [New life]), in *Shimazaki Tōson*, ed. Shimoyama Jōko, vol. 30 of *Nihon bungaku kenkyū ronbun shūsei* (Collected scholarly essays on Japanese literature) (Tokyo: Wakakusa Shobō, 1999), 30:195–212.

61. Michel Foucault, "What is an Author?" in *The Foucault Reader*, ed. Paul Rabinow (New York: Pantheon, 1984), 101–20.

62. It is not surprising, given this turn of events, that criticism of the novel has frequently devolved into moral condemnation of the author. Sekiya Yumiko, in "*Shinsei* no shinwa kōzō: tozasareta shosai no monogatari" (The mythic structure of *Shinsei* [New life]: Tale of the closed-off study), *Nihon kindai bungaku* 45 (October 1991): 147–61, argues

that this focus on moral conduct obscures the connection between the work and its historical moment, a connection she traces through the way the novel relies on a "mythic" structure that invokes a precivilizational "savage" nature as the tonic for the modern, overcivilized intellectual. For other attempts that seek to escape moralistic frameworks by historicizing the novel, see Sekii Mitsuo, "*Shinsei* ron: jiden to iu kokuhaku no yōshiki" (On *Shinsei* [New life]: The confessional form called autobiography), *Kokubungaku kaishaku to kanshō* 55, no. 4 (April 1990), 93–99; and Takahashi Masako, "*Shinsei* ron" (On *Shinsei* [New life]), *Nagoya bungaku kenkyū* 1 (September 1983), 1–16.

63. There is one other novel, *Sakura no mi ga juku suru toki* (When the cherries ripen, 1914–1918), in the series of works depicting the life of Kishimoto. This work (much shorter than either *Haru* [Spring] or *Shinsei* [New life]) is a kind of prequel to *Haru*, depicting Kishimoto's early years as a student at a Christian mission school. No English translation is available.

64. *Shinsei* (New life) comprises the preface and books 1 and 2. It is reprinted in *TZ* 7. No English translation is currently available. The most comprehensive discussion of *Shinsei* in English is contained in Janet Walker, *The Japanese Novel of the Meiji Period and the Ideal of Individualism* (Princeton: Princeton University Press, 1979).

65. This is the extent to which Sonoko's death is described at this point: "his wife at the time she gave birth to their seventh child, a daughter, died due to severe hemorrhaging after the delivery" (*TZ* 7:7).

66. Hence, his send-off onto his voyage is twice compared to a "funeral" (*TZ* 7:94–95).

67. A passage quoted from Kishimoto's travel dispatches is also significant. While this dispatch is written at a time when he is still concealing the reason for his exile to Europe, it nonetheless demonstrates to his newspaper readers (and to the reader of *Shinsei* [New life], aware of the secret from the start) that the trip was motivated by the troubling emergence of Kishimoto's own body: "Savages move in response to necessity. I am the same way. Faced with an unresolvable situation, I went into motion." He describes his nervous, depressed condition prior to his departure, in which he would sometimes remain in bed for as long as two days straight. He concludes, "my own body became too much for me" (*TZ* 7:361–62).

68. Typically, rather than give us a detailed description of the moment of childbirth, the narrator gives us a distanced view of it, indirectly summarizing a description of it from a letter that Setsuko sends Kishimoto. We are told that the letter describes the birth "in detail [*komagoma to kaite yokoshita*]," but those details are not reported to the reader (*TZ* 7:127). For an analysis of Setsuko's illnesses in the context of the discourse of modern medicine and an analysis of her subsequent textual production as connected to her inability to assume the role of "mother," see Iwami Teruyo, "Setsuko no monogatari: *Shinsei* no topogurafii" (Setsuko's tale: The topography of *Shinsei* [New life]) in *Shimazaki Tōson bunmei hihyō to shi to shōsetsu* (Shimazaki Tōson: Cultural critic, poetry, and novels), ed. Hiraoka Toshio and Kenmochi Takeo (Tokyo: Sōbunsha, 1996), 215–29.

69. Chida ("Sei/'kaku' koto no seijigaku: *Shinsei* ni okeru masukyuriniti no senryaku") argues that through the act of writing, Kishimoto acquires not only the pen/penis of the patriarch, but also—with the figuring in the novel of writing as a kind of childbirth—a womb, so that he is able to displace any need for a female body.

70. Nakayama Hiroaki provides a fascinating reading of the letters that are exchanged

between the novel's characters in "*Shinsei* no messēji: tegami to tanka" (The messages of *Shinsei* [New life]: Letters and tanka poems), *Bai* 7 (July 1991): 48–61.

71. Kamei Hideo, "Kyo no dokusha" (The fictional reader), *Bungaku* 57, no. 2 (March 1989), 1–6.

72. Hence they are genres that can be produced by colonial subjects. See Yanagi Sōetsu's 1954 essay, "The Beauty of Irregularity," in Yanagi, *The Unknown Craftsman*, ed. Bernard Leach (Tokyo: Kodansha, 1972), 119–26 . When Yanagi (also known as Yanagi Muneyoshi, 1889–1961) celebrates Korean pottery, it is precisely because its products are not those of individualistic authors: "Korean work is but an uneventful, natural outcome of the people's state of mind, free from dualistic, man-made rules" (123). Folk art, be it from Japan's former colonies or Japan's premodern past (Yanagi equates the two), is inherently maternal: its qualities are "born, not made" (125).

73. Kōno Kensuke, "*Shinsei* ni okeru sensō: Shimazaki Tōson no 'sōsaku' to kokumin kokka" (War in *Shinsei* [New life]: Shimazaki Tōson's creation and the nation-state), *Nihon bungaku* 44, no. 11 (November 1995): 1–10.

74. This notion that the exile in Paris represents a continuation of his father's lifework also appears in Tōson's nonfiction travel writings. In a section of *Umi e* (To the sea, 1918) that is written in the form of a direct address to his father, Tōson declares that his trip to Europe is not a rejection of his father's life, but rather its logical extension: "Your heart stayed with me in the depths of my soul, a light that never dimmed. Forgive me for speaking like this, but I did not launch onto this trip out of a blind admiration for the West. For me, the West was still the Black Ships. An illusion. A phantom. I wanted to see its true nature more clearly" (*TZ* 8:64).

75. At this point Kishimoto again mentally rehearses his previous encounters with death. He recalls the shock he felt when he heard that Katsuko had gotten married and the worse shock when he heard that "barely one year after she married, due to morning sickness from her pregnancy, in the prime of her youth, she died" (*TZ* 7:231). Subsequently, as he walks past the maternity hospital on his way home, he reflects on Aoki's suicide (*TZ* 7:232). Finally, he recalls the death of his wife Sonoko: "Having hemorrhaged after giving birth, Sonoko departed this world almost without time to speak words of farewell to her children; since then, he had become one who simply stared vacantly at this thing called woman" (*TZ* 7:233). This is the most sustained description of death from childbirth in the novels under consideration here.

76. Many of Tōson's friends considered the publication of *Shinsei* (New life) a suicidal gesture, fearing that the novel was an extended suicide note.

77. For an account of all the self-contradictions that must be performed for Kishimoto to reach this conclusion, see Egusa Mitsuko, "Yūwaku to kokuhaku: *Shinsei* no tekusuto senryaku" (Temptation and confession: Textual strategies in *Shinsei* [New life]), in *Dansei sakka o yomu: feminizumu hihyō no seijuku e* (Reading male authors: toward a mature feminist criticism), ed. Egusa et al. (Tokyo: Shinyōsha, 1994), 1–35.

78. Sakai, *Translation and Subjectivity*, 18–19.

79. Sakai, *Translation and Subjectivity*, 27; emphasis in original.

80. Maeda Ai, *Kindai dokusha no seiritsu* (Establishment of the modern reader) (Tokyo: Chikuma Shobō, 1989), 151–98. See also Ericson, "Origins of the Concept of 'Women's Literature.' "

81. See Egusa, "*Kusamakura* no ninshin shussan wo megutte." Chida (in "Sei/'kaku' koto no seijigaku: *Shinsei* ni okeru masukyuriniti no senryaku") notes the relevance of the contemporary *bosei hogo ronsō* (debate over the protection of motherhood) to *Shinsei* (New life) and its depiction of pregnancy. For a recounting of the debate, see Rodd, "Yosano Akiko and the Taishō Debate over the 'New Woman.' "

82. Takano Junko, " '*Chūō kōron*' to 'josei': Meiji yonjūsan-nen 'Joryū sakka shōsetsu jippen' wo yomu" ("*Chūō kōron*" and "women": Reading the 1910 "Women novelist special issue"), *Bungei to hihyō* 7, no. 10 (October 1994): 42–57.

83. Linda Flores, "Subjectivity and the Body: Images of Women in Showa Literature" (unpublished paper, University of California at Los Angeles, 2000).

84. Sugiyama Heisuke, "Geijutsu to moraru" (Art and morals) in *Chūō kōron* 52, no. 5 (May 1937): 391–402. For another critical contemporary reaction to the "second *Shinsei* [New life] incident," see Itō Shirō, "Shimazaki Tōson ron" (On Shimazaki Tōson), *Yuibutsuron kenkyū* 63 (January 1938): 78–96.

85. Part 1 appears in *Fujin Kōron* (May 1937): 282–290, and part 2 in the same journal (June 1937): 200–210. Further references to these works will be cited parenthetically by part and page numbers. A number of Komako's letters as well as relevant newspaper articles from this period are reprinted in Fuji Kazuya, "Shōwa jūni-nen roku-gatsu unmei no 'ibara no michi': Hasegawa (Shimazaki) Komako shoken (Shōwa 11nen-13nen)" (June, 1937, and the "Path of thorns" of fate: Hasegawa [Shimazaki] Komako's correspondence [1936–1938]), *Fuji Kazuya kojinshi Shimazaki Tōson* 12 (December 1999): 26–54.

86. When Japanese women writers in the 1920s published confessional works of prose, their work was not typically assigned to the I-novel genre, but rather to that of *jiden shōsetsu* (autobiographical novel) (Ericson, *Be a Woman*, 27).

87. Komako was not the only woman writer to respond in print to *Shinsei* (New life). See Okamoto Kanoko, "Josei no mitaru gendai sakka no joryū byōsha: Tōson-shi no josei byōsha" (Description of women by contemporary writers as seen by a woman: Tōson's description of women), 1920; reprinted in *TZ* 18:254–55. She complains that the portrait of Setsuko in the latter half of the novel unrealistically has her adopt Kishimoto's views of the world, losing the sense of a real woman that characterized her portrayal in the opening chapters.

88. Gilmour, *Autobiographics*, 12.

89. Iwami, "Setsuko no monogatari." See also Iwami Teruyo, "Setsuko to iu tekusuto: *Shinsei* no sekushuariti" (The text that is Setsuko: Sexuality in *Shinsei* [New life]), *Nihon kindai bungaku* 53 (October 1995), 108–21.

90. Wood, *Writing on the Wall*, 94.

91. On the collaboration of 1930s feminist activists with the state, see Nishikawa Yūko, "Japan's Entry into War and the Support of Women," trans. William Gardner and Brett de Bary, *U.S.-Japan Women's Journal English Supplement* 12 (1996): 48–83; and Oguma Eiji, *A Genealogy of "Japanese" Self-Images*, trans. David Askew (Melbourne: Trans Pacific Press: 2002), 156–171.

92. Wood, *Writing on the Wall*, 119.

93. Cornyetz, *Dangerous Women, Deadly Words*, especially 45–59.

94. Matsushita, "1910 nendai ni okeru *Michikusa* to *Wakai*."

95. In fact, the remainder of Komako's life apparently was fairly happy. Shortly after writing the autobiography, she moved back to Nagano prefecture, where she raised her daughter while pursuing a number of jobs, most notably as a calligraphy instructor—to the end, a writer. In 1958, she paid a symbolic visit to Tōson's grave, delivering an offering of flowers as a way of making peace with her own past. See the entry on "Shimazaki Komako" in *STJ*:189–90.

96. Mizuta Noriko, "Josei jikogatari to monogatari."

97. The "Afterword" is published in *TZ* 7:499–500. For discussions of the 1938 edition, see Egusa "Yūwaku to kokuhaku," and Yabu Teiko, *Tōkoku Tōson Ichiyō* (Tokyo: Meiji Shoin, 1991), 103–35. The revised version of *Shinsei* (New life) never gained wide currency.

98. Sharalyn Orbaugh, "The Body in Contemporary Japanese Women's Fiction," in *The Woman's Hand: Gender and Theory in Japanese Women's Writing*, ed. Paul Gordon Schalow and Janet A. Walker (Stanford: Stanford University Press, 1996), 152.

99. Mizuta, "Josei jikogatari to monogatari," especially 71–72.

Chapter 5. The Times and Spaces of Nations: The Multiple Chronotopes of Before the Dawn

1. *Yoake mae* appears in *TZ* 11 (book 1) and 12 (book 2). It is available in English translation: *Before the Dawn*, trans. William Naff (Honolulu: University of Hawaii Press, 1987).

2. Hayashi Fumio, "Koyomi no bunka shikan," *Chūō kōron* 504 (January 1930): 225–35.

3. Hayashi Fumio, "Koyomi no bunka shikan," 225.

4. Fukuzawa, as quoted in Hayashi Fumio, "Koyomi no bunka shikan," 235.

5. Bergson's *Time and Free Will* appeared in 1889, *Matter and Memory* in 1896. Like many Japanese intellectuals of his day, Tōson was familiar with Bergson's thought and discussed it in "Sei no chōyaku" (The dance of life, 1913; the passage on Bergson is reprinted in *TZ* 6:408–9) and elsewhere. Tōson owned at least two Bergson-related books, one (René Gillouin, *La Philosophie de M. Henri Bergson* [1911]) that he apparently purchased during his years in Paris, and the other a review copy sent to him of a 1936 Japanese translation of Bergson's *The Two Sources of Morality and Religion* (1932). I am indebted to Makino Noriko of the Tōson Kinenkan museum for kindly allowing me to examine Tōson's copies of these books.

6. Stephen Kern, *The Culture of Time and Space, 1880–1918* (Cambridge: Harvard University Press, 1983), 8. On the rise of "clock time" in Meiji Japan see Maeda Ai, "Tō no shisō" (The philosophy of the tower) in *Toshi kūkan no naka no bungaku* (Literature within the space of the city) (Tokyo: Chikuma Shobō, 1982), 141–63. See also Johannes Fabian, *Time and the Other: How Anthropology Makes its Object* (New York: Columbia University Press, 1983).

7. Partha Chatterjee, *The Nation and Its Fragments: Colonial and Postcolonial Histories* (Princeton: Princeton University Press, 1993).

8. Stefan Tanaka, *Japan's Orient: Rendering Pasts into History* (Berkeley: University of California Press, 1993), 34.

9. Okakura Tenshin, *The Ideals of the East* [1903], in *Okakura Kakuzō: Collected English Writings*, (Tokyo: Heibonsha, 1984), 1:3–132. On Okakura, see Karatani Kōjin, "Bijut-

sukan toshite no Nihon: Okakura Tenshin to Fenorosa" (Japan as art museum: Okakura Tenshin and Fenollosa), *Hihyō kūkan* 2d ser., no. 1 (1994): 68–75; and Fred Notehelfer, "On Idealism and Realism in the Thought of Okakura Tenshin," *Journal of Japanese Studies* 16, no.2 (1990): 309–55.

10. Kuki Shūzō, "Tōyōteki jikan" in *Kuki Shūzō zenshū* (Complete works of Kuki Shūzō), (Tokyo: Iwanami Shoten, 1981), 5:11–24.

11. Watsuji Tetsurō, *Climate and Culture: A Philosophical Study*, trans. Geoffrey Bownas (Tokyo: Hokuseido Press, 1961).

12. James A. Fujii, *Complicit Fictions: The Subject in the Modern Japanese Prose Narrative* (Berkeley: University of California Press, 1993), 113–14.

13. Seiji Lippit, "The Disintegrating Machinery of the Modern: Akutagawa Ryūnosuke's Late Writings," *Journal of Asian Studies* 58, no. 1 (February 1999): 27–50.

14. On Miyazawa Kenji (1896–1933) and his relation to Einstein's theory, see Oshino Takeshi, *Miyazawa Kenji no bigaku*(The aesthetic of Miyazawa Kenji) (Tokyo: Kanrin Shobō, 2000), 44–54. On Yokomitsu Riichi (1898–1947) and Einstein, see Gregory Golley, "Voices in the Machine: Technology and Japanese Literary Modernism," (Ph.D. diss., University of California at Los Angeles, 2000). On Yokomitsu, see also Seiji Lippit, *Topographies of Japanese Modernism* (New York: Columbia University Press, 2002), 75–115 and 199–228.

15. Many scholars have previously discussed the concept of time in Tōson's literature. The most extended discussion can be found in Kotani Hiroyuki, *Rekishi to ningen ni tsuite: Tōson to kindai Nihon* (On history and humanity: Tōson and modern Japan) (Tokyo: Tōkyō Daigaku Shuppankai, 1991). See also Sasabuchi Tomoichi, *Shōsetsuka Shimazaki Tōson* (Novelist Shimazaki Tōson) (Tokyo: Meiji Shoin, 1990), 91–96; Ōida Yoshiaki, "*Ie* no jikan: chichi to no kaikō" (The time of *Ie* [The family]: Chance encounters with the father), *Bungei to hihyō* 6, no. 3 (March 1986): 44–55; Sasaki Masanobu, "*Haru* wo megutte: Aoki Shun'ichi zō no ichi" (With regard to *Haru* [Spring]: The position of the image of Aoki Shun'ichi), *Kokugo to kokubungaku* 56, no. 5 (May 1979): 83–94; and Iwami Teruyo, "*Yoake mae* (Shimazaki Tōson): kaiki no kōzu" (*Yokae mae* [Before the dawn] [Shimazaki Tōson]: The structure of return) in *Nihon no kindai shōsetsu II* (Modern Japanese novels II), ed. Miyoshi Yukio (Tokyo: Tōkyō Daigaku Shuppankai, 1986), 113–28.

16. See my "*Yoake mae* to rekishiteki jikan" (*Yokae mae* [Before the dawn] and historical time) in *Sekai ga yomu Nihon kindai bungaku III* (The world reads modern Japanese literature III), ed. Fukuoka UNESCO Kyōkai (Tokyo: Maruzen Books, 1999), 47–64.

17. See, for example, in "Tenmondai no tokei" (The observatory clock) in *Osanaki mono ni* (To the young, 1917), a collection of essays for children, in which Tōson describes a fanciful conversation about time he has with the clock at an observatory in Paris where he often goes to set his watch (*TZ* 8:488–90).

18. The central problem driving the narrative is the narrator's efforts to deliver a clock as a housewarming gift to his son, whom he is helping to establish as a farmer in the rural town the narrator left behind as a child. The opening line of the story: "The children assembled in the parlor where the old clock was hanging up, and I lined them up against the pillar there to compare their heights." "Arashi" appears in *TZ* 10:3–52.

19. "We will give the name *chronotope* (literally, 'time space') to the intrinsic connectedness of temporal and spatial relationships that are artistically expressed in literature. . . .

In the literary artistic chronotope, spatial and temporal indicators are fused into one carefully thought-out, concrete whole. Time, as it were, thickens, takes on flesh, becomes artistically visible; likewise, space becomes charged and responsive to the movements of time, plot and history." Mikhail Bakhtin, *The Dialogic Imagination: Four Essays*, trans. Caryl Emerson and Michael Holquist (Austin: University of Texas Press, 1981), 84.

20. Benedict Anderson, *Imagined Communities: Reflections on the Origin and Spread of Nationalism* (London: Verso, 1983), 29. Further references to this work will be cited parenthetically. Discussions with Joseph Murphy have contributed greatly to my understanding of Anderson's view of temporality.

21. Sasaki Masanobu, "*Haru* wo megutte: seishun to shi" (With regard to *Haru* [Spring]: Youth and death), *Kokubungaku kenkyū* 68 (June 1979): 9–10.

22. Prasenjit Duara, *Rescuing History from the Nation: Questioning Narratives of Modern China* (Chicago: University of Chicago Press, 1995), 29.

23. Included in Homi K. Bhabha, ed., *Nation and Narration* (London: Routledge, 1990), 291–322. Further references to this work are cited parenthetically.

24. On antimodernism as a component of modern Japanese thought, see Suzuki Sadami, *Nihon no "bungaku" gainen* (Japan's concept of "literature") (Tokyo: Sakuhinsha, 1998), especially 179–90 and 313–49.

25. Tessa Morris-Suzuki, *Re-Inventing Japan: Time Space Nation*(Armonk, N.Y.: M. E. Sharpe, 1998).

26. My argument here borrows from Rogers Brubaker, *Citizenship and Nationhood in France and Germany* (Cambridge: Harvard University Press, 1992). Brubaker examines the relationship between two bounded sets that largely, but not completely, overlap: national territory and national citizenship. The boundaries of each set can be defined in a number of ways, and the two sets can interact in a variety of ways. Competing versions of nationalism within a single "nation" can often be distinguished by the way they define the relationship between these two sets.

27. On striated and smooth space, see Gilles Deleuze and Félix Guattari, *A Thousand Plateaus: Capitalism and Schizophrenia*, trans. Brian Massumi (Minneapolis: University of Minnesota Press, 1987), especially 474–500.

28. See Judith Butler, *Subjects of Desire: Hegelian Reflections in Twentieth-Century France* (New York: Columbia University Press, 1987).

29. Carol Gluck, "The Invention of Edo," in *Mirror of Modernity: Invented Traditions of Modern Japan*, ed. Stephen Vlastos (Berkeley: University of California Press, 1998), 262–84.

30. Roughly half of all the films produced in Japan during the prewar era were so-called *jidai-geki* (dramas set in the past, usually the Edo period). Lisa Spalding, "Period Films in the Prewar Era," in *Reframing Japanese Cinema: Authorship Genre History*, ed. Arthur Nolletti Jr. and David Desser (Bloomington: Indiana University Press, 1992), 131–44. On national identity in prewar Japanese film, see Darrell William Davis, *Picturing Japaneseness: Monumental Style, National Identity, Japanese Film* (New York: Columbia University Press, 1996).

31. See, for example, the survey of recent works depicting the Meiji Restoration contained in a highly censored article, Shinoda Tarō, "Bungaku ni okeru ishin-shi no mondai" (The Problem of restoration history in literature), *Kaizō* 15, no. 3 (March 1933): 97–111.

32. See Leslie Pincus, *Authenticating Culture in Imperial Japan: Kuki Shūzō and the Rise of National Aesthetics* (Berkeley: University of California Press, 1996); and Karatani Kōjin, "One Spirit, Two Nineteenth Centuries," trans. Alan Wolfe, in *Postmodernism and Japan*, ed. Masao Miyoshi and H. D. Harootunian (Durham: Duke University Press, 1989), 259–72.

33. See William E. Naff, "Shimazaki Tōson's *Before the Dawn*: Historical Fiction as History and as Literature," in *The Ambivalence of Nationalism: Modern Japan Between East and West*, ed. James W. White, Michio Umegaki, and Thomas R. H. Havens (Lanham, Md.: University Press of America, 1990), 79–114.

34. Bakhtin, *Dialogic Imagination*, 252.

35. This narrative marks some contemporary historical analyses of Meiji as well. See, for example, George M. Wilson, *Patriots and Redeemers in Japan: Motives in the Meiji Restoration* (Chicago: University of Chicago Press, 1992).

36. On the Hirata School and Nativism in general, see H. D. Harootunian, *Things Seen and Unseen: Discourse and Ideology in Tokugawa Nativism* (Chicago: University of Chicago Press, 1988). See also Naoki Sakai, *Voices of the Past: The Status of Language in Eighteenth-Century Japanese Discourse* (Ithaca: Cornell University Press, 1991); Peter Nosco, *Remembering Paradise: Nativism and Nostalgia in Eighteenth-Century Japan* (Cambridge: Council on East Asian Studies, Harvard University, 1990); and Masao Maruyama, *Studies in the Intellectual History of Tokugawa Japan*, trans. Mikiso Hane (Princeton: Princeton University Press, 1974).

37. My argument here derives much from two articles by Takahashi Akinori: "*Yoake mae* no jidai kubun ron" (The theory of historical periodization in *Yoake mae* [Before the dawn]) in *Bungei kenkyū* (Tohoku University) 116 (September 1987): 62–71; and "*Yoake mae* no 'sōsō' o megutte" (On the "grassroots" in *Yoake mae* [Before the dawn]) in *Shimazaki Tōson kenkyū* 17 (September, 1989): 25–41.

38. Konaka Nobutaka, in "*Yoake mae* no hankindai: kyōki no hanten" (Anti-modernism in *Yoake mae* [Before the dawn]: The reverse twist of madness), in *Kōza Shōwa bungaku shi* (Lectures on Shōwa-era literary history), ed. Yūseidō Henshūbu (Tokyo: Yūseidō, 1988), 1:248–56, discusses this calendar reform proposal at length. Konaka maintains that Hanzō's madness represents a sane reaction to a society gone insane with the disease of modernity. The new calendar is symptomatic: it is "nothing more than an inorganic time, a concept of time as measured by the clock that was separated from the daily lives of the farmers that up until then had been deeply attached to the natural climate," and Konaka argues that just "as modernization labors as a force to extinguish cultural differences, that is to say, particular (*koyū*) cultures, the solar calendar functions to strip away all of the various meanings that had grown up in a close relationship with nature" (252–53). Hanzō alone protests this, a protest that ultimately takes the form of his insanity. I have learned much from Konaka's work, but his understanding of modernity (as a "flood" of universal concepts that erase cultural particularity) seems to oversimplify the functioning of ideology in modern societies, where plural categories (such as national cultures or brand names), not monolithic universalities, are the means by which subjects are molded to achieve social reproduction. In this sense, Japanese tradition is not opposed to modernity, but rather is a part and parcel of it.

39. For a useful study of how the rise of railroads reconfigured the experience of time and space in modern Japan, see James A. Fujii, "Intimate Alienation: Japanese Urban Rail

and the Commodification of Urban Subjects," *differences: A Journal of Feminist Cultural Studies* 11, no. 2 (1999): 106–33.

40. *TZ* 6:391. A decade later, as he was preparing to write *Before the Dawn*, Tōson would return to this passage and expand on its significance in the essay, "Zenseiki wo tankyū suru kokoro" (A mind to explore the previous century, 1926; reprinted in *TZ* 9:186–92).

41. Kotani, *Rekishi to ningen*, 141–72.

42. The Kōza faction argued (in conformity with Comintern doctrine) that the Meiji Restoration constituted an incomplete bourgeois revolution, so that the correct strategy for political action in the 1930s was a united front with liberals and others to promote a full bourgeois revolution, only after which a socialist revolution would be possible. Members of the Rōnō faction, on the other hand, argued that the Restoration had effected a sufficient bourgeois revolution, so that the proper political strategy was to agitate immediately for a socialist revolution. On the debate between the two schools, see Yutaka Nagahara, "A Sketch on the Hauntology of Capital: Towards Theory of Community," in *Keizai shirin* 66, no. 2 (October 1998): 143–62; and Germaine A. Hoston, *Marxism and the Crisis of Development in Prewar Japan* (Princeton: Princeton University Press, 1986). In general, Tōson's interpretation resembled that of the Kōza faction (Kotani, *Rekishi to ningen*, 120–21). For a postwar evaluation of *Before the Dawn* by one leader of the Kōza faction, see Hattori Shisō, "Aoyama Hanzō: Meiji zettaishugi no gebu kōzō" (Aoyama Hanzō: The substructure of Meiji absolutism), 1954; reprinted in *Hattori Shisō zenshū* (Complete works of Hattori Shisō), (reprint, Tokyo: Fukumura Shuppan, 1974), 10:327–79. For another useful discussion of 1930s historiography (including *Before the Dawn*) on the Meiji Restoration, see Narita Ryūichi, "Meiji ishin zō: 1935-nen zengo" (Images of the Meiji restoration: Circa 1935), *Edo shisō* 8 (1998): 97–106.

43. Takahashi Akinori, "*Yoake mae* no 'sōsō' o megutte."

44. For a survey of the genre, see Donald Keene, *Dawn to the West: Japanese Literature in the Modern Era: Fiction* (New York: Henry Holt, 1984), 846–905.

45. "*Yoake mae* gappyōkai" (Roundtable discussion of *Yoake mae* [Before the dawn]), originally printed in *Bungakkai* (May 1936), reprinted in *Nihon bungaku kenkyū shiryō sōsho: Shimazaki Tōson* (Collection of research materials on Japanese literature: Shimazaki Tōson), ed. Nihon bungaku kenkyū shiryō kankō kai (Tokyo: Yūseidō, 1971), 288–308.

46. Hara Minoru, "Fuashizumu to Tōson no *Yoake mae*," (Fascism and Tōson's *Yoake mae* [Before the dawn]), *Mita Bungaku* (June 1932): 87–93. Further references to this work are cited parenthetically.

47. Walter Benjamin, "Theses on the Philosophy of History," in *Illuminations: Essays and Reflections*, trans. Harry Zohn (New York: Schocken Books, 1968), 253–64. See Rainer Nägele, *Theater, Theory, Speculation: Walter Benjamin and the Scenes of Modernity* (Baltimore: John Hopkins University Press, 1991), especially 204–5, for a discussion of Benjamin's spatializing of temporality.

48. On Takabatake, see Morris-Suzuki, *Re-Inventing Japan*, 88–90. On the Rōnō-ha, see Germaine Hoston, *The State, Identity, and the National Question in China and Japan* (Princeton: Princeton University Press, 1994), especially 242–56. On Yamada, see Andrew E. Barshay, "'Doubly Cruel': Marxism and the Presence of the Past in Japanese Capitalism," in *Mirror of Modernity*, ed. Stephen Vlastos, 243–61.

49. Morris-Suzuki, *Re-Inventing Japan*, 9.

50. Naoki Sakai, *Translation and Subjectivity: On "Japan" and Cultural Nationalism* (Minneapolis: University of Minnesota Press, 1998), 44.

51. Harry Harootunian, *Overcome By Modernity: History, Culture, and Community in Interwar Japan* (Princeton: Princeton University Press, 2000), xiv.

52. Etienne Balibar and Immanuel Wallerstein, *Race, Nation, Class: Ambiguous Identities* (London: Verso, 1991), 182. See also Duara, *Rescuing History from the Nation*, 12–13.

53. It was not only Marxists who celebrated the spatiality of *Before the Dawn*. Kieda Masuichi, in another early review ("*Yoake mae* shiron" [An attempt at interpreting *Yoake mae* (Before the dawn)], *Kokugo Kokubun* 5, no. 1 [January 1935], 47–70), suggests the multiplicity of levels of national space that must overlap in order to produce the image of an organic, vital community. Kieda compares the maps that were included in two of Tōson's novels, *The Broken Commandment* and *Before the Dawn*, and concludes that the later maps in *Before the Dawn* show a deepening in Tōson's artistry. Whereas the *Broken Commandment* map merely serves as a source of regional color that provides a sense of reality (*genjitsusei*), the maps in *Before the Dawn* demonstrate something more then reality: they lay out the spirituality (*seishinsei*) of the land. The two maps represent a movement from the factual thing (*mono*) to the heart (*kokoro*).

54. Slavoj Žižek, *The Sublime Object of Ideology* (London: Verso, 1989), 142–49. On this issue, I have also learned much from the discussion of the relations between totality and globality in William Haver, *The Body of This Death: Historicity and Sociality in the Time of AIDS* (Stanford: Stanford University Press, 1996).

55. Takayama Shigeru, "Ishin-shi to *Yoake mae* ron" (On Meiji Restoration History and *Yoake mae* [Before the dawn]), *Kogito* 21 (February 1934): 4–19. Further references to this work will be cited parenthetically.

56. Duara, *Rescuing History from the Nation*, 28.

57. Tōson had already developed this interpretation of world history decades earlier. It shows up, for example, in the travel narrative *Umi e* (To the sea, 1918). But Tōson's interpretation shifted in subsequent decades. His denial of 1868 as a breaking point and subsequent discovery of Japan's nineteenth century initially led him to posit instead a break between Japan's eighteenth and nineteenth centuries. But by the late 1930s this break in turn disappeared from Tōson's historical memory. As evidenced by the 1936 lecture "Mottomo Nihonteki naru mono" (The most Japanese of things, *TZ* 13:418–20), Tōson now sought the seeds of Japanese modernity as far back as the Genroku period (1688–1704) and even in the paintings of Sesshu (1420–1506). See Kotani, *Rekishi to ningen*, 152–160.

58. *Tōhō no mon* is reprinted in *TZ* 14. This passage appears on 95–98. For a discussion of the shift in the historical significance assigned to Japan's middle ages between *Before the Dawn* and *Tōhō no mon* (The gate to the East), see Takahashi Akinori, "*Yoake mae* no jidai kubun ron."

59. To my knowledge, the closest Tōson came to publicly making such a statement came in a 1941 roundtable discussion with Hasegawa Nyozekan, Tanikawa Tetsuzō, and Kindaichi Kyōsuke, "Kokugo kokuji no sho mondai" (The various problems of our national language and writing system), originally published in the April 1941 issue of *Chūō kōron* and reprinted in *TZ* 18:505–31. The discussants were asked to make proposals

for standardizing the Japanese language so as to facilitate its use across the Greater East Asia Co-Prosperity Sphere. One of Tōson's remarks during the discussion: "from Manchukuo to Korea and Northern China, all across East Asia, the language of Japan is being diffused; in this sense, [language reform] has extremely deep, timely significance. In India, they use ten different languages now. Bengali is the most superior of these and is spoken by the most people—I understand that Tagore writes in Bengali, for example—but one of the reasons India has been unable to unite is that it lacks a unified language. If you go to another province, you can't communicate, so that it is only by borrowing English that you can make your meaning understood. Because of this, when you think of the present state of affairs, in the sense of the ongoing unification of the entire Orient, it is important for us to tune up [*seibi*] the words of our country, to push them toward a higher degree of excellence" (518–19). Tōson goes onto compare this effort with the *genbun itchi* movement for the creation of a new vernacular literary language in the mid-Meiji period. The private notes Tōson jotted down while preparing to write *Tōhō no mon* (The gate to the East) also contain a number of problematic assertions. See Kotani, *Rekishi to ningen*, 169–72, for a discussion of these notes, such as the following one, dated February 8, 1942: "The fate of the people of the East linked together in world history / China after the Dao Guang Emperor [regnant 1820–1850]—Japan's closed-country isolation and decay / the fall of India, Annam, etc. / the death of the East/until the coming of the Meiji Restoration / the gradual revival from that death" (*TZ* 14:471–72). Another note, dated January 21, 1942: "The seventeenth and eighteenth centuries as the starting point of a fresh modernity, passing through the nineteenth century to arrive at its twentieth-century destination: the Greater East Asian War" (*TZ* 14:467).

60. From Kobayashi's afterword to the 1936 "*Yoake mae* gappyōkai" roundtable: "The transcendent [*zettaiteki*] temperament of a Japanese that the author discovered inside himself at the end of his long literary life is what brings this novel to life. In its depths, beyond notions like individuality or character that modern novelists have struggled over—that Tōson himself has struggled over—what dominates this novel is the blood of the Japanese people that the author has discovered and confirmed.... In fact, no other novel from our nation has expressed in so elevated a tone the idea of Japaneseness" ("*Yoake mae* gappyōkai" 307–8). Kobayashi maps this "blood" onto geography: in praising the novel's depiction of the Mito Loyalists, he writes that "The force of this passage, its compact description, was so powerful that I pulled out a map and gazed at it as I read it" (308).

61. "Today where is the blood of our fathers who drove themselves insane worrying over the fate of Japan?" Kamei Katsuichirō, *Shimazaki Tōson: ippyōhakusha no shōzō* (Shimazaki Tōson: Portrait of a wanderer) (Tokyo: Kōbundō shobō, 1939), 2. I am using a facsimile edition of the 1939 edition, vol. 124 of *Kindai sakka kenkyū sōsho* reprint series (Tokyo: Nihon Tosho Sentā, 1993). On Kamei and the Japan Romantic School of the 1930s, see Kevin Michael Doak, *Dreams of Difference: The Japan Romantic School and the Crisis of Modernity* (Berkeley: University of California Press, 1994); and Tomone Matsumoto, "From Marxism to Japanism: A Study of Kamei Katsuichirō (1907–1967)," (Ph.D. diss., University of Arizona, 1979).

62. Kamei reads Tōson's entire career around the metaphor of life as a journey (*tabi*). According to Kamei, this implies ceaseless struggle, so that the battlefield produces it in

its purest form: "On the boundary between life and death, there is a formless, spotless life. Where it comes from, where it goes to are not known, this great river of life overflowing with screams and courage and wild dreams. There can be no nobler ordeal than that extraordinariness obtained in the backside of the resolve to die. It is also the site where the thought of life as a journey receives its most severe forging. All previously existing principles must die" (Kamei, *Shimazaki Tōson: ippyōhakusha no shōzō*, 3–4). Moreover, "No matter what the field, the resolve to martyr oneself to a single purpose must already by called '*war*.' To throw off the past, to desire a pure eye and to wish to greet a new day burning with a heart of rebirth: this is the figure of a wanderer as he departs. What I want to say is that war produced the figure of the wanderer as a symbol" (Kamei, *Shimazaki Tōson: ippyōhakusha no shōzō*, 4). As I mentioned in chapter 1, the more bloodthirsty elements of Kamei's book were edited out when the work was republished in 1947.

63. Asano Akira, *Romanha henten* (The shifting Japan Romantic School) (Tokyo: Kōbundō, 1988), 153–58. I thank Mark Anderson for bringing this to my attention.

64. Watsuji, *Climate and Culture*, 9–10. Further references to this work are cited parenthetically.

65. Sakai, *Translation and Subjectivity*, 72–152. See also Eiji Oguma, *A Genealogy of "Japanese" Self-Images*, trans. David Askew (Melbourne: Trans Pacific Press, 2002), 260–84.

66. The two in fact had met as early as 1911 but did not become closely involved with each other until the late 1920s, an association spurred on by a close friendship between their wives. See the entries "Watsuji Tetsurō" and "*Fūdo*" in *STJ*: 496 and 384.

67. Watsuji's letter is reprinted in *TZ* 17:515–17. See also two reminiscences of Tōson by Watsuji, "Tōson no omoide" (Remembering Tōson, 1950) and "Tōson no kosei" (Tōson's individuality, 1951), reprinted in *Watsuji Tetsurō zenshū* (Complete works of Watsuji Tetsurō), (Tokyo: Iwanami Shoten, 1962), 3:433–38 and 3:439–47.

68. For Tōson's letters discussing *Climate and Culture*, see *TZ* 17:513 and 515.

69. Harootunian, *Overcome By Modernity*, xxvi; see also 202–21. For another account of Aono's career, see Usui Yoshimi, *Kindai bungaku ronsō* (Disputes in modern literature) (Tokyo: Chikuma Shobō, 1975), 1:215–30.

70. Aono's two essays are: "*Yoake mae* daiichibu o ronzu" (On part 1 of *Yoake mae* [Before the dawn]), *Shinchō* (February 1932); and "*Yoake mae* kanketsu o ronzu" (On the completed *Yoake mae* [Before the dawn]), *Asahi*, September 29–October 3, 1935. They are reprinted in *TZ* 18:305–14 and 315–21, respectively. Subsequent references to these two works are to the *TZ* reprints and are cited parenthetically as "Daiichibu" and "Kanketsu." Aono's interview with Tōson is: "*Yoake mae* o chūshin toshite" (Mainly centered on *Yoake mae* [Before the dawn]), *Shinchō* (December 1935); reprint *TZ* 12:544–53. See also Aono's post-war essay on *The Gate to the East*, "*Tōhō no mon* no Tōson" (The Tōson of *Tōhō no mon* [The gate to the east]), *Meisō* (October 1957); reprint in *Nihon bungaku kenkyū shiryō sōsho: Shimazaki Tōson*, ed. Nihon Bungaku Kenkyū Shiryō Kankō Kai, 1:309–12. Aono also discusses Tōson at length in another essay, "Gendai bungakusha no kaikyūteki seishitsu" (The class-based nature of contemporary writers), *Kaizō* (January 1928); reprint, in *Hirabayashi Hatsunosuke, Aono Suekichi shū*, vol. 3 of *Nihon puroretaria bungaku hyōronshū* (Collection of criticism of proletarian literature) (Tokyo: Shin Nihon Shuppansha, 1990), 3:306–23.

71. Other Marxist critics who were sympathetic to *Before the Dawn* also point out this

"error" in Tōson's understanding of the Meiji Restoration. See, for example, Shinoda, "Bungaku ni okeru ishin-shi no mondai"; and Itō Shirō, "Shimazaki Tōson ron" (On Shimazaki Tōson), *Yuibutsuron kenkyū* 63 (January 1938): 78–96.

72. Many of the points Aono makes are echoed by another Marxist literary figure, Miyamoto Yuriko. Like Aono, Miyamoto points out the limitations of Tōson's approach: his is a subjective account of history masquerading as objectivity. Tōson's understanding of the Restoration may be limited, and yet it is not simply that of an urban, petty-bourgeois intellectual: Tōson contradicts the modern from the standpoint of the rural peasant and is thereby able to locate at least one facet of the hidden violence that accompanied the Restoration. Moreover, despite Tōson's not being a Marxist himself, Miyamoto argues that his subjective sense of responsibility for the present moment in history—and for speaking to a new generation about the truth of the past—is woven throughout the work. See Miyamoto Yuriko, "*Yoake mae* ni tsuite no shishin" (My view of *Yoake mae* [Before the dawn]), *Hihyō* (Sept. 1936); reprint, in *Miyamoto Yuriko zenshū* (Complete works of Miyamoto Yuriko), (Tokyo: Shin Nihon Shuppansha, 1980), 10:471–74. Also see her "Ōgai, Sōseki, Tōson: chichiue-sama wo megutte" (Ōgai, Sōseki, Tōson: Regarding the fathers), *Yomiuri*, October 6–8, 1936; reprint, in *Miyamoto Yuriko zenshū*, (Tokyo: Shin Nihon Shuppansha, 1980), 10:502–8.

73. Calls for a "Shōwa Restoration" were frequently made in the 1930s by fascist ideologues eager to overcome Western modernity and "finish" the supposedly incomplete work of the Meiji Restoration. Tōson, in a 1941 essay, expressed reservations about the notion. See Kotani, *Rekishi to ningen*, 157–58.

74. "*Yoake mae* gappyōkai," 290.

75. No such statement is made either by the narrator or Hanzō in *Before the Dawn*. In fact, the narrator repeatedly and sympathetically cites the testimony of foreign observers in Japan. The sole assertion in the novel that foreigners cannot understand Japan is made by a Frenchman, and it is immediately contradicted by the behavior of another Frenchman, de Cachon, who displays clear familiarity with Japanese ways (*TZ* 12:53–56).

76. "*Yoake mae* gappyōkai," 290–91.

77. See Gilles Deleuze and Félix Guattari, *Anti-Oedipus: Capitalism and Schizophrenia*, trans. Robert Hurley, Mark Seem, and Helen R. Lane (Minneapolis: University of Minnesota Press, 1983), 122–25.

78. Paul de Man, *The Resistance to Theory* (Minneapolis: University of Minnesota Press, 1986), 68. On Benjamin's use of allegory to critique mimesis, see also Nägele, *Theater, Theory, Speculation*.

79. Likewise, in his 1933 survey of recent literary portrayals of the Restoration, Shinoda Tarō ("Bungaku ni okeru ishin-shi no mondai") deliberately denies that *Before the Dawn* should be read as "fascist" or "reactionary" in its politics. Despite inadequacies in Tōson's historical understanding, his position is that of a progressive, bourgeois intellectual. By contrast, Shinoda finds clearer evidence of fascistic tendencies in recent works of popular literature that depicted the Restoration. Ironically, Shinoda praises the novel *Seinen* (Youth, 1933–1934), another fictional version of the Restoration written by the future *tenkōsha* Hayashi Fusao while he was imprisoned for his political activities.

80. It can be argued that Aono fails to recognize the true complexity of the nationalist arguments that in 1930s Japan were constructed through the mode of historical irony

and recognized the need of mediation through Western modernity for any movement that wanted to restore Japanese antiquity. See Doak, *Dreams of Difference*, for a discussion of the ironic nature of 1930s nationalist historical imagination in Japan. Nonetheless, Aono's insistence on the allegorical elements of the novel seriously challenges attempts to read *Before the Dawn* as a celebration of the transcendent space of the Japanese nation.

81. The essay "Shisō no unmei" was first published in 1938 in the *Miyako* newspaper and is reprinted in Hayashi Tatsuo, *Hayashi Tatsuo chosaku shū* (Selected works of Hayashi Tatsuo), (Tokyo: Heibonsha, 1971), 5:97–109.

82. Hayashi Tatsuo, "*Yoake mae* no honshitsu kitei" (Defining the essential nature of *Yoake mae* [Before the dawn]), *Asahi* Tokyo edition, 25 January 1936; reprint, in *Hayashi Tatsuo chosakushū*, 4:258–59.

83. Hayashi Tatsuo, "Tōson Sédentaire," *Bungaku* (August, 1936); reprint, in *Hayashi Tatsuo chosakushū*, 4:260–62. See also Watanabe Kazutami, *Hayashi Tatsuo to sono jidai* (Hayashi Tatsuo and his age), (Tokyo: Iwanami Shoten, 1988), 77–119, for a discussion of Hayashi's activities in the 1930s, including his appraisal of *Before the Dawn*.

84. Likewise, Miyamoto Yuriko complains about Tōson's stance as a passive observer and the lack of dynamism in his portrayal of history: "the characters and their actions seem to float in the narrative rather than take an active part. They are not dynamic. They do not move" (Miyamoto, "*Yoake mae* ni tsuite no shishin," 472). In another article on Tōson published in a Marxist journal, Itō Shirō also complains about Tōson's lack of "sociality": "Rather than go out into the streets to confront society, he has been a mere bystander, closeted away inside his own home. . . . He must come out from his solitary residence and participate in the work needed to bring on the 'storm' [*Arashi*], to bring us 'before the dawn' [*Yoake mae*]" ("Shimazaki Tōson ron," 95–96).

85. Hayashi Tatsuo, "Tōson Sédentaire," 260–61.

86. Deleuze and Guattari, *Anti-Oedipus*, 3. Among Hayashi Tatsuo's 1930s publications was a translation of Bergson's *Laughter* into Japanese.

87. A nomad travels not between fixed points, but rather along a vector that creates its points through the very act of moving. Wherever nomads go, they deterritorialize the preexisting striated space into fluid, smooth space. Therefore, paradoxically, "*they do not move*. They are nomads by dint of not moving, not migrating, of holding a smooth space that they refuse to leave, that they leave only in order to conquer and die." What distinguishes this from the sedentary non-journey of Tōson "is neither a measurable quantity of movement, nor something that would be only in the mind, but the mode of spatialization, the manner of being in space, of being for space." Deleuze and Guattari, *A Thousand Plateaus*, 482.

88. "Forgetting, I would even go so far as to say historical error, is a crucial factor in the creation of a nation, which is why progress in historical studies often constitutes a danger for [the principle of] nationality." Ernest Renan, "What is a Nation?" [1882], trans. Martin Thom, in *Nation and Narration*, ed. Homi K. Bhabha (London: Routledge, 1990), 11.

89. Karatani Kōjin, *Origins of Modern Japanese Literature*, trans. ed. Brett de Bary (Durham: Duke University Press, 1993).

90. Geoffrey Bennington, "Postal Politics and the Institution of the Nation," in *Nation and Narration*, ed. Homi K. Bhabha (London: Routledge, 1990) 130–31; emphasis in original.

91. Quoted in Germaine A. Hoston, "*Ikkoku Shakai-shugi*: Sano Manabu and the Lim-

its of Marxism as Cultural Criticism," in *Culture and Identity: Japanese Intellectuals during the Interwar Years*, ed. J. Thomas Rimer (Princeton: Princeton University Press, 1990), 73. Sano Manabu (1892–1953) was a member of the Central Committee of the Japanese Communist Party; his *tenkō* in 1933 set off the flood of conversions that swept through Japanese Marxism in the following years.

92. Pratt defines "anti-conquest" as "the strategies of representation whereby European bourgeois subjects seek to secure their innocence in the same moment as they assert European hegemony." Mary Louise Pratt, *Imperial Eyes: Travel Writing and Transculturation* (London: Routledge, 1992), 7.

93. I am grateful to Naoki Sakai for pointing out this connection to me. "Politically and ideologically, the liberal creole project involved founding an independent, decolonized American society and culture, while retaining European values and white supremacy" (Pratt, *Imperial Eyes*, 175).

94. See Harootunian, *Overcome By Modernity*.

95. Ernst Bloch, "Nonsynchronism and Dialectics," trans. Mark Ritter, *New German Critique* 11 (Spring 1977), 22–38. Gramsci too faced this problem of "uneven development" in Italy during the same period. See Ernesto Laclau and Chantal Mouffe, *Hegemony and Socialist Strategy: Towards a Radical Democratic Politics* (London: Verso, 1985).

96. Miyamoto, "*Yoake mae* ni tsuite no shishin," 474.

Epilogue. The Most Japanese of Things

1. Tōson published a narrative of his 1936–1937 journey under the title *Junrei* (Pilgrimage, 1937–1940), reprinted in *TZ* 14:121–331. The description of the South Africa stay, on which my account is based, appears on 154–64. For a useful reading of *Junrei* (Pilgrimage) in terms of the diaspora of Japanese laborers abroad, see Sano Masato, "Bungakuteki kokusaishugi to diasupora no unmei: Shōwa jūnendai Tōson Tō-Ajia bungaku" (Literary internationalism and the destiny of diaspora: Tōson's East Asian literature in the 1930s) in *Kindai no yume to chisei: bungaku shisō no Shōwa jūnendai zengo* (The dreams and knowledge of modernity: The mid-1930s of literature and thought), ed. Bungaku Shisō Konwakai (Tokyo: Kanrin Shobō, 2000), 9–27.

2. The Baltimore incident is not depicted in *Junrei* itself but is mentioned in the preparatory notes Tōson produced as he was writing the book. See *TZ* 14:343.

3. The Southern-Advance thesis had first been advocated in the 1880s (in contrast to the Northern-Advance thesis, which argued that Japan's natural sphere of influence centered on Northeast Asia) and had been adopted as official policy in 1936, the same year as Tōson's visit to Cape Town.

4. The lecture itself has been lost, but a Japanese translation of a Spanish-language transcription that appeared in a Buenos Aires newspaper is reprinted in *TZ* 13:418–20.

5. E. J. Hobsbawm, *Nations and Nationalism Since 1780: Programme, Myth, Reality* (Cambridge: Cambridge University Press, 1990), 163.

6. Kenichi Ohmae, *The End of the Nation State: The Rise of Regional Economies* (London: Harper Collins, 1995), 5.

7. Immanuel Wallerstein, *Historical Capitalism with Capitalist Civilization* (London: Verso, 1983); and Etienne Balibar and Immanuel Wallerstein, *Race, Nation, Class: Ambigu-*

ous Identities (London:Verso, 1991). See also Enrique Dussel, "Beyond Eurocentrism: The World-System and the Limits of Modernity," in *The Cultures of Globalization*, ed. Frederic Jameson and Masao Miyoshi (Durham: Duke University Press, 1998), 3–31.

8. Frederick Buell, *National Culture and the New Global System* (Baltimore: John Hopkins University Press, 1994), 9.

9. Yutaka Nagahara, "*Monsieur le Capital* and *Madame la Terre* Do Their Ghost Dance: Globalization and the Nation-State," *The South Atlantic Quarterly* 99, no. 4 (Fall 2000): 931.

WORKS CITED

NOTE: The following abbreviations are used in citations throughout the work:

STJ: Itō Kazuo, ed. *Shimazaki Tōson jiten* (Shimazaki Tōson dictionary) (Tokyo: Meiji Shoin, 1972).

TZ: Shimzaki Tōson, *Tōson zenshū* (Complete works of Tōson), 18 vols. (Tokyo: Chikuma Shobō, 1966–1971).

Akerknecht, Erwin H. "Anticontagionism Between 1821 and 1867." *Bulletin of the History of Medicine* 22 (1948): 562–92.

Anderson, Benedict. *Imagined Communities: Reflections on the Origin and Spread of Nationalism*. London: Verso, 1983.

Anderson, Mark. "National Literature as Cultural Monument: Instituting the Japanese National Community." In *New Directions in the Study of Meiji Japan*, ed. Helen Hardacre and Adam L. Kern, 45–59. Leiden: Brill, 1997.

Andersson, René. *Burakumin and Shimazaki Tōson's* Hakai: *Images of Discrimination in Modern Japanese Literature*. Lund, Sweden: Department of East Asian Languages, Lund University, [2000].

Aono Suekichi. "Gendai bungakusha no kaikyūteki seishitsu." *Kaizō* (January 1928). Reprint, in *Hirabayashi Hatsunosuke, Aono Suekichi shū*. Vol. 3 of *Nihon puroretaria bungaku hyōronshū*, 306–23. Tokyo: Shin Nihon Shuppansha, 1990.

———. "Tōhō no mon no Tōson." *Meisō* (October 1957). Reprint, in *Nihon bungaku kenkyū shiryō sōsho: Shimazaki Tōson*, ed. Nihon Bungaku Kenkyū Shiryō Kankō Kai. Vol. 1, 309–12. Tokyo: Yūseidō, 1971.

———. "*Yoake mae* daiichibu o ronzu." *Shinchō* (February 1932). Reprint, *TZ* 18:305–14.

———. "*Yoake mae* kanketsu o ronzu." *Asahi*, September 29–October 3, 1935. Reprint, *TZ* 18:315–21.

———. "*Yoake mae* o chūshin toshite." 1935. *TZ* 12:544–53.

Arnold, David. *Colonizing the Body: State Medicine and Epidemic Disease in Nineteenth-Century India*. Berkeley: University of California Press, 1993.

Asano Akira. *Romanha henten*. Tokyo: Kōbundō, 1988.

Bakhtin, Mikhail. *The Dialogic Imagination: Four Essays*. Trans. Caryl Emerson and Michael Holquist. Austin: University of Texas Press, 1981.

Balibar, Etienne, and Immanuel Wallerstein. *Race, Nation, Class: Ambiguous Identities*. London: Verso, 1991.

Barnes, David S. *The Making of a Social Disease: Tuberculosis in Nineteenth-Century France.* Berkeley: University of California Press, 1995.

Barshay, Andrew E. " 'Doubly Cruel': Marxism and the Presence of the Past in Japanese Capitalism." In *Mirror of Modernity: Invented Traditions of Modern Japan*, ed. Stephen Vlastos, 243–61. Berkeley: University of California Press, 1998.

———. *State and Intellectual in Imperial Japan: The Public Man in Crisis.* Berkeley: University of California Press, 1988.

Bartholomew, James R. "Science, Bureaucracy, and Freedom in Meiji and Taishō Japan." In *Conflict in Modern Japanese History: The Neglected Tradition*, ed. Tetsuo Najita and J. Victor Koschmann, 295–341. Princeton: Princeton University Press, 1982.

Beichman, Janine. *Masaoka Shiki.* Boston: Twayne, 1982.

Benedict, A. L. "Consumption Considered as a Contagious Disease." *Popular Science Monthly* 48, no. 1 (November 1895): 33–39.

Benjamin, Walter. *Illuminations: Essays and Reflections.* Trans. Harry Zohn. New York: Schocken Books, 1968.

Bennington, Geoffrey. "Postal Politics and the Institution of the Nation." In *Nation and Narration*, ed. Homi K. Bhabha, 121–37. London: Routledge, 1990.

Bhabha, Homi K. "DissemiNation: Time, Narrative, and the Margins of the Modern Nation." In *Nation and Narration*, ed. Homi K. Bhabha, 291–322. London: Routledge, 1990.

Bloch, Ernst. "Nonsynchronism and Dialectics." Trans. Mark Ritter. *New German Critique* 11 (Spring 1977): 22–38.

Bourdaghs, Michael. "Kokusaika no naka no Tōson: Ōbei no baai." *Shimazaki Tōson kenkyū* 29 (2001): 51–59.

———. "*Yoake mae* to rekishiteki jikan." In *Sekai ga yomu Nihon kindai bungaku III*, ed. Fukuoka UNESCO Kyōkai, 47–64. Tokyo: Maruzen, 1999.

Bowring, Richard. *Mori Ōgai and the Modernization of Japanese Culture.* Cambridge: Cambridge University Press, 1979.

Brower, Robert H. "Masaoka Shiki and Tanka Reform." In *Tradition and Modernization in Japanese Culture*, ed. Donald H. Shively, 379–418. Princeton: Princeton University Press, 1971.

Brownstein, Michael C. "*Jogaku zasshi* and the Founding of *Bungakkai.*" *Monumenta Nipponica* 35, no. 3 (1980): 319–36.

Brubaker, Rogers. *Citizenship and Nationhood in France and Germany.* Cambridge: Harvard University Press, 1992.

Buell, Frederick. *National Culture and the New Global System.* Baltimore: John Hopkins University Press, 1994.

Burakumin Kaihō Zenkoku Iinkai. "*Hakai* shohanbon fukugen ni kansuru seimei." 1954. Reprint, *TZ* 2:535–40.

Butler, Judith. *Bodies That Matter: On the Discursive Limits of "Sex."* London: Routledge, 1993.

———. *Gender Trouble: Feminism and the Subversion of Identity.* London: Routledge, 1990.

———. *Subjects of Desire: Hegelian Reflections in Twentieth-Century France.* New York: Columbia University Press, 1987.

Chatterjee, Partha. *The Nation and Its Fragments: Colonial and Postcolonial Histories.* Princeton: Princeton University Press, 1993.

Chida Hiroyuki. "Fusei to dōsei kara no kaihō: *Hakai* no kōzu." In *Shimazaki Tōson: bunmei hihyō to shi to shōsetsu to*, ed. Hiraoka Toshio and Kenmochi Takehiko, 154–66. Tokyo: Sōbunsha, 1996.

———. "Sei/'kaku' koto no seijigaku: *Shinsei* ni okeru masukyuriniti no senryaku." In *Shimazaki Tōson*, ed. Shimoyama Jōko, 195–212. Vol. 30 of *Nihon bungaku kenkyū ronbun shūsei*. Tokyo: Wakakusa Shobō, 1999.

Ching, Leo T. S. *Becoming "Japanese": Colonial Taiwan and the Politics of Identity Formation*. Berkeley: University of California Press, 2001.

Cooter, Roger. "Anticontagionism and History's Medical Record." In *The Problem of Medical Knowledge*, ed. Peter Wright and Andrew Treacher, 87–108. Edinburgh: Edinburgh University Press, 1982.

Copeland, Rebecca. *Lost Leaves: Women Writers of Meiji Japan*. Honolulu: University of Hawaii Press, 2000.

Cornyetz, Nina. *Dangerous Women, Deadly Words: Phallic Fantasy and Modernity in Three Japanese Writers*. Stanford: Stanford University Press, 1999.

Cunningham, Andrew. "Transforming Plague: The Laboratory and the Identity of Infectious Disease." In *The Laboratory Revolution in Medicine*, ed. Andrew Cunningham and Perry Williams, 209–24. Cambridge: Cambridge University Press, 1992.

Date Kazuo. *Ishi toshite no Mori Ōgai*. Tokyo: Sekibundō, 1981.

Davis, Darrell William. *Picturing Japaneseness: Monumental Style, National Identity, Japanese Film*. New York: Columbia University Press, 1996.

de Bary, Brett. " 'Credo Quia Absurdum': *Tenkō* and the Prisonhouse of Language." In *Culture and Identity: Japanese Intellectuals During the Interwar Years*, ed. J. Thomas Rimer, 154–167. Princeton: Princeton University Press, 1990.

de Beauvoir, Simone. *The Second Sex*. Trans. H. M. Parshley. New York: Alfred A. Knopf, 1971.

Deleuze, Gilles, and Félix Guattari. *Anti-Oedipus: Capitalism and Schizophrenia*. Trans. Robert Hurley, Mark Seem, and Helen R. Lane. Minneapolis: University of Minnesota Press, 1983.

———. *Kafka: Toward a Minor Literature*. Trans. Dana Plan. Minneapolis: University of Minnesota Press, 1986.

———. *A Thousand Plateaus: Capitalism and Schizophrenia*. Trans. Brian Massumi. Minneapolis: University of Minnesota Press, 1987.

de Man, Paul. *The Resistance to Theory*. Minneapolis: University of Minnesota Press, 1986.

Derrida, Jacques. *Disseminations*. Trans. Barbara Johnson. Chicago: University of Chicago Press, 1981.

Doak, Kevin Michael. *Dreams of Difference: The Japan Romantic School and the Crisis of Modernity*. Berkeley: University of California Press, 1994.

Dodd, Stephen. "The Railway as Rupture: The Writings of Shimazaki Tōson." In *Disrupted Borders: An Intervention in Definitions of Boundaries*, ed. Sunil Gupta, 42–54. London: Rivers Oram Press, 1993.

Douglas, Mary. *Purity and Danger: An Analysis of the Concepts of Pollution and Taboo*. 1966. Reprint, London: Ark, 1984.

Dower, John. "E. H. Norman, Japan, and the Uses of History." In *Origins of the Modern Japanese State: Selected Writings of E. H. Norman*, E. H. Norman, ed. Dower, 3–101. New York: Pantheon, 1975.

Duara, Prasenjit. *Rescuing History from the Nation: Questioning Narratives of Modern China.* Chicago: University of Chicago Press, 1995.

Dubos, Rene, and Jean Dubos. *The White Plague: Tuberculosis, Man, and Society.* Boston: Little, Brown, 1952.

Dussell, Enrique. "Beyond Eurocentrism: The World-System and the Limits of Modernity." In *The Cultures of Globalization*, ed. Frederic Jameson and Masao Miyoshi, 3–31. Durham: Duke University Press, 1998.

Eagleton, Terry. *Literary Theory: An Introduction.* Minneapolis: University of Minnesota Press, 1983.

Edson, Dr. Cyrus. "The Microbe as Social Leveller." *North American Review* 161 (1895): 421–26.

Egusa Mitsuko. "*Kusamakura* no ninshin shussan wo megutte." *Sōseki kenkyū* 3 (1994): 102–17.

——. "*Shinsei* nōto: Furansu ni iku made." *Nihon kindai bungaku* 49 (October 1993): 61–73.

——. "Yūwaku to kokuhaku: *Shinsei* no tekusuto senryaku." In *Dansei sakka o yomu: feminizumu hihyō no seijuku e*, ed. Egusa et al., 1–35. Tokyo: Shinyōsha, 1994.

Enchi Fumiko. Response to a questionnaire. In *Bungei* 11, no. 12 (September 1954): 227–32.

Ericson, Joan E. *Be a Woman: Hayashi Fumiko and Modern Japanese Women's Literature.* Honolulu: University of Hawaii Press, 1997.

——. "The Origins of the Concept of 'Women's Literature.' " In *The Woman's Hand: Gender and Theory in Japanese Women's Writings*, ed. Paul Gordon Schalow and Janet A. Walker, 74–115. Stanford: Stanford University Press, 1996.

Fabian, Johannes. *Time and the Other: How Anthropology Makes its Object.* New York: Columbia University Press, 1983.

Foucault, Michel. *The Birth of the Clinic: An Archaeology of Medical Perception.* Trans. A. M. Sheridan Smith. New York: Vintage, 1975.

——. *Madness and Civilization.* Trans. Richard Howard. New York: Vintage, 1965.

——. "What is an Author?" In *The Foucault Reader*, ed. Paul Rabinow, 101–20. New York: Pantheon, 1984.

Fowler, Edward. "The *Buraku* in Modern Japanese Literature: Texts and Contexts." *Journal of Japanese Studies* 26, no. 1 (2000): 1–39.

——. *The Rhetoric of Confession: Shishōsetsu in Early-Twentieth-Century Japanese Fiction.* Berkeley: University of California Press, 1988.

Frühstück, Sabine. *Die Politik der Sexualwissenschaft: Zur Produktion und Popularisierung sexologischen Wissens in Japan, 1908–1941.* Vienna: Instituts für Japanologie der Universität Wien, 1997.

Fuji Kazuya. "Shōwa jūni-nen roku-gatsu unmei no 'ibara no michi': Hasegawa (Shimazaki) Komako shoken (Shōwa 11nen–13nen)." *Fuji Kazuya kojinshi Shimazaki Tōson* 12 (December 1999): 26–54.

Fujii, James. A. *Complicit Fictions: The Subject in the Modern Japanese Prose Narrative.* Berkeley: University of California Press, 1993.

——. "Intimate Alienation: Japanese Urban Rail and the Commodification of Urban Subjects." *differences: A Journal of Feminist Cultural Studies* 11, no. 2 (1999): 106–33.

Fujitani, Takashi. "*Minshūshi* As Critique of Orientalist Knowledges." *positions* 6, no. 2 (1998): 303–22.

——. *Splendid Monarchy: Power and Pageantry in Modern Japan*. Berkeley: University of California Press, 1996.

Fukuda Mahito. *Kekkaku no bunkashi*. Nagoya: Nagoya daigaku shuppankai, 1995.

Futabatei Shimei. "Yo ga hansei no zange." In *Meiji bungaku zenshū*. Vol. 17, 112–16. Tokyo: Chikuma Shobō, 1971.

Genette, Gérard. *Narrative Discourse: An Essay in Method*. Trans. Jane E. Lewin. Ithaca: Cornell University Press, 1980.

Gilman, Sander. *Franz Kafka: The Jewish Patient*. New York: Routledge, 1995.

Gilmour, Leigh. *Autobiographics: A Feminist Theory of Women's Self-Representation*. Ithaca: Cornell University Press, 1994.

Gluck, Carol. "The Invention of Edo." In *Mirror of Modernity: Invented Traditions of Modern Japan*, ed. Stephen Vlastos, 262–84. Berkeley: University of California Press, 1998.

——. *Japan's Modern Myths: Ideology in the Late Meiji Period*. Princeton: Princeton University Press, 1985.

——. "The People in History: Recent Trends in Japanese Historiography." *Journal of Asian Studies* 38, no. 1 (November 1978): 25–50.

Golley, Gregory. "Voices in the Machine: Technology and Japanese Literary Modernism." Ph.D. Diss., University of California at Los Angeles, 2000.

Gotō Kōji. "*Wakanashū* no shutai hyōgen ni tsuite." *Gobun ronsō* 8 (September 1980): 46–61.

Graff, Gerald. *Professing Literature: An Institutional History*. Chicago: University of Chicago Press, 1987.

Hara Minoru. "Fuashizumu to Tōson no Yoake mae." *Mita Bungaku* (June 1932): 87–93.

Harootunian, H. D. "America's Japan, Japan's Japan." In *Japan in the World*, ed. Masao Miyoshi and Harootunian, 196–221. Durham, N.C.: Duke University Press, 1993.

——. "Between Politics and Culture: Authority and Ambiguities of Intellectual Choice in Imperial Japan." In *Japan in Crisis: Essays on Taishō Democracy*, ed. Bernard S. Silberman and Harootunian, 110–55. Princeton: Princeton University Press, 1974.

——. *Overcome By Modernity: History, Culture, and Community in Interwar Japan*. Princeton: Princeton University Press, 2000.

——. Review of *An Intellectual History of Wartime Japan* and *A Cultural History of Postwar Japan*, by Tsurumi Shunsuke. *Journal of Japanese Studies* 15, no. 1 (winter 1989): 248–54.

——. *Things Seen and Unseen: Discourse and Ideology in Tokugawa Nativism*. Chicago: University of Chicago Press, 1988.

Hasegawa Komako. "Higeki no jiden." Parts 1 and 2. *Fujin Kōron* 22, nos. 5–6 (May 1937): 282–90; (June 1937): 200–210.

Hasegawa Tenkei. "Handō no genshō." 1906. Reprint, *TZ* 18:102–5.

Hattori Shisō. "Aoyama Hanzō: Meiji zettaishugi no gebu kōzō." *Hattori Shisō zenshū*. Vol. 10, 327–79. Tokyo: Fukumura Shuppan, 1974.

Haver, William. *The Body of This Death: Historicity and Sociality in the Time of AIDS*. Stanford: Stanford University Press, 1996.

Hayashi Fumio. "Koyomi no bunka shikan." *Chūō kōron* 504 (January 1930): 225–35.

Hayashi Fusao. "Tenkō ni tsuite." 1941. In *Shōwa hihyō taikei*, ed. Muramatsu Takeshi, Saeki Shōichi, and Ōkubo Tsuneo. Vol. 2, 239–61. Tokyo: Banchō Shobō, 1968.

Hayashi Tatsuo. *Hayashi Tatsuo chosaku shū*. 6 vols. Tokyo: Heibonsha, 1971–1972.

———. "Shisō no unmei." 1938. Reprint, in *Hayashi Tatsuo chosaku shū*. Vol. 5, 97–109. Tokyo: Heibonsha, 1971.

———. "Tōson Sédentaire," *Bungaku* (August 1936). Reprint, in *Hayashi Tatsuo chosakushū*. Vol. 4, 260–62. Tokyo: Heibonsha, 1971.

———. "*Yokae mae* no honshitsu kitei." *Asahi* Tokyo edition (25 January 1936). Reprint, in *Hayashi Tatsuo chosakushū*. Vol. 4, 258–59. Tokyo: Heibonsha, 1971.

Higashi Eizō. *Hakai no hyōka to buraku mondai*. Tokyo: Meiji Tosho Shuppan, 1977.

Hijiya-Kirschnereit, Irmela. *Rituals of Self-Revelation: Shishōsetsu as Literary Genre and Socio-Cultural Phenomenon*. Cambridge: Council on East Asian Studies, Harvard University, 1996.

Hirano Ken. *Hirano Ken zenshū*. Vol. 2. Tokyo: Shinchōsha, 1975.

Hirata, Hosea. *The Poetry and Poetics of Nishiwaki Junzaburō: Modernism in Translation*. Princeton: Princeton University Press, 1993.

Hirota Masaki. "Nihon kindai shakai no sabetsu kōzō." In *Sabetsu no shosō*, ed. Hirota Masaki. Vol 22 of *Nihon kindai shisō taikei*. Tokyo: Iwanami Shoten, 1990. 436–516.

Hobsbawm, E. J. *Nations and Nationalism Since 1780: Programme, Myth, Reality*. Cambridge: Cambridge University Press, 1990.

Hohendahl, Peter Uwe. *Building A National Literature: The Case of Germany, 1830–1870*. Ithaca, N.Y.: Cornell University Press, 1989.

Hoston, Germaine A. "*Ikkoku Shakai-shugi*: Sano Manabu and the Limits of Marxism as Cultural Criticism." In *Culture and Identity: Japanese Intellectuals during the Interwar Years*, ed. J. Thomas Rimer, 168–86. Princeton: Princeton University Press, 1990.

———. *Marxism and the Crisis of Development in Prewar Japan*. Princeton: Princeton University Press, 1986.

———. *The State, Identity, and the National Question in China and Japan*. Princeton: Princeton University Press, 1994.

Idehara Takatoshi. "Rengeji no kane." *Kokugo kokubun* 56, no. 1 (January 1987): 1–23.

Igarashi, Yoshikuni. *Bodies of Memory: Narratives of War in Postwar Japanese Culture, 1945–1970*. Princeton: Princeton University Press, 2000.

Igari Akira. "Kawakami Bizan no shi: Meiji bunshi no keizai seikatsu." *Nihon kindai bungaku* 12 (May 1970): 89–100.

Ikuta Chōkō. "Tōson-shi no shōsetsu." *Mita bungaku* (June 1911). Reprinted in *TZ* 18:175–86.

Inazō, Nitobe. *Bushido: The Soul of Japan*. 1900. Reprint, Rutland, Vt.: Charles E. Tuttle, 1969.

Irokawa, Daikichi. *The Culture of the Meiji Period*. Trans. Marius B. Jansen. Princeton: Princeton University Press, 1985.

Ishihara Chiaki. " 'Ie' no bunpō." *Kokubungaku kaishaku to kanshō* 55, no. 4 (April 1990): 24–31.

———. *Sōseki no kigōgaku*. Tokyo: Kōdansha, 1999.

Isoda Kōichi, *Hikaku tenkō ron josetsu*. 2nd rev. ed. Tokyo: Sōkōsha, 1980.

Itō Kazuo. ed. *Shimazaki Tōson jiten*. Tokyo: Meiji Shoin, 1972.

Ito, Ken. "The Family and the Nation in Tokutomi Roka's *Hototogisu*." *Harvard Journal of Asiatic Studies* 60, no. 2 (December 2000): 489–536.

Itō Shinkichi. *Shimazaki Tōson no bungaku*. Tokyo: Daiichi Shobō, 1936. Reprint, vol. 5 of *Kindai sakka kenkyū sōsho*. Tokyo: Nihon Tosho Sentā, 1983.

———. "*Shimazaki Tōson no bungaku* shuppan wo meguru kaisō." 1983. In *Shimazaki Tōson no bungaku* by Itō Shinkichi. 1–15.

Itō Shirō, "Shimazaki Tōson ron" *Yuibutsuron kenkyū* 63 (January 1938): 78–96.

Ivy, Marilyn. *Discourses of the Vanishing: Modernity, Phantasm, Japan*. Chicago: University of Chicago Press, 1995.

Iwami Teruyo. "Setsuko no monogatari: *Shinsei* no topogurafii." In *Shimazaki Tōson: bunmei hihyōka to shi to shōsetsu*, ed. Hiraoka Toshio and Kenmochi Takeo, 215–29. Tokyo: Sōbunsha, 1996.

———. "Setsuko to iu tekusuto: *Shinsei* no sekushuariti." *Nihon kindai bungaku* 53 (October 1995): 108–21.

———. "*Yoake mae* (Shimazaki Tōson): kaiki no kōzu." *Nihon no kindai shōsetsu II*, ed. Miyoshi Yukio, 113–28. Tokyo: Tōkyō Daigaku Shuppankai, 1986.

Iwano Hōmei. "Jisatsu ron." 1908. In *Iwano Hōmei zenshū*. Vol. 9, 239–43. Kyoto: Rinsen Shoten, 1995.

Jennison, Rebecca Sue. *Approaching Difference: A Reading of Selected Texts by Shimizu Shikin*. Master's thesis, Cornell University, 1990.

Johnston, William. *The Modern Epidemic: A History of Tuberculosis in Japan*. Boston: Council on East Asian Studies, Harvard University, 1995.

Jusdanis, Gregory. *Belated Modernity and Aesthetic Culture: Inventing National Literature*. Minneapolis: University of Minnesota Press, 1991.

Kakita Tokiya. "Kaisetsu." Afterword to *Shimazaki Tōson no bungaku* by Itō Shinkichi.

Kamei Hideo. "Kyo no dokusha." *Bungaku* 57, no. 2 (March 1989): 1–6.

———. *Transformations of Sensibility: The Phenomenology of Meiji Literature*. Trans. ed. Michael Bourdaghs (Ann Arbor: University of Michigan Center for Japanese Publications, 2002).

Kamei Katsuichirō. *Kamei Katsuichirō zenshū*. Vol. 3. Tokyo: Kōdansha, 1972.

———. *Shimazaki Tōson: ippyōhakusha no shōzō*. Tokyo: Kōbundō Shobō, 1939. Reprinted as *Kindai sakka kenkyū sōsho*. Vol. 124. Tokyo: Nihon Tosho Sentā, 1993.

———. *Shimazaki Tōson ron*. Tokyo: Shinchōsha, 1953.

Kamishima Jirō. *Kindai Nihon no seishin kōzō*. Tokyo: Iwanami Shoten, 1961.

Kano, Ayako. *Acting Like A Woman in Modern Japan: Theater, Gender, and Nationalism* (New York: Palgrave, 2001).

———. "Japanese Theater and Imperialism: Romance and Resistance." *U.S.-Japan Women's Journal English Supplement* 12 (1996): 17–47.

Karatani Kōjin. "Bijutsukan toshite no Nihon: Okakura Tenshin to Fenorosa." *Hihyō kūkan* 2d ser., no. 1 (1994): 68–75.

———. "Nakano Shigeharu to tenkō." In *Hyūmoa toshite no yuibutsuron*, 163–200. Tokyo: Chikuma Shobō, 1993.

———. *NAM: Genri*. Tokyo: Ōta Shuppan, 2000.

———. "One Spirit, Two Nineteenth Centuries." Trans. Alan Wolfe. In *Postmodernism and*

Japan, ed. Masao Miyoshi and H. D. Harootunian, 259–72. Durham: Duke University Press, 1989.

——. *Origins of Modern Japanese Literature*. Trans. ed. Brett de Bary. Durham: Duke University Press, 1993.

Katō, Shuichi. *The Modern Years*. Vol 3 of *A History of Japanese Literature*. Trans. Don Sanderson. Tokyo: Kodansha International, 1979.

——."Tōson to iwayuru shizenshugi." In *Sekai ga yomu Nihon kindai bungaku*, ed. Fukuoka UNESCO Kyōka.Vol. 3, 17–36. Tokyo: Maruzen, 1999.

Kawabata Toshifusa. *Hakai to sono shūhen*. Kyoto: Bunrikaku, 1984.

Kawabata Yasunari."Bungei jihyō." *Bungei shunjū* (August 1929). Reprint, *TZ* 18:297–300.

Kawamura Kunimitsu. "Onna no yamai, otoko no yamai." *Gendai shisō* 21, no. 7 (July 1993): 88–109.

Kawashima Hidekazu. *Shimazaki Tōson ronkō*. Tokyo: Ōfūsha, 1987.

Keene, Donald. *Dawn to the West: Japanese Literature in the Modern Era: Fiction*. New York: Henry Holt, 1984.

——. *Dawn to the West: Japanese Literature in the Modern Era: Poetry, Drama, Criticism*. New York: Henry Holt, 1984.

——. *Modern Japanese Literature*. New York: Grove Press, 1956.

Kern, Stephen. *The Culture of Time and Space, 1880–1918*. Cambridge: Harvard University Press, 1983.

Kieda Masuichi. "*Yoake mae shiron*." *Kokugo Kokubun* 5, no. 1 (January 1935): 47–70.

Kikuchi Kan. "Contemporary Japanese Literature." *Bungei shunjū* 13, no. 12 (December 1935): 236–41.

Kimata Satoshi. "Tōson no romanchishizumu." In *Nihon bungaku kōza 10: shiika II (kindai hen)*, ed. Nihon Bungaku Kyōkai. Tokyo: Taishūkan Shoten, 1988. 103–19.

Kimura Sōta. "*Ie ni tsuite no inshō to kansō*." 1910. *TZ* 18:153–158.

Kitahara Daisaku. "*Hakai* to buraku kaihō undō." In *Nihon bungaku kenkyū shiryō sōsho: Shimazaki Tōson*, ed. Nihon Bungaku Kenkyū Shiryō Kankō Kai, 220–24. Tokyo: Yūseidō, 1971.

Kō Yonran. "*Hakai* kaitei katei to minzokuronteki gensetsu." *Gobun* 100 (March 1998): 70–82.

——." 'Tekisasu' wo meguru gensetsu ken: Shimazaki Tōson *Hakai* to bōchō keifu." In *Disukūru no teikoku: Meiji sanjū nendai no bunka kenkyū*, ed. Kaneko Akio, Takahashi Osamu, and Yoshida Morio, 273–302. Tokyo: Shinyōsha, 2000.

Kobayashi Akiko. "Shimazaki Tōson no joseikan: Iwamoto Yoshiharu no joseikan to no kakawari." *Tōkyō Joshi Daigaku Nihon bungaku* 76 (September 1991): 38–49.

Kobayashi Hideo. *Kobayashi Hideo zenshū*.Vol. 3. Tokyo: Shinchōsha, 1968.

——. *The Literature of the Lost Home: Literary Criticism, 1924–1939*. Trans. Paul Anderer (Stanford: Stanford University Press, 1995).

Komori Yōichi. "*Yuragi*" *no Nihon bungaku*. Tokyo: NHK Books, 1998.

Konaka Nobutaka. "*Haru* ron: shinwa no shūen." *Nihon kindai bungaku* 36 (October 1987): 30–43.

——. "Ie no chiyuryoku." *Nihon kindai bungaku* 53 (1995): 96–107.

——. "*Yoake mae* no hankindai: kyōki no hanten." In *Kōza Shōwa bungaku shi*, ed.Yūseidō Henshūbu.Vol. 1, 248–56. Tokyo:Yūseidō, 1988.

Kōno Kensuke. "Joshi kyōiku to *Wakanashū*: ren'ai no seijigaku." *Nihon no bungaku* 12 (December 1993): 27–44.

——. "Onna no kaiwa, otoko no kaiwa: *Ie* ni okeru kaiwa no gihō." In *Shimazaki Tōson: Bunmei hihyō to shi to shōsetsu to*, ed. Hiraoka Toshio and Kenmochi Takehiko. 167–81. Tokyo: Sōbunsha, 1996.

——. " 'Seishun' to iu tekusuto: Shimazaki Tōson *Haru* wo megutte." In *Bungaku ni okeru nijūdai*, ed. Satō Yasumasa, 123–44. Tokyo: Kasama Shoin, 1990.

——. "*Shinsei* ni okeru sensō: Shimazaki Tōson no 'sōsaku' to kokumin kokka." *Nihon bungaku* 44, no. 11 (November 1995): 1–10.

——. *Shomotsu no kindai: media no bungakushi*. Tokyo: Chikuma Shobō, 1992.

Koschmann, J. Victor. "Intellectuals and Politics." In *Postwar Japan as History*, ed. Andrew Gordon, 395–423. Berkeley: University of California Press, 1993.

——. *Revolution and Subjectivity in Postwar Japan*. Chicago: University of Chicago Press, 1996.

Koseki Kazuhiro. " 'Ren'ai' to iu gensō: ren'ai shi no ken'iki." *Kokubungaku* 41, no. 13 (November 1996): 42–48.

Kotani Hiroyuki. *Rekishi to ningen ni tsuite: Tōson to kindai Nihon*. Tokyo: Tōkyō Daigaku Shuppankai, 1991.

Kristeva, Julia. *Powers of Horror: An Essay on Abjection*. Trans. Leon S. Roudiez. New York: Columbia University Press, 1982.

Kuhnast, Jutta. *Das Epische im Fruhwerk des Shimazaki Tōson; die Gedichtsammlung*. Hamburg: Gesellschaft fur Natur- und Volkerkunde Ostasiens, 1973.

Kuki Shūzō. "Tōyōteki jikan." 1936. In *Kuki Shūzō zenshū*. Vol. 5. Tokyo: Iwanami Shoten, 1981.

Kurokawa Midori. *Ika to dōka no aida: hisabetsu buraku ninshiki no kiseki*. Tokyo: Aoki Shoten, 1999.

Laclau, Ernesto, and Chantal Mouffe. *Hegemony and Socialist Strategy: Towards a Radical Democratic Politics*. London: Verso, 1985.

Lamarre, Thomas. "Bacterial Cultures and Linguistic Colonies: Mori Rintarō's Experiments with History, Science, and Languages." *positions* 6, no. 3 (Winter 1998): 597–635.

——. "The Deformation of the Modern Spectator: Synaesthesia, Cinema, and the Spectre of Race in Tanizaki." *Japan Forum* 11, no. 1 (1999): 23–42.

Latour, Bruno. *The Pasteurization of France*. Trans. Alan Sheridan and John Law. Cambridge: Harvard University Press, 1988.

Lippit, Seiji. "The Disintegrating Machinery of the Modern: Akutagawa Ryūnosuke's Late Writings." *Journal of Asian Studies* 58, no. 1 (February 1999): 27–50.

——. *Topographies of Japanese Modernism*. New York: Columbia University Press, 2002.

MacCannell, Juliet Flower. *The Regime of the Brother: After the Patriarchy*. London: Routledge, 1991.

Maeda Ai. *Kindai dokusha no seiritsu*. Tokyo: Chikuma Shobō, 1989.

——. "Tō no shisō." In *Toshi kūkan no naka no bungaku*, 141–63. Tokyo: Chikuma Shobō, 1982.

Maeda Akira. "*En to Gisei* gōhyō: egaku saku to kataru saku." 1911. Reprint, *TZ* 18:164–66.

Makino Noriko. "Tōson to fujin undō: *Shojochi* o chūshin toshite." In *Tōson Kinen Kan kōen shū*, ed. Tōson Kinen Kan, 176–84. Magome, Nagano Pref.: Tōson Kinen Gō, 1994.

Mao, Douglas. "The New Critics and the Text-Object." *ELH* 63, no.1 (1996): 227–54.

Maruyama, Masao. *Studies in the Intellectual History of Tokugawa Japan.* Trans. Mikiso Hane. Princeton: Princeton University Press, 1974.

Matsumoto, Tomone. "From Marxism to Japanism: A Study of Kamei Katsuichirō (1907–1967)." Ph.D. diss., University of Arizona, 1979.

Matsushita Hiroyuki. "1910 nendai ni okeru *Michikusa* to *Wakai*: sono 'shussan' ga imi suru mono." *Meiji Daigaku daigakuin kiyō: bungaku hen* 30 (February 1993): 47–66.

May, Katharina. "Das Motiv des Aussenseiters in der modernen japanischen Literatur." *Bochumer Jahrbuch zur Ostasienforschung* 4 (1981): 110–29.

McClellan, Edwin. "Tōson and the Autobiographical Novel." In *Tradition and Modernization in Japanese Culture*, ed. Donald H. Shively, 347–78. Princeton: Princeton University Press, 1971.

——. *Two Japanese Novelists: Sōseki and Tōson.* Chicago: University of Chicago Press, 1969.

McNeill, William H. *Plagues and Peoples.* Garden City, N.Y.: Anchor Press, 1976.

Miyamoto Yuriko. *Miyamoto Yuriko zenshū.* Vol. 10. Tokyo: Shin Nihon Shuppansha, 1980.

Miyasaka Yasuko. " 'Osan' no shakai shi." In *Bosei: Nihon no feminizumu* 5, ed. Inoue Teruko, Ueno Chizuko, and Ehara Yumiko, 89–124. Tokyo: Iwanami Shoten, 1995.

Miyoshi Yukio. *Shimazaki Tōson ron.* 1966. Reprint, vol. 1 of *Miyoshi Yukio chosaku shū.* Tokyo: Chikuma Shobō, 1993.

Miyoshi Yukio et al. "Shimazaki Tōson to Nihon no kindai." *Kokubungaku* 16, no. 5 (April 1971): 8–49.

Mizukami Ryūtarō. "Shimazaki Tōson sensei no ashiato (kaigara tsuihō)." *Chūō kōron* 44, no. 7 (July 1929): 289–302.

Mizuta Noriko. "Josei no jikogatari to monogatari." *Hihyō kūkan* 1st ser., no. 4 (1992): 64–79.

Mori Ōgai. "Nihon heishoku ron taii." 1886. In *Ōgai zenshū.* Vol. 18, 11–18. Tokyo: Iwanami Shoten, 1974.

Morita, James R. "Shimazaki Tōson's Four Collections of Poems." *Monumenta Nipponica* 35:3–4 (1970): 325–69.

Morris-Suzuki, Tessa. *Re-Inventing Japan: Time Space Nation.* Armonk, N.Y.: M. E. Sharpe, 1998.

Mosse, George. *Nationalism and Sexuality.* Madison: University of Wisconsin Press, 1985.

Murai Osamu. "Kokubungaku no jūgonen sensō." Parts 1 and 2. *Hihyō kūkan* 2d ser., no. 16 (1998): 170–87; no. 18 (1998): 170–81.

——. *Nantō ideorogii no hassei.* Rev. ed. Tokyo: Ōta Shuppan, 1995.

Muta Kazue. "Images of the Family in Meiji Periodicals: The Paradox Underlying the Emergence of the 'Home.' " Trans. Marcella S. Gregory. *U.S.-Japan Women's Journal English Supplement* 7 (1994): 53–71.

Naff, William E. "Shimazaki Tōson: A Critical Biography." Ph.D. Diss., University of Washington, 1965.

——. "Shimazaki Toson's *Before the Dawn*: Historical Fiction as History and as Literature." In *The Ambivalence of Nationalism: Modern Japan Between East and West*, ed. James W.

White, Michio Umegaki, and Thomas R. H. Havens, 79–114. Lanham, Md.: University Press of America, 1990.

Nagahara, Yutaka. "*Monsieur le Capital* and *Madame la Terre* Do Their Ghost Dance: Globalization and the Nation-State." *The South Atlantic Quarterly* 99, no. 4 (Fall 2000): 929–61.

——. "A Sketch on the Hauntology of Capital: Towards Theory of Community." *Keizai shirin* 66, no. 2 (October 1998): 143–62.

Nägele, Rainer. *Theater, Theory, Speculation: Walter Benjamin and the Scenes of Modernity*. Baltimore: John Hopkins University Press, 1991.

Nairn, Tom. *Faces of Nationalism: Janus Revisited*. London: Verso, 1997.

Najita, Tetsuo and H. D. Harootunian. "Japan's Revolt Against the West." In *Modern Japanese Thought*, ed. Bob Tadashi Wakabayashi. Cambridge: Cambridge University Press, 1998. 207–72.

Nakamura Mitsuo. "Tenkō sakka ron." 1935. In *Shōwa hihyō taikei*, ed. Muramatsu Takeshi, Saeki Shōichi, and Ōkubo Tsuneo. Vol. 2, 314–29. Tokyo: Banchō Shobō, 1968.

Nakamura Seiko. "Hitotsu no me to tasū no me." 1911. Reprint, *TZ* 18:166–68.

——. "Shimazaki-shi no *Ie* to Shusei-shi no *Kabi*." *Waseda bungaku* (March 1912). Reprint, *TZ* 18:203–7.

Nakano Shigeharu. "Iwayuru geijutsu no taishūka ron no ayamari ni tsuite." 1928. Reprinted in *Nakano Shigeharu zenshū*. Vol. 6, 148–56. Tokyo: Chikuma Shobō, 1959.

Nakayama Hiroaki. "*Ie* no shikaku: 'jigyō' to 'kannen.' " *Kokubungaku kenkyū* 89 (June 1989): 57–67.

——. "Kettō no monogatari: *Ie* no 'yamai' ron." In *Shimazaki Tōson: bunmei hihyōka to shi to shōsetsu*, ed. Hiraoka Toshio and Kenmochi Takeo, 182–97. Tokyo: Sōbunsha, 1996.

——. " 'Komoro' to iu basho: Shimazaki Tōson ni okeru kinsen to gensetsu." *Nihon bungaku* 42, no. 7 (July 1993): 54–66.

——. "*Shinsei* no messēji: tegami to tanka." *Bai* 7 (July 1991): 48–61.

——. " 'Shōsetsu' no shihonron: Kōzu Takeshi no patoronēji." *Bungei to hihyō* 7, no. 10 (October 1994): 67–80.

——. "*Wakanashū* no juyōken: Tōson-chō to iu seido." *Kokugo to kokubungaku* 70, no. 7 (July 1993): 26–41.

Narita Ryūichi. "Kindai toshi to minshū." In *Toshi to minshū*, ed. Narita Ryūichi, 1–56. Tokyo: Yoshikawa Kirofuni-kan, 1993.

——. "Meiji ishin zō: 1935-nen zengo." *Edo shisō* 8 (1998): 97–106.

——. "Women and Views of Women Within the Changing Hygiene Conditions of Late-Nineteenth- and Early-Twentieth-Century Japan." *U.S.-Japan Women's Journal English Supplement* 8 (June 1995): 64–86.

Natsume Sōseki. *Sōseki zenshū*. Vol. 14. Tokyo: Iwanami Shoten, 1966.

Neary, Ian. *Political Protest and Social Control in Pre-War Japan: The Origins of Buraku Liberation*. Atlantic Highlands, N.J.: Humanities Press International, 1989.

Ninkovich, Frank A. "The New Criticism and Cold War America." *The Southern Quarterly* 20, no. 1 (fall 1981): 1–24.

Niranjana, Tejaswini. *Siting Translation: History, Post-Structuralism, and the Colonial Context*. Berkeley: University of California Press, 1992.

Nishikawa Yūko. "Japan's Entry into War and the Support of Women." Trans. William Gardner and Brett de Bary. *U.S.-Japan Women's Journal English Supplement* 12 (1996): 48–83.

——. *Shakuya to mochiie no bungakushi.* Tokyo: Sanseidō, 1998.

Nolte, Sharon, and Sally Ann Hastings. "The Meiji State's Policy Toward Women, 1890–1910." In *Recreating Japanese Women, 1600–1945,* ed. Gail Lee Bernstein, 151–74. Berkeley: University of California Press, 1991.

Nosco, Peter. *Remembering Paradise: Nativism and Nostalgia in Eighteenth-Century Japan* (Cambridge: Council on East Asian Studies, Harvard University, 1990).

Notehelfer, Fred. "On Idealism and Realism in the Thought of Okakura Tenshin." *Journal of Japanese Studies* 16, no. 2 (1990): 309–55.

Oguma, Eiji. *A Genealogy of "Japanese" Self-Images.* Trans. David Askew. Melbourne: Trans Pacific Press, 2002.

Ohmae, Kenichi. *The End of the Nation State: The Rise of Regional Economies.* London: Harper Collins, 1995.

Ohnuki-Tierney, Emily. *The Monkey as Mirror: Symbolic Transformations in Japanese History and Ritual.* Princeton: Princeton University Press, 1987.

Ōida Yoshiaki. "*Haru ni okeru komyunikeishon no mondai.*" *Bai* 7 (July 1991): 33–47.

——. "*Ie no jikan: chichi to no kaikō.*" *Bungei to hihyō* 6, no. 3 (March 1986): 44–55.

Okakura Tenshin. *The Ideals of the East.* 1903. Reprint, in *Okakura Kakuzō: Collected English Writings.* Vol. 1. Tokyo: Heibonsha, 1984.

Okamoto Kanoko. "Josei no mitaru gendai sakka no joryū byōsha: Tōson-shi no josei byōsha." *Shinchō* (October 1920). Reprint, *TZ* 18:254–55.

Okazaki Yoshie. "Tōson ron joshō." *Bungaku* 4, no. 8 (August 1936): 1–12.

Ōkubo Tsuneo. "*Hakai: sono soko ni aru mono.*" *Kokubungaku* 16, no. 5 (April 1971): 109–115.

Olson, Lawrence. *Ambivalent Moderns: Portraits of Japanese Cultural Identity.* Savage, Md.: Rowman & Littlefield, 1992.

Ōnuki Shōsen. "*Gisei wo yomite.*" 1911. *TZ* 18:158–60.

——. "*Ie o yomu.*" 1910. *TZ* 18:149–53.

Orbaugh, Sharalyn. "The Body in Contemporary Japanese Women's Fiction." In *The Woman's Hand: Gender and Theory in Japanese Women's Writing,* ed. Paul Gordon Schalow and Janet A. Walker, 119–64. Stanford: Stanford University Press, 1996.

Oshino Takeshi. *Miyazawa Kenji no bigaku.* Tokyo: Kanrin Shobō, 2000.

——. "'Yamai': Tayama Katai 'Shōjobyō.'" *Kokubungaku* 40, no. 11 (September 1995): 72–76.

Oyama, Sayuri. "Shimazaki Tōson's *Hakai*: (Re)writing and (Re)reading the Canon." *Issues of Canonicity and Canon Formation in Japanese Literary Studies: Proceedings of the Association for Japanese Literary Studies* 1 (2000). 59–75.

Parker, Andrew, et al. "Introduction." In *Nationalisms and Sexualities,* ed. Parker et al., 1–18. New York: Routledge, 1992.

Pincus, Leslie. *Authenticating Culture in Imperial Japan: Kuki Shūzō and the Rise of National Aesthetics.* Berkeley: University of California Press, 1996.

Pratt , Mary Louise. *Imperial Eyes: Travel Writing and Transculturation.* London: Routledge, 1992.

Pyle, Kenneth. *The New Generation in Meiji Japan: Problems of Cultural Identity, 1885–1895.* Stanford: Stanford University Press, 1969.

Rabson, Steve. "Shimazaki Tōson on War." *Monumenta Nipponica* 46, no. 4 (1991): 453–81.

Renan, Ernest. "What is a Nation?" 1882. Trans. Martin Thom. In *Nation and Narration*, ed. Homi K. Bhabha, 8–22. London: Routledge, 1990.

Robinson, Jennifer. "It Takes a Village: Internationalization and Nostalgia in Postwar Japan." In *Mirror of Modernity: Invented Traditions of Modern Japan*, ed. Stephen Vlastos, 110–29. Berkeley: University of California Press, 1998.

Rodd, Laurel Rasplica. "Yosano Akiko and the Taishō Debate over the 'New Woman.'" In *Recreating Japanese Women, 1600–1945*, ed. Gail Lee Bernstein, 175–98. Berkeley: University of California Press, 1991.

Roggendorf, Joseph. "Shimazaki Tōson: A Maker of the Modern Japanese Novel." *Monumenta Nipponica* 7, nos. 1–2 (1951): 38–66.

——. "Yōroppajin no mita Shimazaki Tōson." *Bungei* 11, no. 12 (September 1954): 23–29.

Rubin, Jay. *Injurious to Public Morals: Writers and the Meiji State*. Seattle: University of Washington Press, 1984.

Ryan, Marleigh Grayer. *Japan's First Modern Novel: Ukigumo of Futabatei Shimei*. Ann Arbor: Center for Japanese Studies, University of Michigan, 1965.

Saeki Yūichirō. "Tōson kenkyū bunken." *Bungaku* 4, no. 8 (August 1936): 156–69.

Sahlins, Marshall. *Stone Age Economics*. Chicago: Aldine Publishing, 1972.

Said, Edward. *Culture and Imperialism*. New York: Knopf, 1993.

——. *Orientalism*. London: Routledge, 1978.

Saitō Minako. *Ninshin shōsetsu*. Tokyo: Chikuma Bunko, 1997.

Sakai, Naoki. *Translation and Subjectivity: On "Japan" and Cultural Nationalism*. Minneapolis: University of Minnesota Press, 1998.

——. *Voices of the Past: The Status of Language in Eighteenth-Century Japanese Discourse*. Ithaca: Cornell University Press, 1991.

Sakaki, Atsuko. *Recontextualizing Texts: Narrative Performance in Modern Japanese Fiction*. Cambridge: Harvard University Asia Center, 1999.

Sand, Jordan. "At Home in the Meiji Period: Inventing Japanese Domesticity." In *Mirror of Modernity: Invented Traditions of Modern Japan*, ed. Stephen Vlastos, 191–207. Berkeley: University of California Press, 1998.

——. "House and Home in Modern Japan, 1880s–1920s." Ph.D. Diss., Columbia University. 1996.

Sano Masato. "Bungakuteki kokusaishugi to diasupora no unmei: Shōwa jūnendai Tōson Tō-Ajia bungaku." In *Kindai no yume to chisei: Bungaku shisō no Shōwa jūnendai zengo*, ed. Bungaku Shisō Konwakai, 9–27. Tokyo: Kanrin Shobō, 2000.

Sas, Miryam. *Fault Lines: Cultural Memory and Japanese Surrealism*. Stanford: Stanford University Press, 1999.

Sasabuchi Tomoichi. *Shōsetuka Shimazaki Tōson*. Tokyo: Meiji Shoin, 1990.

Sasaki Masanobu. "*Haru* wo megutte: Aoki Shun'ichi zō no ichi." *Kokugo to kokubungaku* 56, no. 5 (May 1979): 83–94.

——. "*Haru* wo megutte: Kishimoto Sutekichi zō no ichimen." *Nihon kindai bungaku* 25 (October 1978): 168–79.

——. "*Haru* wo megutte: seishun to shi." *Kokubungaku kenkyū* 68 (June 1979): 1–11.

——. "*Ie* no josetsu: kōsei wo megutte." *Kokubungaku kaishaku to kanshō* 55, no. 4 (April 1990): 82–87.

Sato, Hiroaki, and Burton Watson, eds. *From the Country of Eight Islands*. New York: Columbia University Press, 1986.

Seaman, Louis Livingston. *The Real Triumph of Japan*. New York: D. Appleton, 1906.

Sedgwick, Eve Kosofsky. *Between Men: English Literature and Male Homosocial Desire*. New York: Columbia University Press, 1985.

——. "Nationalisms and Sexualities in the Age of Wilde." In *Nationalisms and Sexualities*, ed. Andrew Parker et al., 235–45. New York: Routledge, 1992.

Seki Reiko. "Tatakau 'chichi no musume': Ichiyō tekusuto no seisei." In *Onna ga yomu Nihon kindai bungaku: feminizumo hihyō no kokoromi*, ed. Egusa Mitsuko and Urushida Kazuo, 31–54. Tokyo: Shinyōsha, 1992.

Seki Ryōichi. "*Ie*: maboroshi no sanbusaku." In *Nihon bungaku kenkyū shiryō sōsho: Shimazaki Tōson II*, ed. Nihon Bungaku Kenkyū Shiryō Kankō Kai, 152–64. Tokyo: Yūseidō, 1983.

Sekii Mitsuo. "*Shinsei* ron: jiden to iu kokuhaku no yōshiki." *Kokubungaku kaishaku to kanshō* 55, no. 4 (April 1990): 93–99.

Sekiya Yumiko. "Kanyu toshite no *Ie*." *Kokugo to kokubungaku* 66, no. 4 (April 1989): 46–59.

——. "*Shinsei* no shinwa kōzō: tozasareta shosai no monogatari." *Nihon kindai bungaku* 45 (October 1991): 147–61.

Seltzer, Mark. *Bodies and Machines*. New York: Routledge, 1992.

Senuma Shigeki. "Chi ni tsunagaru furusato." *Taiyō* 195 (March 1972): 45–48.

——. *Shimazaki Tōson: sono shōgai to sakuhin*. Tokyo: Kaku Shobō, 1953.

Shibata Michiko. *Hisabetsu buraku no denshō to seikatsu: Shinshū no buraku korō kikigaki*. Tokyo: San'ichi Shobō, 1975.

Shimazaki Tōson. *Before the Dawn*. Trans. William Naff. Honolulu: University of Hawaii Press, 1987.

——. *The Broken Commandment*. Trans. Kenneth Strong. Tokyo: University of Tokyo Press, 1974.

——. *The Family*. Trans. Cecilia Segawa Seigle. Tokyo: University of Tokyo Press, 1976.

——. *Tōson zenshū*. 18 Vols. Tokyo: Chikuma Shobō, 1966–1971.

"Shinkan shōkai." *Katei zasshi* 4, no. 5 (May 1906): 51.

Shinoda Kōichirō. *Shōsetsu wa ika ni kakareta ka*. Tokyo: Iwanami Shoten, 1982.

Shinoda Tarō. "Bungaku ni okeru ishin-shi no mondai." *Kaizō* 15, no. 3 (March 1933): 97–111.

Shirane, Haruo. "Introduction: Issues in Canon Formation." In *Inventing the Classics: Modernity, National Identity, and Japanese Literature*, ed. Shirane and Tomi Suzuki, 1–18. Stanford: Stanford University Press, 2000.

Sibley, William F. "Naturalism in Japanese Literature." *Harvard Journal of Asiatic Studies* 28 (1968): 157–69.

Sievers, Sharon L. *Flowers in Salt: The Beginnings of Feminist Consciousness in Modern Japan*. Stanford: Stanford University Press, 1983.

Silverberg, Miriam. *Changing Song: The Marxist Manifestos of Nakano Shigeharu*. Princeton: Princeton University Press, 1990.

Sontag, Susan. *Illness as Metaphor and AIDS and its Metaphors*. New York: Doubleday, 1990.

Sorgenfrei, Carol Jay. "Shuji Terayama: Avant Garde Dramatist of Japan." Ph.D Diss., University of California at Santa Barbara, 1978.

Spalding, Lisa. "Period Films in the Prewar Era." In *Reframing Japanese Cinema: Authorship Genre History*, ed. Arthur Nolletti Jr. and David Desser, 131–44. Bloomington: Indiana University Press, 1992.

Stallybrass, Peter, and Allon White. *The Politics and Poetics of Transgression*. Ithaca: Cornell University Press, 1986.

Steinhoff, Patricia. *Tenkō: Ideology and Societal Integration in Prewar Japan*. New York: Garland, 1991.

Strychacz, Thomas. *Modernism, Mass Culture, and Professionalism*. London: Cambridge University Press, 1993.

Suga Hidemi. "Bungaku wo yōgo shi, shi wo hoshu suru: posutokoroniaru hihyō/karuchuraru sutadiizu to 'bungaku.'" *Gendai shi techō* 40, no. 9 (September 1997): 38–46.

——. "Kokumin to iu sukyandaru: 'Teikoku' no bungaku 1." *Hihyō Kūkan* 2d ser., no. 13 (1997): 226–46.

——. *Nihon kindai bungaku no "tanjō": genbun itchi to nashonarizumu*. Tokyo: Ōta Shuppan, 1995.

——. " 'Onna' to iu hikokumin: 'teikoku' no bungaku 2." *Hihyō kūkan* 2d ser., no. 14 (1997): 229–46.

Sugiyama Heisuke. "Geijutsu to moraru." *Chūō kōron* 52, no. 5 (May 1937): 391–402.

Suzuki Sadami. *Nihon no "bungaku" gainen*. Tokyo: Sakuhinsha, 1998.

Suzuki, Tomi. "Gender and Genre: Modern Literary Histories and Women's Diary Literature." In *Inventing the Classics: Modernity, National Identity, and Japanese Literature*, ed. Haruo Shirane and Tomi Suzuki, 71–95. Stanford: Stanford University Press, 2000.

——. *Narrating the Self: Fictions of Japanese Modernity*. Stanford: Stanford University Press, 1997.

Takagi Takeo. *Shinbun shōsetsu shi: Meiji-hen*. Tokyo: Kokusho Kankōkai, 1974.

Takahashi Akinori. "*Yoake mae* no jidai kubun ron." *Bungei kenkyū* (Tōhoku University) 116 (September 1987): 62–71.

——. "*Yoake mae* no 'sōsō' o megutte." *Shimazaki Tōson kenkyū* 17 (September 1989): 25–41.

Takahashi Masako. "*Ie* no jojutsu." *Nagoya kindai bungaku kenkyū* 2 (December 1984): 22–35.

——. "*Shinsei* ron." *Nagoya bungaku kenkyū* 1 (September 1983): 1–16.

——. "Taishō-ki no ryōsei mondai: ren'ai ron to *Shinsei*." *Nagoya Daigaku kindai bungaku kenkyū* 3 (November 1985): 10–23.

Takano Junko. " '*Chūō kōron*' to 'josei': Meiji yonjūsan-nen 'Joryū sakka shōsetsu jippen' wo yomu." *Bungei to hihyō* 7, no. 10 (October 1994): 42–57.

Takayama Chogyū. *Chogyū zenshū*. Vol. 2. Tokyo: Hakubunkan, 1926.

Takayama Shigeru. "Ishin-shi to *Yoake mae* ron." *Kogito* 21 (February 1934): 4–19.

Tanaka, Stefan. *Japan's Orient: Rendering Pasts into History*. Berkeley: University of California Press, 1993.

Terayama Shūji. *Iede no susume*. Tokyo: Kadokawa, 1972.

Togawa Shinsuke. *Shimazaki Tōson*. Tokyo: Chikuma Shobō, 1980.

Tokieda Motoki. "Chōsen ni okeru kokugo seisaku oyobi kokugo kyōiku no shōrai." *Nihongo* 2, no. 8 (July 1942): 54–63.

Tōkoku Atsushi." 'Haiboku' no mukō: Itō Shinkichi to tenkō. *Shakai Bungaku* 18 (2003): 26–37.

Tokutomi, Kenijro [Roka]. *Nami-ko: A Realistic Novel.* Trans. Sakae Shioya and E. F. Edgett. Boston: Herbert B. Turner, 1904.

Tomiyama Ichirō. "Kokumin no tanjō to 'Nihon jinshu.' " *Shisō* 845 (November 1994): 37–56.

Tsurumi, Patricia. *Japanese Colonial Education in Taiwan, 1895–1945.* Cambridge: Harvard University Press, 1977.

Tsurumi Shunsuke. *An Intellectual History of Wartime Japan, 1931–1945.* London: KPI Limited, 1986.

———. *Tsurumi Shunsuke shū.* 12 volumes. Tokyo: Chikuma Shobō, 1991.

Ueno Chizuko. "Kaisetsu." In *Fuzoku sei.* Vol. 23 of *Nihon kindai shisō taikei,* ed. Ogi Shinzō, Kumakura Isao, and Ueno Chizuko, 505–50. Tokyo: Iwanami Shoten, 1990.

———. *Kindai kazoku no seiritsu to shūen.* Tokyo: Iwanami Shoten, 1994.

Ueno Chizuko, Ogura Chikako, and Tomioka Taeko. *Danryū bungaku ron.* Tokyo: Chikuma Shobō, 1992.

Umezawa Toshihiko, Hirano Eikyū, and Yamagishi Takashi. *Bungaku no naka no hisabetsu buraku zō: senzen hen.* Tokyo: Akashi Shoten, 1980.

Usui Yoshimi. *Kindai bungaku ronsō.* Vol. 1. Tokyo: Chikuma Shobō, 1975.

Vernon, Victoria V. *Daughters of the Moon: Wish, Will, and Social Constraint in Fiction by Modern Japanese Women.* Berkeley: Institute of East Asian Studies, University of California, 1988.

Vincent, J. Keith. "Masaoka Shiki to yamai no imi." *Hihyō kūkan* 2d ser., no. 8 (1996): 160–87.

Walker, Janet. *The Japanese Novel of the Meiji Period and the Idea of Individualism.* Princeton: Princeton University Press, 1979.

Wallerstein, Immanuel. *Historical Capitalism with Capitalist Civilization.* London: Verso, 1983.

Washburn, Dennis. *The Dilemma of the Modern in Japanese Fiction.* New Haven: Yale University Press, 1995.

Watanabe Hiroshi. *Shimazaki Tōson wo yominaosu.* Tokyo: Sōjusha, 1994.

Watanabe Kazutami. *Hayashi Tatsuo to sono jidai.* Tokyo: Iwanami Shoten, 1988.

Watanabe Naomi. *Kindai Nihon bungaku to "sabetsu."* Tokyo: Ōta Shuppan, 1994.

Watsuji Tetsurō. *Climate and Culture: A Philosophical Study.* 1935. Trans. Geoffrey Bownas. Tokyo: Hokuseido Press, 1961.

———. "Tōson no kosei." 1951. Reprinted in *Watsuji Tetsurō zenshū.* Vol. 3, 439–47. Tokyo: Iwanami Shoten, 1962.

———. "Tōson no omoide." 1950. Reprinted in *Watsuji Tetsurō zenshū.* Vol. 3, 433–38. Tokyo: Iwanami Shoten, 1962.

Wilson, George M. *Patriots and Redeemers in Japan: Motives in the Meiji Restoration.* Chicago: University of Chicago Press, 1992.

Wolfe, Alan. *Suicidal Narrative in Modern Japan: The Case of Dazai Osamu.* Princeton: Princeton University Press, 1990.

Wood, Mary Elene. *The Writing on the Wall: Women's Autobiography and the Asylum.* Urbana: University of Illinois Press, 1994.

Yabu Teiko. "Meiji bungaku to kazoku: oboegaki." *Nihon kindai bungaku* 41 (October 1989): 80–93.

———. *Tōkoku Tōson Ichiyō.* Tokyo: Meiji Shoin, 1991.

Yamamoto Yoshiaki. " 'Chichi' no shōzō: Tokutomi Roka *Hototogisu*." *Kokubungaku* 40, no. 11 (September 1995): 42–49.

Yamashita Etusko. *Mazakon bungakuron.* Tokyo: Shinyōsha, 1991.

Yanagi, Sōetsu. *The Unknown Craftsman*, ed. Bernard Leach. Tokyo: Kodansha, 1972.

Yanagita Izumi. "Meiji jidai ni okeru josei bungaku." *Kokubungaku kanshō to kaishaku* 6, no. 12 (December 1941): 48–56.

"Yoake mae gappyōkai." *Bungakkai* (May 1936). Reprint, in *Nihon bungaku kenkyū shiryō sōsho: Shimazaki Tōson*, ed. Nihon bungaku kenkyū shiryō kankō kai, 288–308. Tokyo: Yūseidō, 1971.

Yoshida Seiichi. *Shimazaki Tōson.* Vol. 6 of *Yoshida Seiichi chosakushū.* Tokyo: Ōfūsha, 1971.

Yoshie Takamatsu. "Jōnetsu no shijin Tōson." *Bunshō ōrai* 1, no. 4 (April 1925): 16–18.

Yoshimoto Takaaki. "Tenkō ron." 1958. Reprinted in *Seiji shisō*, vol 3 of *Yoshimoto Takaaki zenshūsen*, 9–34. Tokyo: Yamato Shobō, 1986.

Yoshino, Kosaku. *Cultural Nationalism in Contemporary Japan.* London: Routledge, 1992.

Young, Robert. *Colonial Desire: Hybridity in Theory, Culture, and Race.* London: Routledge, 1995.

Yuval-Davis, Nira. *Gender And Nation.* London: SAGE Publications, 1997.

Žižek, Slavoj. *The Sublime Object of Ideology.* London: Verso, 1989.

abject, 131, 145
abortion, 123–24
Akita Ujaku, 1–2, 12
Akutagawa Ryūnosuke, 156
allegory: in *Before the Dawn*, 179–81; in *The Family*, 85–86, 90, 224n. 87
Anderson, Benedict, 2, 14, 15, 84, 158–61, 164, 167, 168
animals, 62–64, 212n. 38
anti-conquest, 188
antimodernism, 4, 161, 163, 238n. 38
anti-Semitism, 60, 195, 211n. 30
Aono Suekichi, 178–82, 188, 189
Arishima Takeo, 23
Asahi (newspaper), 107–8, 124, 133
Asano Akira, 176, 213n. 43
autobiography, 147, 148, 151, 152–53

Balibar, Etienne, 14, 112, 172
Bakhtin, Mikhail, 157, 164
Barthes, Roland, 229n. 40
Bashō. *See* Matsuo Bashō
Benjamin, Walter, 158, 171, 180–81
Bennington, Geoffrey, 186–87
Bergson, Henri, 155, 161, 235n. 5, 244n. 86
Bhabha, Homi, 69, 160–61, 171
Black Ships, the, 165, 174, 184, 186, 195, 233n. 74; in *The Family*, 98
Bloch, Ernst, 189
blood: and discrimination, 56–57, 60–62, 212n. 38; of family, 79, 100; of nation, 69, 96, 121, 162, 174; in Tōson criticism, 32–33, 37–38, 175–6, 206n. 56, 241n. 60

body and bodies: of animals, 63–64; of *burakumin*, 56–58, 63–65; and colonization, 70; ethnic, 140; female, 152; and gender, 9–10, 115, 136–37, 149; and ideology, 50, 51, 52; masculine, 125, 134–35; maternal, 116, 123, 131, 137, 228n. 25; and modernity, 51; nation as, 49, 51, 52, 58, 69, 71, 73, 75, 76, 173; as possession of national community, 50; and race, 135, 141; sexual, 136, 140; and state policy, 68, 123–4, sublime, 173; and vaccination, 69–70
brothers, 82, 85, 104, 217n. 14
Buell, Frederick, 196
Bungakkai (journal), 119, 120, 124, 125
Bungaku (journal), 25, 26, 183
burakumin, 34, 47, 49–50, 56–76, 205n. 43, 208n. 5; in literature, 56–57, 62, 65–66, 71–72, 212n. 34; and migration, 213n. 41, 213n. 42; origins of, 211n. 33; and race, 76
Buson. *See* Yosa Buson
Butler, Judith, 46, 85, 117, 124

calendars, 154–55, 158, 159, 166–67, 188, 238n. 38
canon formation, 19–25, 32, 39; and gender, 116
capitalism, 14, 17, 21, 172, 188–89, 196–97; definition of, 112; and family life, 87, 101–5, 221n. 60, 222n. 66; in *The Family*, 92, 217n. 17; in *Hototogisu* (Tokutomi), 217n. 17; in Japan, 6–7, 173–74; and literature, 80, 101–5; and patri-

archy, 101, 103–5; and tuberculosis,
    53–54, 211n. 29
Chatterjee, Partha, 15, 155
Chikuma Shobō publishing house, 33
childbirth: death in, 115–17, 131–32; in
    The Family, 114; in I-novels, 231n. 55;
    and medicine, 123; in Shinsei, 232n. 68;
    and writing, 123–24, 150–51, 232n. 69.
    See also pregnancy
China, 71, 73, 108, 152, 173–75, 225n. 3
chronotopes, 157, 164, 236–37n. 19
Chūō Kōron (journal), 23, 24, 80, 147, 154,
    175
Civil Code, Meiji, 3, 86, 87
climate, 37, 121, 156, 167, 176–77, 182–83
Cold War, 21–22, 34, 35, 40, 41, 65
contagion, 53, 57–61, 64–68, 209n. 13,
    211n. 31, 212n. 34
Cornyetz, Nina, 124

death, 115; in childbirth, 114–15, 135; and
    national imagination, 2; and preg-
    nancy, 127; representation of, 114–15
de Bary, Brett, 42–43, 111
deconstruction, 46
Deleuze and Guattari, 17, 77; on "becom-
    ing-animal," 95; on capitalism, 112; on
    "infinite debt," 188, 218n. 24; on
    minor literature, 112–13; on
    nomadism, 71, 214–15n. 63, 244n. 87;
    on Oedipus, 79, 92, 101–2; on Proust,
    106; on "schizo," 180, 183; on smooth
    and striated space, 162, 189, 244n. 87
Derrida, Jacques, 66, 161, 214n. 54
dictation, 138, 145–46
diet, 51, 55, 68
divorce, 86, 99, 218n. 29
Doi Bansui, 8
Duara, Prasenjit, 160

Eagleton, Terry, 21
Edo period, in historical memory, 163–64
Edson, Cyrus, 53
Educational system, 87
Einstein, Albert, 155, 156

Ellis, Havelock, 122
emperor, 8, 32, 48, 57, 71; in Before the
    Dawn, 166, 183–84, 185–88; in The
    Broken Commandment, 56, 110; as par-
    ent to nation, 85, 86, 96
Enchi Fumiko, 39

family, 10, 18, 36, 77–113, 222n. 66; and
    blood lineage, 37; and dining rituals,
    99; and empire, 112; ie (extended fam-
    ily) and katei (nuclear family), 83,
    85–86, 88, 90–91, 98–104, 111, 217n.
    17; and sacrifice, 85; state policies on,
    86–87, 88; and tradition, 88–89, 112; as
    trope for Japan, 38, 88–89; uchi (inside)
    and soto (outside) in, 36, 89–98, 111–12
fascism, 2, 16, 180, 188–89, 194–95, 243n.
    79; and Before the Dawn, 170–73, 181;
    and blood, 56–57; and hygiene, 54
father: in The Broken Commandment,
    62–63; and capitalism, 87; in The Fam-
    ily, 82, 102–3, 216n. 9, 221n. 59; in
    Meiji literature, 82; in Shinsei, 137,
    141–42, 144. See also patriarchies
femininity, 121, 227–8n. 23
feminism, 38, 122
Fitzgerald, F. Scott, 2
Flores, Linda, 147
forgetting, 185–87, 244n. 88
Foucault, Michel, 133, 209n. 10, 222n. 65
Fujii, James, 63, 66, 110, 156
Fujin Kōron (journal), 147, 151
Fujitani, Takashi, 8, 35, 87
Fukuzawa Yukichi, 155
furusato (hometown), 36, 37
Futabatei Shimei, 106–9, 223–24n. 76

genbun itchi, 4, 106, 108, 109, 119, 120,
    240–41n. 59
gender, 122, 124, 132; and genre, 117–18,
    120–24, 149, 153, 227–28n. 23
germ theory, 51–54, 58, 64, 70, 209n. 11,
    211n. 31
Gilmour, Leigh, 122, 148
Gluck, Carol, 35, 59, 85, 163

Gotō Shimpei, 55
Gramsci, Antonio, 245n. 95

Haga Yaichi, 3, 8
Hani Gorō, 169
Haniya Yutaka, 43, 111
Hara Minoru, 170–73, 181
Harootunian, Harry: on Aono Suekichi, 178; on capitalism, 172, 188–89; on the family in Japan, 88; on postcolonialism, 16; on Takayama Chogyū, 8; on Tsurumi Shunsuke, 43
Hasegawa Komako, 118, 133, 147–53, 235n. 95
Hasegawa Tenkei, 212–13n. 40
Haver, William, 117
Hayashi Fumio, 154–55
Hayashi Fusao, 14, 28, 32, 35, 243n. 79; on Before the Dawn, 170, 179–80
Hayashi Tatsuo, 182–83, 188, 189, 244n. 86
Heidegger, Martin, 176–77
heredity, 51, 69, 175; and burakumin, 60–62, 64, 68; and disease, 56–58, 60, 67, 68
Higuchi Ichiyō, 8, 116, 229–30n. 41, 230n. 47
Hirabayashi Taiko, 146, 147
Hirano Ken, 22, 44, 90
Hirata School. See Nativism
Hirotsu Ryūrō, 116
Hobsbawm, E. J., 196
Hohendahl, Peter, 25
Hokkaido, 161
homosexuality, 141, 210–11n. 28
homosociality, 132–33, 177, 211n. 29; in The Family, 84; in Haru, 125; in Shinsei, 141, 144, 145
hybridity, 17, 79, 91,; in colonial discourse, 96–98, 214n. 55, 220–21n. 56; of verandah, 92–98, 110, 111
hygiene 50–56; and burakumin, 62–64, 65; and the family, 88; and fascism, 54; and imperialism, 55; in Japan, 49, 76; and nationalism, 54–55, 69; and socialism, 53–54, 65, 67, 209n. 15

Ibsen, Henrik, 122, 124
Ihara Saikaku, 4, 37, 230n. 47
Ikuta Chōkō, 109
Imperial Rescript on Education, 85
impressionism, 109–10, 216n. 10
incest, 101–2; in The Family, 79, 94, 100; in Shinsei, 97, 143–44, 221n. 58
infinite debt, 85, 100
India, 70, 173–75, 192, 240–41n. 59
Inoue Tetsujirō, 85
I-novel, 28, 31, 204n. 31, 226–27n. 15; as commodity, 102, 103–4; and gender, 121, 124, 145–46, 148–49, 152; and the family, 82–84; and Japanese tradition, 202–3n. 6; in literary history, 30, 109, 118–19; and national literature, 120–21; and pure literature, 225n. 3; and pregnancy, 231n. 55; and suicide, 131, 135; and tenkō literature, 169; by women writers, 218n. 18, 234n. 86
Irokawa Daikichi, 34–35, 46, 48, 85
irony, 243–44n. 80
Isoda Kōichi, 44
Ito, Ken, 88
Itō Shinkichi, 6, 26–32, 33, 37
Ivy, Marilyn, 16, 39
Iwami Teruyo, 148
Iwamoto Yoshiharu, 227n. 20
Iwano Hōmei, 14, 115–16
Izumi Kyōka, 22, 121, 150

Japan: and blood, 38; in the Cold War, 21; cultural tradition of, 3, 40, 88–89, 175, 194, 227–28n. 23, 238n. 38; educational system in, 87; emperor of, 8, 32, 57, 77; empire of, 3, 11, 48, 55, 70–71, 95–98, 152, 162, 163, 187, 188, 192–94; family in, 10, 36, 38, 57, 79, 83, 85–89; honorary "white" status of, 193–94; minority groups in, 70–71, 74, 214n. 60; and suicide, 115–16, 225n. 3
Johnston, William, 54
Jogaku Zasshi (journal), 120, 122, 227n. 20, 228n. 28
joryū bungaku. See women's literature

Katō Shūichi, 37

Kamei Hideo, 62, 116, 137

Kamei Katsuichirō, 12, 22, 33, 241–42n. 62; and "blood," 32–33, 37, 175–76; and *tenkō*, 25

Kano, Ayako, 124

Karatani Kōjin, on Futabatei Shimei, 109; on germ theory, 52; on "landscape," 186; on *tenkō*, 44–45; on tuberculosis, 53, 58, 60, 211n. 31

Katayama Sen, 214n. 62

Katei zasshi (journal), 75–76

Kawabata Yasunari, 20, 21, 121, 203n. 18

Kawakami Bizan, 127

Keene, Donald, 20–21, 120

Key, Ellen, 122, 132

Kikuchi Kan, 119

Kimura Sōta, 109, 216n. 10

Kinoshita Naoe, 53–54

Kitamura Tōkoku, 10, 11, 35; in *Haru*, 119, 125, 126, 127

Kita Sadakichi, 71

Kitasato Shibasaburō, 52, 54, 58, 71

Kobayashi Hideo, 30, 176, 241n. 60

Koch, Robert, 51, 52, 58, 60, 71, 73

Kōda Rohan, 4, 25

Kogito (journal), 173

kokka (state), 77–78. *See also* state

Kokubungaku kaishaku to kanshō (journal), 25

kokugaku. See Nativism

kokutai (national polity), 77

Konaka Nobutaka, 129, 238n. 38

Kōno Kensuke, 9, 129, 221n. 59

Korea, 74, 75, 173, 193–94; annexation of, 71, 95–96, 220n. 54; in *Before the Dawn*, 187; in *The Family*, 221n. 57; folk art in, 233n. 72; Japanese language in, 96; in *Shinsei*, 97, 145

Koschmann, J. Victor, 35

Kō Yoran, 71, 213n. 41, 214n. 62

Kristeva, Julia, 129, 228n. 26

Kuki Shūzō, 34, 156, 163

Kurokawa Midori, 61

Laclau and Mouffe, 58, 213n. 45

landscape, 62–63, 186

Latour, Bruno, 52, 64

Levick, H., 194–5

Lippit, Seiji, 111, 156

literature: academic study of, 24–25, 26; as commodity, 101–5, 107, 110, 112; concept of, 7; gender in, 8–9, 18, 117–18, 135; in *Haru*, 125, 128; and sexuality, 125; in *Shinsei*, 135, 137–39, 143–44;and suicide, 126–27; value in, 80, 107

literary history: I-novel in, 48, 90, 118–19; and national imagination, 19–26, 32; naturalism in, 30–31, 106, 109, 305n. 34; proletarian literature in, 30–31, 305n. 34; realism in, 106, 108–10

love, romantic concept of, 10, 125–26, 132, 138, 143, 148

Lu Xun, 225n. 3

MacCannell, Juliet Flower, 82, 85, 104, 217n. 14

Marinetti, F.T., 194–95

marriage, 87–88; between Japan and Korea, 95–96, 220n. 54

Marxism, 27; in the Cold War, 21; and historical debates over Meiji Restoration, 169, 172, 178; in Japan, 28, 31–32, 35, 39–45, 170, 172, 188; and literary theory, 106, 111; and national imagination, 112; view of history, 170–74, 180, 189. *See also* proletarian literature; socialism; *tenkō*

Masamune Hakuchō, 109, 181

Masaoka Shiki, 7, 9, 62, 104, 200n. 13

masculinity, 118, 134–35, 139, 153

Matsuo Bashō, 7, 25, 200n. 13

McClellan, Edwin, 202–3n. 6

McNeill, William, 70

medicine 51; clinical, 52; military, 48–49, 52, 55; and pregnancy, 123

Meiji emperor, 48, 71; in *Before the Dawn*, 183–4, 187, 188; in *The Broken Commandment*, 56; gendering of, 8, 121; marriage of, 87; as parent to nation, 85

Meiji Restoration, 6, 34–35, 168; in *Before the Dawn*, 13–14, 154, 164, 166, 173, 183–89; in literature, 237n. 31, 243n. 79; Marxist interpretations of, 169, 172, 178, 239n. 42; in *Tōhō no mon*, 175

men's literature, 121–2, 226n. 12

migration, 193, 213n. 41, 213n. 42, 214n. 62, 245n. 1; in *The Broken Commandment*, 50, 64–68, 70–71, 212n. 38; and nomadism, 71, 214–15n. 63

minor literature, 112–3

minorities, 66, 70–71, 74, 214n. 60. *See also burakumin*

Mishima Yukio, 20, 21

Miyamoto Kenji, 40

Miyamoto Yuriko, 40, 146, 152, 189, 243n. 72, 244n. 84

Miyazawa Kenji, 156

Miyoshi Yukio, 22, 36, 119, 120–21

Mizuta Noriko, 151, 152, 227–28n. 23

modernism, 106, 110–11

modernization theory, 21–22, 35, 41, 76, 173

Mori Ōgai, 25, 52, 55, 68, 116, 209n. 17

Morris-Suzuki, Tessa, 16, 38, 66, 75, 85, 96, 161–2, 172

motherhood, 149, 150–51, 153, 234n. 81; and modernity, 123–24; in *Shinsei*, 232n. 68; in Tōson's works, 115, 217n. 12

Murai Osamu, 35, 95

Murō Saisei, 27

Nagahara Yutaka, 196

Nagai Kafū, 163

Nagatsuka Takashi, 23

Nakamura Mitsuo, 109, 205n. 34

Nakano Shigeharu, 23, 27, 41, 44–45; and modernism, 111, 223n. 73; on realism, 105–6

Nakarai Tōsui, 8

Nakayama Hiroaki, 8, 80, 102

Nakazato Kaizan, 163

Narita Ryūichi, 50–51

narrative, 156, and national imagination,

16, 43, 159–61, 172, 187; in Marxism, 171–73

national imagination, 13–17, 195–97; and antinational thought, 17, 32, 45, 112, 197; and body, 49–52, 58, 76, 79; critique of, 46, 58, 76, 189–90, 197; and empire, 11; and family, 10, 18, 78, 84–89, 111–12; and forgetting, 185–87; and gender, 8–9, 132–33, 141; and historical memory, 38–39; and hybridity, 17, 69, 75; and hygiene, 54–55, 58; and literature, 7, 19–26, 32; multiplicity of, 4, 44; and narrative, 16, 43; and patriarchy, 135; and poetry, 1–2, 6–12; in prewar and postwar Japan, 26, 34–39; and romantic love, 10; and space, 18, 157–58, 161–62, 172–73, 186–88; and *tenkō*, 39, 45, 169; and time, 2, 10–12, 18, 157–62; and tradition, 3, 12, 88–89

national literature (*kokubungaku*), 3, 37, 119, 152, 227n. 18; and gender, 8–9, 18, 120–22, 152–53

nationalism: anticolonial, 15–16, 192, 196; and body, 68–72; and capitalism, 6–7, 14, 17, 196–97; cultural, 3–4, 7, 34, 36–37, 39, 43; fascist, 28; and feminism, 149; "good" and "bad" strains of, 2, 13–14, 33–34, 36, 40, 43, 46; and irony, 243–44n. 80; mass, 41; and minorities, 66; multiplicity of, 15; popular, 3, 34, 35, 38; in postwar Japan, 34–39; and race, 75; revolutionary, 3, 86; state, 16, 32, 37, 149

Nativism (*kokugaku*), 7, 31, 141–42, 166, 179, 181, 184, 186, 189

Natsume Sōseki, 22, 25, 37, 104, 202–3n. 6; *Kokoro*, 116; *Michikusa* (Grass by the wayside), 231n. 55; *Mon* (The gate), 220n. 49; *Nowaki* (Autumn storm), 80; *Wagahai wa neko de aru* (I am a cat), 156

naturalism, 20; in Japan, 22, 23, 106, 109, 305n. 34

New Criticism, 20–21

New Left, 35–36

Nietzsche, Friedrich, 4
Niranjana, Tejaswini, 110
Nishikawa Yūko, 82–84, 86
Nitobe Inazō, 116
Nogami Yaeko, 146
nonsynchronicity, 189

Oedipus, 79, 92, 101–2, 110, 112, 210–11n.
    28
Oguma Eiji, 4, 35, 69, 75, 96
Ogura Chōrō, 71
Ohmae, Kenichi, 196
Okakura Tenshin, 156, 176
Okamoto Kanoko, 234n. 87
Okazaki Yoshie, 25
Okinawa, 74, 161, 214n. 60
Okubo Tsuneo, 36–37
Olson, Lawrence, 42
Onuki Shōsen, 109, 224n. 85
Orbaugh, Sharalyn, 152
Orientalism, 21, 22, 45, 56, 110
Ozaki Kōyō, 4, 230n. 47

Pasteur, Louis, 51, 54, 58, 71, 73
patriarchies 82, 112, 217n. 14; in
    The Broken Commandment, 62–63; in
    The Family, 38, 100–105, 221n. 59; in
    Hototogisu (Tokutomi), 217n. 17; in
    national literature, 122; and writing,
    133, 232n. 69
PEN Club, 26, 108, 191, 194–95
People's Rights Movement, 86, 90
pharmakos, 66
physical education, 51, 56
Pincus, Leslie, 34
poetry; and national imagination, 1–2,
    6–12; new-style (shintaishi), 5, 7, tradi-
    tional forms of, 7, 138–39
postcolonialism, 16
Pratt, Mary Louise, 188
pregnancy: in Haru, 127; in I-novels,
    231n. 55; in literature, 116; as modern
    construct, 123–24; in Shinsei, 133,
    134–37; and writing, 150–51. See also
    childbirth

proletarian literature, 27, 30–31, 105–6,
    111, 112, 169, 205n. 34
Proust, Marcel, 106, 110
public space and private space, 89–98
publishing industry, 4, 25, 80, 103, 107,
    146–47
pure literature, 116–7, 120, 125, 225n. 6,
    228n. 26

quarantine, 55, 64–68, 69, 70–75, 212n. 38

race, 51, 76, 135, 174, 191–95; 220–21n. 56
realism, 102, 105; in literary history, 106,
    109–10
representation, 43, 78, 102, 106, 110–12;
    and childbirth, 115, 116, 131–32; in
    Nakano Shigeharu, 45; of nation,
    160–61, 180; and suicide, 116, 131–32
Robertson, Jennifer, 36
Roggendorf, Joseph, 20, 202n. 4
romanticism, 6, 12; in Europe, 4, 58; in
    Japan, 10, 22, 119
Rossetti, Dante Gabriel, 228n. 31
Rubin, Jay, 23
Ruskin, John, 4
Russo-Japanese War, 47, 48–49, 73, 80, 90,
    91, 108

sacrifice, 85, 104–5, 115, 117, 188
Said, Edward, 95
Saigyō, 200n. 13
Saikaku. See Ihara Saikaku
Saitō Minako, 116
Sakai, Naoki, 145–46, 177
Sakai Toshihiko, 215n. 72
Sand, Jordan, 88, 92, 99
Sanger, Margaret, 122
Sano Manabu, 188, 244–45n. 91
Sasabuchi Tomoichi, 11–12
Sasaki Masanobu, 159–60
Seaman, Louis, 48–49
Sedgwick, Eve, 15, 132
Seitō (journal), 228n. 28
Sekiya Yumiko, 93
Seltzer, Mark, 69

Senuma Shigeki, 36, 37
Sesshu, 194
sexology, 122, 229n. 34
Shiga Naoya, 150, 231n. 55
Shimazaki Fuyuko, 81, 95
Shimazaki Tōson: and Bergson, 235n. 5; on
burakumin, 47, 60, 212n. 35; critical
reception of in Japan, 22–26, 32–39, 44,
45–46; critical reception of in the West,
20–22, 45–46; on The Family, 89–90;
family lineage of, 37–38; and feminism,
122; and Futabatei, 106–8; and Ibsen,
122; on imperialism, 240–41n. 59; as an
intellectual, 181–83; on Japanese history, 168, 175, 188, 239n. 42, 240n. 57;
on Japanese literature, 108; and Kitamura Tōkoku, 119; life of, 29–30,
38–39, 47, 78, 81, 133–34, 191–94; and
Marinetti, 194–95; and nationalism,
13–14, 46, 195–96, 168–69; and naturalism, 21, 22, 109; and Okakura Tenshin,
176; as poet, 1–2, 4–12, 130, 199n. 7,
216n. 5; as publisher, 80, 216n. 4; rediscovery of in 1930s, 14, 24–34; rediscovery of in 1960s, 14, 36–39; and romanticism, 12, 22; and Sendai, 26, 130; and
Shimizu Shikin, 212n. 34; and Shojochi,
122–23; in Singapore, 108; and sociality,
27–28; in South Africa, 191–93; in
South America, 26, 108, 192–94; and
suicide, 233n. 76; and tenkō, 169–70;
translation of, 20, 152; in the United
States, 192, 194–95; and Watsuji Tetsurō,
177; writing style of, 222n. 64; and
women's writing, 122–24
Major Works
Before the Dawn (Yoake mae), 13–14, 18,
86, 154–5, 157, 162, 164–90; as allegory, 179–81; critical reception of,
20–21, 30, 31–32, 169–75, 177–83,
204n. 29; film version of, 34;
impact on historical studies of
Japan, 34–35, 154, 164; as I-novel,
30, 31, 179; publication history of,
23, 26, 32, 154

The Broken Commandment (Hakai), 13,
17–18, 47–50, 55–76, 157; critical
reception of, 6, 36, 47–48, 64–65,
75–76; 205n. 43, 212–13n. 40; in literary history, 109, 118; film version
of, 34, 65; publication history of,
26, 33–34, 72–75, 80, 215n. 65,
215n. 68
The Family (Ie), 18, 77–113, 114–5; as
allegory, 85–86, 90, 224n. 87; critical reception of, 22–23, 38, 78, 81,
89–91, 105–6, 216n. 10; in literary
history, 90, 109; publication history
of, 80–81
Haru (Spring), 18, 78, 124–31, 159–60;
body language in, 230n. 43; critical
reception of, 29, 35, 118–20; in literary history, 118–19; publication
history of, 107–8, 124
Shinsei (New life), 18, 97, 116–17,
133–46; 211n. 31; critical reception
of, 29, 44, 120–21, 231–2n. 62,
234n. 87; and Hasegawa Komako,
147–53; in literary history, 109;
publication history of, 32, 133,
151–52, 235n. 97
Other Works
"Arashi" (The storm), 157, 236n. 17;
"Chosaku to shuppan" (Writing
and publishing), 80; "Eagle's Song"
(Washi no uta), 7; "Hasegawa
Futabatei-shi wo itamu" (Mourning Hasegawa/Futabatei), 224n. 79;
"Hatsu koi" (First love), 9; Hitohabune (A leaflike boat), 1; Junrei (Pilgrimage), 108, 176, 190–95, 225n.
3; "Komoro naru kojō no hotori"
(By the old castle of Komoro), 11;
"Mebae" (Seedlings), 223n. 72;
"Mottomo Nihonteki naru
mono" (The most Japanese of
things), 194; "Nihon kindai bungaku no hatten ni tsuite" (On the
development of modern Japanese
literature), 108; "Nobijitaku"

Other Works (*continued*)
(Preparations for growth), 228–9n.
32; "Okakura Kakuzō," 176;
"Okinu," 5–6, 9, 10; *Rakubaishū*
(Fallen plum blossoms), 1; *Sakura
no mi ga juku suru toki* (When the
cherries ripen), 232n. 63; "Sōnen
no uta" (Song of a man in his
prime), 9–10; "The Sound of
Tides" (Chōon), 11–12; "Tenmondai no tokei" (The observatory clock), 236n. 17; *Tōhō no mon*
(The gate to the East), 175, 176,
178, 240–41n. 59; "Toki" (Time),
154; *Umi e* (To the sea), 233n. 74,
240n. 57; *Wakanashū* (A collection
of seedlings), 1, 2, 5–6, 11, 28;
"Yamakuni no shinheimin" (New
commoners in the mountain districts), 61; "Yashi no mi"
(Coconut), 11

Shimizu Shikin, 71, 212n. 34
Shinchōsha publishing house, 26, 33,
216n. 4
Shirane, Haruo, 19
Shojochi (journal), 122–3, 228n. 28
Shōwa Restoration, 179, 181–82, 243n. 73
Silverberg, Miriam, 111
Singapore, 108, 144
Sino-Japanese War, 3, 7, 211n. 29
socialism, 74, 75, 163; and hygiene, 53–54,
65, 67, 71, 209n. 15; and migration,
214n. 62. *See also* Marxism
sociality, 27–28, 30, 37, 91, 204n. 29
South Africa, 144, 191–93
Southern-Advance thesis, 192–93, 245n. 3
space, 18, 155–57; in *Before the Dawn*,
240n. 53; in historical understanding,
176–77; of nation, 95, 157, 161–62,
172–73, 174–75, 186–8; as performative, 183, 187, 188; as smooth or striated, 162, 189, 244n. 87
Spivak, Gayatri Chakravorty, 46
Stalinism, 173, 179
state, 16, 77–78, 88

Suga Hidemi, 2, 7, 11, 37, 160, 207–8n,
215n. 67
suicide: in *The Broken Commandment*, 50;
in *The Family*, 115; in *Haru*, 126–28,
129–31, 230n. 50; and Japan, 115–16,
153, 188, 225n. 3; and literature, 116,
126–27, 131; in *Shinsei*, 134, 135, 137,
139, 142–43
Suiheisha, 72, 74, 212n. 35
Suzuki Sadami, 24
Suzuki, Tomi, 119

Taishō (Emperor), 87
Taiwan, 3, 55, 96, 133, 194; in *Before the
Dawn*, 187; in *Shinsei*, 97, 139, 143,
145, 152
Takabatake Motoyuki, 172
Takahashi Akinori, 169
Takayama Chogyū, 8, 9
Takayama Shigeru, 173–75
Tanaka, Stefan, 156
Tanizaki Junichirō, 20, 21
tanka, 7, 9, 138–39
Tayama Katai, 80, 90, 109, 118–19, 120
tenkō (political apostasy), 18, 157, 162, 169;
305n. 34; and Aono Suekichi, 178; and
Before the Dawn, 169–70, 188; literature
of, 23, 40, 43, 45, 169–70; and Tōson
criticism, 24, 25–32; postwar discourse
on, 39–45
Terayama Shūji, 111, 218n. 19
time, 155–62, 189; in *The Broken Commandment*, 157; cyclical, 161, 164–65; filled
and empty forms of, 158–59, 161, 168;
lived, 92, 110; linear, 155, 159, 161–62,
164, 171, 172–73, 179; in literature, 156;
in modernization theory, 76; and
national imagination, 2, 18; pedagogical
and performative forms of, 160–61,
178–79, 186–87; and poetry, 10–12
Tokieda Motoki, 96
Tokuda Shūsei, 57
Tokutomi Roka, 58, 60, 211n. 29, 217n. 17
Tsubouchi Shōyō, 107, 223–24n. 76
Tsurumi Shunsuke, 41–44, 46, 169

tuberculosis, 49, 52, 56, 58–60, 63–65, 69; and anti-Semitism, 211n. 30; in cows, 63–64, 212n. 38; in France, 209n. 15; and Mori Ōgai, 209n. 17; and romanticism, 58–60, 115, 211n. 31

Ueda Kazutoshi, 3, 8, 96, 220n. 55
Ueno Chizuko, 10, 84
Unequal Treaties, 3, 55, 212n. 38
university system, 3; study of literature in, 24–25, 26
Uno Chiyo, 146

vaccination, 55, 68–75
verandah, 92–98, 110, 111, 220n. 49
violence, 184–87, 189
visuality, 56–58, 61, 62–63

Wallerstein, Immanuel, 17, 87, 196
Watanabe Hiroshi, 38, 82
Watanabe Naomi, 56–58
Watsuji Tetsurō: on climate, 34, 156, 176–77, 182; on the family, 88; on Tōson, 39
Whitman, Walt, 7
Wolfe, Alan, 116, 126, 131
women's literature, 8–9, 18, 117–18, 120–24, 125, 145–47, 149, 226n. 12, 148; and childbirth, 124, 146–47, 150–51; critical reception of, 22, 228n.

25; and female body, 152; in *Haru*, 128–29; in *Shinsei*, 133, 137–39, 142
women's magazines, 146–47
Wood, Mary Elene, 150
Wordsworth, William, 4
world system, 15, 87, 196
World War I, 139–40
World War II, 32–33, 72–75, 176, 215n. 67

Yamada Bimyō, 108
Yamada Moritarō, 172
Yamashita Etusko, 38, 217n. 17
Yanagi Sōetsu, 233n. 72
Yanagita Kunio, 34, 35, 61, 206n. 47
Yasuda Yojūrō, 11
Yokomitsu Riichi, 156
Yomiuri (newspaper), 80
Yosa Buson, 7
Yosano Akiko, 9, 146, 200–201n. 19
Yosano Tekkan, 7, 9
Yoshida Seiichi, 22, 36
Yoshikawa Eiji, 163
Yoshikuni Igarashi, 33
Yoshimoto Takaaki, 46, 207n. 67; on *tenkō*, 40–41, 169
Yu Miri, 111
Yuval-Davis, Nira, 16, 91–92

Žižek, Slavoj, 65, 173, 213n. 45

STUDIES OF THE EAST ASIAN INSTITUTE
Selected Titles

Taxation Without Representation in Rural China: State Capacity, Peasant Resistance, and Democratization, Thomas P. Bernstein and Xiaobo Lu. Modern China Series, Cambridge University Press, 2003

Spanning Japan's Modern Century: The Memoirs of Hugh Borton, Hugh Borton. Lexington Books, Inc., 2002

The Reluctant Dragon: Crisis Cycles in Chinese Foreign Economic Policy, by Lawrence Christopher Reardon. Seattle: University of Washington Press, 2002

Korea Between Empires, 1895-1919, Andre Schmid. New York: Columbia University Press 2002

The North Korean Revolution: 1945-50, Charles Armstrong. Cornell University Press, 2002

Abortion before Birth Control: The Politics of Reproduction in Postwar Japan, by Tiana Norgren. Princeton University Press, August 2001

Japan's Imperial Diplomacy: Consuls, Treaty Ports, and War with China, 1895-1938, by Barbara Brooks. Honolulu: University of Hawai'i Press, 2000

Japan's Budget Politics: Balancing Domestic and International Interests, by Takaaki Suzuki. Lynne Rienner Publishers, 2000

Cadres and Corruption: The Organizational Involution of the Chinese Communist Party, by Xiaobo Lu. Stanford University Press, 2000

Assembled in Japan: Electrical Goods and the Making of the Japanese Consumer, by Simon Partner, University of California Press 1999

Nation, Governance, and Modernity: Canton, 1900-1927, by Michael T. W. Tsin. Stanford: Stanford University Press, 1999

Civilization and Monsters: Spirits of Modernity in Meiji Japan, by Gerald Figal, Duke University Press, 1999

The Logic of Japanese Politics: Leaders, Institutions, and the Limits of Change, by Gerald L. Curtis. New York: Columbia University Press, 1999.

Trans-Pacific Racisms and the U.S. Occupation of Japan, by Yukiko Koshiro. New York: Columbia University Press, 1999

Bicycle Citizens: The Political World of the Japanese Housewife, by Robin LeBlanc. Berkeley: University of California Press, 1999

Alignment despite Antagonism: The United States, Japan, and Korea, by Victor Cha. Stanford: Stanford University Press, 1999

Contesting Citizenship in Urban China: Peasant Migrants, the State and Logic of the Market, by Dorothy Solinger. Berkeley: University of California Press, 1999

Order and Chaos in the Works of Natsume Sōseki, by Angela Yiu. Honolulu: University of Hawai'i Press, 1998

Driven by Growth: Political Change in the Asia-Pacific Region, 2d edition, edited by James W. Morley. Armonk, NY: M. E. Sharpe, 1998

Japan's Total Empire: Manchuria and the Culture of Wartime Imperialism, by Louise Young. Berkeley: University of California Press, 1997

Honorable Merchants: Commerce and Self-Cultivation in Late Imperial China, by Richard Lufrano. Honolulu: University of Hawai'i Press, 1997

Print and Politics: 'Shibao' and the Culture of Reform in Late Qing China, by Joan Judge. Stanford: Stanford University Press, 1996